TANKER WAR

TANKER WAR
America's First Conflict with Iran, 1987–1988

By
LEE ALLEN ZATARAIN

CASEMATE
Philadelphia & Newbury

Published in the United States of America in 2008 by
CASEMATE
1016 Warrior Road, Drexel Hill, PA 19026

and in the United Kingdom by
CASEMATE
17 Cheap Street, Newbury RG20 5DD

ISBN 978-1-932033-84-7

Cataloging-in-publication data is available from the Library of Congress
and the British Library.

Printed and bound in the United States of America.

For a complete list of Casemate titles please contact:

CASEMATE PUBLISHERS
Telephone (610) 853-9131, Fax (610) 853-9146
E-mail: casemate@casematepublishing.com
or
CASEMATE UK
Telephone (01635) 231091, Fax (01635) 41619
E-mail: casemate-uk@casematepublishing.co.uk

CONTENTS

INTRODUCTION   1

1 / THE *STARK* DISASTER   7
2 / TARGET: KUWAIT   27
3 / RAISING QUESTIONS   39
4 / OPERATION EARNEST WILL   55
5 / AMBUSH   63
6 / RETHINKING   77
7 / THE INVISIBLE HAND STRIKES AGAIN   87
8 / *IN FLAGRANTE*   101
9 / FORT APACHE—THE GULF   125
10 / "TURN AND ENGAGE"   137
11 / "WE WILL COMMENCE FIRING"   151
12 / "WE ARE THE BIG WINNERS IN THE GULF NOW"   175
13 / "NO HIGHER HONOR"   187
14 / "A ONE-DAY WAR"   205
15 / "STOP, ABANDON SHIP, I INTEND TO SINK YOU"   223
16 / "NONE OF THESE LADIES HAS A SCRATCH ON HER"   241
17 / "MULTIPLE SILKWORMS INBOUND"   261
18 / POLICEMAN OF THE GULF?   291
19 / "UNKNOWN, ASSUMED HOSTILE"   297
20 / "I DEEPLY REGRET THE RESULT, IF NOT
        THE DECISION   315
21 / SEA OF LIES?   329
22 / "GIVE ME THE KEY. GIVE ME THE KEY."   357
23 / "THEY DON'T FIGHT LIKE IRANIANS ANYMORE"   379

END NOTES   389
INDEX   411

INTRODUCTION

In 1987 and 1988, the United States fought an undeclared naval war with the Islamic Republic of Iran in the Persian Gulf. That war is little remembered, even though it involved the largest surface battle fought by the U.S. Navy since the Second World War, a mark which still stands. Perhaps it is mostly recalled today in connection with the Navy warship USS *Vincennes*' accidental shoot-down of an Iranian commercial airliner, killing nearly 300 innocent civilians.

For a variety of policy reasons, the U.S. decided to intervene in the Gulf in 1987 to protect Kuwaiti-owned tankers from Iranian attack. Shipping in the Gulf had come under increasing attack from both Iran and Iraq in what became known as the "tanker war." That war was an offshoot of the brutal Iran-Iraq war begun in September 1980. The Iran-Iraq war was predominately a grinding land struggle. It was nominally fought over the ownership of the disputed Shatt al-Arab waterway, which ran from the confluence of the Tigris and Euphrates rivers for some nine miles down to the Gulf. The waterway formed the southern border between Iran and Iraq, and was the latter's only outlet to the Gulf. Iraq claimed full ownership of the waterway, Iran claimed ownership to its centerline. Iraq had been forced to accept the Iranian claim via an agreement known as the 1975 Algiers Accords.

Iran's monarch, the Shah, had been overthrown by an Islamic-dominated revolt in 1979, resulting in the radical Islamic prelate, the Ayatollah Ruollah Khomeini, seizing the reins of power. Iraq's secular dictator, Saddam Hussein, was directly threatened by the bubbling cauldron of the Iranian revolution on his doorstep. Khomeini described Saddam as a "puppet of Satan." In 1980, he called on Iraqis to over-

1

throw Saddam and cleanse the country of his atheistic rule. An increase in armed clashes along the border mirrored the escalating rhetoric. On September 17, 1980, Saddam appeared on Iraqi television, tore up the 1975 Algiers agreement, and claimed sovereignty over the entire Shatt al-Arab. Faced by the threat of a militant Islamic revival in his own country and presented with the opportunity of the Iranian military built up by the Shah having been greatly weakened by the Iranian revolution, Saddam decided on war.

On September 22, 1980, nine Iraqi Army divisions attacked across the Iranian border. Iraqi forces seized a sizeable foothold in the valuable oil producing southern Iranian province of Khuzestan. Iraq's war aims were relatively limited. Saddam thought he could take advantage of a tilt in the regional balance of power from Iran to Iraq to resolve the territorial disputes in Iraq's favor. He could also put an end to the threat to his rule by putting Khomeini in his place, perhaps even precipitating a collapse of the clerical regime. Unfortunately, he had made a near fatal error. He was indeed attacking a weakened regional rival, but he was also attacking a revolution.

Following the overthrow of the Shah, a tide of fundamentalist Islamic terror had swept over Iran. Those suspected of anti-revolutionary activities were arrested by groups of students and workers organized around a mosque or a mullah. Zealots threw acid in the faces of women who failed to wear veils, or slashed them with razors. Revolutionary tribunals did a brisk business in trials and executions. Khomeini's grim vision of a true Islamic society was imposed on Iran. He declared music to be corrupting. Swimming pools and sports clubs were closed. Revolutionary Guards raided homes, looking for "objects of corruption" such as playing cards and chess sets.

In November 1979, some 80 students seized the U.S. embassy in Tehran. While not ordered by Khomeini, he found that the students' act played so well that he "got behind his followers" and gave the seizure his blessing. The resulting prolonged hostage crisis led to the humiliating failure of a U.S. rescue attempt. Public frustration in the face of U.S. inability to resolve the crisis took a heavy political toll on the Carter administration. That frustration helped propel Ronald Reagan to the White House.

Absorbed in internal power struggles and in the midst of defying the U.S. with the embassy hostage seizure, Khomeini's regime did not feel much threatened by the limited Iraqi attack. Believing himself in a position of strength with the initial success of Iraq's invasion, Saddam Hussein announced his willingness to negotiate a settlement. Iran refused. The Iraqi army continued its plodding advance against stiffening Iranian resistance. The Iranian defense really took hold at the city of Khorramshahr. The Iraqis were finally able to take the city, but losses were horrendous on both sides. By early 1981, the Iraqi advance had stalled. Given breathing space, Iran regrouped and counterattacked.

Starting in the fall of 1981, the Iranians completely wrestled the initiative away from Iraq with a series of advances. By May 1982, Khorramshahr was retaken. Saddam tried to declare a unilateral cease fire and withdrew his remaining forces from Iranian territory back to Iraq, where they assumed a defensive position. Iran was not so anxious to call it quits. Khomeini had a personal hatred for Saddam. He also saw the utility to his regime of an ongoing war with an external enemy. Calling it an "imposed war," the regime sought to rally the populace against the invader, and behind it. The clerical regime could use the war to further consolidate its power and to provide a convenient rationale to suppress remaining domestic opponents by labeling them as traitors. Iran demanded impossible terms from Iraq as the price for peace, including the removal of Saddam Hussein and his trial as a war criminal. With its back to the wall, the Iraqi regime hunkered down.

If Iraq made a mistake "attacking a revolution," Iran was now making one of its own: attacking a ruthless dictator who could and would deploy the resources of his state to the maximum extent possible to protect his position. Inflated by oil revenue, Iraq's financial resources were enormous. Its human resources were less impressive. Iraq had only one-third of Iran's population, and its people also lacked enthusiasm for the war that Saddam's gambit had plunged them into.

In 1982, Iran launched its first major assault into Iraqi territory, near the southern city of Basra. Others would follow. The attacks made headway and inflicted significant causalities on the Iraqis. However, the Iraqis were able to hold on by the skin of their teeth and prevent any major breakthroughs. What captured the attention of the world, and badly unnerved the Iraqis, was the nature of the Iranian attacks. Tsunami-like human waves, driven by the winds of surging Shiite religious fervor, repeatedly crashed against Iraqi lines. The attacks were made with what appeared to be a complete disregard for human life.

One Iranian attack was described by an Iraqi officer as looking like a crowd pouring out of a mosque. Advancing lines of Iranians were blown up by mines, blasted by mortars, and swept away by machine gun fire. Still, they kept coming. Even when they successfully beat off the Iranians, such sights were profoundly disturbing to many young Iraqi soldiers. Particularly bothersome was the fact that many of the Iranians were young boys down to the age of twelve. On one occasion, Iraqi soldiers broke out laughing when they saw Iranian kids on bicycles pedaling towards their position. The laughter stopped when the young boys started throwing hand grenades. The Iraqis shot them down.[1]

Playing to traditional Shiite themes, the Khomeini regime fostered a cult of martyrdom. Young volunteers were promised instant access to heaven upon death. They wore "keys to paradise" around their necks. The plastic imitation-brass keys, made in Taiwan, were sometimes handed out by Khomeini himself. Iran seemed to flaunt the human cost of the war. Pictures of mutilated wounded were posted in hotels. There was a Martyrdom Sports Foundation in which teams were named after soldiers killed in action and a Martyrdom Video Library where videotapes of funerals were made available to families.

Many of Iran's fallen fighters were buried in the huge Behest-e-Zahara cemetery, which featured a fountain whose waters were dyed red to symbolize the blood of martyrs. A flower arrangement on the grave of one young soldier carried the inscription: "We congratulate you on your martyrdom."—[signed] Students and Staff of the Tehran University of Science.[2]

The Iraqis responded to the Iranian tactics by adopting a defense in depth, consisting of multiple defensive lines. The Iraqis made extensive use of barbed wire and engineering obstacles to slow Iranian attacks, and used massive artillery support. Many observers likened the Iraqi defenses to World War I entrenchments. Iraq went on a binge of weapons buying in a desperate effort to acquire the wherewithal to hold Iran at bay.

Massive Iranian attacks in 1983 and 1984 did not result in much movement of the front. The Iranians suffered truly enormous losses for their limited gains. In 1984, Iraq began employing chemical weapons against the Iranians on a large scale and extended the war into the Gulf with attacks on Iranian tankers. In 1985, Iran pulled back from major offensive operations. However, the war took an ugly turn with bombing and missile attacks directed against civilian populations on both sides.

In February 1986, in a well-planned amphibious assault, Iranian forces overran Iraq's Al-Faw peninsula in less than 24 hours. The site of Iraq's only port on the Gulf (closed by the war), Al-Faw was itself of little military value. However, the successful Iranian offensive was a serious psychological setback for Iraq. It also set the stage for an attack on Basra, Iraq's second largest city. If Basra fell, the traumatic blow might set in motion political upheavals which could topple the Saddam regime. The Iraqis dug in around Basra in anticipation of the coming storm. The Iranians unleashed their massive human wave assaults on Basra in late 1986 and early 1987. They failed, with huge losses. However, at times, it was a near-run thing. Before the January 1987 assault, Iraqi general Al-Duri promised Saddam Hussein "a harvest of rotten heads." He got his harvest all right but the situation still looked grim, with more Iranian assaults anticipated.

Back in 1982, Iran could have made peace based on the pre-war status quo. Starting in mid-1987, a series of events would eventually force Iran to accept those same terms, some six years, hundreds of billions of dollars, and over one million casualties later.

ACKNOWLEDGMENTS

This book relies greatly on author interviews with individuals directly involved in the events recounted. It would simply have been impossible to write it without the cooperation of so many who generously gave of their time to submit to interviews, and, in many cases, to provide their feedback on draft chapters they reviewed. These individuals include William Dallas Bethea, Paul X. Rinn, James McTigue, David Yonkers, James F. Chandler, James Perkins, Gary L. Bier, Harold L. Bernsen, Tom Wetherald, Jonathan Roark, Paul Evancoe, Gary Stubblefield, Guy Zeller, Doug Bracca, James F. Schork, Peter I. Wikul, Jim Engler, A.N. "Bud" Langston, Tom Matthews, Steve Chilton, Daniel Larsen, Chris Dodd, and Rick Francona. I would like to thank former *Vincennes* commander Will Rogers for his written responses to my questions. In particular, I would like to thank Reuben S. Pitts III, Head, Warfare Systems Department NSWC Dahlgren Division, along with Trish Hamburger, for their wonderful cooperation on my research into the *Vincennes* incident. I would also like to thank the Office of Senator Kay Bailey Hutchison for their assistance in prying loose certain previously classified material. Thanks, too, to Jeff Calder for his assistance in researching newspaper articles, and last but not least, my wife Terry for her diligent typing efforts, without which this book would have taken much longer to complete.

CHAPTER 1

THE *STARK* DISASTER

Under a clear evening sky, on Sunday, May 17, 1987, the guided missile frigate USS *Stark* cruised slowly through the Persian Gulf. The *Stark* was on a routine patrol in international waters, some 80 miles northeast of Bahrain. Commanded by Captain Glen Brindel, 43, a 21-year Navy career officer, the 445-foot long ship carried a crew of 200 officers and men. Brindel's tour as the *Stark*'s CO was rapidly winding down, with his replacement due on board in six days.

Iraq was hitting tankers carrying Iran's oil exports, while Iran was attacking ships carrying oil from Kuwait and Saudi Arabia, who were extending financial aid to Iraq. There had been misdirected attacks by both sides. However, so far, no U.S. ships had been involved. Iranian attacks had usually been mounted in the southernmost part of the Gulf. Iraqi attacks were usually mounted in northern areas.

The *Stark* was sailing in the central Gulf, in an area in which no attacks had occurred to date. Still, there was reason to worry. Iraqi anti-shipping strikes had been creeping further south. Three days earlier, on May 14, an Iraqi fighter had hit a tanker with a French-made Exocet missile barely sixty miles away from the area the *Stark* was now sailing in. Capt. Brindel had been warned about the Iraqi attack. However, on the evening of the 17th, he seemed to be preoccupied with readying his ship for an upcoming inspection.

Shortly before 8:00 P.M., a U.S. Air Force E-3A "Sentry" Airborne Warning and Control aircraft (AWACS) flying in Saudi Arabian airspace picked up an Iraqi aircraft on its powerful surveillance radar. The AWACS was part of what was dubbed the "ELF-1" force, based in Dhahran, Saudi Arabia. The Iraqi aircraft was flying on a relatively rare, for the Iraqis, nighttime mission toward the central Gulf. The Iraqi aircraft's course took it over water in a southeasterly direction, threading through the relatively narrow strip in international waters between an Iranian declared "exclusion zone" and Saudi Arabian territory. Iraqi fighters often took this route for their ship attacks. American officers sometimes called this strip "Mirage Alley."

As a precaution, the AWACS called in air cover in the form of two Saudi Arabian Air Force F-15 fighters. It didn't call on them to intercept the Iraqi aircraft, since it appeared to be flying the kind of mission the Iraqis usually flew against Iranian shipping targets. The Iraqi aircraft picked up by the AWACS was outside the detection range of the *Stark*'s own air search radar. However, the *Stark* was quickly alerted to the Iraqi's presence by the AWACS, which began feeding data on the contact to the USS *Coontz*, sitting dockside in the port of Manama, Bahrain.

The *Coontz*, whose own radars were not operating, relayed the AWACS information to the *Stark* over a Navy data link. The *Stark* could, in effect, see through the eyes of the AWACS and follow the path of the oncoming aircraft. The AWACS confirmed that it was tracking an Iraqi military aircraft, a French-made Mirage F-l fighter. Iranian-U.S. antagonism was still strong following the fall of the U.S.–supported Shah and the embassy hostage crisis. To counter expansion by Iran's revolutionary government, the U.S. was even extending "soft" support to Iraq's war effort. Given the circumstances, the AWACS classified the Iraqi track as a "friendly strike/support aircraft."

Captain Brindel briefly stopped by the *Stark*'s Combat Information Center (CIC) and was told that an Iraqi aircraft was headed south. Brindel told his Tactical Action Officer, Lieutenant Basil Moncrief, to keep a close eye on the contact, noting that the Iraqis had been coming further south recently. The *Stark* was scheduled to participate in an Atlantic Fleet Mobile Training Team exercise and inspection in a few days. In preparation for the inspection, the *Stark* then began a "full power run" engineering test, running up to a speed of 30 knots. Capt. Brindel continued on to the bridge. He had the CIC contacted to find out why the *Stark*'s own radar had not yet picked up the Iraqi fighter.

His inquiry prompted the CIC to shift the *Stark*'s air search radar to a shorter- range (80-mile) mode, focusing on contacts lower and closer to the ship. The mode switch did the trick and the *Stark*'s own radar now detected the Iraqi fighter about 70 miles out. When the full power run ended, Capt. Brindel left the bridge and went to his cabin to make a head call.

The AWACS now saw the Iraqi fighter ending its run down the Gulf and swinging around to the east. The Iraqi pilot had either spotted a likely target or was searching for one. If the fighter kept to its new course, it would pass within approximately 11 nautical miles of the *Stark*. Shortly thereafter, the Iraqi jet turned even more toward the *Stark*. The frigate's radar operator told Lieutenant Moncrief that the Iraqi's course would now take it to a closest approach point of only 4 nautical miles from the ship. At the same time, an Electronic Warfare Technician in the *Stark*'s CIC began to pick up radar signals which correlated with emissions from the Cyrano IV radar carried on Iraqi Mirage fighters. A minute later, the *Stark*'s radar operator requested permission to transmit a standard warning on the Military Air Distress Frequency to the Iraqi fighter, which had now closed to a distance of 43 nautical miles from the ship. Lieutenant Moncrief responded, "No, wait."

Not aware that anything special was going on, the *Stark*'s Executive Officer, Lieutenant Commander Ray Gajan walked into the CIC to discuss some administrative matters with Lieutenant Moncrief. Seeing the activity, he waited, watching events from a position near the chart table. About the same time that Lt. Commander Gajan entered the CIC, the Duty Officer on board the Middle East Force flagship, USS *LaSalle*, docked in Bahrain, radioed an inquiry to the *Stark*. He wanted to know if it was copying the details on the AWACS track of the Iraqi aircraft. Lieutenant Moncrief replied that it was, noting that the track had been evaluated as an Iraqi Mirage F-1EQ.

Unknown to the U.S. forces tracking it, the Mirage had been specially modified to carry two French-made Exocet anti-ship missiles rather than its normal load of one Exocet. The fighter also carried a centerline fuel tank for extended range. The overloaded Iraqi aircraft was aerodynamically unstable and was proving to be a handful for its pilot to fly. The AWACS could see that the plane's track was erratic, indicating that the pilot was having difficulty in fully controlling it. Reportedly, the overloaded Mirage was going so slow at one point that it almost stalled out and crashed.

At a range of 32-1/2 nautical miles, the Iraqi fighter began flying directly toward the *Stark*, rapidly closing the distance between them. No one in the *Stark*'s CIC seemed to notice that the Iraqi jet was now headed straight at them. At 9:07 P.M., the pilot of the Mirage fired one of his Exocet missiles at a blip on his radar screen. The missile was launched at a range of 22 nautical miles and would take some two minutes to reach its target. The *Stark* was running with its navigation lights blazing, completely unaware that an Exocet was now streaking toward it at 550 miles per hour.

The frigate was operating at what the Navy called Readiness Condition III: its air and surface sensors were operating, and its weapons could be put into action on short notice. One third of the crew were at their stations. Still, the ship wasn't quite as ready as it should have been. All of the consoles in the CIC were supposed to be manned but they were not. A crewman assigned to a .50 caliber machine gun was lying down at his post.

The *Stark*'s forward lookout saw a bright light flare on the horizon when the Iraqi missile was launched, but he assumed that the light was from something on the surface. Around the time that the first missile was launched, Lieutenant Moncrief noticed on the radar display the course change which had been made earlier by the Iraqi jet. The situation was apparently getting more serious and Lieutenant Moncrief had Captain Brindel summoned to the CIC. He also ordered the radio operator to issue warnings to the Iraqi pilot. About a minute after firing its first missile, the Mirage fired another Exocet at the *Stark*. The second missile was launched at a range of 15 nautical miles. At about the same time, the *Stark* finally broadcast a warning on the Military Air Distress Frequency:

> "Unknown aircraft, this is a U.S. Navy warship at your 078 . . . (pause), for 12 miles, request you identify yourself, over."[1]

Also, around this time, the Electronic Warfare Technician in the CIC detected what he thought was the F-1EQ's radar "locking-on" the *Stark*. The technician turned up the volume on his console and a steady, high-pitched signal of the radar "lock-on" sounded throughout the darkened CIC. Virtually all of the men in the CIC paused and turned their heads toward the console that was the source of the signal. About 10 seconds later, the signal abruptly ceased. It may actually have been the first Exocet missile's seeker locking on the *Stark*. A concerned crewman got permission from Lieutenant Moncrief to go topside and arm the Super Rapid Bloom Off Board Chaff (SRBOC) launchers. That system consisted of clusters of mortar-like tubes which fired packages of metallic strips, or chaff. The strips dispersed in the air and reflected back a signal to a missile's guidance radar, mimicking a ship. Hopefully, a missile would be distracted into the cloud of chaff and away from its intended target. The *Stark* then issued its second warning on the Military Air Distress Frequency:

> "Unknown aircraft this is US Navy warship on your 076 at 12 miles . . . (pause), request you identify yourself and state your intentions, over."[2]

There was no reply.

Two of the deadly 15-foot long Exocet missiles, each tipped with a 300-pound warhead, were now streaking toward the *Stark*. Their blue rocket exhausts reflected off the waters of the Gulf as they bobbed up and down slightly, maintaining a sea-skimming altitude about 10 feet above the surface. The frigate's low alert status had not changed and off-duty crewmen, some in the last moments of their lives, remained settled in their bunks.

Lieutenant Moncrief moved to the console controlling the Phalanx Close In Weapon System (CIWS). The Phalanx is a short-range "last ditch" anti-missile defense in the form of a self-contained, radar-directed, 20-mm multi-barrel "Gatling" gun. The weapon was capable of firing up to 3,000 rounds per minute, using very dense, depleted uranium ammunition. The rounds could penetrate a missile's warhead, detonating it, or damage the missile's fuselage and control surfaces, knocking it into the sea. Lieutenant Moncrief inserted his key in the console and brought the Phalanx into "stand-by" mode, which meant that it was warmed up, but its internal radar was not operating. If the Phalanx had been set on "automatic" it would have tracked and fired on any target it detected.

Lieutenant Moncrief then told the fire control technician to "lock-on" the Iraqi jet with the long-range search radar of the ship's MK92 Fire Control System. When a radar "locks-on" a target, it continuously tracks it rather than just periodically picking it up as it searches in all directions. If the aircraft detects that it has been "locked-on," it would assume that the source of the "lock-on" has targeted him and might be preparing to fire. Accordingly, "locking-on" a plane serves as a definite attention-getter and warning, even if the ship does not intend to actually fire at that point. The radar "lock-on" would also indicate to an Iraqi pilot on an attack mission that the source of the radar signal was a warship and not a tanker, which would most likely have been his intended target.

However, the *Stark*'s radar was unable to lock-on to the Iraqi since its signal was blocked by the ship's superstructure, which fell between the radar antenna and the location of the Iraqi fighter at the time. Lieutenant Moncrief then ordered another radar at a different location be used to "lock-up" the Iraqi. This had finally been accomplished at a range of about 10 nautical miles. Observing the proceedings, Lt. Commander Gajan said, "Let him know who we are." It was way too late.

The *Stark*'s forward lookout had seen the flash of the first Exocet launch without realizing what it was. He then observed a small blue dot on the horizon, moving erratically up and down. The dot resolved itself into a blue fireball, which became steady as it neared the ship, coming in at an angle of 10 to 15 degrees off the port bow. Seconds before impact, the lookout realized just what the approaching fireball of missile exhaust meant and screamed, "Inbound missile! Inbound missile!" on the sound powered phone circuit. He then dived to the deck. Bernard Seely was standing watch at the helm when he saw a nearby fog bank suddenly turn an eerie blue color. A ball of light streaked out of the mist and seemed to head straight for the bridge. At the last second, the missile dove into the hull of the ship.

The Exocet slammed into the *Stark* with a loud thud rather than an explosion, indicating that its warhead had failed to detonate. Seely was jolted into a compass in the console behind him. Alarmed by the impact, the men around him began shouting, "What the hell is going on?"[3] Most crewmen, including those in the CIC, did not even realize that a missile had just hit their ship. Men at the aft end of the ship thought that a fire pump or some other piece of operating machinery had torn itself apart. Others thought that maybe the ship's 76mm cannon had fired or that chaff had been launched from the SRBOC tubes.

The Exocet's warhead may not have exploded, but the missile easily sliced though the thin, unarmored hull of the *Stark*. Propelled by its still burning rocket motor, it tore its way deep into the body of the ship, ripping its way through the portside fire main, the ship control berthing area, the barbershop, the mail room and the Chief Petty Officer's quarters. The missile started to break up as it careened through the ship, with one piece passing entirely through the hull and finally punching a small exit hole in the starboard side. The unexploded warhead itself came to rest in a passageway near that hole. Tragically, the still burning rocket motor came to a stop in a heavily occupied crew berthing area. Because the Exocet had been launched well short of its maximum range, it was still carrying a large quantity of solid rocket fuel when it hit.

A few seconds before, the rocket motor had been powering the 1,500-pound Exocet over the Gulf at 550 mph. Now, fueled by 300 pounds of remaining propellant, it was spewing an intense jet of flame like a gigantic blowtorch inside the relatively small confines of the berthing compartment. What it was like for the men trapped in there is unimaginable. Sailors screamed as they were incinerated in their bunks.

The bridge finally sounded General Quarters. Lieutenant (jg) William A. Hanson, Junior Officer of the Deck, saw the second missile streaking in and shouted into the mike, "Inbound missile, Portside!" Captain Brindel ran to the CIC from his stateroom. With no explosion following the first missile hit, the forward lookout picked himself up only to see another blue dot incoming. He started running but was tossed across the deck when the second Exocet hit about 20 to 30 seconds after the first. The warhead on this one did explode. From the time the Iraqi aircraft had been detected by the *Stark*'s radar to the time the second missile hit, the *Stark* had been plowing through the Gulf on a steady course and speed, seemingly oblivious to what was happening.

The second Exocet hit about eight feet forward of the first, penetrating only about three feet into the ship before its warhead detonated. Having traveled a shorter distance, the second missile had even more fuel onboard than the first. The exploding warhead ravaged an area with a radius of about 30 feet into the ship. Fortunately for the *Stark*, the quick warhead detonation also blew a large hole in the ship's hull, venting some of its blast energy to the outside. Still, the explosive combustion of the exploding warhead, and propellant shed by the first missile, released a near instantaneous wave of heat energy.

A searing fireball raced along the path punched through the ship by the first missile. Bernard Seely had been headed to a lower deck to man his general quarters station when the second Exocet exploded. "All I remember is seeing little red balls of fire flying all over the place and people screaming," he said. "It was completely dark and there was fire everywhere."[4] One off-duty sailor had been hurled from his bunk when the first missile hit. He picked himself up and headed for an upper deck.

He had scrambled up one ladder and was halfway up the next when the second missile hit. He saw the sailor behind him cut in two when a bulkhead collapsed.

In the living quarters near the area struck by the missiles, there was pandemonium. Hull Technician Michael O'Keefe was in Engineering Support Berthing, directly below the missile impact area. "There was an explosion and I was thrown out of my rack," recalled O'Keefe, who thought the ship's engines might have blown up. "I heard them saying 'General Quarters, General Quarters, all hands man your battle stations.' I started yelling and pulling people out of their racks. I made it to the exit but there were flames already there. I told everybody to go to the emergency escape hatch. We got there and we had water already pouring in."

The second missile then hit and exploded. O'Keefe saw the fireball but kept trying to get men out through the escape hatch. "There were no lights . . . It was hard to get around and check [bunks] so we could get everybody out of the compartment." O'Keefe later said, "I grabbed them by their head and their pants, just shoving them out."[5]

James Wheeler, a 28-year old Petty Officer from Texas, was asleep in his bunk at the time of the attack. "I heard the alarm and I didn't know where it was coming from at first," he later reported. "Then I heard whistling and there was nothing but fire."[6] Lieutenant Carl S. Barbour, who dragged him away from the area of raging fires, saved Wheeler. Some of the *Stark*'s crew died in the searing flames of the first missile's burning rocket motor as it rampaged on its angular, 100-foot long swath through the ship. Most of the men lost in the attack perished in the berthing area, where the burning rocket motor came to rest. They were either burned to death or were suffocated.

Michael O'Keefe tried to save three Senior Chief Petty Officers, getting to within six feet of their location before being driven back by the intense heat. Twenty-three-year-old Mark Bareford recalled the horror when the missile hit. "I was screaming, everybody was screaming. The guys behind me, they died. They screamed until they died. . . . If I had stopped to get somebody out of their bunk, If I had waited the five seconds to say, 'Hey, Pete, get up,' that missile would have gone through me and blown me into 50,000 little pieces."[7] Both Wheeler and Bareford were badly burned. Many of the surviving crewmen were driven out of enclosed spaces by the dense smoke and found refuge on the open helicopter deck located aft.

As the inferno raged below decks, individual crewmen fought to save their buddies and their ship. Electronics Technician Wayne Richard Weaver, from Bethlehem, Pennsylvania, kept pulling men from the wreckage and supervising their evacuation from Combat Systems Berthing. He could have easily escaped, but remained to aid as many men as possible. Weaver may have pulled as many as a dozen men to safety before succumbing to his injuries. He was later found clutching the body of another man he had been trying to rescue.

The explosion severed the leg of Seaman Mark Robert Caouette, from Fitchburg, Massachusetts. He also had shrapnel wounds and was severely burned. Nevertheless, he refused to let his crewmates pull him away from the burning area. Instead, he somehow dragged himself around, desperately shutting off valves to the fire main, which had been ruptured by the initial missile impact. Unless that line could be shut down, there would be inadequate water pressure to fight the raging fires. *Stark* officer Lieutenant William A. Conklin later recalled, "Caouette knew he was going to die, that's what he said to people who passed by him."[8] Mark Caouette's charred body was later found slumped over one of the valves.

Petty Officer William Morandi had been sleeping in the Combat Systems Berthing compartment when the missiles hit. "There were a lot of us in the berthing compartment at the time, but we couldn't go out the main hatch because of the fire and smoke, and the escape hatch was blocked," he recalled. "Then the compartment started filling with water."[9] Trapped with 28 others in the darkened compartment, Morandi, along with crewmen Timothy Porter, William McLeod, and Timothy Gable donned hooded Emergency Escape Breathing Devices (EEB's). These provided a limited oxygen supply and were available for every sailor on Navy ships.

The men climbed through the main hatch into the compartment above, the one that had been hit by the missile. They staggered out through the thick smoke, jolted by electric shocks from torn, arcing cables. The dangling, live cables would electrocute some other crewmen. Virtually blinded, Porter, McLeod, and Morandi stumbled through the huge hole blasted in the portside hull by the second Exocet and fell out of the ship into the Gulf. "I got disoriented," Morandi said. "The smoke was getting in my head. I ended up actually falling out the hole on the side of the ship. When I surfaced, I saw the ship cruising away over the horizon."[10] He found himself in the water less than 15 minutes after the missiles hit. Gable jumped out deliberately. Another sailor in the same berthing area, Gary Mahone, discovered two bodies face down in the water on the deck. He too fell into the Gulf trying to escape. The week before the attack, the crew had participated in an egress exercise to test their ability to move from berthing areas to topside while blindfolded. A crewmember later said that he wouldn't have made it out that day if it hadn't been for the practice provided by that blindfold drill.

In spite of the two Exocet hits, the *Stark*'s engines were still running. However, the bridge lost control of the ship's steering, which had to be shifted to a control station in the aft engineering room. The stricken ship headed back to Bahrain at 15 knots. Course changes had to be relayed from the bridge to the aft control station. The *Stark* had also lost outside radio communication. However, crewmen improvised and used small battery powered helicopter aircrew survival radios to contact the USS *Waddell* and the AWACS. They called on the same Military Air Distress Frequency on which the *Stark* had futilely attempted to warn off the Iraqi attacker.

In Bahrain, U.S. Ambassador Sam H. Zakhem and Rear Admiral Harold Bernsen, commander of the Middle East Force, were having dinner together on board the flagship USS *LaSalle*. A few minutes after their meal had begun, a duty officer reported to Admiral Bernsen that the AWACS had picked up an Iraqi Mirage heading south. Bernsen had told him to make sure that the *Stark* was talking to the AWACS and receiving good information on the Iraqi track. The two were just having after-dinner tea when one of the bridge officers came in. "We sensed something was wrong," said Zakhem. Admiral Bernsen left and was informed that the *Stark* had been attacked. "Oh my God," was his reaction. Admiral Bernsen quickly returned and tersely told the ambassador, "The *Stark* got hit."[11]

The two Exocets had severely damaged the *Stark* and inflicted a heavy loss of life, though the immediate destruction caused by the missile hits did not threaten to sink the ship. But now, super hot fires, ignited by the missiles and sustained by their propellants, were growing and consuming more of the ship. The water pressure available to firefighters was drastically reduced because the portside fire main had been ruptured by the missile impacts. Hoses would have to be brought all the way forward from the aft fire mains. Extremely dense smoke blocked all visibility in workspaces adjacent to the fires. Unless those fires could be contained, the *Stark* might well share the fate of HMS *Sheffield* during the Falklands War. A single Exocet, whose warhead had also failed to explode, had hit that Royal Navy destroyer. Fires ignited by the missile had gotten out of control, causing the loss of the ship.

Nearly one fifth of the *Stark*'s crew was dead within a short time after the attack. Others had been badly burned, were suffering from serious smoke inhalation, or had received shrapnel wounds. Several had fallen overboard. Many senior crewmen with damage control experience had been lost. The battle to save the ship was just beginning. It would last some 18 hours.

Captain Brindel stationed himself on the bridge to monitor firefighting efforts fore and aft of the missile hits. Communication with the aft part of the ship was difficult because of the damage and fires. Accordingly, Lieutenant Moncrief went to the flight deck at the stern to direct efforts on that side of the missile hits. Lieutenant Moncrief had to scramble over the bridge wing to avoid the twisted port side blast hole and a white-hot deck on the starboard side. The *Stark* carried munitions which could well be ignited by direct contact with the flames, or even by the intense heat radiated by the fires at a distance. Exploding munitions would cause more ship damage and casualties.

Lieutenant Commander Gajan had been wounded in the shoulder and the hand by shrapnel when the second Exocet exploded. Nevertheless, he went to the bridge and ordered crewmen to jettison the hand-held Stinger anti-aircraft missiles and .50 caliber machine gun ammunition located topside.[12] Those items were dangerous enough, but the real threat to the *Stark* was in the forward missile magazine, located under a deck-mounted launcher. That magazine housed nearly 40 Standard anti-aircraft and Harpoon anti-ship missiles, each of which had warheads and propellant loads roughly comparable to the ones on the Exocets that had hit the *Stark*. If they detonated, like a string of gigantic firecrackers, the *Stark* would simply be blown apart and most of her surviving crew lost.

The *Stark*'s Damage Control Assistant was 27-year-old Lieutenant William A. Conklin. The evening of the attack, he had settled into his bunk in a T-shirt and a pair of gym shorts. When the first missile hit, he heard the sound of grinding metal and at first thought the *Stark* had collided with another ship. He grabbed his shoes and clothes and ran out of his room. The adjacent passageway was already filled with blinding smoke. Conklin was trying to make his way aft when the second missile hit. He saw the passageway buckle under him from the warhead blast.

Conklin managed to reach Damage Control Central around 9:30 P.M. He and his team began to evaluate the ship's situation and plan their actions. Increasingly intense fires, fed by the missile propellants, were raging in the forward parts of the ship struck by the Exocets. The compartments in which the fires were raging were turning into a kind of giant, super hot burner within the ship, roasting compartments above it. The intense heat was already reaching up to parts of the ship's box-like aluminum superstructure, which rose above the hull on the main deck.

The first order of business was to close off the damaged fire main sections. Water was gushing out of shattered fire main sections, seriously reducing line pressure and greatly hampering efforts to fight the fires. The valves, which had to be shutdown, were located in the burning, smoke-filled crew berthing area. Determined to reach them, Conklin took off the T-shirt from under the coveralls he was now wearing, soaked it in seawater, wrapped it around his otherwise exposed face, and made his way back into the berthing area. Conklin kept his eyes closed to protect them from the intense heat. He figured, better to lose the eyelids than the eyes themselves. He felt his way along the scalding pipes, relying on his memory for their layout. "Every time I touched a pipe," Conklin recalled, "it was like striking a hot griddle." He used the backs of his hands, tapping on the burning hot pipes to locate and turn off valves. Sometimes his hands stuck to a pipe. When he pulled them away, he left behind strips of skin sizzling on the metal.

Bulkheads and the deck were glowing from the heat. Conklin thought that being in the berthing compartment was like being inside a pizza oven. "Stand in front of one sometime, then imagine walking inside it," he said. Brass keys in his pocket melted together from the heat. Two days after the attack, when Conklin was finally able to remove his coveralls and to take a shower, he discovered that his nylon gym shorts had melted into his body like candle wax.[13]

The crew was now fighting a fire later described by a Navy panel as a "shipboard inferno the like of which had never been experienced."[14] At least by the modern U.S. Navy, which trained for fires generating temperatures up to 1,800 degrees Fahrenheit. The Stark's fires reached 3,000 degrees, stoked by the missile propellant and modern materials used in the ship's construction. Water being used for firefighting sometimes flashed instantly into steam or formed scalding pools, lapping around the shoes of the men.

Sailors found that their Navy uniforms were better suited to inspection than safety. Shiny corfam shoes and wrinkle-resistant polyester clothing melted in the intense heat. Standard issue fire helmets had to be tossed aside because they absorbed too much heat. The smoke was so thick that the firefighters were forced to use Oxygen Breathing Apparatuses (OBA's). The sheer volume of smoke would keep them from isolating the actual sources of the fire for several hours.

The blaze began to grow and started to climb vertically. Combustible materials in compartments above the fire were heated to their "flashpoints" and burst into flames, starting fires in new locations. Hose teams tried to attack the fire from adjacent compartments, but were driven back by the heat and smoke. Heat from the furnace below was beginning to melt portions of the ship's superstructure above deck. The vinyl covering on exposed wires and cables burned with billowing clouds of acrid smoke, which were then spread throughout the ship by its air re-circulation system. Within an hour, the spreading fire consumed the Combat Information Center. Finally, in the face of the fires, even the bridge had to be abandoned. Areas of the main deck and the starboard side of the ship were glowing cherry red. The deck was so hot that crewmen's feet were being burned through the soles of their boots.

Extreme exertion in near unbearable heat forced the men on the firefighting teams to be spelled every 10 to 15 minutes. Freshwater pumps were down, and desperately thirsty firefighters used axes to break into mess deck vending machines. They even resorted to drinking the bagged IV fluids from medical supplies to try to slake their thirst. The Oxygen Breathing Apparatus (OBA) worn by the men uses replaceable canisters, which generate oxygen through a chemical reaction. Because of an upcoming inspection, the *Stark* had over 300 OBA canisters, three times its normal supply. It still was not enough. Within a few hours the *Stark*'s supply was exhausted and fresh canisters had to be brought in by helicopter from the Middle East Force flagship and from other ships. Ultimately, over 1,200 canisters would be used up. Without the new supplies, it is doubtful if the *Stark*'s damage control teams could have continued fighting the fires.

As the fires spread upward, the teams counterattacked by cutting holes into the overheads of compartments and jamming in hose nozzles from above to try to extinguish the flames. They discovered that an additional advantage to this technique was that superheated air and smoke vented upward and out of compartments, eventually making it easier to gain lateral access to them. The thick smoke roiling through the ship continued to be a vexing problem.

The *Stark* tried several course changes in an attempt to use the wind to clear the smoke out, but it didn't really help much. Even worse, the ship's speed made it difficult to keep the intake hoses feeding the auxiliary fire pumps in the water. The *Stark* finally came to a dead stop about 11:00 P.M. Capt. Brindel ordered the endangered missile magazine flooded. However, crewmen couldn't carry out the order because the loss of the forward fire main prevented them from getting the water supply they needed.

The first ship to come to the *Stark*'s aid was a Dutch-owned commercial salvage tug, which pulled alongside the stricken frigate around 11:30 P.M. Salvage tugs loitered near areas in the Gulf where tankers were frequently attacked by either side and then rushed to the scene, offering their services to the victim. The salvage vessels were sometimes called "vulture tugs," and were said to arrive with a fire hose in one hand and a salvage contract in the other. Nonetheless, to the *Stark*, this circling "vulture" had to be a very welcome sight. Without its help, the missile magazine might well have blown up, sinking the ship. Lieutenant Gajan directed the tug forward, on the starboard side, to play its water cannon in the vicinity of the missile magazine. A 2-1/2 inch hose was also run over from the tug and down into the magazine to spray the missiles with cooling water. Gunner's Mate Mark Samples would courageously sit inside the magazine for over 12 hours, using the hose to cool the missiles.

Water was itself turning out to be a big problem for the *Stark*. So much of it had accumulated in the upper decks and the superstructure, from firefighting efforts and ruptured mains, that the *Stark* began taking on a severe list to port. Eventually, the ship would reach a maximum angle of 36 degrees. Pictures of the *Stark*, heeled way over under the weight of all that water, probably communicated its distress to the public more than any other visual aspect of the disaster. If the water kept accumulating, the ship threatened to capsize.

Lieutenant Gajan organized a "dewatering" party to cut and punch holes in bulkheads to allow water to drain out, preventing any increase in the angle of list. In the early morning hours of Monday the 18th, the USS *Waddell* arrived on the scene with damage control supplies and medical aid. The survivors of the *Stark*'s crew, with the aid of supplies from other ships, were slowly able to prevail in their battles against the fires and flooding. By Monday afternoon, the fires were mostly extinguished, although small fires, "reflashes," continued to ignite up to 48 hours after the attack. The *Stark*'s crew worked continuously until around 5:00 P.M. on Monday, when men from other ships finally relieved them.

Swimming in the Gulf, unknowingly left behind by the *Stark* after they fell overboard, Timothy Porter and Timothy Gable found life rings which had been tossed out earlier. The others in the water, William McLeod and William Morandi, used their EEB's as improvised floats. Porter worried about rescue after being in the water for several hours. "I was praying for the sun to come up," he said. "When the sun came up and I saw the sharks, I wanted the sun to go down."[15] The four men were picked up a few hours later by a Bahrain Defense Forces Search and Rescue helicopter, which had been dispatched to the scene. Gary Mahone was still in the water. He managed to stay afloat by swimming on his back until picked up by the USS *Waddell* later in the morning. On one of his backstrokes, he brought up a poisonous sea snake in his hand. Mahone hurled it away from him.[16]

The first Exocet's unexploded warhead had remained intact on the *Stark* and was discovered by firefighters from USS *LaSalle* on the 18th. The men ignored the live warhead as they went about their work. An Explosive Ordnance Disposal (EOD) team flown in to render the *Stark*'s own missiles and torpedoes safe also removed and disarmed the warhead. The EOD personnel got assistance from the French Naval Attaché Staff in Washington in order to devise a procedure to disarm it. The information on the French-made missile was radioed to the Gulf. It was still a dicey business because the right wires had to be cut. Unfortunately, they had all been blackened by the fire and smoke and couldn't be identified by their color-coding. The EOD team somehow did manage to cut the right ones and safe the warhead. It was taken away and is still being used as a training aid in Fort Story, Virginia. It was fortunate that the warhead did not "cook-off" from all of the heat it had been exposed to.

The *Stark* was taken under tow by USS *Conyngham* and brought to anchorage Tuesday night near the flagship *LaSalle* in Sitra Bay, Bahrain. Teams went onboard the ravaged ship the next day to recover the bodies of the crewmen killed in the attack—a total of 37. Most of the men lost in the attack had been in the forward berthing compartments. The scene there was appalling. Eight-inch solid steel pipes had been twisted like pretzels by the heat. The body of one crewman was found melted into his bunk. Three bodies were found with EEBD's on near a hatch. One sailor reported finding a severed arm with a letter still clutched in the hand.

"It's hard, very hard," crewman Dwayne Massey recalled. "When we looked down in the hole and saw all the bodies lying down there, it was an empty feeling, like an empty shell outside. You don't have any emotions."[17]

Bodies were identified visually. In some cases, the preliminary identification could only be made from clues such as clothing stencils, jewelry initials and bunk positions in the compartment. The body of one seaman, who had last been seen wandering around injured after the attack, was not recovered. He was presumed to have been lost overboard. Several of the men who had gone overboard and were later recovered thought they had heard someone screaming or yelling in the water that night. In Bahrain, telephones were set up on the *Waddell* for surviving crewmen to call relatives.

At the *Stark*'s home base, Mayport Naval Station near Jacksonville, Florida, Navy officers had the solemn task of notifying the families of sailors killed in the attack. Eighty-six *Stark* sailors made their homes in the area. Sixteen of them died in the attack. While awaiting news of their loved one's fate, Navy families leaned heavily on each other. A dozen families conducted an all-night prayer vigil in the base chapel. Relatives in the Base Community Center held an emotional three-hour meeting.

"The tension increased with every second that passed," said Chaplain Bill Perry. "It was like taking a guitar string and winding it ever more taut."[18] One wife gave birth to a baby girl not knowing her husband's fate. The Red Cross sent the news to the *Stark*. The presence of reporters trying for stories caused some resentment in Mayport. One reporter attempting to interview an off-duty sailor in a pool hall was threatened with a cue stick and told, "You wouldn't be here if it wasn't for the *Stark*."[19] A few reporters angered families and officials by visiting or phoning homes where word was still being awaited on the fate of their relatives.

Resentment against some in the media was justified. One reporter went to the home of the father of a *Stark* sailor who was unaccounted for. Asked to phone in her notes, she told her editor that she didn't want to tie up the family's phone. "Why not?" asked the editor. The son was dead. The newspaper knew, but the family had not yet been informed. The editor told the reporter to make sure she stayed there so she could get the big story on how the family reacted when told of their son's death. Instead, the reporter left and called in her notes from a pay phone. Unable to stomach her callous assignment, she did not return and quit her job the next day.[20]

For most, the waiting came to an end Monday and Tuesday when the news, terrible or joyful, came to one family after another. Betty Belton sent her three children to school at Mayport Elementary on Monday, not knowing if their father had survived the attack. She told them not to pay attention to rumors. At 1:00 A.M. Tuesday, she learned that her husband Mack was alive. Ernestine Foster, who had three of her seven children attending the same school as the Belton children, was told by a naval officer knocking on her door that her husband, Vernon, had been killed on the *Stark*. At the school, the principal asked the pupils to pray for the Foster family. Many of the children, 90 percent from military families, began to worry aloud about their own fathers' safety.[21]

Some families were understandably bitter. "They were like sitting ducks," said Robert DeAngelis, fighting to hold back tears over the death of his son Christopher, an electronics technician who had celebrated his 23rd birthday aboard the *Stark* on May 8.[22] "If someone is shooting at you," Susan Ryals told reporters gathered at her home, "you have the right to defend yourself."[23] Her husband Earl was missing and presumed dead. Most relatives were too lost in their grief to immediately go into reasons why.

The shadow of the *Stark* fell across the U.S. Naval Academy at Annapolis in the middle of the celebration marking the graduation of the Class of 1987. Flags were lowered to half-staff on the grounds. Navy Secretary James H. Webb urged the 1,022 graduates to remember the men killed and injured in the *Stark* attack. The survivors of that attack stood at attention on the hot tarmac at Bahrain International Airport on May 20 as a Navy helicopter appeared out of the haze over Manama harbor. The helicopter was ferrying aluminum caskets containing the remains of their crewmates for transfer to an Air Force C-141 Starlifter transport. The caskets, borne by *Stark* crewmen, were moved one by one to the Air Force transport in a simple, 15-minute ceremony.

An emotional focus for many present that day was Barbara Kiser and her five-year-old son John. Barbara had traveled 9,000 miles from Florida to rent an apartment in Bahrain to be close to her husband, Chief Petty Officer Steve Kiser. The couple had been able to enjoy several short leaves together, the last of which ended when Barbara took her husband to the wharf for the *Stark*'s departure at 8:00 A.M. Sunday morning, May 17th. Steve Kiser died that evening in the attack. Three days later, Barbara Kiser stood with her son between Captain Glen Brindel and Middle East Force Commander, Rear Admiral Harold J. Bernsen, as the caskets were loaded onto the Air Force transport. Wives of dignitaries present came up and hugged Mrs. Kiser. Bahraini officials lined up to shake hands and express their condolences.

While the adults talked, five-year-old John Kiser sat alone on a chair by his mother. When Ambassador Zakhem bent down to speak to him, the boy shyly hid his face in his mother's dress. As the last of the flag-draped caskets were loaded on the waiting jet, a Navy bugler played "Taps," Bahraini jets flew overhead, officers saluted and the honor guard presented arms. Mrs. Kiser whispered to her son, who put his hand over his heart. Photographs of the tow-headed youngster made papers around the world the next day. Later, Ambassador Zakhem stated that Mrs. Kiser had given him a letter and an Arabic language New Testament. The package was addressed to "The men who attacked the *Stark*, Dad's ship." Zakhem said he could not bring himself to read the letter out loud but described it as "a message of eternal peace."[24]

On Friday, May 22, in a sweltering hangar at the Naval base in Mayport, Florida, a crowd of 2,000, including 350 grief-stricken relatives of the men killed on the *Stark* gathered for a memorial service attended by President Ronald Reagan and his wife Nancy. The President personally embraced every sobbing mother in the crowd. His own eyes became red and swollen. His shirt was wet from tears and his suit stained with tears and makeup. Nancy Erwin, whose son Steve had died on the *Stark*, said, "The President greeted all of us personally, and it meant a lot to me that he said, 'I'm sorry about your son.'" She said that Reagan's look and the caring he showed "were genuine. I'll remember that for the rest of my life."[25]

The President eulogized the *Stark*'s dead as heroes who "stood guard in the night." President Reagan mentioned Senior Chief Petty Officer Gary Clinefelter, who volunteered to work at a base coordinating center for families when he was told his own son, 19-year-old

Seaman Brian Clinefelter, previously listed among the missing, had been confirmed dead. "I need to keep working," Reagan quoted him as saying. "He stayed at his post," the President said. "He carried on. Well, so, too, we must carry on. We must stay at our post."[26]

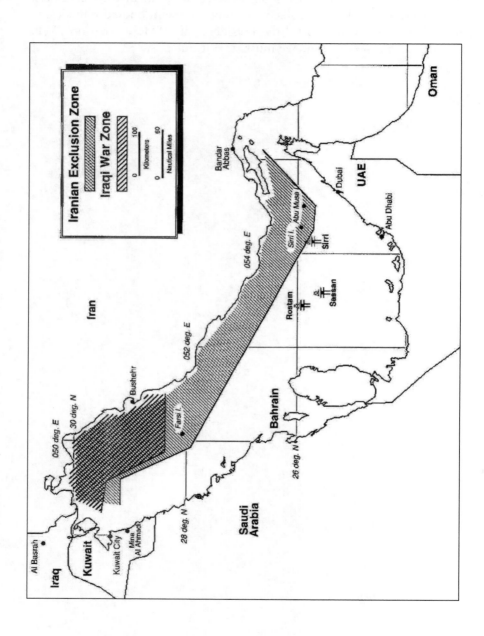

CHAPTER 2

TARGET: KUWAIT

At the time of the *Stark* attack, the United States was on the verge of a large and unprecedented commitment of naval forces to the Persian Gulf. The upcoming operation was in response to the most recent developments in the so-called "tanker war," which was itself an offshoot of the Iran-Iraq war. Both sides in that war depended on oil revenues to sustain their efforts. Iran's oil production was concentrated in fields north and east of the northernmost tip of the Gulf. Most of the oil was pumped from the mainland via underwater pipelines to the Kharg Island terminal, where it was the loaded into huge deep-draft tankers. These ships carried some 90 percent of Iran's oil down through the Gulf and then on to its ultimate destinations. In contrast, Iraq was able to flow its oil exports through overland pipelines that ran into Saudi Arabia and Turkey. This was an option which geography and politics denied to Iran.

The tanker war was generally considered to have begun in March 1984, when an Iraqi jet hit the Greek tanker *Filikon L* with an Exocet missile. The missile failed to explode, which was just as well, since the tanker was carrying oil for Iraq's supporter, Kuwait. Hitting the wrong target with a dud missile did not exactly mark an auspicious start for Iraq's anti-shipping campaign. Things, however, would change. In rapid succession, other Iraqi strikes followed for a total of 53 attacks in 1984. Iran responded in May that year by launching air attacks on ships traveling to and from Saudi Arabian, Kuwaiti and other non-belligerent ports. Attacks by both sides continued through 1985.

In 1986, Iran began using its navy frigates to fire relatively small Seakiller missiles at targeted ships. Iranian Revolutionary Guard Corps

(IRGC) naval elements joined in the attacks in 1987. The IRGC used a
fleet of small speedboats, often based on islands and oil platforms. They
fired machine guns and shoulder-launched anti-tank rockets in their
attacks on tankers. The Iranians also began a stop and search operation
near the entrance to the Strait of Hormuz, looking for war material destined for Iraq.

When the "tanker war" began in 1984, it had marked the first sustained military operation directed against merchant shipping since the
Second World War. The results had been a bit surprising. The super-
tanker-size crude carriers turned out to be difficult targets to sink or
even seriously damage. In fact, in many cases, the price Iraq paid for its
Exocet missiles actually exceeded the cost of repairing the damage
inflicted on the tankers.

While a missile or rocket might punch a hole in the hull of a tanker,
the cargo of thick crude tended to muffle the explosion of the warhead.
One military analyst compared it to "shooting a bullet into mud."[1] The
unrefined crude was also unlikely to ignite from the blast. If the ship
was traveling empty, it used exhaust gas from its diesel engines to flush
fire-sustaining oxygen from empty crude compartments. Some ships,
coming into the Gulf to pick up cargoes of crude, were hit in compartments that had been filled with water ballast. Needless to say, little damage was done.

Many of the rockets and missiles fired at ships by the Iranians did
not carry large warheads, and were incapable of doing any serious
structural damage. Even the large-warhead Exocets used by the Iraqis
might damage one or at most a couple of up to 17 compartments on an
ultra-large crude carrier. This sort of damage might cause some flooding, but was unlikely to sink a ship. The steel plating used for the hulls
of supertankers was a fair amount thicker than the plating used on warships, and would usually stop the rifle-caliber machine gun bullets fired
by the IRGC from small boats. Probably the greatest threat to large
tankers was posed by their own fuel supply. That fuel was substantially
more volatile than the crude cargo. A fuel-fed fire could cause extensive
damage or even the loss of the ship.

The less numerous gasoline tankers were in a great deal more danger since their volatile cargo was much more likely to be ignited by even
a minor hit. Even empty compartments on such ships posed a serious
threat since they were likely to contain a potentially explosive mix of air
and gasoline fumes. Liquid Petroleum Gas (LPG) tankers faced some-

what similar hazards since their pressurized cargo was highly inflammable, though their double hulls offered some protection. "Dry" bulk cargo carriers were not particularly vulnerable, although the ships were much smaller than the crude carriers. One 30-year-old Indian cargo vessel carrying onions and potatoes to Iran was hit by an Iraqi Exocet missile. It was quickly patched up and returned to service.

The radar-guided Exocets fired by the Iraqis had a tendency to home in on the high profile accommodation blocks rising above the hulls of ships, particularly on the outbound journey, when the laden hull sat low in the water. A hit on the accommodation block was unlikely to cause the ship's cargo to catch fire, but was more likely to cause crew casualties. Iran did develop a simple, but sometimes effective, countermeasure to the Iraqi Exocet. Radar reflectors were placed on barges or small boats, and either towed behind ships or placed near them when they were anchored for loading. Wrecks were also reportedly fitted with the reflectors. The devices returned a stronger signal to the Exocet's radar than a ship, leading the missile to go after the reflector. Some of these reflectors were spotted with holes punched clear through them by decoyed Exocets.

This evidence did not prevent Aerospatiale, the manufacturer of the Exocet, from claiming that the missile was resistant to such countermeasures. "The whole idea of the Iranians spoofing them makes me burst out laughing," said an Aerospatiale executive.[2] The French government insisted that it had received a personal assurance from Iraqi President Saddam Hussein that the Exocet-carrying Super Etendard fighters it had leased to Iraq would only be employed against military targets and not civilian shipping.[3] There were no reports of civilian tanker crewmen bursting out laughing at that assertion.

When its shipping came under attack by Iraq, Iran looked around the Gulf for a target to retaliate against. There was one obvious one: Kuwait. A supporter of Iraq, and lacking any real military capability, the small country looked like a ripe candidate for intimidation. Unlike Saudi Arabia, Kuwait was totally dependent on Gulf shipping for its petroleum exports. Thus, the tankers sailing to and from Kuwait fully exposed its exports and served as a highly sensitive pressure point for possible Iranian action.

Faced with large and threatening neighbors, "like a Finland with two Russias," said one diplomat,[4] Kuwait found little to choose between Iran and Iraq prior to the outbreak of the war. Now, fearing that an Iraqi defeat would allow the Iranian Islamic revolution to wash up to and probably over it, Kuwait threw its support behind Iraq. Kuwaiti efforts on Iraq's behalf included extending large loans, allowing the use of its ports to unload the mostly Soviet war material destined for Iraq, and may even have included allowing Iraqi aircraft to pass through its airspace on their way to strike targets in the Gulf.

Frustrated at Kuwait's support of Iraq, and demanding that the Emirate "repent" by ending it, Iran alternated between threats and conciliatory gestures. For its part, Kuwait alternated between periods of apprehension over apparently imminent Iranian battlefield breakthroughs and then relief when the Iraqis were able to hold. The Iranian capture of the Faw Peninsula in February 1986 brought Iranian forces right opposite to Kuwaiti territory at Bubiyan Island. Iran wasted little time in pointing out the obvious implications. Iranian prime minister Rafsanjani ominously noted, "These countries should remember that we are now on their borders."[5]

Iran also called on its subversive network among Kuwaiti Shias to conduct terrorist strikes and sabotage in order to put additional pressure on the beleaguered country. In 1984, there had been an assassination attempt against the Emir. In mid-June 1986, major fires broke out at the Mina Al-Ahmadi petroleum complex. A nervous Emir dissolved the Kuwaiti parliament in July 1986. Iran began singling out of Kuwaiti-bound ships in late 1986, further tightening the screw. Three Kuwaiti-flag tankers and ten others bound for the country were hit in 1986. The attacks only increased as 1987 dawned. Some ships were refusing to sail to Kuwaiti destinations in the face of the sustained Iranian attacks. A Kuwaiti diplomat later said, "Faw had intoxicated the Iranians. They wanted to impose a siege on Kuwait which would lead to a domestic uprising against Kuwait's support for Iraq."[6]

Under heavy pressure, an increasingly desperate Kuwait turned to the major powers for relief. In late 1986, it approached both the United States and the Soviet Union on the subject of re-flagging half of the 22 tankers belonging to the government-owned Kuwaiti Oil Tanker Company. More important to Kuwait than the protection of some of its ships was the idea that a commitment to re-flagging would draw one, and likely both, superpowers more deeply into the Gulf. The ultimate goal was to use their involvement to help force an end to the war. Kuwait apparently had long held the view that only the superpowers could resolve the conflict.

"I don't think it has anything to do with shipping," said a Western diplomat. "The goal is to get the superpowers involved."[7] The Kuwaitis subsequently approached the other permanent members of the UN Security Council (Britain, France, and China) on re-flagging Kuwaiti ships or chartering their national-flag ships.

With its invasion of Afghanistan and its record of support for the Communists in various internal struggles in the region, the Soviet Union had generally found itself shut out of the Gulf. The Iran-Iraq war, however, gave the Soviets an opportunity to do some fishing in troubled waters, with an eye to expanding their tenuous position in the region. Moscow sought to maintain relationships with both Baghdad, which it heavily supplied with weapons, and Tehran, which it supplied to a much more limited extent. From a Cold War strategic perspective, taking on responsibility for protecting Kuwaiti tankers would give the previously unwelcome Soviets entry into an area of great strategic importance to the West. Accordingly, the Soviets agreed in principle to re-flagging Kuwaiti ships by the end of 1986.

What appeared to be a deepening Soviet involvement in the Gulf was made apparent in other ways. In January 1987, a Soviet warship entered the Gulf to escort merchant ships for the first time. In early May, a small Soviet freighter, the *Ivan Koroteyev*, was attacked off of Dubai by Iranian speedboats, which raked it with machine gun and rocket propelled grenade fire. It was the first attack on the merchant ship of a superpower and may have drawn a superpower-type reaction. Some 50 Soviet warplanes were reported to have flown across the Iranian border shortly after the *Ivan Koroteyev* was attacked. "This was a field warning to the Iranians who were told later that Moscow would not allow another incident of this type, even if it meant direct Soviet military intervention," an Eastern European diplomat told a Kuwaiti newspaper.[8]

For its part, the United States had looked to its so-called "Twin Pillars" policy of depending on Iran and Saudi Arabia, suitably armed and trained by the U.S., to maintain stability in the region following the British withdrawal from "East of Suez" in 1968. The Iranian revolution had tumbled one of those pillars into the sand. Thus the U.S. had no particular brief for either party in the Iran-Iraq war. Henry Kissinger summed up the U.S. attitude pretty well with his quip that it was a shame that both sides couldn't lose.

Nevertheless, as the war continued along with the apparently increasing prospect of an Iranian victory, the threat presented to U.S.

interests by the spread of the Iranian revolution to the nearby Gulf states became sharper. The overthrow of the generally pro-Western rulers in a region that contained nearly two-thirds of the world's oil reserves would be a major setback for U.S. interests. Another concern was the need to keep the international sea lanes open to facilitate the flow of world oil. Periodic Iranian threats to close the Strait of Hormuz, if Iraq seriously interfered with its oil export operations, had certainly gotten U.S. attention.

In October 1983, before the tanker war started, but with the air thick with threats against shipping by Iran and Iraq, President Reagan had asserted that America's vital interest required that the sea lanes be kept open and the oil flowing. Asked how far the U.S. was prepared to go, the President replied, "That's for them to wonder about."[9] Most U.S. and Western European officials doubted that Iran would make good on its threat to close the Strait. "No rational government would try to close the Strait," said an official, "but, as recent history has shown, we are not dealing with a rational government. . . ."[10]

The U.S. maintained an official neutral stance in the war and prohibited the export of weapons to both Iran and Iraq, but it did extend covert support to Iraq in the form of intelligence sharing. The information mainly consisted of data on Iran obtained by U.S. reconnaissance or "spy" satellites. The decision to begin furnishing the information was prompted by fears in 1984 that Iran was about to overrun Iraq. The information was apparently not supplied on a regular basis in the earlier stages of the effort, but by 1986 it was reported that a link had been established directly between the U.S. and Iraq to facilitate the flow of better and timelier data. The move resulted from heightened U.S. concerns over Iran's breakthrough at Al-Faw.

Revelations about the U.S. intelligence link to Iraq caused a stir, but the real bombshell hit in November 1986 with the first disclosures in what was to become known as the Iran-Contra scandal. In Cold War terms, with its wealth and population, Iran remained the pre-eminent strategic prize in the region. Thus, there was a kernel of sense in the U.S. moving toward a more regular relationship to succeed the sometimes fervent hostility on both sides produced by the Iranian revolution and the embassy hostage crisis. However, the forces shaping the affair, including the desire to secure the release of U.S. hostages in Lebanon, the Iranian need for weapons and spare parts, the U.S. strategic interest in a rapprochement, and the personal agendas of some distinctly odd key players, led to an exercise in a kind of Surrealpolitik. The United States ended up trading arms for hostages and opening a door to nowhere with Iran.

Hedging one's bets was normal practice in the Middle East; however, the affair, when cast against President Reagan's no-compromise, tough-on-terrorism image, as well as the long-established U.S. goal of preventing an Iranian victory, revealed U.S. policy as incoherent. The diversion of funds from Iran to the Nicaraguan Contras was the rancid icing on the cake.

One who was there as a chief actor on the U.S. side was Reagan's National Security Advisor Robert C. McFarlane. Following his impressive contribution to the recent U.S. fiasco in Lebanon, McFarlane went on to deliver a bravura performance in Iran-Contra as the Inspector Closseau of American foreign policy. At one point, a jetliner stuffed with American weapons landed at Tehran. As low-level Iranians milled about in confusion outside, McFarlane sat in the plane with his gifts for the leaders of the Islamic Republic: a Bible signed by President Reagan and a baked-in-Israel kosher cake.

Another key figure was the middleman, Iranian arms dealer Manucher Ghorbanifar, who had been administered a polygraph test at the insistence of the CIA. The examiner judged him to be lying on almost every response except when he was asked his name.[11] Naturally, he remained a key player. It also came out that the U.S. had been giving intelligence data to Iran as well as Iraq. Not to worry: some of it had been "doctored" and was bogus. McFarlane eventually resigned.

Official Iraqi reaction to the disclosures was muted, probably because of the intelligence support it was continuing to receive from the U.S. However, revelation of the affair dealt an enormous blow to U.S. credibility in the Gulf region. President Reagan's protective layer of domestic popularity was pierced. Opponents and critics who had ground their teeth in frustration for years now poured in through the breach.

By the time the Kuwaitis made an official inquiry to the U.S. embassy in December 1986, the U.S. was aware of the Kuwaiti request made to the Soviets in November. On January 13, 1987, a formal request was made to Secretary of State George Schultz, who was also advised of a Soviet offer to transport all of Kuwait's crude oil out of the Gulf using Soviet tankers or Kuwaiti tankers under the Soviet flag. Kuwait wanted to know if the U.S. was prepared to re-flag Kuwaiti tankers to match the Soviet commitment. When the Kuwaiti request was received, Washington was initially reluctant to act on it, and the request languished. "Frankly, our initial response [to Kuwait] was that we can't charter ships. . . .We told them that there would be a lot of inspections and that it would take a year or two," said a White House official. "The thing got trapped in a bureaucratic swirl. . . . Our reaction, frankly, was bureaucratic inertia."[12]

The specter of Soviet involvement, however, brought an end to U.S. vacillation. "Once we knew that the Kuwaitis were negotiating with the Soviets, it sped up the process tremendously, and we said, 'Let's do it all,'" an administration official said. "We don't want to see the Soviets coming into the Gulf en masse."[13] The decision had not been reached without debate within the administration. The National Security Council supported the re-flagging, and Defense Secretary Caspar Weinberger was a strong proponent of the plan. Secretary of State George Schultz was a notable opponent, because of what he later said were serious reservations about America's ability to see it through.

One of the factors that contributed to the U.S. decision was the need to rebuild American credibility in the region after the fall of the Shah, the withdrawal from Lebanon (after the death of 241 Marines in a terrorist bombing in October 1983), and the Iran-Contra revelations. There was also Iran's acquisition of Silkworm anti-ship missiles from the People's Republic of China. By September 1986, it had become clear that Iran was acquiring the missiles and was going to deploy them along the Strait of Hormuz where launch sites were under construction. The Silkworm was a Chinese-made version of the relatively old Russian Styx anti-ship missile. With a range of approximately 50 miles and a warhead weight of 1,100 pounds (three times as large as the Exocet's warhead), the Silkworm gave Iran the realistic potential to sink large tankers for the first time, putting teeth into its threat to close the Gulf.

In late January, the U.S. relayed its willingness to re-flag all eleven of Kuwait's tankers. "It was a pre-emptive strike," said one official. "We'd keep the Soviets out. We'd take all 11. . . .When we told them, they were astounded. They didn't think we'd do it."[14] For Kuwait, the U.S. decision came at a good time. With 21 Moslem heads of state scheduled to attend the summit of the Organization of the Islamic Conference being hosted by Kuwait in late January, Iran intensified the pressure. It seemed particularly incensed by the fact that the conference was being held in Kuwait

While it was never publicly acknowledged, the Iranians actually began firing their Silkworm missiles into Kuwaiti territory beginning that January 1987. An Iranian "shell" which reportedly had hit an uninhabited area of Failaka Island on January 21, was, in fact, a Silkworm missile fired from a launch site on the newly captured Faw Peninsula.

On January 24, 1987, on the eve of the Kuwaiti-hosted Organization of the Islamic Conference Summit, another Silkworm exploded at near midnight in the waters off Failaka Island. The Iranians followed up with yet another Silkworm launch on February 11, 1987. This time the missile exploded in the waters off Kuwait's coast. The missiles appear to have been fired into Kuwaiti territory without specific targets and to have detonated when they hit land or the water.[15]

In May, the Iranian pressure on Kuwait would tighten yet another notch. Sea mines were discovered at the entrance to the Mina Al-Ahmadi deep-water channel used by large tankers to reach Kuwaiti loading facilities. The Soviet tanker *Marshal Chuykow* hit one of the mines, which blew a sizeable hole in its starboard side.

There were also reports that Iran was planning direct military action against Kuwaiti territory. Reportedly, Iranian "invasion plans" had been obtained by the U.S. in late 1986 or early 1987. Robert Oakley, a National Security Council official at the time, later stated, "They [Iran] apparently had a plan to use small boats and things to attack Bubiyan Island, and we were trying to help the Kuwaitis, once we'd made the decision that they were worth helping."[16]

In March 1987, Kuwait formally notified the U.S. of its acceptance of the proposal to re-flag with the Stars and Stripes all eleven of its ships, but then went on to cover its superpower bases by chartering three long-haul Soviet-flagged tankers. The British government brushed off the Kuwaiti request for protection, stating that re-flagging was a commercial, not a governmental matter. That approach did not stop the opposition Labor Party from heckling the government with taunts of "rent-a-flag" during Parliamentary debate on the subject.

The U.S. still hoped to maintain an appearance of neutrality. It did not want to push Tehran toward Moscow and did want to at least keep open the possibility of normalizing relations with Iran sometime in the future. The U.S. would pursue a "two track" policy, with one track running on the diplomatic front to galvanize greater international pressure on Iran to end the war. The other track would be the re-flagging operation designed to protect U.S. interests in the strategic oil region against

Iranian domination through victory over Iraq and against a substantial increase in Soviet influence.

The re-flagging policy would be publicly justified as a high-minded one of upholding freedom of navigation so that the oil supplies the West was so dependent on could flow unimpeded. In a May statement referring to the '70's oil shock, with its gas lines, economic dislocation, and "international humiliation," President Reagan said:

> Mark this point well: the use of the sea lanes of the Persian Gulf will not be dictated by the Iranians. These lanes will not be allowed to come under the control of the Soviet Union. The Persian Gulf will remain open to navigation by the nations of the world.[17]

The U.S. was only getting 15 percent of its oil imports (five percent of its total oil consumption) through the Strait of Hormuz. Moreover, the total flow of oil through the Gulf was really not being seriously reduced by the Iranian, or for that matter, Iraqi attacks. Only a very small percentage of the 800–1,000 ships entering the Gulf monthly were being attacked. Observers thought that, since Iran was dependent on the Gulf for its oil exports, whereas Iraq was not, any attempt to close the Strait was likely to be held back by Iran unless Iraq succeeded in drastically reducing Iran's oil exports for a sustained period of time. On the other hand, from Saddam Hussein's point of view, pushing Iran too far by cutting its fiscal lifeline might draw a ferocious battlefield response and lead to increased attacks on the shipping of Iraq's Gulf financial supporters.

With the possibility of a complete shutdown in the Gulf rather distant, the U.S. strategic interests of preventing an Iranian victory in the war, firming relations with the Gulf States, and, above all, minimizing Soviet presence and influence in the region remained the paramount considerations behind the re-flagging decision. In short, Kuwaiti tankers weren't the only things being re-flagged. America's national interest would sail into the Gulf flying "Freedom of Navigation" as a flag of convenience.

The Reagan administration's decision to re-flag had been revealed to Congress in March and April 1987 briefings. At the time, Congress was deeply involved in its investigations of the Iran-Contra scandal.

Preoccupied, it did not show a great deal of interest in the re-flagging decision. Defense Secretary Caspar Weinberger described Congressional reaction as running from positive to indifferent. That relaxed situation had been radically changed by the two Exocet missiles that hit the *Stark*.

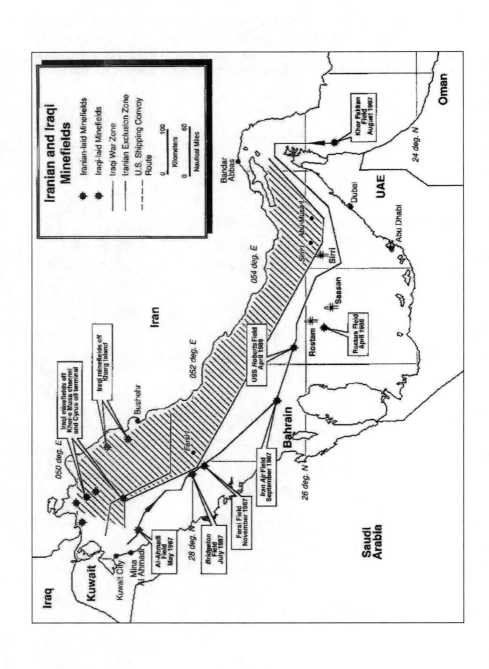

CHAPTER 3

RAISING QUESTIONS

The *Stark* attack brought home the Iran-Iraq War to most Americans for the first time. Pictures and stories on the stricken ship and its casualties appeared at the top of the news on TV screens and were splashed across the front pages of newspapers. The attack raised a whole series of questions which rippled outward from the ravaged ship: Had the *Stark*'s officers and men failed to prevent the attack when they could have? Were there faults in the performance and design of the ship and its systems? Why had the Iraqis attacked it? Just what national interest justified the risks to which American ships and sailors were going to be exposed in the upcoming re-flagging operation?

Many voices, some of them angry, were demanding answers. With the *Stark* attack seizing national attention, the sound of various axes being grinded rose steadily in the background.

Rear Admiral Grant Sharp, who convened an investigation panel in Manama, Bahrain, headed the formal Navy investigation into the *Stark* attack. A declassified version of the Sharp report was released in October 1987. The most serious issue addressed by that report was the conduct of the *Stark*'s commanding officer, Captain Eric Brindel, and that of his two subordinates, Lt. Basil Moncrief and Lt. Commander Ray Gajan.

The report found that Captain Brindel had not appreciated the significance of the intelligence information provided to him about the threat from inadvertent Iraqi attacks, particularly in connection with the recent Iraqi move into the Central Gulf, the area in which the *Stark* was operating at the time of the attack. The Captain's failure to appreciate the potential Iraqi air threat to his ship led to a "cascade" of other failures that day. The report tallied failures to fully man watch stations at all times, to keep weapons at appropriate readiness levels, and a failure to implement the Rules of Engagement properly. The cumulative result of these failures was described as a "total collapse of the ship's defensive readiness posture."

The ultimate source for this "cascade" of failures was attributed to Captain Brindel's perception that the prospect of an accidental Iraqi attack on his ship did not present the kind of critical threat which demanded a high level of alertness to detect, evaluate, and if necessary, make the appropriate response. Captain Brindel had certainly been informed about that threat. He had been given an intelligence briefing and a Rules of Engagement briefing prior to the *Stark* having been attached to the Middle East Force (MEF). On May 15, Captain Brindel had gone recreational sailing in the Gulf with the MEF Commander, Admiral Harold Bernsen. On that occasion, Admiral Bernsen had told him about an incident on the previous day when the Iraqis had attacked a ship just 60 miles from the *Stark*'s intended position.

On May 16, 1987, the day before the attack, Captain Brindel had been specifically directed by Admiral Bernsen to get a briefing by the MEF's Assistant Intelligence Officer. In that briefing, the recent Iraqi moves into the Central Gulf, near the area the *Stark* would operate in, were discussed. Messages mentioning Iraqi moves in the Central Gulf had been sent to the *Stark* within a few days prior to the attack. One message, received the day before the attack, had highlighted the possibility of an indiscriminate attack.

The Rules of Engagement in effect on May 17, 1987 were not declassified. However, the Sharp report concluded that they were sufficient to have enabled the *Stark* to properly warn the Iraqi aircraft and, if the warning was not heeded, to defend itself without taking the first hit. These rules, issued by the MEF, provided that both Iranian and Iraqi aircraft were to be regarded by U.S. forces as potentially hostile. As air contacts approached within specified distances of U.S. ships, identification, warnings, and other actions were required to keep the contact clear. If the contact then took hostile action or demonstrated hostile intent, the U.S. commanders were authorized to defend themselves with appropriate means.

Much of the failure of the *Stark* to prevent the attack or to defend itself could be directly attributed to the actions or, more properly, inactions of the Tactical Action Officer, Lt. Moncrief, operating in the

Combat Information Center. To a somewhat lesser extent, similar failures could be attributed to the ship's Executive Officer, Lt. Commander Gajan, who came by the CIC on other business while events were unfolding. He had not taken over from Lt. Moncrief or otherwise directed any actions by the watch team. (One officer who investigated the incident noted reports that Gajan had his feet up on a console and was munching popcorn at the time.)

On the sound theory of command responsibility, those failures were laid at the feet of Captain Brindel. The Sharp report cited his failure to train his watch teams correctly and his failure to impress upon his Tactical Action Officers and his Executive Officer the need to properly implement the Rules of Engagement.

There was really more to it than that. The recent Iraqi strike runs down into the area in which the *Stark* would be sailing marked a distinct and significant change in Iraqi behavior, one that drew a lot of attention from Admiral Bernsen and the MEF intelligence staff. Those concerns had been directly transmitted to Captain Brindel. And there they had stopped. Amazingly, Captain Brindel had not passed on any of the information to his officers. Not one of them was aware of the recent Iraqi actions. Captain Brindel's failure to inform his officers, including those who ended up on duty in the CIC at the time of the attack, was the critical element in the decision to court martial him. The results of the CIC officers' lack of preparedness were woeful.

The *Stark*'s Tactical Action Officer, Lt. Moncrief, had failed to "lock-on" the Iraqi aircraft with the ship's fire control radar as the jet approached and entered Exocet launching range. He thought that action would be interpreted as a hostile act. Voice warnings to the Iraqi pilot were made too late. When the Mirage was 43 miles away, Lt. Moncrief had turned down a request to contact it. This may have been an absolutely critical decision which spelled doom for the *Stark*. If the Iraqi jet had been warned at this point, it very well might not have fired on the ship.

When warnings finally were made, they were not made in the correct form. Not that it would have made any difference in this case, since they came too late. Radar lock-on should hardly have been considered provocative. U.S. ships had been instructed that they should not hesitate to lock-on to aircraft at maximum range, since that appeared to be the only way to get a pilot's attention. Even passive defense measures were taken too late or not at all. Those defensive measures would have included maneuvering to unmask weapon and radar systems, and arming the chaff launching system.

The *Stark*'s Phalanx anti-missile defense gun had been put in the "stand-by" mode and it did indeed stand by as one Exocet, then the other, slammed into the ship. Under the circumstances of the *Stark* attack, with no other surface contact within 10 nautical miles of the ship and a potential threat closing rapidly, it is hard to see why the gun was not set on automatic. Likewise, mounting an anti-aircraft missile on its launcher seems like a prudent defensive measure, the value of which outweighed any offense it might theoretically give to possible observers. The *Stark* had been so concerned about not giving an aggressive impression that the ship had refused to mount even a blue-colored dummy training missile on its launcher for tests, except at night.

The *Stark*'s Combat Information Center had also failed to sound General Quarters prior to the first missile's impact. Aside from getting the crew to their stations earlier and facilitating damage control, that action would have had the fortuitous effect of getting crewmen out of the berthing quarters in which most of the casualties were sustained. If hatches had been shut, the smoke, which had billowed through the ship in the aftermath of the attack, would have been contained in the immediate areas of the fires.

Another failure was the delayed decision to arm the SRBOC chaff launchers. The chaff required some 30–45 seconds to launch to height, disperse, and settle low enough to be mistaken by a missile seeker for a ship. This lead-time made it clear that, in the face of a potential incoming threat, the launchers should have been armed well before the missiles were actually fired on the *Stark*.

A benchmark ship performance against which the *Stark*'s could be measured was cited by several sources: that of the USS *Coontz* on May 14, 1987, three days before the *Stark* attack. In that incident, an Iraqi Mirage F-1 had flown on a course similar to the one taken in the *Stark* attack. When the Iraqi approached within 39 miles of the *Coontz*, the ship transmitted a warning message. It also mounted an anti-aircraft missile on its launcher, armed its chaff launcher, and altered course to bring itself broadside to the Mirage. Because the Iraqi fighter's radar never left the surveillance mode, the *Coontz* did not lock its radar on to the Iraqi jet as it flew within 10 miles of the ship on its way to attack a tanker. The *Coontz*'s actions were not a guarantee against accidental attack. However, they did indicate that the ship was alert and reacting positively to a potential threat. The same could not be said for the *Stark*.

During the investigation, Lt. Cdr. Gajan and Lt. Moncrief's legal counsel worked together. The two officers felt like they maintained their loyalty to Captain Brindel, but that it was not reciprocated.[1] Possibly on the advice of his Navy attorney, Captain Brindel took an unappealing position for a Commanding Officer who would normally be considered fully responsible for the actions of those under him: It was his subordinates' fault. Moncrief and Gajan had acted contrary to Brindel's training and procedures, preventing him from defending his ship. In particular, Brindel felt that he should have been notified when the Iraqi fighter had been picked up on the ship's radar.[2]

It was true that Captain Brindel had not been present during any events leading up to the Iraqi attack. It was also true that he should have been called when the *Stark*'s own radar picked up the Iraqi fighter. However, the investigating officer properly saw the operation of the *Stark*'s CIC watch as a reflection of the ship's captain, even in the absence of his physical presence. "Would you not," he asked Brindel, "expect the watch to act identically to the way you yourself would act?"[3] As has been said, a Captain may delegate his authority but not his ultimate responsibility.

The investigating panel, headed by Rear Admiral Sharp, recommended that charges of dereliction of duty against Captain Brindel and Lt. Moncrief be referred to General Courts-Martial and that charges against Lt. Commander Gajan be referred to Admiral's Mast, a closed door non-judicial hearing. A little more than two weeks previously, Lt. Cdr. Gajan and Lt. Moncrief had each been awarded the Navy/Marine Corps Medal for their post-attack efforts to save the ship.

The Sharp report, in effect, laid out an indictment of the conduct of the three *Stark* officers. There were, however, mitigating factors to be considered. It was true that the *Stark*'s captain had been thoroughly briefed on the Rules of Engagement and that those rules provided that an Iraqi aircraft was to be regarded as potentially hostile. The rules made no distinction between Iranian and Iraqi contacts. However, U.S. personnel in the Gulf generally perceived Iran as the likely real "enemy" and Iraq as a quasi-ally. This perception was logical. Aside from the recent history of antagonism between Iran and the U.S., the Navy was at least partially in the Gulf to help bolster allies of Iraq who were being threatened by Iran. The Iraqis were simply not perceived as serious a threat as the Iranians. AWACS operators reportedly referred to the Iraqi fighters as "strike command general" rather than potentially hostile aircraft. The Iraqi Mirage had been classified as a "friendly strike/support aircraft" by the AWACS, a classification that was reflected in the symbology superimposed over the video displayed on the *Stark*'s radarscopes.

Hundreds of Iraqi strikes had been mounted against shipping in the Gulf since the start of the Tanker War, with more than 100 Exocets fired. No U.S. warships had been attacked by Iraq or Iran. Iraqi overflights of U.S. ships were common. A naval source noted that standard tactical doctrine said that the best defense against a missile is to knock down the launch platform before it can fire, but if the *Stark*'s captain had shot down the Iraqi Mirage at a range of 30 miles, "We'd be hanging his ass today."[4]

Familiarity with Iraqi flybys, along with the overall political situation in the Gulf, had to have had a certain dulling effect on the perception of potential threats from that source. It is also worth remembering that not only was the U.S. not at war, it was only then on the verge of entering an operation short of war, which did involve the potential for significant military action. The distinction between the mental attitudes held by commanders in wartime and those held in even a moderately threatening "peacetime" environment can be crucial. A ship reacting in wartime against a known enemy the way the *Stark* did in the Gulf is almost unimaginable.

"Combat is much more straightforward than what they have here," said a senior naval officer. "You never have a problem with classification or judgment calls—a thing coming at you is hostile and you shoot it down."[5] Perhaps at least some of the blame for the *Stark*'s fate should be borne by those who send ships to sail in such uncertain seas. A 1988 article in U.S. Naval Institute *Proceedings* by Dr. Michael Vlahos put the proposition succinctly:

> There are really two U.S. Navies—one for peace and one for war. The difference is mental readiness. In war, one's senses are honed for battle; in peace, even where the threat of inadvertent attack' is considered, one's senses must be leashed. The peacetime Navy remains a key instrument of U.S. foreign policy. The commanders and crews of its ships cannot assume the 'dangerous' mental edge of warriors when engaged in delicate diplomacy. . . . If our society does not want to nurture the mental

edge for combat while we are 'at peace,' then we should confess at least our role, however indirectly sensed, in the tragic consequences of sending mentally disarmed men into harms way.[6]

Between the society, which sends its ships on such missions, and the crews who carry them out, there stood the institution of the Navy. That institution had found failures on the part of the *Stark* officers sufficient to warrant courts-martial. Granted that the *Stark*'s officers had not passed the rigorous test of the Gulf, the question was—had the Navy?

After the *Stark* attack became the focus of national attention, critics of various stripes rushed in. Some claimed that in its push for a 600-ship fleet, the Navy had ignored the important, but more mundane, task of seeing that each ship was properly equipped and outfitted. Others argued that the small, relatively limited-capability frigate design itself was a mistake. Observers claimed that the demonstrated readiness deficiencies in the surface Navy would not have been tolerated in the aviation and submarine communities, owing to the much more unforgiving environments the latter two routinely operated in.

The Sharp report's critique of the *Stark*'s failure to use its Phalanx anti-missile gun highlighted the importance of that system in missile defense. Because the option of shooting the "archer," i.e. the attacking aircraft, rather than the "arrow," i.e. the missile, was severely restricted by the political situation in the Gulf, last-ditch defenses such as the Phalanx carried a large burden in preventing a potential missile hit on a ship.

The Navy noted that, since 1984, all Navy ships scheduled to receive the Phalanx system had been equipped with it prior to their being sent to the Middle East. However, the Navy managed not to mention that older ships, ones not scheduled to receive the system, had been dispatched without it. Indeed, the night of the *Stark* attack found three of the six Navy destroyers or frigates deployed in the Gulf—the *Conyngham*, the *Coontz*, and the *Waddell*—without the Phalanx close-in weapons systems installed. After the *Stark* incident, those ships were hastily withdrawn and replaced by Phalanx-armed warships.[7]

Some thought that part of the *Stark*'s lack of a "combat mindset" could be attributed to the Atlantic Fleet's emphasis on peacetime administrative requirements, such as the ship's upcoming power plant examination. Certainly, the routine requirements imposed on a forward-deployed ship could be a burden and a distraction. In a 1992 article, published in the USNI *Proceedings*, the author claimed that "the dilution of attention from the threat at hand to what should be a routine peacetime evolution was the proximate cause of the tragedy that struck the *Stark*."[8]

This is going too far. At the end of the day, Captain Brindel was commanding a warship in an operational situation. He had to make a decision over where his priorities lay: protecting his ship and its crew against accidental attack, or preparing for an inspection. If he felt like he couldn't sort that out on his own, he could have gone to the Middle East Force for a request to Atlantic Fleet to put off the inspection. Further, the upcoming pre-inspection exercise in no way prevented Captain Brindel from warning his subordinate officers about the recent, and threatening, Iraqi moves down the Gulf.

The *Stark* attack also ignited a debate about the adequacy of the ship's defenses against missile attack. Questions were raised over whether or not they detected the launching of the Exocets and whether they had seen the missiles as they streaked toward the ship. The *Stark* hadn't detected the Exocets being launched, since neither the ship's air search radar nor its surface search radar were designed to pick up the separation of a missile from an aircraft. Aside from the eyeballs of the ship's lookouts, the only system on the *Stark* that might have detected the incoming Exocets in time to warn the crew was the electronic countermeasures system, the SLQ-32, sometimes called the "Slick-32."

That equipment was designed to passively receive radar signals and give a bearing (i.e. angle relative to the ship) on the source of the signal. The system could also compare a given signal it was receiving against a preprogrammed "library" of threats and identify the kind of threat. The Exocet's radar signal was in the *Stark*'s SLQ-32 "library" and, thus, the system theoretically should have identified the incoming missiles if it had detected them. The system could also pick up and identify the radar employed by Iraqi F-1 Mirage fighters.

In fact, the *Stark*'s electronic warfare (EW) operator, manning the SLQ-32, did pickup the electronic emissions from the Iraqi Mirage's Cyrano-IV radar operating in a search mode. He detected the changes which he identified as the radar "locked-on" the *Stark* briefly, returned to the search mode, "locked-on" a second time and finally returned to search mode. All of these actions taking place in a matter of less than one minute. In retrospect, it is likely that each "lock-on" meant an Exocet was being fired at the *Stark*. The "lock-on" was of enough concern to one of the EW technicians that he asked for and was granted permission to arm chaff launchers.

The Exocet missiles were guided by data from the launch aircraft to within a few miles of the *Stark*, whereupon small radars in the missiles' noses turned on and guided them to final impact. Thus, for a very brief period—less than a minute, the *Stark*'s SLQ-32 system might have picked up the emissions from the missiles' radars. We do not know if it did so. The EW operator, who was experienced with the system, claimed he never detected the missiles. If the SLQ-32 had picked up the missiles, it would normally have sounded an audible alert and displayed a video symbol. However, the EW Operator admitted that he had turned off the audible alert because it was distracting him from his duties with too many false alarms.

This action left only the possibility of a video signal being displayed on the EW Operator's screen, which he claimed not to have seen. Either the SLQ-32 did not pick up the Exocet and did not display the symbol or it did so and the operator missed it. Many observers felt that, under the circumstances, with a great deal of activity taking place in the CIC, and the EW Operator having to converse with the Tactical Action Officer, that the operator overlooked the video symbol. We will never know for sure since the *Stark*'s CIC and any electronic records were destroyed in the fire.

The Oliver Hazard Perry frigate class to which the *Stark* belonged was designed to provide relatively low cost, low capability ships that could be procured in large numbers. Some derisively referred to them as "K-Mart ships."[9] As Navy warships moved up the size scale, their capabilities generally rose as well. Partly this was a result of increasing size accommodating more equipment, and partly the result of higher value ships being allocated more protection. As a "low-end" ship, the *Stark* had a fairly minimal electronic warfare suite, consisting only of a signal receiving system, which could correlate signals to a threat "library." What was completely lacking in the system was the ability to jam or deceive the radars of threats such as the Exocet or the Iraqi Mirage fighter. A jamming capability would have cost more money but would not have added that much weight nor occupied that much space, both commodities being in tight supply on frigate-size ships. While there has to be a trade-off in capability and cost between "high-end" and "low-end" ships, it seems that the Navy simply set the electronic warfare standard for the *Stark* too low.

One problem with the perception of a *Stark*-type frigate as a "low end" ship is that while it may have been at the low end of the scale of U.S. fleet combatants, objectively, it was quite a large sized ship and would have been at the top of the scale of all but a few of the world's navies. In most navies, such a ship would have received the best electronic warfare and other defensive systems. After all, the ship carried a crew of 200, and America puts a very high value on the lives of its young men. The *Stark* also carried America's prestige in the Gulf. The attack took a heavy toll on both.

The Phalanx was a critical defensive system on the *Stark*. It is a 20mm Gatling-type gun designed for short-range "last-ditch" defense against incoming missiles. The Phalanx gun on the *Stark* was located atop the helicopter hanger near the stem of the ship, producing a so-called "blind-zone" approximately 30 degrees to either side of the bow, where the ship's superstructure blocked the gun and its radar. The incoming Exocets' paths apparently took them along the edges of this "blind zone," leading to speculation that the Phalanx did not detect them and did not have an opportunity to fire. Maneuvering the ship would have moved this "blind zone" so that it no longer fell between the ship and the threat aircraft.

Not that it would have mattered anyway, since the Sharp report makes it clear that the Phalanx was still in "standby" mode when the missiles hit and could not have fired on them. While censored as to details, the report stated that neither Lieutenant Moncrief nor the fire control technician brought the Phalanx into the "AAW Manual" mode. It appears that they desperately tried to do so in the last moments before the first missile hit, but were unsuccessful in the attempt. Again, no details were made available in the Sharp report. In fact, the technician had been allowed to go to the head carrying the key to the system with him. When he returned to the CIC, it was too late, despite the frantic attempt to get the weapon on line.

The *Stark* attack gave the U.S. Navy its first experience with the effects of actual missile hits on one of its modern surface ships. The results were mixed. On the positive side, the ship had survived the two hits and subsequent fires, whereas, in comparison, the larger Royal Navy destroyer HMS *Sheffield* was lost to fire in the Falklands after a hit by a single Exocet which did not explode. Further, no one aboard the ship died in the long and dangerous battle against the fires following the initial impacts—no small achievement considering their intensity.

Still, there were some serious shortcomings. Navy firefighting doctrine was based on maximum 1,800-degree temperature fires rather than the 3,000-degree maximum actually encountered on the *Stark*. Emphasis in Navy training was more on containing the horizontal spread of fires rather than the vertical-type spread on the *Stark*. There was one really critical piece of fire fighting gear that had not been aboard the *Stark*: a thermal imager. Firefighters repeatedly entered compartments that were full of smoke only to find that the fire was not in those spaces. If the *Stark*'s firefighters had been equipped with the thermal heat imagers, they could have pinpointed the fire sources much earlier, significantly limiting further damage. While reports concentrated on the efforts of the crew, not enough credit was given to the critical fire fighting intervention of the Dutch-owned salvage tug. Captain Brindel said that the *Stark* would have been lost without the tug's efforts.

It turned out that the Navy had experienced many of the same problems encountered in fighting the fires on the *Stark* some four years previously. Then, a damaged and out of control target drone had struck the USS *Antrim* off of Virginia. The problems, which reoccurred on the *Stark*, had included a severe shortage of Oxygen Breathing Apparatuses and a lack of the power tools needed to clear wreckage. "They still didn't correct that problem?" asked the Petty Officer who led the fire fighting on board the *Antrim*. "How many more lives do they have to lose before they figure this stuff out?" When questioned after the *Stark* attack, the Navy said that the investigators' reports on the *Antrim* incident had been put in "long term storage."[10]

While the *Stark* controversy was raging at home, an eight-man Defense Department team, led by Rear Admiral David N. Rogers, flew to Baghdad to begin an inquiry into the circumstances of the attack with Iraqi cooperation. However, that cooperation had its limits: the Rogers team was refused access to the Mirage pilot.

In a meeting with Iraqi Foreign Minister Tariq Aziz, Admiral Rogers urged that the pilot be made available in order to make the investigation complete. As to the disposition of the Iraqi pilot, there had been some speculation, not in jest, that he would be beheaded. Iraq, however, indicated that no action was to be taken against him. Aziz explained that the subject of the pilot had been discussed intensively at the highest levels, but the pilot had been following orders and, by Iraqi military tradition, responsibility for the matter rested not with the pilot but his military superiors. The Iraqis were also concerned with the "human side."

The pilot was said to have been deeply grieved that he had killed inno-cent American sailors.

The State Department reported, with apparent seriousness, that the "human argument" had swayed Saddam Hussein. The Iraqis did claim that the pilot never heard the radio warnings from the *Stark*, even though he understood English and should have been monitoring the fre-quency used by the ship to broadcast its warnings. The Iraqis told their American visitors that the pilot was experienced, having accumulated 1,300 hours of flying time, including 800 hours in Mirage fighters. Flying Mirages, the pilot had made fifteen previous successful missile attacks on tankers in the Gulf. The Iraqis said that the returning pilot was debriefed by his commander and stated that he had attacked an Iranian vessel inside the Exclusion Zone declared by Iraq. Reportedly, only upon reading news reports the next day did he realize that he had attacked the *Stark*.

As to the Iraqi pilot, one U.S. publication made the unsubstantiated claim in 1989 that he had been decorated, and given $43,000 in cash and a Mercedes for the *Stark* attack.[11] A veteran Iraqi pilot, who defect-ed to the West, reported a far different fate in 1991: The *Stark* attack pilot had been "purged"—that is, executed. The defecting pilot's protest against this action landed him in serious trouble and put him on the road that ultimately led to his defection.[12] While impossible to verify, it seems entirely possible that Saddam would have made a point of not publicly appearing to bend to U.S. pressure by punishing the pilot, but in private had lashed out in typical fashion at the individual who sub-jected him to tens of millions of dollars in compensation costs while jeopardizing his relationship with the U.S. at a critical moment.

The Iraqis claimed that their pilot had attacked the ship five to ten nautical miles inside their Exclusion Zone, within which they consid-ered any vessels fair game. The Iraqis provided the Americans with a map showing the track of their fighter. The map was in accord with U.S. data on the long path down the Gulf taken by the Iraqi pilot and agreed on the point at which the plane swung to the east across the Gulf. There, the Iraqis claimed that their data, derived from the Mirage's inertial nav-igation system, showed the plane's flight path diverging from the one indicated by the U.S. data.

The Iraqis showed the plane's course as 12 degrees off from the U.S. version and moving at a faster speed, taking it further across the Gulf. This flight path would have put the relative location of the plane's target, the *Stark*, inside the Exclusion Zone when the Mirage fired its Exocets.

U.S. data contradicted the Iraqi version. The Pentagon said it had a "wealth of positive data" on the *Stark*, both from the ship itself and other sources such as the AWACS plane, the USS *Coontz*, and USS *LaSalle*, all of which had monitored the attack. Based on the data, the Pentagon maintained, "We are convinced that the *Stark* was 10 to 15 nautical miles outside" the Exclusion Zone.[13] Supported by multiple sources, the Americans really had the better version of the events that day.

It also seems possible that, in an air force not known for its professional competence, a very tired pilot nearing the end of his fuel "tether" after a long and difficult night flight simply "dumped" his missiles at the first target he saw and scooted for home. It was reported that Iraqi pilots were subject to arrest for bringing home their missiles unused. Further, landing an aircraft with unused Exocets could have been a difficult prospect. Such a situation may have caused the crash of an Iraqi Super Etandard in one instance.

In July, the Iraqi ambassador to the U.S., Nizar Hamdoon, claimed that the Iraqi pilot had made a simple technical error with his radar system, wrongly setting the switch controlling the scale on which he could view potential targets relative to his own position on his radar screen. As a result of this error, the pilot would have thought that the relative location of his target placed it inside the Exclusion Zone.

A former Mirage pilot without links to either the U.S. or Iraqi governments thought that the new explanation was "quite feasible," noting that it would be easy to turn the radar scale switch to the wrong position under combat conditions. A knowledgeable U.S. official agreed. "That's right; it was as simple as the wrong switch being thrown on the radar system of the Iraqi fighter. We have known that but had not intended to discuss it publicly."[14] Ultimately, the Iraqis agreed to pay $27.3 million in compensation to the families of the *Stark* victims.

While by no means absolutely certain, the wrongly positioned radar range scale switch stands as a plausible explanation for the attack.* This is rather more than could be said for a series of theories, ranging from the improbable to the bizarre, that began to surface in the Gulf region. One story making the rounds among shipping executives in Dubai had it that the *Stark* was stalking an Iranian frigate on behalf of the Iraqis, as was the AWACS, which guided the Iraqi to the attack in which he mistakenly fired on the wrong ship.[15] There were other reports that two Mirages, piloted by foreign mercenaries, had actually been involved in the attack.

Iran jumped in, claiming involvement in the attack. Parliamentary Speaker Ali-Akbar Hashemi Rafsanjani claimed: "Our officers devised a plan which caused trouble in (implementation of) the joint U.S.-Saudi-Iraqi plot and resulted in the U.S. frigate being hit. This is a military secret which we cannot reveal. But if, one day the U.S. nation wanted to follow up the matter in a court, we are prepared to present some evidence."[16] No model of consistency, Speaker Rafsanjani had previously claimed that the attack on the *Stark* had been deliberately staged as part of a conspiracy by Saudi Arabia and the U.S. to blame the incident on Iran.[17] Teheran radio urged Washington to order more flags "to drape the coffins containing the bodies of the dead U.S. servicemen" and warned that the U. S. was stepping into a military swamp.[18]

Other theories had it that Iraq deliberately attacked the *Stark*, either in revenge for the American arms transfers to Iran or to draw the U.S. deeper into the Gulf war. Iraqi bitterness over the massive U.S. arms "sales" to Iran was certainly justified. Thousands of TOW antitank missiles, Hawk anti-aircraft missiles, Phoenix air-to-air missiles and critical spare parts for Iran's fleet of American made F-4 and F-14 fighters were bolstering Iranian forces facing Iraq on the battlefield. The problem with the "revenge" rationale for a deliberate attack is that, because of the Iran-Contra revelations, Baghdad had the U.S. in an awkward situation and was seeking to exploit the political debt incurred by Washington's perfidy. With the *Stark* attack, "Debt Cancelled" was stamped across the whole Iran-Contra affair. It is hard to believe that, in desperate straits vis-à-vis Iran, Baghdad would have deliberately given up its "Washington Card" in exchange for spilling some American blood in the Gulf.

In late July 1987, after both *Stark* officers wrote letters accepting responsibility for the ship's failure to take defensive action, the Navy allowed Captain Brindel to retire and Lieutenant Moncrief to resign, rather than face court-martials. Letters of reprimand were issued to both men. Brindel retired one step down in rank, costing him some $7,000 per year in retirement pay. Moncrief resigned his commission.

Lt. Commander Gajan was allowed to stay on in the Navy, with a letter of admonition placed in his permanent service record stating that he had been found derelict in his duties. The letter effectively killed any chance of promotion, and he retired from the Navy in 1993. Admiral Frank B. Kelso II, commander of the Atlantic Fleet, said that he had imposed the non-judicial punishment because, "The degree of culpability is mitigated by the unique circumstances of the incident and its aftermath."[19] The latter was a reference to the officers' actions in saving the ship after it was hit.

Captain Brindel did not go quietly. He publicly blamed the ship's failure to defend itself on its electronic equipment, not the inactions of its officers, and accused the Navy of having conducted a distorted and misleading investigation into the incident. In what was apparently a reference to the Rules of Engagement under which he had operated, Captain Brindel said that, "The investigation didn't go high enough, but that's all I'll say about it."[20] He also said that ships shouldn't be allowed to conduct engineering tests of their engines in the Gulf since such activities impeded combat readiness. Captain Brindel noted that Pacific Fleet ships were not allowed to perform that kind of training in the Gulf while the Atlantic Fleet, to which the *Stark* belonged, were.[21]

The Navy's decision not to prosecute the *Stark* officers, but rather to make them pay with their careers, seems generally reasonable. Although, in view of the fact that he bore the ultimate responsibility for his ship's catastrophic level of un-preparedness, Captain Brindel appears to have gotten off very lightly indeed. Still, while the *Stark*'s officers had failed, they had done so in a difficult situation, which invited such failures. The Exocet missiles that had hit the *Stark* may have traveled along the line of the "blind zone" of the Phalanx system, but they also traveled along the line dividing a near-wartime environment from a politically charged peacetime one. The incoming missiles may have been physically masked from ship's radar system by its superstructure, but they were also masked by the common perception that Iraq was a "virtual ally" who would not attack a U.S. ship. The *Stark* demonstrated the hazards of inaction in such a situation. What about the hazards on the other side of the coin? Retired Rear Admiral and former Chairman of the Joint Chiefs of Staff Thomas H. Moorer's prophetic, if inelegantly phrased, warning was that: "You don't get anything free. If they shoot down a friendly aircraft in the area or something . . . then that will cause a big rhubarb."[22]

The Reagan administration moved quickly to point an accusing finger at its preferred culprit in the Iraqi attack on the *Stark*: Iran. Two days after the attack, President Reagan said that Iran "was the real villain in the piece" because of its refusal to negotiate an end to the long and costly war. The administration did not find it particularly expedient to apportion any blame to Saddam Hussein's Iraq for actually attacking the *Stark* or for starting the war by invading its neighbor. For their part, the Iranians gloated over the tragedy. "The great Satan is trapped," exulted Iranian Prime Minister Mir Hussein Moussavi. "The Persian Gulf is not a safe place for the Superpowers, and it is not in their interest to enter these quicksands," he warned.[23] It was a warning that would go unheeded.

The *Stark* attack had the subsequent effect of drawing the U.S. deeper into the Gulf. Plans to provide naval escorts for the Kuwaiti oil tankers were accelerated, with the planned re-flagging moved up from August to the end of June. Defense Secretary Caspar Weinberger warned that "armchair strategists, self-styled defense gurus, and maritime theologians" would use the attack to second-guess the U.S. presence in the Gulf."[24]

A furious debate broke out in Congress. "Why is American treasure and U.S. blood being expended to safeguard these oil lifelines to Japan and Europe?" demanded Senator James Sasser (D-TN).[25] The administration did not back down in the face of Congressional pressure. The aircraft carrier *Constellation* sailed into the Arabian Sea and positioned itself so that its jet fighters could provide air cover for U.S. ships in the Gulf. In another sign of a more interventionist U.S. policy, four U.S. Navy warships took turns escorting a Kuwaiti-registered freighter, the *Ibn Rashid*, loaded with U.S. M-60 tanks, artillery, and ammunition bound for Bahrain. The latter country had requested the U.S. escort out of fear that Iran might intercept the freighter and confiscate or destroy its cargo.

In advancing the tanker re-flagging and escort missions, President Reagan defended them as "vital." Iran was indicating that it would continue to attack Kuwaiti tankers, whatever flag they flew, because of Kuwait's support for Iraq. If that was its intent, Iran now had a formidable means with the installation of its huge Chinese-made Silkworm anti-ship missiles near the Strait of Hormuz. Congressman Robert Toricelli (D-NJ) summed up the feelings of many when he said, "We're on a collision course with the Iranian government."[26]

CHAPTER 4

OPERATION EARNEST WILL

The *Stark* attack cast a very harsh light on the potential risks involved in the United States carrying out its plan to re-flag Kuwait's tankers. The Reagan administration's Gulf plans had drawn little attention prior to that attack. Some Congressional committees had even failed to make the time to receive proffered briefings. No overt opposition had appeared. According to Defense Secretary Weinberger, a member of the Senate Foreign Relations Committee even offered to change the re-flagging laws to speed up the process.[1] Following the *Stark* disaster, the administration's policy became the focus of an intense debate. A previously quiescent Congress suddenly seethed with urgent concerns over the upcoming Gulf operation. Senator Ted Kennedy charged that, "Once again, the administration has leaped before it looked on a sensitive issue in the Middle East, with reckless disregard of the consequences for our military policy and for our foreign policy in the region."[2]

Administration critics argued that the U.S. had casually stepped into a major, open-ended commitment without adequately studying the implications and fully assessing the risks. Because the tempo of Iranian attacks on shipping was roughly linked to the level of Iraqi strikes, in a "tit-for-tat" fashion, the potential exposure of U.S. forces to Iranian retaliation depended a great deal on Iraqi actions over which the U.S. had no say.

In this view, the U.S. position in the Gulf was hostage to Iraq's decisions on when and how it would choose to conduct its anti-shipping campaign. It was also said that U.S. intervention could only inflame an already bad situation in the Gulf. By so publicly flaunting its backing for Iraq's quasi ally, Kuwait, critics charged that the U.S. was rubbing

Tehran's nose in the dirt and practically inviting Iran to challenge the U.S. in some way. Confrontation with Iran ultimately risked the U.S. being drawn into the Iran-Iraq war.

Some critics charged that Kuwait had "played" the Soviet Union against the United States in order to secure U.S. intervention. There is little doubt that the Soviet offer to Kuwait had given the U.S. a strong incentive to act. Indeed, it seems fair to say that it was the concern over a Soviet opening in the Gulf, when added to other concerns, such as rebuilding U.S. credibility and propping up Kuwait in the face of Iranian intimidation, that pushed the U.S. across the threshold to act. As to the Kuwaitis, it was no mere play on their part. They saw themselves in a very dangerous situation and were desperately looking for help. They may have had a preference for the U.S. over the Soviet Union, but if the U.S. had not acted, they would certainly have turned to the Soviets. Even with the U.S. commitment to re-flag all eleven Kuwaiti tankers, and an expressed willingness to re-flag any number of others, the Kuwaitis went ahead and spread their bets by chartering three Soviet tankers.

Administration officials were now grilled in hearings before Congressional committees, with the discussion occasionally becoming heated. While many Congressmen worried about the possibility of suicide attacks by fanatical Iranians against U.S. ships, administration officials took a more sanguine view. Secretary Weinberger testified that Iran "has assiduously avoided even the mere hint of a threat towards U.S. ships," and said that "we do not expect that situation to change."[3] Admiral William J. Crowe, Jr. told the Senate Armed Services Committee that escorting the Kuwaiti tankers would not be a high-risk undertaking, although, "There were no guarantees that such an operation will be casualty free." He characterized the Gulf as "a thriving and busting commercial crossroads, not a no-man's land."[4]

If the administration was pursuing a two-track policy of diplomacy along with the military re-flagging operation to protect U.S. interests, it also appeared to be pursuing a two-track policy in selling the operation to a skeptical Congress and public. Here, though, the tracks ran in opposite directions. On the one hand, painting the situation in dark tones, the re-flagging was necessary because of the ominous developments in the Gulf, particularly Iran's acquisition of the Silkworm missiles, which presented a grave threat to shipping and the vital flow of world oil. On the other hand, as to the threat to American ships and sailors, the dark Gulf skies suddenly lightened and the roiled waters became calm. Why no, there was little risk of U.S. ships being attacked or casualties being incurred.

Needless to say, the U.S. re-flagging decision had few critics in Iraq. On the eve of the U.S. convoy effort, Iraq even suspended its anti-shipping attacks, reducing the likelihood of Iranian retaliatory attacks on U.S. escorted ships. The Iraqi suspension was officially done in order to give Iran time to accept a U.N. ceasefire resolution. It also smoothed the way for the commencement of the U.S. escort operation. One U.S. official said that, although there wasn't any explicit linkage, "The Iraqis understand us."[5]

For its part, Iran appeared angry over the American decision to protect the re-flagged Kuwaiti tankers. As an observer later noted, "Having so recently been courted by the Americans on bended knee, the Iranians were now confronted with bewildering rapidity by a sword-wielding, quasi-adversary, apparently aligned with Iraq." From Iran's point of view, its ship attacks were only tit-for-tat responses to Iraqi strikes against Iranian shipping. It was Iraq which had been responsible for initiating the tanker war, and it was Kuwait, which was providing critical financial support to Iraq. Now, by shielding Kuwaiti tankers, the U.S. was depriving Iran of a legitimate target for its retaliation. The re-flagging, taken together with a renewed U.S.-sponsored arms embargo directed at Iran, and the increasing diplomatic pressure to force an end to the war, all seemed to indicate a deliberate U.S. decision to side with Iraq. The U.S. move also brought something Iran was loath to see: a superpower military buildup in its own backyard. The Iranians could only view these developments as serious setbacks. The question was, how would they react?

Responsibility for carrying out the re-flagging operation would fall to the U.S. Central Command. One of five geographically defined unified Commands at the time, Central Command was responsible for planning and conducting U.S. military operations in a region consisting of 19 countries in Northeast Africa and Southwest Asia. Marine General George W. Crist had taken over Central Command in November 1985. General Christ had served as an advisor to the Vietnamese Marine Corps during that war. Those who knew him considered him to be highly intelligent and an excellent organizer. The chain-smoking General was thin to the point that some thought he looked sickly. A driving personality, he seemed capable of working an unlimited number of hours. However, the intensity he brought to the job quickly generated turbulent waves in his Command.

According to one observer, General Crist had a flinty personality which made him a terrifying boss, who:

> . . . in the words of one subordinate officer "ate colonels for breakfast." Stories were legion at MacDill of how Crist would fire on the spot any briefing officer who did not have an immediate answer to a question. The officers, while looking for new assignments, tended to gather at an area of the base known as the "mole hole," where according to one former CENTCOM officer, "They played a lot of golf." He said that after awhile it became something of a badge of honor to have been fired by the fire-breathing Marine.[6]

According to one source, so many staff officers were being relieved and replacements assigned at CENTCOM, that some officers were quietly "recycled" back into the command several months after they had been relieved. Reportedly, General Crist never noticed their reappearance among the crowds coming and going.

With the U.S. offer to re-flag eleven tankers and the Kuwaiti acceptance in March, CENTCOM planning for the escort operation went forward under the code name "Private Jewels." The name was ultimately changed to operation "Earnest Will." The plan called for convoys entering the Gulf to form up in the Gulf of Oman with an escort of at least two Middle East Force (MEF) warships equipped with surface to air missiles and Phalanx close-in weapons systems. The aircraft carrier battle group steaming in the Arabian Sea (CTG 70) would provide air cover. The U.S. brought in several electronic reconnaissance aircraft in a special configuration code-named "Reef Point." These planes were modified P-3C Orion maritime patrol aircraft, based in Oman. The Navy aircraft would fly through the "Silkworm Envelope" at the Strait, monitoring it for electronic signals indicating Silkworm activity. In a highly classified operation in support of the re-flagging effort, the CIA stationed two turboprop surveillance aircraft in Dhahran, Saudi Arabia. These aircraft were used to monitor Iranian activity in what was dubbed the "Eager Glacier" program.

Kuwait was shipping about 12 percent of the total crude going through the Strait (Saudi Arabia accounted for 52 percent). The re-flagging agreement would cover seven crude carriers and four LPG carriers. These tankers had been carrying roughly one third of Kuwaiti crude exports (by volume) and constituted half of its fleet. The initial plan was to use ten of the re-flagged tankers for long haul trips to the crude or LPG's ultimate destination, and one as a Gulf "shuttle." Escorts would drop off their charges in international waters outside the Mina Al Ahmadi Channel. Protection of the re-flagged ships would be the responsibility of Kuwait once they reached its territorial waters. Kuwait would provide refueling and allow provisioning of U.S. escort ships. Because of the mines discovered at the entrance to the Al Ahmadi Channel, the U.S. ships were directed to stay clear of that area.

For Operation Earnest Will, U.S. forces would be beefed up by the addition of a guided missile destroyer and two frigates. Despite its rather sprawling nature, as far as the seas went Central Command only had authority over the Persian Gulf and the Red Sea. The Navy had balked at this commitment of additional resources to Central Command, arguing that the bolstering the Middle East Force would generate turbulence in fleet operating schedules. Central Command's General Crist observed of the Navy that, "To them it represented a challenge to the Pacific Command and threatened a diversion of resources from the traditional Navy strategic focus on the North Atlantic and Pacific."

The Navy-perceived threat to the Pacific Command was due to a split between the Middle East Force inside the Gulf, which reported to Central Command (through Naval Command Central in Honolulu) and the carrier battle group steaming in the Arabian Sea, which reported to the unified Pacific Command, headed by a Navy Admiral. The re-flagging operation would have to draw on forces from two different unified commands, hardly an ideal situation. The Navy also had its nose out of joint because Central Command was headed by a Marine General, not a Navy Admiral. Joint Chiefs Chairman Admiral Crowe bitingly observed that, "The prospect of a Marine commanding an almost exclusively Navy mission was deeply disturbing to many in the naval community. A maritime operation of these dimensions, they believed, was far too significant to be left to a Marine, regardless of what the command structure of the United States called for."[7]

Admiral Crowe himself was a highly intelligent, politically savvy officer who was well tuned to foreign policy concerns. He was well suited to oversee the operation at the highest military level. Another point in his favor was that some observers thought that he truly wore a "purple suit" as Joint Chiefs Chairman. That is, he truly was a joint forces commander. In contrast, some JCS Chairmen were said to have retained their Navy blue, Army green, or Air Force blue suits, which meant that they had continued to pursue their parochial service concerns, even as JCS Chairman.

American Navy warships had been stationed in the Gulf since January 1949 as part of the U.S. Middle East Force. Their missions included training, air and sea surveillance, monitoring U.S. shipping, and rendering humanitarian assistance. However, the basic purpose of the force was to maintain a U.S. presence in a region of strategic importance.

Reporting to CENTCOM, the Middle East Force would actually conduct operations in the Gulf. There were some in the Navy who had their doubts about the Middle East Force (MEF). As opposed to the other, more "cutting edge" commands, which had been rigorously training for World War III against the Soviet Navy at sea, the MEF was seen as little more than a show-the-flag force. One officer described it as a "sleepy hollow." He thought it lacked first-rate people and was over its head with the hazardous operations it was undertaking. Time would tell.

In the wake of the *Stark* attack, the U.S. worked out de-confliction procedures with the Iraqis. Their aircraft were to turn on their radars when they flew down the Gulf and reached the 29th parallel, alerting U.S. ships to their presence. A UHF monitoring frequency was provided to the Iraqis on a monthly or bi-monthly basis by the U.S. military attaché in Baghdad. Any Iraqi plane closing to within 50 miles of a U.S. ship would receive a warning on this frequency. If the Iraqi aircraft did not respond and closed to within 30 miles, he was subject to being fired on by the U.S. ship. For its part, the U.S. supplied Iraq with the convoy routes in advance. This fairly extensive U.S.-Iraqi cooperation was kept very low profile.[8]

The U.S. had four E-3A AWACS radar surveillance aircraft stationed in Riydah, Saudi Arabia. Along with some aerial tankers, they were known as the Elf-One force. The Saudis had themselves purchased five AWACS aircraft and eight KC-135 tankers. The Saudis had agreed to use their AWACS aircraft to help provide radar coverage over the southern Gulf, while the U.S. would continue to operate in the northern Gulf. The Saudis had agreed to fly their AWACS for 100 hours a month in the south. They would mostly orbit over the United Arab Emirates, covering the critical Gulf area in the vicinity of the Strait of Hormuz.

The Iranian acquisition of Chinese-made Silkworm missiles had been cited by the administration as a significant factor in its decision to re-flag. The U.S. disclosed the Iranian acquisition of the missiles in March 1987, and critics saw the sudden U.S. trumpeting of the Silkworm threat as an attempt to justify the re-flagging decision. A Kuwaiti official claimed that the Americans had known about the missiles since the previous summer. A Western diplomat noted, "It's very interesting the Americans are making such a fuss over it now."[9] The need to sell its re-flagging policy to Congress and the public caused the administration to emphasize the threat to the flow of world oil presented by Iran's growing ability to close the Strait of Hormuz. In this, the administration was helped by Iran's shrill rhetoric. The U.S. certainly knew about the Silkworms well in advance of the March 1987 disclosure. U.S. reconnaissance had observed the missiles and associated equipment at the Bandar Abbas Naval Ammunition Depot through December 1986.

Domestic political considerations aside, there is no doubt that the administration took the Silkworm threat seriously indeed. By the spring of 1987, the National Security Council was looking seriously at a preemptive strike to destroy the missiles rather than wait for them to be deployed around July. A preemptive strike had the obvious drawback of attacking Iran when the U.S. was declaring itself neutral in the Iran-Iraq war and making the U.S. look like the aggressor. However, holding back until a missile was actually fired risked it getting through the ships' defenses and hitting. The U.S. Navy actually thought it had a high probability of shooting down or jamming Silkworms fired at U.S. warships, but was not confident that it could stop a missile from hitting a ship under escort. In the end, the U.S. decided that it would attack the Silkworm missile sites if they showed evidence of hostile intent, but would not attack them preemptively. The U.S. warned the Iranians through diplomatic channels that it would take appropriate action to protect its ships if threatened.

In early July, the U.S. detected preparations to make the missiles operational at launch sites along the Strait of Hormuz. Strike aircraft roared off the deck of the aircraft carrier USS *Constellation*, steaming outside the Strait in the Arabian Sea. The Navy aircraft orbited near the Strait of Hormuz, prepared to bomb the missile sites. The Iranians stopped their preparatory work on the launch sites, and the aircraft returned to the carrier with their bombs and missiles still hanging under their wings. It was unclear if the Iranians stopped the work because they detected the U.S. aircraft. White House spokesman Marvin Fitzwater said that the launching of the planes "had nothing to do with the Silkworms."[10] It looks suspiciously like the aircraft were sent aloft in case the Silkworms were about to be used, which they were not. The administration then, in a manner that would become increasingly common during the U.S. involvement in the Gulf, sought to downplay the seriousness of the incident.

In a Congressional statement, Richard W. Murphy, Assistant Secretary for Near Eastern and South Asian Affairs, had said of administration re-flagging policy, "Our goal is to deter, not to provoke."[11] As Operation Earnest Will prepared to get underway, concerns were running strongly in the direction of provocation. Analogies were being made to the disastrously unfocused U.S. policy in Lebanon, which had left U.S. Marines exposed to the terrorist bombing of their barracks. Some on Capitol Hill were openly dubbing the operation "Beirut II." A Western diplomat said, "It's Lebanon once more, but on a much bigger, more dangerous scale."[12]

In early July, Iranian Parliamentary Speaker Hajatolislam Hashemi Rafsanjani warned that "If the enemy got crazy," Iran was ready for a confrontation. "We are ready to sink American ships," he said.[13] Barely a week before the first re-flagged convoy was scheduled to get underway, a U.S. Navy sailor in the Gulf observed, "You can just feel things getting more tense." Due to return to the U.S. in two months, the sailor said, "I'm glad that I'm short. I'm looking forward to getting out of here."[14] That was no longer an option enjoyed by the U.S.

CHAPTER 5

AMBUSH

U.S. Navy Captain David Yonkers gazed upward from his small launch to the massive bulk of the supertanker *Bridgeton* looming high above him. The 401,000-ton ship was the sixth largest tanker in the world. It was Yonkers' first close up view of a supertanker, and he was staggered by the sheer size of the thing. Yonkers had spent a lot of time on aircraft carriers, the Navy's largest warships, but this was something else. To Yonkers, the hull seemed to soar above him like the Empire State Building. Disembarking from the launch, he began the laborious climb up the accommodation ladder leading to the main deck. It seemed to take an eternity before he made it all the way to the top.

Captain Yonkers had been handed the command of the very first Earnest Will convoy. He had gone to the *Bridgeton* to meet with the commanding officers of three U.S. warships and the civilian masters of two re-flagged tankers. Those five ships would make the high-profile first convoy run. The meeting between the ship commanders would go over convoy issues such as the route, how close together the ships would sail, and communications procedures.

Yonkers probably shouldn't have been surprised that he had ended up commanding this first re-flagged convoy. Throughout his naval career, he always seemed to be turning up at the scene of action. In 1962, as a young Ensign recently commissioned out of the Naval Reserve Officers Training Corps (NROTC) at the University of Michigan, he had been aboard the destroyer USS *Joseph Kennedy* when it made the first stop of a Russian freighter headed into the quarantine zone imposed around Cuba at the height of the October missile crisis. He did two tours off of North Vietnam, conducting "Sea Dragon" shore

bombardments north of the Demilitarized Zone. During the 1983 invasion of Grenada, he was the surface operations officer for Cruiser/
Destroyer Group 8. He was offshore Lebanon in 1986, at the time of
the U.S. intervention, and had passed on the command for the battleship
Missouri to open fire for the first time. As commander of Destroyer
Squadron 14, based in Mayport, Florida, he had taken three warships
into the Gulf on a normal rotation. He was in Bahrain, anticipating his
return home, when he was informed that he would be staying to command the convoy escort groups for Operation Earnest Will.

The escort group for the first convoy would consist of the cruiser
USS *Fox* (CG-33), the destroyer USS *Kidd* (DDG-993) and the frigate
USS *Crommelin* (FFG-37). U.S. Naval Reserve liaison officers (LNO's)
would be stationed on board each of the tankers to act as intermediaries
between the convoy group commander and the merchant vessel captains. Civilian ships' masters were unlikely to have had any experience
operating in concert with warships. The *Bridgeton*'s captain, former
U.S. Navy Captain Frank C. Seitz, was a welcome exception. The
LNO's function was to explain military procedures to civilian crews and
help in coordinating transit details. There weren't enough officers from
the escort ships to go around, so reserve officers were called up and
assigned the duty.

The two tankers in the first convoy were the 401,000-ton *Bridgeton*
(formerly *Al Rekkah*) and the 48,233-ton *Gas Prince* (formerly *Gas Al
Minagish*). The *Bridgeton* was capable of carrying a load of nearly three
million barrels of oil—all of Kuwait's production for three full days. The
huge ship was some 1,200 feet long. Officers on the bridge, located at
the aft end of the ship, had to use binoculars to inspect the bow. The
Kuwaiti ships were now owned on paper by Chesapeake Shipping, Inc.,
a U.S. company that had been incorporated in May for the sole purpose
of taking title to the ships. One U.S. official described the company as a
post office box in Delaware. The Kuwaiti Oil Tanker Company in turn,
controlled Chesapeake Shipping. The names of the ships had been
picked out on a road map from small towns across the Delaware River
in South Jersey.

U.S. flags had been raised over the ships in a brief ceremony outside the Gulf. Nobody seemed to be worried about operational security.
In fact, the Navy turned the re-flagging ceremony into a media event
with press helicopters flying overhead and the Navy ships maneuvering
to ensure that good pictures could be taken of the newly flagged tankers

against the dramatic backdrop of their escorting U.S. warships.

The re-flagged ships, empty and riding high in the water, would start from a point in the vicinity of Khor Fakkan, the United Arab Emirates port outside the Gulf. They would proceed through the Strait of Hormuz, and then sail the balance of the 550-mile Gulf route to the Kuwaiti oil port of Mina Al-Ahmadi. There, they would take on their loads of crude oil and liquefied natural gas for the return leg. The U.S. plan was to run convoys once every two weeks in July and August, going slowly in the initial stages of the effort in order to test Iranian reaction and to shake out any kinks in the escort operation. To guard against an accidental Iraqi attack, the U.S. agreed to provide Baghdad with continuously updated location information on the ships.

On the night of July 21, 1987, Captain Yonkers received a presidential order to begin the operation. The convoy assembled about 13 miles off the port of Khor Fakkan in the Gulf of Oman and weighed anchor about 9:30 A.M. on Wednesday, July 22. The USS *Fox* took the point position in a diamond formation with the USS *Kidd* to port and behind and the USS *Crommelin* to starboard and behind. The *Bridgeton* completed the diamond to the rear, and was in turn followed by the *Gas Prince* a mile back. Captain William Mathis of the *Fox* announced over the ship's loudspeakers, "Remember, this is the real thing, this is not a drill."[1]

The 476 crewmen of the *Fox* were in a grim and determined mood as that ship bore down on the Strait of Hormuz, and probably didn't need any reminders. One Petty Officer said, "I think everybody here has the feeling that something is going to happen, I'm just trying to talk about it with other sailors and keeping my mind busy so I don't think about it too much."[2] Jets from the *Constellation* weaved continuous patrols over the convoy while crews on the ships and aircraft tensely monitored their electronic displays, looking for any sign that the Iranians were locking their missile fire control radars on the ships. Topside, sailors wearing helmets and orange life vests manned deck-mounted machine guns and scanned the heat-shimmered horizon for trouble.

As the ships entered the 50-mile long Strait of Hormuz and came within range of Iran's Silkworm missiles, three Iranian F-4 fighter-bombers took off from an airbase near Bandar Abbas. The fighters initially flew a "racetrack" pattern between Kuhestak and Surek over Iranian territory, then they suddenly darted straight toward the

American convoy some 60 miles away. The Iranians streaked over the Gulf at a 10,000-foot altitude. Warnings were read out to them over the radio, but there was no response. Finally, the *Fox* locked on to the jets with its fire control radar. That got the Iranians' attention and the F-4's broke off their approach about 17 miles away from the U.S. ships and returned to land.

Operators hunched over radar displays in the *Fox*'s darkened combat information center could see six letter "X's" on their screens. Each indicated an Iranian Silkworm anti-ship missile site. "There are more than these. But these are the ones we're most concerned about," said the *Fox*'s tactical information officer. Two of the sites were located on the Iranian mainland, while four others were on two islands in the strait which the convoy would pass close by.[3] The warships moved within 1,200–1,300 yards of the tankers to be in the best position to respond to a Silkworm attack. It was believed that a Silkworm's radar seeker would lock onto the larger target when ships were that close together, so the tankers' huge radar signature gave some protection to the more vulnerable warships.

It was a beautiful day and the waters in the Strait were calm. However, as the convoy proceeded into the Strait it looked to Captain Yonkers like "the world had stopped." The normally bustling passageway was absolutely empty of both northbound and southbound traffic. None of the commercial operators wanted to take a chance on being around if the balloon went up. Ninety-five degree temperatures, combined with eighty-five percent humidity took its toll on the escort crews standing at general quarters through the Strait. Watertight doors between compartments were secured, making travel from one part of the ship to another difficult. Below decks on the *Fox*, almost 100 sailors, many outfitted with oxygen breathing equipment, stood ready in damage control parties in case the ship took a hit. Damage control was serious business, and the crewmen were not allowed to play cards or otherwise find any distraction as they sweated and waited.

The U.S. escorts had orders to knock out any individual ships or aircraft that attacked, but retaliation against Iran would only be undertaken if there was a loss of American lives. Targets for possible retaliatory strikes included the Silkworm sites, speedboat bases at Abu Musa and Farsi Island, and Iranian air and naval bases along the Gulf. "Enough feathers have been pulled out of the American eagle by Iran," said a belligerent senior State Department official. "People are getting damned pissed. If there has to be widespread urban renewal in Iran as a result of our military action, then so be it."[4]

In fact, Iran did not appear to be looking for a direct confrontation with the U.S. Parliament Speaker Rafsanjani said America was looking for an "excuse" to launch massive air attacks against Iran, implying nothing would be done to give the Americans a pretext for retaliatory raids.[5] "I personally believe they [Silkworms] will not be used," said Captain Yonkers." If they were to launch one, that would probably be the last one."[6] An intelligence analyst on board the *Fox* noted that, "If the Iranians are smart, they will stay cool. If they are not, then things are going to get pretty heated for them pretty quickly. It will be a quick kill."[7]

As the convoy passed through the Strait and moved beyond range of the Silkworm batteries, Captain Mathis of the *Fox* told his crew over the ship's intercom, "It's been a very quiet transit, which I'm sure we're all thankful for."[8] Safe passage through the Silkworm "envelope" covering the Strait of Hormuz was an important milestone for the convoy. However, it still had the majority of its voyage in front of it and would be vulnerable to other forms of Iranian attack virtually up until it entered port in Kuwait. Iran retained the initiative. If it wished to strike against the ships, it was free to choose the time, the place, and the method. And so it would.

The convoy sailed swiftly up the Gulf at night after passing through the Strait. The Silkworm threat, which had gotten almost all of the publicity, was now well behind the ships, but an attack by small, high-speed boats was still a danger. The first night, the convoy ran past Iran's Abu Musa Island, where armed speedboats were based. Normally, U.S. ships stayed about 22 miles away from the island. However, because of the deep draft of the tankers, the convoy had to use a deepwater passage, which ran only some 14 miles off the island. Yonkers found the night passage "agonizing" since it took the ships through shoals of fishing boats. There was simply no way to sort out any potential attackers hiding among them. The ships were at maximum alert status. All searchlights were on, their long, thin white fingers probing the darkness ahead and around the convoy. Both available helicopters were in the air for spotting purposes. Still, Yonkers felt virtually helpless to prevent a small boat attack if the Iranians decided to mount one. They didn't.

After another day of sailing on the 23rd, the convoy would be able to make the northernmost leg into Kuwait in daylight on the 24th. In addition to the Iranian threat, passage through the northern Gulf brought the threat of accidental Iraqi attack. "Daylight is really good because if the Iraqis come down and see this gaggle, they can't mistake us for anybody else—three Navy-gray ships surrounding two big tankers. It's hard to say, 'Oh, I made a mistake,'" said Captain Mathis of the *Fox*. "We want to make this a daylight run so we can see the sur-face [radar] contacts, so that we can maneuver if necessary," he said. "All these little marks here," Capt Mathis said, pointing to a map on his stateroom wall, "indicate either oil platforms, buoys, or places where small boats can hide [in] narrow confined waters—it's a real hairball up here, so we want to make sure we go up here in the daylight hours.[9]

As the convoy continued up the Gulf, reaching its halfway point on Thursday, July 23rd, Iranian officials made an ominous declaration that the re-flagged tankers were carrying "prohibited goods" being used to support Iraq.[10] Iran's declaration notwithstanding, the Middle East Task Force Commander, Rear Admiral Harold Bernsen, was clearly relieved that the convoy had made it past the Silkworms and on to its current location without incident. "So far," he told reporters, "it has gone precisely the way I thought it would—smoothly, without any con-frontation on the part of Iran."[11] Admiral Bernsen's relief would short-ly prove premature.

During the night of July 23/24, the U.S. AWACS orbiting in the northern Gulf, along with naval sources, began picking up signs of trou-ble near Farsi Island. Numbers of Iranian small boats were detected maneuvering in the area. The U.S. convoy was due to pass through a deepwater channel near the island in the still dark early morning hours of Friday, July 24. It now looked like the Iranians were preparing for a nighttime gunboat attack on the U.S. ships. Advised of the Iranian activ-ity, Admiral Bernsen ordered the convoy to hold up near Bahrain until first light, then to proceed. If the ships were going to face a small boat attack, they would stand a lot better chance in daylight, when it would be much easier to spot and engage the gunboats.

With daylight, the convoy came on. Expecting an attack, over 1,000 sailors on the three escorting warships manned their battle sta-tions as the convoy approached the deepwater channel near Farsi. Anxious lookouts peered through their binoculars and saw . . . nothing. The waters were empty. No Iranian speedboats could be detected, visu-ally or on radar. Captain Mathis told the crew of the *Fox*, "If you were on the bridge with me, you'd see that the horizon is virtually unlimited and it's open. We intend to turn over the tankers at approximately noon to the Kuwaitis. So, we're on our last leg here. We've got about eight more hours, and things look very good."[12] The convoy was now running about 18 miles west of Farsi Island, some 80 miles south of its Kuwaiti destination. The morning was calm and clear. The mercury had already hit 100 degrees Fahrenheit at 6:55 A.M. Breakfast was being brought up to the bridge crew on the *Bridgeton*. Suddenly, the tanker was rocked by a huge blast.

The Captain of the *Bridgeton*, Frank Seitz, said, "It felt like a 500-ton hammer hit us up forward."[13] As the shock wave traveled through the vast and empty ship, crewmen located nearly a thousand feet away had to grab hold of something so they weren't knocked off their feet. Loose objects went flying through the air. All of the stays on the radar mast snapped. The Navy liaison officer on the *Bridgeton*, Lieutenant Richard Vogel, radioed excitedly from the supertanker: "We've been hit! We've been hit!" Lieutenant Vogel later recalled that, "All of a sudden, the whole ship shuddered and rocked for about 15 to 20 seconds. It actually lifted us off our feet three or four inches."[14] Shrapnel propelled by the explosion was driven upward with such force that it sliced through several decks, penetrating all the way to the main deck, some 90 feet above the blast. Fortunately, none of the 31 people on board, including the wives of two crewmen, were injured. *Bridgeton* crewmen looked over the stern and saw a trail of oil from the ship and a bulge in the wake from the explosion.

Captain Seitz thought that there wasn't much question that his ship had hit a mine. He slowed but didn't stop the huge ship, which kept going deeper into what seemed to be a minefield. Given its momentum, the massive tanker would have taken a full half-hour, traveling a distance of some three miles, to come to a complete stop from a speed of 16 knots. In this case, it slowed to three knots, "bare steerageway," to evaluate the damage. The *Bridgeton* radioed, "We have flooding in . . . a tank at the bow. It goes all the way from port to starboard. We have flooding that filled, to sea level, one inner port in about three minutes. We have gradual flooding in one port, which is the outboard tank of one inner port, over." A few minutes later, the *Bridgeton* radioed its Navy escorts, "Have the helicopters take a low pass over our stern—look at the propeller and see what he can see above the waterline." An SH-60 helicopter from the *Crommelin* flew over and reported: "No damage to your rudder or screw." After a few minutes the tanker's officers had gotten a better idea of the extent of the damage and radioed, "The hit is port amidships, 100 to 200 feet of the bow. There is no danger to the ship, plenty of reserve buoyancy here."[15]

A 15- by 30-foot hole had been ripped in the tanker's hull below the water line. Thousands of tons of water were gushing into ruptured compartments. Emergency pumps kicked in to try contain the inrush of water. Four of the ship's 31 compartments were flooded, but the remaining 27 were dry and intact. These compartments would easily provide the buoyancy needed to keep the massive ship afloat. Captain Seitz radioed to the Navy escorts, "I don't know if you realize the force of the explosion here. "I would strongly advise that the escorts get in behind the *Bridgeton*."[16]

Captain Yonkers' major concern with the damaged *Bridgeton* was its mobility, which Captain Seitz reported was unimpaired. The convoy closed ranks in a compact single file, with the *Bridgeton* in the lead and the last ship, the destroyer *Kidd*, only two miles behind. The ships picked up speed and continued to head to Kuwait. The escort ships posted sailors with M-14 rifles on their bows to shoot at any suspicious objects in the water. The *Gas Prince* brought up more lookouts on deck to intently search the water. The logic of closely trailing the *Bridgeton* was plain enough. A mine blast of the type just shrugged off by the huge and empty *Bridgeton* could be fatal to one of the much smaller escorts.

The Navy ships carried hull plating only 5/8 of an inch thick, as opposed to the 1-1/8 inch thick plating on the *Bridgeton*. They were densely packed with fuel, equipment, and explosive ordnance. The relatively small warships also lacked the reserve buoyancy of the empty supertanker, which had just taken on 20,000 tons of water, more than the combined displacements of all three of the escorting warships. The *Bridgeton* purposely took on even more water to correct a list toward its damaged side. Aboard the *Fox*, Captain William Mathis announced over the loudspeaker, "This is the Captain. We have been ordered to form behind the *Bridgeton*. Basically, that means that the *Bridgeton* will be acting as a deep draft minesweeper for us, which I am very grateful for."[17]

Captain Yonkers felt that the convoy had probably not hit a mine "field," but rather a mine "line," which had been laid perpendicular to its path, across the fairly narrow deep-water passage. He figured that, while it was possible that there were successive mine lines, given the relatively short time period over which the mines had likely been laid, there was probably only one line. Accordingly, he didn't view the mines as a "persistent" threat once the ships had gotten past the immediate area of the *Bridgeton*'s impact. He had made a reasonable assessment of the situation. However, the Iranians had actually managed to lay two separate mine lines. Fortunately, the convoy didn't strike any in the second line, and was able to continue on without further incident. It reached Kuwaiti waters some seven hours later. On its way, it encountered a small Soviet convoy headed south. The convoy was composed of two merchant ships escort by a "Natya"-class minesweeper, apparently headed for the same mined channel the U.S. ships had just passed through. The Soviet minesweeper did not respond to calls, but one of the merchantmen did. "I want to report to you the location of a known mine," Commander Murphy told the Soviet captain. Then he read out the longitude and latitude of the mine site. The Soviet Captain answered, "Thank you American warship."[18]

The first convoy of the U.S. re-flagging operation had sailed in the bright glare of the media spotlight. When the *Bridgeton* struck the mine, reaction was immediate and intense. President Reagan was awakened at 2:00 A.M. with the news. Joint Chiefs of Staff Chairman Admiral William Crowe's bedside phone jolted him awake with the report. Within twenty minutes, he was in a grim Pentagon war room. A crowd of Iranians worshipping on the Moslem Sabbath in Tehran rejoiced, chanting "Death to USA!" and "Persian Gulf of Iran, the graveyard of Reagan." Oil and gold market prices jumped at the news, anticipating U.S. retaliation. The Iranian "sting" in the Gulf, and nobody really doubted the culprit, was widely viewed as a great humiliation for the U.S., which had invested so much effort and prestige in the re-flagging operation.

What had started out as a highly publicized media event suddenly became an embarrassment. Proposed press trips in Kuwait to the newly arrived *Bridgeton* were cancelled. Visa extensions promised to journalists in Kuwait were not forthcoming. A Press Information Center, which had been set up all week at the Kuwait Hilton, disappeared. The administration sought to put the best face on the fiasco. America's Ambassador to Kuwait, Anthony Quainton, called the mine strike "a matter of considerable regret," but added, "I don't think you can characterize the mission as having failed."[19] White House spokesman Marvin Fitzwater even tried to turn the tables on critics by citing the mining "as a good example" of the U.S. need to escort vessels in the Gulf.[20]

Others saw the event differently. While it had made operational sense under the circumstances for the *Bridgeton* to lead the convoy as a "deep draft minesweeper," the televised sight of Navy warships seemingly cowering in the wake of the tanker they were supposed to be protecting invited worldwide ridicule. "Who is escorting whom?" snorted Senate Majority Leader Robert Byrd. "This patently absurd and ridiculous result of the first escort mission is embarrassing to the nation."[21] Shipping agents and salvage operators in the Gulf were privately scornful about the convoy operation. They saw the mining as having left the U.S. Navy a red-faced laughingstock. Critical newspaper editorials appeared in several Arab capitals.

Iranian Prime Minister Mir Hussein Moussavi said, "The U.S. schemes had been foiled by invisible hands."[22] Moussavi crowed that the mining was "an irreparable blow to America's political and military prestige, proving how vulnerable Americans are despite their huge and unprecedented military expedition in the Persian Gulf to escort Kuwaiti tankers."[23] While not specifically claiming credit for the mining, Iran was giving broad hints. An Iranian military spokesman said that Iranian forces had carried out "special operations in the Gulf" the night before the incident.[24] Iran's ambassador to the United Nations, Said Rajaie Khorassani, said Iran was "pleased to see the tanker hit," but that, "Those mines might have been there months and probably years. It might be ours; it might be somebody else's."[25]

While there was little real doubt as to the origin of the mines, the White House said the U.S. would not retaliate. One diplomat said retaliation would only occur if American lives were lost. Not retaliating was probably the right call, given the dangers of igniting an escalating tit-for-tat exchange with Iran. Still, U.S. inaction was not to everyone's taste. "We should have pulverized Farsi Island," fumed Zbigniew Brzezinski, Jimmy Carter's National Security Adviser. "All this power cringing in the area is a terrible embarrassment."[26] Certainly the episode was immensely satisfying to Iran. As a Middle East expert put it: "The constant agonizing demonstration of American ineffectiveness and its inability to act are what give the Iranians their greatest gratification."[27]

If the *Bridgeton* mining had rocked the administration's Gulf policy, the U.S. Navy was left standing with egg all over its face. The Navy was quickly accused of blatant incompetence in anticipating every contingency except the one that actually happened. "U.S. Navy's Incompetence Blown Open by a Single Mine" ran a searing headline in

The Times (London).[28] Aboard the Middle East Force flagship *LaSalle*, when the *Bridgeton* had hit the mine, MEF Commander Admiral Bernsen's first thought had been, "Oh my God, now I know what they were up to last night!" His second thought was, "I guess I'm fired." Nevertheless, he went on to publicly defend the Navy, saying, "We had no indications that there were mines in that area." He added that, "Never have we seen a moored mine in that area. We don't normally sail into a minefield. That's not the way we do business."[29]

Three fully loaded tankers had passed through the channel the day before the *Bridgeton* was hit. It looked like the *Bridgeton* had been the victim of what might be described as a "mine ambush," set up in the night only hours before its expected early morning passage through the narrow one-and-a-half to two-mile-wide channel off Farsi Island. If the channel had been checked the day before, nothing would have been found.

With its mind concentrated on defending against the much greater threat posed by direct Iranian attacks with Silkworm anti-ship missiles and armed speed boats, as well as contingency plans for retaliatory strikes, the Navy hadn't thought to look for mines where they hadn't shown up before. Failure to check narrow "choke points" immediately before the passage of the high profile first convoy was clearly a serious mistake, but it was not gross incompetence. For that, a look at the state of the Navy's mine countermeasures was required.

Actually, looking around the Gulf, one wouldn't find any at all. Incredibly, the Navy had zero minesweeping capability in the Gulf. Neither minesweeping ships nor helicopters were available to support the re-flagging operation. Asked why the task force was not equipped with minesweeping ships or helicopters, Commander Murphy of USS *Kidd* haplessly replied, "I don't know."[30] Others had seen the potential threat more clearly. The Senate Armed Services Committee Report of June 29, 1987 had noted that mines were a form of indirect attack that Iran might favor and that, "The United States must be prepared well in advance to counter any mine threat."[31] The Navy's glaring failure to anticipate the mine threat triggered an avalanche of criticism.

"I was astonished to find out that they sailed the first convoy without any minesweeping capability at all," said retired Rear Admiral Robert Hanks, who once headed U.S. naval forces in the Gulf.[32] "John Moore, editor of the authoritative *Jane's Fighting Ships*, found it "quite staggering that the forces it [the U.S.] has called upon to carry out the task were unsuited for the operation because of a complete lack of mine countermeasures." He noted that, over three years before, Iran had warned that it was prepared to use mines and that the failure to provide any form of MCM support in the Gulf was incomprehensible.[33]

Mine countermeasures capability was not the only issue raised by the *Bridgeton* incident. The circumstances under which the Iranians had mined the tanker led to recrimination over lapses in operational security. Captain Seitz of the *Bridgeton* was convinced that his convoy route had been compromised. He also blamed U.S. politicians for giving out the information that the convoy was underway to reporters. With the route, departure time, and speed of the convoy known, Captain Seitz thought the Iranians were presented with a relatively simple problem in targeting the convoy with a small minefield laid in a choke point.[34]

Revelations about the convoy's departure were not the only Congressional lapses. Some ten days before the convoy sailed, Defense Secretary Weinberger, National Security Aide Frank Carlucci, and Joint Chiefs Chairman Admiral Crowe had held a briefing for key Congressional leaders. At the meeting, Admiral Crowe had specifically stated that the information to be briefed was extremely sensitive and should be treated accordingly. However, the lure of open microphones proved too much for the politicians. Immediately following the meeting, Les Aspin, Chairman of the House Armed Services Committee, held a press conference divulging exact details on the upcoming first convoy, including place and date of departure, number of ships, etc. The next day, the details appeared on the front page of the *Washington Post*. After the *Bridgeton* struck the mine, military members of Weinberger's staff resurrected a modified version of the old World War II slogan, "Loose lips sink ships." For several days, the phrase, "Les' lips sink ships," was heard in the corridors of the Pentagon.[35]

In order to minimize the fallout from the mine hit on the *Bridgeton*, Kuwaiti and American authorities were anxious to get the tanker back in operation as soon as possible by loading it with crude and sending it on the return leg of the trip. Shipping sources in Dubai estimated that, in its damaged state, the *Bridgeton* could still fill about 65 percent of its tanks and sail without repairs, if the load were carefully balanced. Even if the *Bridgeton*'s owners had wanted to have the hull repaired before proceeding, all of the docks big enough to handle the ship were booked through August. The *Bridgeton* was inspected by divers in Kuwait, and some temporary repairs were made to internal piping. Tanks next to those awash with seawater were not loaded, forming a sort of "coffer dam" between the damaged areas and the cargo of crude, which was loaded in the rest of the tanks.

There was, of course, another problem facing the return journey—the mines. Trying to avoid mines by depending on ship bow watches and helicopters to visually spot them was obviously not good enough. With no minesweepers available, the U.S. turned to Saudi Arabia, which was equipped with four modem U.S.-built minesweepers, for assistance. They declined. As an expedient, the Navy flew over a minesweeping cable from the United States for use by two 150-foot commercial oilfield tugboats. While a minesweeper would normally tow the cable streamed out behind it to either side, supported by floats, the tugs would simply drag the cable between them, covering a 400-meter-wide stretch. Dubbed the "Hunter" and the "Striker," the Kuwaiti boats were provided at that country's expense through the efforts of Oil Minister Sheik Ali. Some one third of the civilian boat crews balked at the minesweeping task and had to be replaced by U.S. Navy volunteers. On August 1, the *Gas Prince* quietly slipped out of Kuwait, escorted by the USS *Kidd* and USS *Crommelin*, and sailed unscathed on a shoreline-hugging run back through the Gulf.

However embarrassing the *Bridgeton* strike and the exposure of the Navy's dismal mine countermeasures situation had been, the truly critical aspect of the incident was the fact that the Iranians had shown their willingness to challenge the United States. Deterrence had failed. Indeed, according to a State Department source whose contacts in Tehran were felt to be in a position to know, only Rafsanjani's last-minute intervention had prevented a full-blown assault on the *Bridgeton* convoy. A local commander had supposedly mined the waters near Farsi as a "spite" action following the cancellation of the operation, which had already gotten underway.[36] Whatever the truth of those reports, there had been no guarantee whatsoever that the Farsi minefield would not sink a U.S. warship with the loss of lives.*

Admiral Bernsen later said that he believed that the Iranians had looked at what was going on in Washington and concluded that the escort operation did not enjoy solid political support. They had also looked at recent history and seen an apparent pattern of U.S. inability to sustain its commitments when the going got rough, obvious examples being South Vietnam, the Shah of Iran, and Beirut. Admiral Bernsen said:

I think they came to a decision, and I think they bet. The bet that they made was that there was better than a 50-50 chance that if they successfully mined a United States ship, not necessarily a tanker, but a warship, that we might just turn around and leave. Those mines, the mine that hit the *Bridgeton*, were set at a depth such that the USS *Kidd* or anyone of the other escorts could just as likely have been hit and blown sky-high.[37]

Such an event would have precipitated a major U.S. strike against Iran. Joint Chiefs Chairman Admiral Crowe found the thought truly sobering, and realized that the entire nature of the operation had now changed. As he later put it, "I thought . . . if this is an indication of what the Iranians are going to do, that, yes, we may be involved in a real sea war here."[38] Captain David Yonkers somberly noted, "A lot of people are going to have to do some rethinking about this thing."[39]

CHAPTER 6

RETHINKING

Navy Commander Paul Evancoe assumed command of Special Boat Unit (SBU) 20 in early August 1987. That unit, based in Little Creek, Virginia, operated relatively small patrol boats for shallow water operations. A SEAL officer, Evancoe was fresh from a seven-month deployment as the commander of a Special Operations task unit, which was part of what was called a Marine Expeditionary Unit, Special Operations Capable [MEU (SOC)]. The first of its kind, the MEU (SOC), had deployed to the Mediterranean. Within that unit, Evancoe had commanded a force consisting of a Marine rifle company, a SEAL platoon, a special boat squadron and helicopter elements. The idea was to incorporate a SpecOps capability within a regular Marine amphibious unit.

Evancoe assumed command of the Special Boat Unit 20 at the usual formal ceremony, relieving the prior CO, Stan Holloway. The ceremony was followed by an informal get-together for a charcoal grill cookout on a small hill nearby. Kegs of beer were provided for the occasion. Barely six minutes after the change of command ceremony had ended, the Quarterdeck Watch Orderly approached the men gathered at the cookout and called for the commander of SBU 20. Both the freshly minted Evancoe and the just-relieved Holloway responded, "Yes?" Evancoe was told that he had a "red phone call." He thought it was some kind of joke. "No sir, it is not," was the orderly's sobering reply. On the line was Commodore Gormly, commander of Naval Special Warfare Group 2. He told Evancoe that his SBU was being committed to the Middle East Force. Their mission was to be anti-mining and containment of the Iranians should they come out into the Gulf.

Evancoe was only one of two SEALs up to that time who had gone through the Navy's Mine Warfare School in Charleston, South Carolina. He had also done extensive testing and evaluation work on weapons and equipment which might be adopted by the SEALs. Some of these also had anti-mine applications. This background, plus the fact that he had apparently been judged as having done well as the first Marine Special Operations Task Unit commander, probably got him recommend for the job in the Gulf.

Evancoe didn't have the least hesitation in accepting the task. "How could anybody turn this down?" he thought. He asked about his deployment time frame and was told he had four days to get out for what looked like a three-month tour. He would take four Mark III Patrol Boats (PB's) along with three small wooden-hulled minesweeping boats (MSB's). His first problem was trying to load out his new command for transportation to the Gulf. The plan was for the four 60-ton Mark III PB's to be transported in cradles mounted on the deck of the amphibious assault ship USS *Raleigh* (LPD-l), something that had never been done before.

Naval architects were consulted on whether it would work or not. Their confidence-inspiring verdict was, "We think so." The three MSB's were carried inside the ship. They were loaded by the expedient of attaching jury-rigged steel cradles to the hulls, putting the boats in the water and floating them into the *Raleigh*'s flooded well deck. Weighed down with the heavy cradles, the boats barely had any freeboard above the water's surface. After they were maneuvered into the *Raleigh*, the water in the well deck was drained, leaving the MSB's sitting in their cradles on the now dry deck.

The urgency of the situation in the Gulf following the *Bridgeton* mining was being transmitted down the chain of command. The *Raleigh* was loaded at Norfolk with the patrol boats, equipment, fuel, ammunition and other supplies in less than 48 hours. Normally, the process would have taken a leisurely 30 days. The ammunition being loaded had to come from the Yorktown ammunition depot on the other side of the James River. Vehicles carrying ammunition were prohibited from using the convenient tunnel under the river, so they normally had to take a circuitous 75-mile route to get to the base. Given the priority assigned to getting the unit to the Gulf, however, the safety procedures were waived. Big 18-wheelers, loaded with ammunition, went rumbling through the confined spaces of the tunnel.

The deployment was kept a closely held secret. The men wore their camouflage uniforms "slick," i.e. without any rank or unit insignia. Loading was only allowed during a daily one-and-a-half-hour "window" during which Soviet reconnaissance satellites were not overhead. The men were not allowed to tell their wives or sweethearts where they were going. To his regret, Evancoe had to stay behind when the *Raleigh* and most of his men sailed. He would remain to be more fully briefed on the mission and to receive the latest intelligence updates. Evancoe also got orders to send along two "Seafox" naval special warfare boats. These were to be flown to Rota, Spain aboard an Air Force C-5A Galaxy transport plane. There, they would catch up with the *Raleigh* and be loaded on the ship for the final leg of the voyage to the Gulf.

The Seafoxes, too, could only be transported and loaded during the one-and-a-half-hour-long window, which avoided Soviet satellite observation. Unfortunately, as the boats were slowly being towed on their long trailers to the airport, one was rear-ended by an overtaking automobile. The tractor-trailers carrying the boats stopped and the police were summoned. By the time they arrived and had begun their accident investigation, the officer in charge of the two special warfare craft was becoming increasingly worried as the satellite window began to close on him. Anxious to get on his way, he tried to talk the Virginia police into letting him proceed on to the airport. The police refused to let him leave the scene of the accident. The driver who hit the boat trailer apparently was intoxicated. Finally, with most of the police paper work done, the boat officer could stand it no longer. He told the police, "Sorry, we're going to war," and drove off.

Evancoe caught up with the *Raleigh* at Rota, and the Seafoxes were loaded aboard there. The four Patrol Boats sitting on the ship's deck were now impossible to hide from observers, but a bit of misdirection on their armament was employed. Angle iron frames in the distinct ribbed rectangular shape of French-made Exocet anti-ship missile containers were mounted on the boats and covered with canvas. The props were very convincing. So much so that, when some French naval officers came on deck while visiting the *Raleigh* during a stopover at Port Suez, they were certain that the patrol boats were equipped with Exocets. At sea, the boat crews underwent vigorous twice-a-day training sessions. Fire hoses were used to spray seawater directly into cooling intakes so that the boat engines and other systems could be run with the craft mounted in their cradles. Crewmen were even able to fire all of the boats' weapons over the side. By the time they reached Bahrain, the crews had undergone an extensive practice regimen. When the men from the special boat units arrived in the Gulf on the *Raleigh*, the on-scene commander greeted them. He looked over the boats and growled, "Who's ready to go to war?"[1]

Navy Special Boat Units weren't the only Special Forces being rushed to the Gulf. Major Tom Mathews commanded "B" Company of the U.S. Army's 160th Special Operations Aviation Regiment, which was mainly based at Fort Campbell, Kentucky. "B" Company was a "gun" company, equipped with the AH-6 attack version of the 160th's "Little Bird" helicopters. "A" Company had the MH-6 observation version, equipped with a Forward Looking Infra-Red (FLIR) viewing device. Mathews was told that there was a possibility that detachments from the 160th would be sent to the Gulf following the *Bridgeton* mining. The problem, he was told, was that the Navy's ships were at risk from night attack by small boats. The ships lacked the ability to consistently detect the small craft or to discriminate between potential threats and the sometimes hundreds of civilian fishing and cargo boats that were commonly encountered in certain areas. What the Navy needed, he was told, were some nighttime eyes out there for self-protection and escort operations.

Feasibility tests for using the special operations helicopters at sea would be run out of Norfolk, with the "Little Birds" embarked on the USS *Antrim*. Mathews figured there was little likelihood that the Army unit would actually deploy to the Gulf. He expected that the Marines or the Navy would much prefer to use their own helicopters for the mission rather then to have to call on the Army. Still, the tests went so well that they were discontinued after two days rather than continue for a scheduled third day. Instead, the detachment flew back to Fort Campbell. When he got back, Mathews was surprised by the news that detachments from the 160th would be deploying to the Gulf after all—in two days. He found it hard to believe, but amusedly thought to himself, "I'll bet the Marines are really pissed."

Mathews would go as the Officer in Charge (OIC) of one of two detachments being deployed. He was personally excited about the opportunity to go. He had trained with the Navy in joint exercises for several years. In fact, a few months earlier, in May 1987, he had taken a 160th detachment out to the West Coast for a Navy training exercise. In light of the upcoming Gulf mission, the nature of that exercise was a fortunate coincidence. During the exercise, the Army helicopters had been able to fire their weapons at salvaged small boats provided by the Navy as targets. This was exactly the practice the 160th crews needed to prepare for upcoming mission in the Gulf.

Six helicopters were to be sent: two MH-6 observation craft and four AH-6 gunships. The small helos were to be carried over on one of the Air Force's huge C-5A Galaxies. The plan was for the C-5A to land at Bahrain, quickly offload the helicopters, and have them fly out to the USS *LaSalle* at sea. Bahrain allowed the U.S. to transship general supplies through the country, but it forbade munitions transshipment. High-level pressure was applied, and the rules were bent a bit. The armed helicopters were allowed to take what they could carry. This meant that each of the AH-6's could mount their basic weapons-load of seven 2.75- inch rockets and 2,000 rounds of 7.62 mm minigun ammunition, along with one identical reload stuffed in the aft cabin behind the seats.

The 160th's arrival in Bahrain was kept very hush-hush. The C-5A landed at 2:00 A.M. in the morning on August 5. The AH-6's and MH-6's were rolled out of the big transport and quickly prepared for flight. Waiting on the runway was a civilian Bo-105 helicopter, piloted by a robed Bahraini prince. When the Army helicopters were ready, the Bahraini prince called the central tower and requested take off clearance for his aircraft only. He got it and lifted off. Observing complete radio silence, the six blacked-out U.S. Army Special Forces helicopters followed him aloft. The control tower was never aware of their presence. The Bahraini helicopter led the six "Little Birds" part of the way toward the *LaSalle* before pulling away and returning to the airfield. The U.S. helicopters flew on to the *LaSalle*, where they landed and were whisked under cover. By dawn, there was nothing visible to observers that would have indicated the unit had arrived and deployed. The Iranians didn't have a clue that they were in the Gulf.

The various U.S. Special Forces headed to the Gulf would have a role to play in preventing future Iranian mine attempts. Unfortunately, most of the mines that had been laid were still bobbing somewhere under the Gulf's surface. Many thought that the Iranian mine that had exploded under the *Bridgeton* had done more damage to the reputation of the U.S. Navy than it had done to the supertanker. Aside from exposing the Navy's failure to even prepare for a possible mine threat in the Gulf (a *Newsweek* article at the time was chidingly entitled: "Oops, We

Forgot the Minesweepers"[2]), the incident turned the spotlight of public attention on the Navy's mine countermeasures (MCM) forces. It was not a pretty sight. At the time, the U.S. confronted a Soviet Union that had accumulated an enormous mine stockpile, estimated to contain some 300,000 to 400,000 mines. Many of these mines were of a vastly more sophisticated design than the simple contact type that had holed the *Bridgeton*. Recognizing that mines presented a threat to themselves as well, the Soviet Navy deployed 390 mine countermeasures vessels. America's allies in the 14 NATO navies, also sensitive to the mine threat, deployed some 319 MCM vessels. The U.S. Navy, the most powerful fleet in the world, had three.

To be fair, the Navy did have a few other MCM assets: seven small minesweeping boats (MSB's), ineffective in all but protected waters, and 23 RH-53D minesweeping helicopters of limited endurance and capability. The reserve force had 19 minesweepers of the same type as the three in active service. Wooden-hulled, some suffering from dry rot and leaks, not all of the vessels were ready to perform their mission. That was it. The Navy had allowed its mine countermeasures capability to deteriorate into a critical condition. That fact was hardly a secret. Vice Admiral Robert L. Waters, then deputy chief of naval operations for surface warfare, had testified before Congress in 1983 that "no segment of naval warfare has been under-funded for so many years as the mine warfare community."[3]

As one frustrated naval mine warfare officer pungently noted: "If you look back through CNO's [Chiefs of Naval Operations] going back 20 years, they have all said it is time to revitalize Mine Warfare, and it has never been done. . . . It's all been lip service, as far as I am concerned, and it's a lot of crap also."[4] Following the *Bridgeton* mining, Senator John W. Warner (R-VA.), a former Secretary of the Navy, wrote in a newspaper commentary that, "Faced with declining defense budgets and the need to modernize an overage fleet, naval planners (including this former Secretary of the Navy) decided to rely primarily on our NATO allies to provide the required mine countermeasures capability."[5] The idea had been to entirely pass on the MCM task to U.S. allies in a kind of military specialization of labor. This scheme may have led to an efficient utilization of naval resources in a major conflict involving NATO, but, in anything less, it left the U.S. with no assets of its own.

Critics asserted that the problem with mine warfare was that, despite threat analysis and some bitter real world experience, it constituted a backwater of operations for the U.S. Navy. For officers, a long association with mine warfare was not considered "career enhancing." In contrast, the Soviet Navy and America's allies took mine warfare much more seriously. Unlike the U.S., their MCM forces received solid funding and the field was considered a viable professional career path for officers. On the naval aviation side, MCM pilots were seen as spending all their time tediously dragging sweeps back and forth through the water.[6] One mine warfare officer described the field as the Rodney Dangerfield of the U.S. Navy. A reference to the comedian whose signature line was, "I don't get no respect."

In 1979, mine warfare expert Dr. Gregory K. Hartmann had written, "Many persons in positions of decision in the U.S. Navy do not understand the characteristics or principles of mine warfare," and that he was not sure if mine warfare "even exists in the U.S. Navy." Among the reasons cited by Dr. Hartmann for this state of affairs was that military people are mostly "platform" (i.e. aircraft, ship, etc.) oriented and mines were not associated with a particular platform or vehicle. Further, there was no tactical excitement in the use of mines—no satisfying "Bang!" when they were laid.[7]

The U.S. did have an Explosive Ordnance Disposal (EOD) team in the Gulf, helping to clear the mines discovered in Kuwait's Al Ahmadi channel in May. Working off a Kuwaiti tug in strong tidal currents and in water temperatures exceeding 115 degrees Fahrenheit, the EOD divers destroyed eight of the mines and towed two of them to the beach. The mines were rendered safe and "exploited." They turned out to be a 1908 Russian design, which floated beneath the surface while moored by cable to a heavily weighted base resting on the sea bottom. The mines had 115-kilogram (about 250-lb.) explosive charges that were detonated when a ship struck one of the five "horns" projecting from its spherical case. The mines usually floated at a depth of about four to twenty feet below the surface, and had to be laid at least 120 feet apart to prevent an exploding mine from detonating its neighbor. It was believed that Iran had manufactured the mines, using a North Korean model, which was itself based on the Russian design. The *Bridgeton* had struck an identical mine off Farsi. Iran claimed to have a factory, which "could make mines like seeds."[8]

The U.S. Navy's only active duty minesweeping boats were located on the East Coast, while reserve ships were located on both the East and West Coasts. It would take some time to crew, ready, and move the craft to the Gulf. The earliest help that could be expected would be the minesweeping helicopters. Squadron HM-14 was stationed in Norfolk, Virginia. Its eight helicopters were embarked two at a time onboard Air Force C-5A Galaxy transports and flown to the base on the British island of Diego Garcia, located in the Indian Ocean.

The helicopters would operate in the Gulf from the USS *Guadalcanal*, an *Iwo Jima*-class amphibious assault ship with a 603-foot flight deck. The delicate political situation in the Gulf dictated against high-profile shore bases in Saudi Arabia or Kuwait, neither of whom wished to risk Iranian wrath by allowing the semi-permanent basing of U.S. forces. The Reagan administration evasively insisted that neither Saudi Arabia nor Kuwait had turned down U.S. requests to base aircraft on their soil, claiming rather that no such requests had been made. The administration found itself caught in an uncomfortable position between the reluctance of the Gulf States to expose themselves to possible Iranian retaliation and the domestic political need to show that the countries the U.S. was supporting were sharing the burden of the escort effort.

The *Guadalcanal* had been conducting training exercises in the Arabian Sea when it was directed to steam to Diego Garcia and pick up the helicopters. A Navy SEAL team also came aboard. Rigged with running lights to look like a commercial ship, and maintaining radio silence, the *Guadalcanal* slipped into the Strait of Hormuz on the night of August 14, in the company of USS *Fox* and USS *Reeves*. During its passage through the Strait, an Iranian warship interrogated the *Guadalcanal*. The radio exchange was piped throughout the amphibious assault ship over the intercom. Anxious crewmen heard the *Guadalcanal* identify itself as a civilian ship to the Iranians, who seem to have bought the story and ended the questioning without further action.

The helicopters carried by the *Iwo Jima* would help with minesweeping efforts; however, the helicopters were maintenance intensive and lacked endurance. What was really needed to deal with the mines was mine countermeasures ships. The Navy's three active, and eighteen reserve-force minesweepers (MSO's), were 172-foot-long, 830-ton vessels with a top speed of only 14 knots. Crewed by about 75 men and seven officers each, the ships were equipped with mine-hunting SQQ-14 sonars. The Navy urgently dispatched six MSO's to the Gulf. Three were from the Pacific Fleet and three were from the Atlantic Fleet.

Coming from both sides of the North American continent, the Atlantic and Pacific based ships headed in opposite directions to reach the same Gulf destination.

The West Coast ships were lucky to miss two typhoons that swept across the Pacific, and generally encountered calm seas. The Atlantic crossing was much rougher, with the ships rolling 30 to 35 degrees in high seas. The Atlantic Fleet ships took nearly 60 days to reach their destination. The rough seas knocked equipment and crewmen about, making sleep difficult. One seaman described the experience as having made him feel like he'd been run over by a truck.[9] When he met the arriving ships, the Middle East Force Mine Countermeasures Commander later said he "was amazed at the lack of casts on people's arms or other indications of broken bones."

The new situation in the Gulf required that new kinds of units, including Army helicopters, Special Boat Units, SEALs, and mine countermeasures vessels and helicopters, be added to the tactical mix of U.S. forces. That new situation also required some rethinking on the command structure needed to manage the various units. General Crist wanted a joint force, under one commander, which integrated all of the forces in the region. The joint commander would head a staff composed of members from all services and which would be constituted in proportion to the resources those services had committed to the area. It would also cut out the command layer of the Naval Forces Central Command, with General Crist's line of authority running directly to the joint commander.

General Crist ran into a great deal of hostility from the Commander of the 7th Fleet, Admiral James A. Lyons, who was insisting that he control the entire naval battle. The Commander of Pacific Command, Admiral Ronald J. Hays, and Admiral Crowe backed up General Crist. The latter, as JCS Chairman, had the authority under the Goldwater-Nichols Defense Reorganization Act to create a joint command structure, which he did—although only after what General Crist later described as some "bloody infighting."

On September 20, 1987, the new joint command was formed. The Navy Middle East Force in the Gulf and detachments from other armed forces in the area were to report to a new unified command: The Joint Task Force Middle East (JTFME). A two-star Navy Admiral, Dennis M. Brooks, would command the JTFME. It was hoped that the new command structure would reduce some of the frustration felt by the predominantly Navy forces in the region that had to report to what they viewed as a land-oriented Central Command. Admiral Brooks would initially fly his flag from the cruiser USS *Long Beach*. The new JTFME commander would coordinate activities in and around the Gulf and report to the Central Command, which in turn reported to the Joint Chiefs of Staff. Both the command arrangement and the choice of the individual to head it were to prove less than ideal.

While the U.S. was rethinking its force mix and command structure for the escort operation, the strategic situation in the Gulf also needed a sober reappraisal. With the *Bridgeton* mining, the Iranians had demonstrated that they were willing to risk challenging the U.S. in the Gulf. That is not what the administration had expected when it undertook its commitment to Kuwait. The U.S. belatedly realized that the anticipated low-key re-flagging effort was turning into a major and possibly open-ended operation, one that risked a serious confrontation with Iran. Unfortunately, that looked like a risk that now had to be run. A pull-out would have utterly wrecked any credibility the U.S. had in the region, and likely have driven friendly Gulf states to cut deals with Iran in order to ensure their own survival.

"We've made a tactical error going in," said a U.S. official. "Now we're stuck. We can't pull out. We've got to do the best we can."[10] Accordingly, the U.S. began a major buildup of the kind of conventional naval forces needed for a possible direct confrontation with Iran. A surface battle group built around the battleship USS *Missouri* arrived in the northern Arabian Gulf on August 28, joining the carrier battle group already there. With additional ships still on the way, the U.S. was now assembling the largest flotilla deployed by the Navy since the Vietnam War. However, as Iranian Prime Minister Mir Hussein Moussavi would warn, "It is easier entering the Gulf than leaving it."[11]

CHAPTER 7

THE INVISIBLE HAND
STRIKES AGAIN

In an August 3 message, the U.S. Office of Naval Intelligence ominously concluded, "A number of indirect indicators taken together imply that within the immediate future . . . Iran will initiate combat actions against U.S. interests in the Gulf. . . . [The] threat would most likely come in the form of mines, terrorist attacks, Revolutionary Guard attacks." Nevertheless, escorted by the USS *Kidd* and USS *Crommelin*, the supertanker *Gas Prince* was able to make its return voyage through the Gulf without incident. However, as the re-flagged tanker approached the Strait of Hormuz, several truck-mounted Silkworm missile launchers were positioned by Iran at a previously unknown missile site near Khuzistan along the Strait.

Iranian targeting radar illuminated the ship, possibly in a pre-firing drill to obtain bearing and range. U.S. forces detected the Iranian action, and Navy EA-6B Prowler electronic warfare aircraft flying escort for the convoy jammed the Iranian radars. Admiral Crowe, Chairman of the Joint Chiefs of Staff, was roused from his bed in the early morning hours by Pentagon duty officers and rushed to the Pentagon. It turned out to be a false alarm. No active missiles or crews were detected at the site and everyone breathed a sigh of relief. The Iranians appear to have been engaging in a war of nerves with U.S. forces. They had directed missile search radars at U.S. vessels on several other occasions and had been jammed each time.

Iran also announced that it would conduct military maneuvers code-named "Operation Martyrdom." Iran said that its airspace and territorial waters along the littoral of the Gulf and into the Sea of Oman would be closed to foreign ships and aircraft for three days. Iran said that the exercises would help prepare Iranian forces for possible aggression by the "arch-Satan." The maneuvers began on August 4, 1987, and were the first held offshore by the IRGC, as opposed to the regular Iranian navy. Tehran radio said that the exercises showed a portion of its military power able "to carry out martyrdom-seeking attacks against international arrogance in the Gulf."[1] The exercises were extended an additional day and ended in the Strait of Hormuz with Iranian President Ali Khamenei reviewing regular navy vessels and dozens of IRGC speedboats from the deck of a command ship. Looking incongruous in a nautical setting, turbaned mullahs wearing long robes lined the rails as the crews of boats passing in review chanted, "The Persian Gulf is the burial place of Reagan."[2]

Iran was obviously engaging in some high profile threat posturing. However, one expert noted, "It is vital to see Iranian threats for what they are—a substitute for war, not a prelude to it."[3] While reluctant to escalate the conflict with the U.S., the revolutionary regime thrived on confrontation and saw the U.S. presence as a golden opportunity to deflect domestic attention from the sacrifices demanded by the war with Iraq. "People were starting to complain that the cost of the war was too high," said a long-time Western resident of Tehran. "But the Iranians have a strong nationalistic streak, and they are masters at using external incidents to direct attention from domestic problems."[4]

Events, however, were rapidly moving beyond the posturing stage. On August 8, the U.S. fired its first shots at Iranian military forces in the Gulf. The second convoy up to Kuwait weighed anchor before dawn on Saturday, following the end of Iranian maneuvers at midnight on Friday. The convoy was composed of two tankers, the *Sea Isle City* and the *Ocean City*, and an LPG carrier, the *Gas King*. Three U.S. Navy warships, USS *Kidd*, USS *Crommelin*, and USS *Jarett* escorted the tankers. For its transit through the Strait of Hormuz, a fourth warship, the guided-missile cruiser USS *Valley Forge*, accompanied the convoy. Normally part of the carrier battle group sailing in the Gulf of Oman, the *Valley Forge* was equipped with the highly sophisticated Aegis air defense system—the Navy's, and probably the world's, most advanced. The *Valley Forge* was a logical choice to shield the convoy through the Silkworm envelope in the Strait, after which the ship would return to its carrier battle group.

Because of concerns over operational security, and possibly because of the bad publicity that resulted from the *Bridgeton* fiasco, no media pool was embarked on the second convoy north. The tugs *Hunter* and *Striker* would be employed to sweep mine danger areas before the convoy's passage.

The convoy made its way through the Strait of Hormuz with one of the specially configured Navy Lockheed P-3C Orion "Reef Point" aircraft based in Oman flying a Silkworm surveillance patrol ahead of the ships. The Orion is a relatively slow, long-range four-engine turboprop aircraft, originally designed primarily for antisubmarine work. It normally carried a crew of ten. F-14 Tomcat fighters from the USS *Constellation* had been escorting Navy P-3C reconnaissance aircraft on their "Reef Point" runs through the Strait. Sometimes, Iranian F-4 Phantom fighters rose from Bandar Abbas airbase, but they did not look like they wanted to challenge the American aircraft. Still, there had been at least one incident when an F-14 came very close to firing on approaching Iranian fighters before the latter had veered away. The Iranian jets would head toward American aircraft but then turn parallel to the coast and stay overland. Recently, though, a few Iranian fighters had begun venturing out over the water before pulling back in the face of American warnings.

As the convoy passed through the Strait, two Iranian aircraft took off from an airbase and were tracked by U.S. forces on radar. Given their point of origin and performance, the aircraft were identified as American-made F-4 Phantom fighters. The Aegis radar on the *Valley Forge* tracked the Iranian jets, as did a *Constellation*-based Navy E-2C Hawkeye radar-warning plane. The Iranian fighters began closing from the rear on the P-3C in what the Orion pilot took to be a threatening manner. Warnings were broadcast to the Iranian fighters by the *Valley Forge* to stay clear of the P-3C. The warnings were ignored. "It kept coming, coming, coming," a Pentagon official later said.[5]

Two U.S. Navy F-14A fighters based on the *Constellation* and flying cover were now called up by the E-2 Hawkeye. The flight leader was Lieutenant Commander Robert Clement; Bill "Bear" Ferran piloted the other F-14. The day was hazy and neither the P-3C nor the F-14's streaking to the scene could actually see the Iranian aircraft. Events were to play out on radar screens only. Ferran had the better radar picture on the two Iranian fighters, which were coming in at a low 700-foot altitude, and was passed the flight lead. The American and the Iranian aircraft closed head-on at high speed. As the U.S. jets reached a 10-mile range of the Iranian fighters, within which their ROE's allowed

them to fire, they decided that they were facing a hostile threat. Ferran
fired an AIM-7 Sparrow air-to-air missile at one of the Iranian F-4's.
The missile was a dud. Its rocket motor failed to ignite and it plunged
into the sea. Clement then fired a Sparrow and Ferran fired his second.
Clement thought he saw his missile explode and called for a "break
turn."

"We go screaming down to the deck," said Ferran, "and I'm of
course looking behind me trying to find somebody and pumping out
chaff and flares."[6] It was not clear to him if one of the Iranian aircraft
had been hit and damaged or even shot down by the exploding missile.
The Iranian F-4's were probably equipped with radar warning receivers,
which would have allowed them to detect the F-14s' missile guidance
radars locking on to them.

Under the circumstances, with repeated warnings being ignored and
the aircraft closing rapidly, the American pilots' split-second decision to
fire on the F-4's was understandable. The increasing tension in the Gulf
had to have played its part. Still, it seems unlikely that the Iranian jets
were actually going to attack the Navy electronic surveillance plane. An
obvious, direct blow against the U.S. invited retaliation, which was not
what Iran was looking for. It was just as well that the Sparrow missiles
apparently did not knock down their targets.

The shooting incident was kept quiet for several days by the Reagan
administration, which was clearly concerned with the potential impact
on a Congress which was then considering invoking the War Powers
Act. In an apparent effort to downplay the incident, officials even raised
the possibility that the aircraft weren't Iranian or that the radar contacts
weren't aircraft at all. Administration spokesmen played a contorted
game of talking about the incident but refusing to confirm that it had
actually occurred. When White House Spokesman Marvin Fitzwater
told reporters that President Reagan was informed "soon after the incident happened," reporters tried to trap him by quickly asking what incident. "The incident I'm not confirming," replied Fitzwater with a
wink.[7]

The bad news was that another incident was on the way. By early
August, U.S. intelligence had determined that the Iranians were plan-
ning another mining in the Gulf. The big unanswered question was,
"Where were they going to do it?" The intelligence community was
divided. The Central Intelligence Agency, the Defense Intelligence
Agency, and the National Security Agency believed that the mining

would take place inside the Gulf. However, Middle East Force (MEF) intelligence believed the indications were that the mining would take place where "things gather." The MEF interpretation was that the likely Iranian target was the Khor Fakkan anchorage, where U.S. convoys assembled outside the Gulf. That anchorage was not far from the Iranian base at Bandar Abbas, where the mines were stored.[8]

Admiral Bernsen, the MEF commander, now had a decision to make. Which of the conflicting intelligence interpretations would he go with? In the end, he decided to go with the MEF intelligence call, and assume that the mining would take place at Khor Fakkan. He ordered the next Earnest Will convoy going into the Gulf to form up 100 miles south of Khor Fakkan, and to delay its run by one day. It was the right decision.

Shortly before dusk on Monday, August 10, 1987, the U.S.-owned, Panamanian-registered, supertanker *Texaco Caribbean* was slowly steaming through the Gulf of Oman outside the Strait of Hormuz. The 274,375-ton tanker had taken on a load of oil at Iran's Larak Island terminal in the Gulf. As the ship cruised about eight miles off the United Arab Emirates port of Fujariah, it was rocked by an explosion which ripped a 12-foot hole in its hull. As crewmen hosed down the decks, the *Texaco Caribbean* pulled farther away from shore to prevent contaminating nearby beaches. Some 8,000 barrels of oil would eventually leak through the ship's ruptured hull before its cargo could be transferred to other tankers. The damaged ship eventually limped into Fujairah for emergency repairs.

The *Texaco Caribbean* hit the mine near what had always been considered a safe anchorage. At first, it was unclear to shippers if the mine had been deliberately planted or had merely drifted down from the Gulf. Within a few days, however, additional mines were spotted in the area, one by the crew of an ABC News helicopter. There was now no question that the mines had been deliberately laid. The shipping community was shocked, because for the first time mines had been planted outside the Gulf in an area considered the last safe assembly point prior to making the perilous voyage through the Gulf itself. "No one thought it could happen here—this has always been the safest place in the Gulf," said a Fujairah shipping agent. "Now, after this, everyone is afraid." Alarmed harbor officials closed off part of the anchorage to shipping.[9]

UAE coastguardsmen, aided by helicopters, located and defused two mines. The mines found in the Gulf of Oman were of the same M-

08 type that the *Bridgeton* had hit, leaving little doubt as to their origin. One Pentagon official said, "It looks like the same modus operandi. The invisible hand strikes again."[10] Possibly they had been laid a few days earlier, using the "Operation Martyrdom" naval exercise as cover. The *Texaco Caribbean* had struck the mine not too far from the point off the small UAE port of Khor Fakken, just north of Fujairah, where U.S. Navy-escorted tankers and their escorts marshaled for convoy runs up the Gulf to Kuwait. Admiral Bernsen's call had proved to be the correct one.

The UAE was concerned since it derived a major part of its income from the port of Fujairah."[11] Defensive over the presence of the mines, the UAE hastily and prematurely declared the Fujairah anchorage mine-free. When a ship captain later spotted a mine and notified UAE authorities, they dismissed the sighting as the hump of a bloated dead camel floating in the water.[12] Tragically they were wrong.

Shortly after noon on August 15, the *Anita*, a 156-foot supply boat owned by a Swedish services company, headed for a supertanker off Fujairah on a re-supply mission. The *Anita* was captained by Gerry Blackburn, a 38-year-old Briton who was coming to the end of his five-month tour and looking forward to a holiday with his wife and 13-year-old son. Captain Blackburn had earned a reputation for courage in the Gulf, staging daring rescues of sailors after Iraqi or Iranian attacks.

Plowing through calm waters, the *Anita* struck an M-08 type mine in the bow, just above the crew compartment. Two hundred and fifty pounds of explosives blew the small ship in half. The *Anita* sank within three minutes, taking Captain Blackburn and four crewmen to the bottom. Four other crewmen were rescued. The Fujairah port manager and the harbormaster, both also Britons, had lifted the exclusion zone the day before after being told by the Emirates Coast Guard that the area had been cleared of mines.

The new Iranian mining quickly produced some unexpected consequences. After the *Bridgeton* mine strike, the U.S. had found its mine countermeasures (MCM) cupboard virtually bare. The U.S. turned for immediate help to its NATO allies, several of whom had first-rate MCM forces. The Reagan administration had originally solicited allied support for its build-up in the Gulf back in May and June and had been turned down. The Europeans took a rather dubious view of U.S. Gulf policy. Wanting to maintain their neutrality, they had no desire to be drawn into a confrontation with Iran that might escalate out of control.

The U.S. tried again after the *Bridgeton* incident, specifically appealing for the desperately needed minesweepers. To the embarrassment of the Reagan administration, the second U.S. request was also refused.

British Prime Minister Margaret Thatcher was sympathetic to the U.S. request, but her military advisors were dead-set against any action. When the original request for support had been made, she had also been seeking a third term in mid-June national elections. She had no wish to appear to be, in the words of a British journalist, "Ronald Reagan's poodle."[13] France wished to maintain its traditional foreign policy independence. Germany could argue that its constitution forbade the dispatch of ships, though in fact, this was less clear as to minesweepers only. Italy, a waggish Italian official remarked, had a navy but not a government.[14] As to the U.S. plea for minesweepers following the *Bridgeton* strike, the Europeans had no wish to operate as a minesweeping adjunct to the U.S. Navy, in pursuit of U.S. foreign policy objectives.

Britain and France did have warships in the region, but they were careful about committing them to the cockpit of the Gulf itself, making limited escort runs into the southern portion. Mostly they maintained a presence in the Gulf of Oman. Relations between France and Iran, however, were deteriorating because of Iranian shipping attacks. Following a July 13, 1987 attack on the French-flagged cargo ship *Ville d'Avers*, France broke diplomatic relations with Iran. Later in the month, it dispatched four ships from its Mediterranean Squadron: two guided missile armed escorts, an oiler, and the aircraft carrier *Clemenceau*. The carrier group sailed under what was dubbed "Operation Promethee," with the *Clemenceau* departing Toulon on July 30.

President Reagan's ringing declaration with regard to the Gulf in early June that, "Free men should not cower before such challenges, and they should not expect to stand alone,"[15] had left America's European allies unmoved. The appearance of mines just outside the Persian Gulf now caused a surprisingly quick change of heart on the part of Britain and France. On August 11, Britain announced that it would send four minesweepers and a support ship to operate in the Gulf of Oman. Later that same day, in a move not coordinated with Britain, France announced that it too would be sending two minesweepers and a support vessel. The rapid reversal of both countries' previous positions was actually brought about by military necessity. The British and French ships sailing in the Gulf area had the same vulnerability to the mines as did their U.S. counterparts. As a British demolitions expert put it, "If a warship hit one of these mines, it would be the *Anita* story all over again: massive damage and loss of life."[16]

The mines discovered there now directly threatened the French and British warships operating in the Gulf of Oman. Those countries' naval officials thought it was imperative to protect their ships from the mine threat. Concerns about appearing to bend to American pressure were ultimately outweighed by the risk of having one of their ships sunk by a mine.

Carefully distancing themselves from American policy in the Gulf, Britain and France both emphasized that they would operate independently of the U.S. "We do not foresee carrying out any combined operations," said French Defense Minister Andre Giraud in response to a question about cooperation with the U.S.[17] Nevertheless, the Reagan administration was pleasantly surprised by the French and British decisions. "It just fell out of a tree," said one U.S. diplomat.[18]

The announcements from London and Paris were viewed as important symbolic steps toward a claim that the U.S. was not going it alone in the Gulf, but to at least some extent, was acting in concert with its major European allies. That claim would help neutralize domestic critics who argued that the European nations, much more dependent on Gulf oil than the U.S., were not doing their "fair share" to keep the Gulf open. Indeed, observers thought that once operations actually got underway, it would, as a practical matter, be difficult to avoid coordinating them. Britain's decision to send minesweepers came with a bonus: Prime Minister Margaret Thatcher brought pressure to bear on Germany, the Netherlands, Belgium, and Italy to join in the effort as well. Radio Tehran accused Britain of using minesweeping as a pretext to drag the West European allies into a Gulf "powder keg" that could destroy them.

The Netherlands and Italy had supported the concept of a U.N. minesweeping force, but this option was now mooted by the French and British decisions to act independently. Eventually in September, Italy, the Dutch, and then the Belgians came around and dispatched minesweepers. Italy had been prompted to move when IRGC gunboats had attacked the Italian container ship *Jolly Rubino* on September 3. The next day, Rome announced the dispatch of a formidable force of eight ships, including three *Lerici*-class minesweepers and three *Maestrale/ Lupo*-class frigates. The Italian flotilla did not sail under joint European auspices but under the direct command of an Italian Navy admiral. The

Dutch dispatched two minesweepers. The Belgians dispatched two more along with a support vessel, the *De Zinnia*. The joint task force had a Belgian on-scene commander acting under the authority of a bi-national command structure established at Den Helder (the Netherlands). Eventually, the three European countries would form an integrated MCM force code-named "CALENDAR." Germany agreed to send ships to the Mediterranean to replace ships being moved out of that area by NATO members.

Prior to the appearance of the mines outside the Gulf, an American diplomat who had served in Tehran noted Iran's ability to "judge the threshold" in provoking the West and to "go right up to it but not over."[19] With the mining of the anchorage area off Fujairah and the port of Khor Fakkan, located slightly to the north, Iran had made a serious misjudgment and finally stepped over the line. The action had fueled an atmosphere of international crisis and pushed the Western allies to send in minesweeping ships. Exuberant over its success in mining the *Bridgeton*, Iran may have thought it could humiliate the U.S. again with another mining in an unexpected location. If so, it had very badly overplayed its hand.

With additional Western forces on their way to the Gulf, Iran scrambled to undo the damage. Implausibly accusing the U.S. of sowing the mine which had blasted the *Texaco Caribbean*, Iran proposed to the United Arab Emirates that it work with them to "clear the area of mines planted by the United States, either directly or through its agents." The UAE Foreign Ministry politely thanked Iran for the offer but stated that the Emirates would rely on their own resources. Obviously anxious to make their point, the Iranians then announced that they would go ahead and unilaterally sweep for mines in international waters.

Iran did admit for the first time that it had planted mines inside the Gulf to protect coastal installations, but denied trying to block free navigation. A spokesman for the Iranian Supreme Defense Council disingenuously stated, "We believe there are different kinds of mines in the Persian Gulf. Some may be U.S. mines, some may be Iraqi mines, and some may be Iranian mines. In order to defend ourselves, we use mines."[20]

The third Earnest Will convoy sailed into the Gulf on August 19 and made it to Kuwait without interference. As if to make up for its lack of action, heated rhetoric continued to spew from Iran. Parliament Speaker Hashemi Rafsanjani told a Tehran crowd that they should be ready for war with U.S. forces, and that every U.S. warship in the Gulf would become a target if Iran were attacked. Rafsanjani said that President Reagan had lost his power. Gripping a rifle barrel in his hand, he added, "His nose is affected by cancer; he's uncontrollable. All his speeches are made by others. He only reads them after many rehearsals."[21]

Meanwhile, U.S. warships had successfully dropped off the third convoy and picked up the partially loaded *Bridgeton*, which was finally ready for the return run down the Gulf. The repaired supertanker traveled in the company of the *Ocean City*, *Sea Isle City*, and the *Gas King*, departing from their anchorage off of the Al Ahmadi terminal only hours after the third convoy had docked in Kuwait. The return convoy, actually the fifth one-way convoy, made it down the Gulf without difficulty. The *Bridgeton* finally unloaded its oil to a Swedish tanker and returned to the Gulf, this time to a Dubai shipyard for extensive hull repairs, which would take a month. Four convoys in a row had now safely made it through the Gulf (two to Kuwait, two back out) and another was on the way.

There was some hope that things were settling down a bit in the troubled waters, when, on August 29, Iraq broke its 45-day-long, self-imposed cease-fire and launched air raids against Iranian shipping. "From now on we will strike them in the sea and destroy all the economic arteries which finance their military aggression," said Saddam Hussein in a radio broadcast.[22] The 237,807-ton Iranian supertanker *Alvand* was set on fire at the oil-loading platform on Sirri Island. Iran promised a "crushing response" to the attacks.

While the United States was definitely not seeking a confrontation with Iran, encounters between U.S. and Iranian warships could be tense affairs. There were several incidents in which Iranian naval vessels seemed to make a point of ignoring warnings from U.S. ships who thought that they were approaching too closely. With U.S. fingers on the trigger, it was a dangerous business. As Bahrain's Minister of Information observed, "The greatest danger is somebody making a false move, something which can be misinterpreted."[23] On one occasion, during the course of a strained radio exchange between a U.S. warship and an Iranian vessel, a voice came over the radio informing the Iranian ship, "Now, I'm going to blow your ass out of the water."[24] The American ship hastily got on the radio and overrode the warning. The "Filipino Monkey" had struck again.

Most shipping sources recollected first hearing the Monkey around 1984. "He started out playing music and taunting seamen, usually Filipinos, with curses in the night," an official recalled.[25] The Monkey sometimes sang songs, but mostly it was barnyard noises, screams, and obscene taunts. Sometimes bored seamen responded in kind and the airwaves were filled with a bizarre round of insults delivered in heavily accented English.[26] During the monotonous nighttime runs, seamen didn't mind their "monkey friend" too much, since his silly activities at least served as a mildly entertaining diversion from their tedious duties. However, increasing numbers of Iranian challenges and outright attacks, along with the arrival of U.S. warships escorting convoys, ratcheted tensions upward. Things weren't quite so funny any more.

"He's dangerous," said a Gulf shipping source. "He gets on the radio when ships are being challenged and some of the things he tells the Iranians could provoke an attack."[27] Breaking into radio traffic in the midst of Iranian interrogations, the Filipino Monkey caused consternation among ship captains. In one instance, an Iranian naval officer challenged a merchant ship, demanding to know its cargo and destination. He heard a radio voice reply, "Rockets, grenades, tanks, missile launchers; all bound for Iraq." The ship's captain frantically radioed, "That was not me! That was not me!"[28] Another time, a container vessel halted by an Iranian gunboat demanding information on its cargo heard the Monkey break in and reply, "Oh, bombs rockets . . . atom bombs."[29]

"I don't know whether he's trying to make trouble or whether he's simply an idiot who doesn't understand the implications of what he is doing, but either way he is a real hazard to commercial shipping," said a former ship captain.[30] The Monkey operated in the southern Gulf around the Strait of Hormuz, possibly out of the United Arab Emirates. He did not much care for the Iranians. Once, when an Iranian warship challenged a vessel, demanding to know its destination, the Monkey broke in and replied, "I go to your mother's house."[31]

The hazards presented by this not-so-funny monkey business prompted Emirates officials to mount a search for him, checking out shore-based two way radios to make sure they were licensed. Given that there were hundreds of possible broadcast sites, including tugs, supply boats, oil platforms, barges, shore facilities, etc., it is not surprising that the Monkey was never found.[32] Indeed, to make matters worse, the original may have inspired several others to imitate his antics. Officials, seamen, and reporters all had theories on how many monkeys there were and where they were based. Some even claimed to know the Monkey's true identity.

The arrival of the U.S. Navy in force meant new opportunities for the Monkey to sow mischief. He was not slow to take advantage of them. When, during a convoy escort mission in October 1987, the USS *Guadalcanal*, USS *Crommelin*, and USS *Jarrett* confronted an Iranian landing ship, a voice in the background on the radio could be heard saying, "American warship, shut up. American warship, shut up."[33] In early October, an Iranian warship provocatively locked its fire control radar onto the USS *Hawes*. Three times the *Hawes* radioed stern warnings to the Iranian ship to shut down its radar. The Filipino Monkey gleefully broke in: "Iranian warship, Iranian warship, you're gonna get it now!"[34]

In 1988, by which time the Monkey's act had worn thin indeed, listeners overheard a voice with a southern drawl from a U.S. warship calling on an unidentified ship to identify itself and state its intentions. With no response, the U.S. warship got increasingly testy, demanding, "Who are you and what are your intentions? You have one-zero seconds to respond." A high-pitched cackle suddenly filled the airwaves.

"It's the Fil-i-pino mon-kee. Who wants some of my Fil-i-pino ba-naaan-a?" The radio then reverberated with screams. "The monkey is horn-eeeeeee! Who wants some bananaaaaa?"

Another voice broke in and shouted, "Monkey, we will find you and you will die!"[35]

The Filipino Monkey wasn't the only "animal" trouble the Navy was having in the Gulf. Following the *Bridgeton* strike and other mine hits in the area, ship's lookouts strained their eyes searching for the deadly devices floating on or near the surface of the water. It was easy to mistake various floating objects for mines. One object in particular bore an uncanny resemblance to a floating mine: a dead sheep. A bloated dead sheep, blackened by the sun, floating upside down with its legs thrust out like the detonating horns on a mine, looked a lot like the real thing. The Middle East was a large market for the consumption of sheep, and to meet the demand, big Australian boats shuttled thousands of live ones from down under. When sheep died en route, they were unceremoniously pitched overboard. The bobbing "mutton mines," floating on the surface, could raise pulse levels whenever they were spotted.

The sheep boats were large, multi-deck vessels, packed with the animals. One officer said that they looked to him like cruise ships. Particularly in the heat of the Gulf summer, the floating livestock pens reeked to high heaven. When one passed by near the mobile seabases, the stench would linger in the air for hours until dispersed by Gulf breezes. The fetid boats were usually accompanied by an immense swarm of flies, which hung like a black cloud around the boats and trailed up to a half-mile behind them. When a sheep boat passed nearby, some of the flies would manage to find their way over to the mobile seabases, infesting them for several days.

The floating sheep not only caused problems for the large warships and tankers, but also for the Navy's small patrol boats. The boats usually patrolled after dark, using night vision goggles. Seen through the goggles, the bobbing sheep carcasses looked even more like mines than they did during the day.

When the patrol boat crews determined that the floating object was a sheep, they would usually fire an M-16 rifle round into it. The bullet would puncture the carcass, allowing the gasses trapped within to escape. Deflated, the carcass would then sink. Unfortunately for the boat crews, an intense odor of bodily decay was released from the punctured sheep and a nauseating wave of it would roll over the nearby sailors. One officer said of this experience in the Gulf that, over twelve years latter, he was still unable to stomach mutton.

Incredibly, the Filipino Monkey, or his spiritual successor, is still at it twenty years later. And his irresponsible troublemaking still has the potential to spark a serious if not tragic incident between the U.S. and Iran. As of this writing, with tensions between the countries running high, the Strait of Hormuz has again become a potential flashpoint. On December 19, 2007, USS *Whidbey Island*, an amphibious warship, fired warning shots at a small Iranian boat approaching at high speed. On January 6, 2008, three U.S. warships transiting the Strait were approached by Iranian speedboats which "maneuvered aggressively" close to the U.S ships. Warnings were issued by the U.S. ships.

The Iranian speedboat maneuvers could be seen as threatening in themselves, but what really increased the pucker factor were radioed warnings that "I am coming at you" and "you will explode." The U.S. ships conducted evasive maneuvers and were reportedly on the verge of

firing on the Iranian boats. Fortunately, they did not and the incident
did not escalate. Excerpts of video of the incident, with added-in sound
recording of the radio threats, was released by the Defense Department
shortly afterward. Critics of the Pentagon video were quick to note that
the voice issuing the threats sounded different than the voice of an
Iranian officer who called the U.S. ships. Further, the threat radio transmissions were relatively clear, without any of the background sounds of
throbbing motors and rushing air one might have expected from a small
boat maneuvering at speed.

An official at the U.S. Fifth Fleet headquarters in Bahrain said that
it was common knowledge that hecklers often got on the VHF ship-to-
ship channel and made threats or rude comments. He said they were
often referred to as the Filipino Monkey.[36]

CHAPTER 8

IN FLAGRANTE

The Army MH-6 observation copter swung in for a close look at the unidentified surface contact. It was nighttime in the Persian Gulf, but the MH-6 was equipped with a Forward Looking Infrared (FLIR) system, which didn't depend on visible light. Instead, it was sensitive to heat radiation in the infrared band. The FLIR provided a TV-like black and white picture on a display screen in the copter. The hotter areas of an object being viewed showed up as lighter on the image, the cooler ones, darker. There were two other Army helicopters from Task Force 160 backing up the observation copter. Both were AH-6 gunship models. Army Warrant Officer Dave Chitwood (not his real name), who held his AH-6 in a low orbit, keeping it at a discreet distance from the surface contact, was piloting one of them.

Chitwood was a 32-year-old Chief Warrant Officer 3rd Class. Born and raised in the mountains of northern Georgia, he had joined the Army in 1977. He had volunteered for jump training and become a paratrooper in the 82nd Airborne Division. In 1980, he had gone to Army flight school and qualified as a UH-1 "Huey" helicopter pilot. During a tour in Korea, he had become one of a limited number of pilots authorized to fly into the Demilitarized Zone between North and South Korea. Following his Korean tour, he had volunteered and been accepted into the Army's 160th Special Operations Aviation regiment, the "Night Stalkers."

That unit had been formed in the aftermath of the disastrous failure of the "Desert One" Iranian embassy hostage rescue mission in April 1980. The need for a highly trained, specially equipped helicopter capability dedicated to Special Forces-type operations had been made appallingly obvious by the debacle in the Iranian desert. Better known as Task Force 160 (TF-160), the unit was organized in October 1981. Headquartered at Ft. Campbell, Kentucky, it recruited experienced volunteer pilots for a three-year tour. With its motto, "Death waits in the dark," low-level nighttime operations were the specialty of the 160th. Using aviators' night vision goggles (NVG's), which amplify the faint amount of starlight or moonlight available, some companies flew exclusively at night. The NVG's in use at the time were restricted to a narrow, 40-degree field of view. Some described it as like looking through two of the cardboard tubes inside rolls of toilet paper. The goggles also provided limited depth perception.

In 1983, a spate of accidents claimed four helicopters and sixteen TF-160 soldiers. A veteran recalled "going to the chapel all the time" for funerals. A "Blue Ribbon" panel had been set up to examine the causes of the accidents and to recommend solutions. One approach, which seemed to make a big difference, was to form a dedicated training company. The new safety measures did dramatically reduce the accident rate after 1983.[1]

The safety record may have improved, but as far as Dave Chitwood was concerned, TF-160 was still a "balls to the walls" outfit. He really liked the "knockdown bunch of guys" that flew the helicopters with him. These men were overwhelmingly Warrant Officers who had been promoted from the enlisted ranks. Chilton thought they were the spirited heart and soul of TF-160 in its formative years. Later, he thought that spirit would ebb as career-minded commissioned officers flooded into the unit. There really hadn't been that many officers early on, and Chitwood thought that the senior Warrant Officers really ran the outfit. As more officers came in, he saw standards lowered. On occasion, he saw commissioned officers displace Warrant Officers from their seats in the cockpit so they could fly the missions, looking for awards and promotions. As far as he was concerned, the worst were the West Point graduates, while the better ones came through the Officer Candidate School (OCS).

Chitwood participated in several operations with TF-160, actions that cannot be discussed. The Earnest Will mission had come up on short notice. Briefed on the Gulf deployment, Chitwood was given a day and a half to say "bye." He couldn't tell his wife or two daughters where he was going or when he would be returning. Still, he was "tickled to death" at the chance to go to the Gulf. It was what he did for a living. He went with the very first group of six helicopters, which had been landed at night in a C-5A and had then stealthily flown to the *LaSalle*. The "Little Birds' had split into two three-ship groups and deployed to Navy ships. His group went to the frigate USS *Jarrett*.

The helicopter teams immediately began flying nighttime patrols off the Navy ships. The warships were escorting re-flagged tanker convoys on their runs from outside the Strait of Hormuz up to Kuwait and back. The TF-160 helicopters would fly out ahead of the convoys checking on suspicious contacts. The long nighttime missions could be wearying. However, Chitwood found the actual low-level flying to be a piece of cake. He credited the superb training the unit's pilots had received for their ability to quickly adapt to Gulf conditions.

Superb training or not, the idea of flying Army helicopters off of Navy ships had not gone down very easily with the Navy. The driving force behind the notion of putting them on ships was Admiral William J. Crowe, Chairman of the Joint Chiefs of Staff. With the need urgent, he intervened and pushed the Navy into accepting the Army helicopters. "At a certain point, Crowe became incensed," said a knowledgeable source. "He said, 'Damn it, I don't care whether those are Air Force or Army assets; we've got to have some of those out there.'"[2] The deployment of Army helicopters to the Gulf was dubbed Operation "Prime Chance." The units sent to the Gulf were designated as Detachment 160 Aviation Group (DET 160 AVGP).

Central Command's General Crist had remained skeptical about the use of Army helicopters from Navy ships. As mentioned earlier, he had required TF-160 to conduct a trial run from the frigate USS *Antrim* off the Virginia coast. Over July 28–30, 1987, a MH-6 and two AH-6's flew with a Navy LAMPS Mark I helicopter in the test. The helicopters practiced nighttime target acquisition and attacks against Navy patrol boats, as well as smaller Seafoxes and Zodiacs. The small boats simulated attack runs against the *Antrim*, and in the war games the helicopters stopped every simulated attack. In fact, the helicopters were so effective that the trials were discontinued after only two of the three nights allotted for testing.

The TF-160 pilots did learn some lessons, though. Three helicopters flying independently in the same limited area at night made for the real possibility of a mid-air collision. Accordingly, the helicopters flew together in a group except for attack runs. On those, one of the AH-6's would run in to the target, reverse 180 degrees and fly back to the group. The other AH-6 covered the target with its weapons while the attacking AH-6 returned, then made its own run.

The light (gross weight under 3,000 lbs.) MH/AH-6's ("Little Birds") were small and difficult to detect on radar. The helicopters had a five-bladed main rotor and a four-bladed tail rotor, which produced a subdued whirring sound rather than the loud thumping of larger helicopters. In addition to the special rotors, the engine itself was relatively quiet, making the helicopters inaudible at a distance of about a quarter-mile. Even if audible, their steady whirring was much more likely to fade into general background noise than the peaky "whump-thump" of most helicopters. The MH/AH-6's were ideal for short-notice, long-range deployment by transport aircraft since they required only minor disassembly for loading and could quickly be made ready on arrival. Their folding rotor blades and their small size allowed a team of three of them to be squeezed into the hangers on a Navy frigate.

The MH-6 was equipped with the FLIR and a videotape system. It would serve as the flight lead to spot and vector AH-6 models to a target. The AH-6 was a gunship, armed with a Mark 27 7.62mm mini-gun, a multi-barrel Gatling-type machine gun, and 2.75-inch rockets.[3] Both models had a crew of two pilots. In service, the MH/AH-6's would turn out to be very reliable in the Gulf environment and required only minimal support. Despite the heat, dust, and salt air, they performed flawlessly. In fact, during their deployment, no mission would ever be cancelled for maintenance reasons. The helicopters could react quickly, requiring only about eight minutes from alert to launch. The crews discovered that in some ways, over-water flying conditions in the Gulf were more benign than those encountered by the unit in its "normal" low-level overland flights. Altimeters gave steady height readings, allowing crews to confidently fly over the water at 30-feet without worrying about the hazards posed by terrain features, power lines, towers, or other obstacles. The helicopters definitely stayed low. One frigate captain, who flew on an MH-6, recalled that, when his aircraft drifted up to all of 45 feet above the surface, the trail helicopter facetiously inquired if the MH-6 crew had started using oxygen yet, since they were flying at such a high altitude.

There were some practical problems arising from the use of the Army helicopters on Navy ships. Warships put out a lot of electromagnetic radiation from sources such as radio and radar. The electronic signals might cause the Army's 2.75-inch rockets mounted on the helicopters to fire aboard ship, with disastrous consequences. In testing prior to deployment, all ships' electromagnetic emissions had to be shut down when the Army helicopters were arming, taking off, landing, or even flying close by. The solution turned out to be to replace the Army rocket motors with Navy motors, which were safe for shipboard use.

When TF-160 arrived on board the *LaSalle* in early August, Middle East Force commander Admiral Bernsen had been briefed on the detachment's capabilities, and had agreed to use the helicopters on nighttime patrols only. This would reduce the risk of the Iranians being able to figure out how they were operating, and then developing tactics to counter them. The initial group was divided into two three-helicopter teams, with the call sign SEABAT. Each of the SEABAT teams consisted of one MH-6 and two AH-6s. The SEABAT moniker was derived from a prank sometimes played on new guys aboard Navy ships. The men were told to report any sightings of "sea bats" flying near the ship in the dark. Then, they were told that one of the "sea bats" had been caught and was being kept in a box. When the gullible sailor bent over to look in the box, he was whacked in the rear with a board. When the Navy asked about a call sign for the Army helicopters, which were small, black, and operated at night, just like the mythical "sea bats," the name seemed a natural fit. SEABATS it was.

Following the *Bridgeton* mining, U.S. intelligence had been studying the Iranian mine laying equipment and methods. The U.S. was giving special attention to those Iranian ships that had been reconfigured with mine laying racks. Radio intercepts of communications were being used extensively to monitor Iranian activity. The U.S. was clearly gathering a lot of information on Iranian activities. Still, the raw information had to be collated and evaluated. The Chief Intelligence officer for the Middle East Force was Navy Captain Conway Ziegler. Admiral Bernsen thought that the smart, hard-working Ziegler had developed a kind of sixth-sense about what the Iranians were up to. What they were up to now was another mining operation.

Ziegler had pinpointed what they were going to do, when they were going to do it, and where they were going to do it. When Admiral Bernsen heard about the probable location, a chill went up his spine. The location the Iranians had targeted was a sea lane used by the U.S. convoys and warships. It also happened to be the area in which his flagship, the *LaSalle*, was scheduled to conduct amphibious exercises the day after the expected mining operation. There was little chance that the

Iranians knew about the planned exercise and were aiming at the
LaSalle. They had probably simply planned on mining a sea lane traf-
ficked by U.S. forces. Still, if not for U.S. intelligence, they might have
gotten lucky. Admiral Bernsen promptly moved the *LaSalle* north, away
from the target area.

On September 18, a nine-year-old 1,662-ton Japanese-built "ro-ro"
(roll off/roll on) landing ship left the Iranian port of Bandar Abbas and
headed into the Gulf. The ship, the *Iran Ajr*, was listed under commercial registry as being owned by the Iranian National Shipping Lines.
Now, it was operating under new management: the Iranian Navy.
Powered by two diesel engines, the *Iran Ajr* had been used as a coastal
transport. On this trip, it wasn't hugging the coast and it wasn't carrying its usual cargo. The ship had been kept under a careful watch, which
was rewarded when U.S. intelligence spotted and photographed mines
being loaded aboard the vessel in port. As the vessel proceeded into the
Gulf, AWACS and P-3C maritime surveillance aircraft flying out of
Saudi Arabia tracked it on radar. On the night of Monday, September
21, the *Iran Ajr* left the normal Iranian coastal shipping routes and
crossed the Gulf. The Iranian ship was heading to an area about 30
miles from Ra's Rakan, a small island off the northernmost tip of Qatar.
That area lay in the path of the U.S. Earnest Will convoys.

Dave Chitwood and the other five pilots of his three-helicopter
SEABAT team had run an early evening patrol and had returned to their
temporary home on the frigate USS *Jarrett*. The patrol had been ho-
hum, without even a single contact to check out. The TF-160 pilots had
put up their gear and were just getting ready to call it a night when the
General Quarters alarm sounded. The warship's twin turbine engines
whined as it went to full power. The *Jarrett* had gone charging into the
night at high speed for some thirty minutes before the TF-160 crews
were alerted to launch and check out a surface contact. Surprisingly,
they weren't told that it was a suspected minelayer. As far as they knew,
it was just another surface contact.

The three-helicopter SEABAT team launched from the *Jarrett* at
10:00 P.M. The contact was now some 15 miles away. Each of the AH-
6s was armed with seven 2.75-inch rockets, two with flechette warheads
and five with high-explosive warheads. They also had 2,000 rounds of
7.62mm mini-gun ammunition. While the two AH-6 gunships provided
cover from an over-watch position, the MH-6 flew undetected to within 200 meters of the Iranian ship. It was a cloudless, moonless night.

Hovering invisibly in the dark, the MH-6 observed the Iranian ship through its FLIR. As one of the MH-6 pilots later described it:

> The *Iran Ajr* was going directly into the wind, which was good and . . . they [its crew] were just carrying on normal conversations . . . . It was steaming away from us, and we made a run down the port side and we reported . . . what we were seeing on the ship. . . . Reported a bunch of 55-gallon drums down the port side, a canvas-covered area in the middle, and a Zodiac-type boat—I remember it had an LST or flat front like an amphib front, on it. We made a left turn. I think we made another pass. They said, "Have you been seen?" I said, "No, there is just normal deck activity."[4]

The pilots had been told that the suspect vessel was 50 to 75 feet long. It was actually 176 feet long. No radar antenna could be seen on the ship. The *Jarrett* ordered the helicopters to pull back and continue to observe the ship. The SEABAT team remained within one nautical mile of the *Iran Ajr*. At 10:50 P.M., the Iranian ship suddenly darkened itself and reversed course. The *Jarrett* ordered the helicopters to go back in and take another look. Visibility was poor, with a foggy haze in the air. If one of the helicopters flew away from the ship for five seconds too long without turning, it would lose sight of it. The AH-6s provided cover from well back off the stern, while the MH-6 flew down the port side of the ship. Through the FLIR, ship crewmembers could be seen removing the tarpaulin, which covered the center deck area. With that cover gone, the helicopter could see 12 to 18 objects, which at first looked like Mk-6 life rafts. Those rafts are stored uninflated, in cylindrical plastic shells.

When the *Iran Ajr* had extinguished its deck lights, it actually became easier for the MH-6 to distinguish activity on the deck with its FLIR. The helicopter pilots could now see the Iranians pushing one of the previously covered objects over the side. Busy with their task, the Iranian crewmen appeared to be completely unaware of the presence of the helicopters. Ten Iranians were on the bridge. The *Jarrett* asked if any of the objects were being pushed over the side. The MH-6 replied that three crewmembers had just pushed a cylindrical "mine-like" object into the water from an eight-foot "gang plank" on the starboard side of the ship. The *Jarrett* relayed this information to the *LaSalle* command center where Admiral Bernsen was monitoring the action. Admiral Bernsen was in the Command Center on the flagship with his operations boss, his intelligence chief, Conway Ziegler, the watch officer and several others. The instant that the CIC (combat information center) reported to him that mine-like objects were being pushed into the water, his response was, "Take them under fire!" The operations officer was hesitant and cautioned the MEF Commander that the objects only appeared to be mine-like. Thanks to his intelligence staff, Admiral Bernsen had no doubts about what the Iranians were up to. "Bullshit," he said, "They're mines!"

The hovering helicopters were in contact with the *Jarrett* when Admiral Bernsen gave the order to open fire. The *Jarrett* relayed the order: "You are cleared to engage." In accordance with the Rules of Engagement, no warnings were given to the Iranians prior to opening fire. That's what Dave Chitwood wanted to hear. As far as he was concerned, the Rules of Engagement under which they usually operated were so tight that "you couldn't blow your nose."

At 11:02 P.M., the MH-6 cleared out of the line of fire, and the AH-6s went into the attack. Chitwood's orbit had him pointed at the Iranian ship when the order came. He radioed, "Inbound hot." At a range of 600 to 700 meters out from the ship, he opened fire with the AH-6's mini-gun. He sprayed the deck with 7.62mm fire in order to drive crewmen away from the mines and the two .50 caliber machine-guns which armed the ship, as well as to "cause chaos." As he closed to 200 meters, he fired two 2.75-inch rockets fitted with high explosive warheads into the stem area of the hull, looking to disable the ship by knocking out its engines. Chitwood ended his attack run, breaking right, as the second AH-6 bored in. It hit the deck area and bridge with mini-gun fire. The second AH-6 also punched out two 2.75-inch rockets, one of which hit a paint locker causing a secondary explosion.

The second AH-6 broke right and Chitwood now made his second firing run. He fired the mini-gun until he exhausted its ammunition supply and then launched two more rockets at the stern. At least one of these hit, causing an even larger secondary explosion than the previous hit. Chitwood broke right again and the other gunship made its second attack run. Chitwood swung back around for his third pass, launching his remaining 2.75-inch rockets.

He fired a rocket with a high explosive warhead, and then moved in closer to the ship. He punched out two rockets with flechette warheads.

Each of the 17-pound warheads on these rockets carried 2,200 of the flechettes, which looked like finned nails. The flechette rockets were "fired flat" at targets, with a minimal vertical angle, stretching the zone beaten by the flechettes. That way, more of them were likely to hit the target. The warheads detonated after the rockets had traveled some 700–1,000 meters, spraying the darts like a gigantic shotgun blast for another several hundred meters.

The flechette rockets were aimed at the pilothouse, which was hit by hundreds of the lethal steel darts. Before the second helicopter could begin its third run, the SEABAT team received a call from the *Jarrett* to cease fire and report. Admiral Bernsen had been waiting anxiously on the *LaSalle* for word. Although the initial engagement had lasted only a few minutes, Admiral Bernsen said it seemed as if, "about 20 or 30 minutes went by while we all sat wondering what the hell we had done— sort of on tether hooks." Five minutes after the attack ceased, there was a secondary explosion on the ship's bow. The break in the action allowed Chitwood to return to the *Jarrett* to rearm. The MH-6 stayed on the scene and continued to watch the ship through its FLIR. The second AH-6 still had two rockets and 500–700 7.62mm rounds on board, so it stayed in the vicinity to provide cover.

When the TF-160 SEABAT team had first arrived on board the *Jarrett*, it had taken some time to convince the ship's CO that the unit was not just another naval aviation detachment. The SEABATs had to be given the leeway to operate their way. Some tension had developed between the Navy crew, particularly the officers, and the TF-160 team. In fact, Chitwood thought that the Army aviators were being treated like "redheaded stepchildren." At first, the TF-160 pilots had eaten with the ship's officers in their mess. However, after a while, some of the pilots started going to eat in the enlisted mess instead. They felt like they got along better with the crewmen than the officers.

When he landed on the *Jarrett* after the first attack, Chitwood could see Navy crewmen voluntarily joining in with the TF-160 ground crew to rearm and refuel the copter. Navy guys were passing rockets and belts of machine gun ammunition to the Army guys. Other Navy crewmen handed drinks and sandwiches, which had been made by the ship's cook, to the Army pilots. In the midst of the action against the *Iran Ajr*, the Army and Navy crews had pulled together. It was a kind of breakthrough moment. Afterward, relations between the men of the two services steadily improved.

The first helicopter attack on the *Iran Ajr* had not discouraged the Iranians from their mine-laying mission. They may have thought the helicopters had completely withdrawn following the initial attack. Around 11:17 P.M., the MH-6 saw lights come on in the bridge area and the ship get underway, moving erratically at about five or six knots. Some 10 to 15 Iranians were standing near the bow. Each time the U.S. helicopter made a close-in pass, the Iranian ship changed course. Sixteen "objects" were still seen on board, with Iranian sailors working around them. The MH-6 reported they were moving from the bow of the vessel back to the suspected mines. It looked like they were preparing to push them overboard. The MH-6 watched as three of the objects were pushed overboard into the water. Obviously, the Iranians hadn't gotten the message. The SEABATS requested permission to open fire again. They were told to use whatever means necessary to prevent further mining.

Once again, the MH-6 observation chopper pulled aside as the second AH-6 opened up. The AH-6 fired one of its remaining 2.75-inch rockets at the ship's stem and sprayed the deck with its mini-gun. In order to confuse the Iranians, the AH-6 made its next two passes from random directions. The helicopter aimed its mini-gun fire at lighted areas on the ship and at any movement it saw. Meanwhile, the USS *Jarrett* was closing at best speed to get within 76mm gun range of the Iranian ship. The AH-6 fired its last rocket and exhausted it mini-gun ammunition on the last pass. Its last rocket had been fired in close, and its flechette warhead detonated on impact, spraying the deck.

The second AH-6 radioed that it had used up its ammunition, but Chitwood was now back in the air. He responded that he was inbound and told the second AH-6 to break away. In his rearmed AH-6, Chitwood ran in toward the *Iran Ajr* bow-on. Commencing at a range of 800 to 900 meters, he fired some 500 to 800 7.62mm mini-gun rounds along with two rockets at the ship's bridge. He came around on a second pass, raking the deck and firing two rockets, which just missed the ship and exploded in the water.

One of the 2.75-inch rockets fired during the second engagement had hit the stern area and punched into the engine room. The rocket caused a secondary explosion when it detonated a propane tank. Shrapnel from the explosion of the tank mortally wounded an Iranian sailor in the engine room. The crew of the *Iran Ajr* had now had enough. They began abandoning ship—either getting into life rafts or jumping overboard with life rings. The *Jarrett* issued the order to cease fire.

The MH-6 and Chitwood in the AH-6 held station, continuing to observe the ship while the other AH-6 was rearming on the *Jarrett*. The *Iran Ajr* now appeared to be mostly abandoned. It was dead in the water. Oil was leaking from the starboard side. A fire was burning at the stern. Two dead Iranian crewmen lay sprawled on deck. A body could also be seen lying on the bridge. The ship did not respond to radio calls made to it on Channel 16. A few Iranian crewmen were still aboard and could be seen moving around at the bow.

When the second AH-6 returned from the *Jarrett*, the MH-6 finally took its turn to go back and refuel. While on its way back to the *Jarrett* to refuel and rearm, the other AH-6 had spotted something in the water: a Zodiac inflatable boat. It was a motorboat, not a life raft. However, its outboard motor must have stalled, because an Iranian sailor on the boat could be seen trying to restart it. A Zodiac had been spotted earlier on board the *Iran Ajr*. With all the activity during the attack, no one had seen it being launched or pulling away from the ship. The MH-6 went over for a quick look with its FLIR and reported that the boat looked like it was adrift. The MH-6 then returned to the *Iran Ajr* in order to keep the minelayer under close observation. Chitwood flew his AH-6 over to the Zodiac for a close-in visual inspection.

He approached the boat low and slow. He held at a distance, searching the surrounding water for any threat. Seeing nothing, Chitwood gave the controls to his copilot. He told him to fly within about 10 feet of the boat so he could focus one of the tubes of his night vision goggles to see at close range. The copilot brought them in near the aft starboard side of the Zodiac. Through his focused night vision goggle tube, Chitwood couldn't see anyone on board. Maybe the Iranian sailor had abandoned ship. There was a lot of water sloshing around inside the craft. It looked like it was around a foot deep. Floating on the water inside the boat was a gas can and some papers. Those looked interesting. The Iranian sailor had escaped the *Iran Ajr* while it was under attack, but had taken the trouble to grab the papers and bring them with him. Chitwood figured that they might well have some intelligence value. The copilot nosed the helicopter's left skid over the Zodiac as Chitwood held at the ready with his 9mm MP5K submachine gun. That was a short barreled, folding-stock version of the standard Heckler and Koch weapon.

Suddenly, from under the surface of the water in the boat, the Iranian sailor jumped up "like the Creature from the Black Lagoon." The Iranian was so close that he could have easily grabbed hold of the helicopter's skid. He was holding something in his hands and brought both arms up toward the American helicopter. Chitwood's heart was in his throat as he swiveled his MP5K toward the Iranian sailor and squeezed the trigger. He fired an extended burst into the man. The Iranian was knocked backward and fell overboard. Chitwood held the trigger down until his entire 32-round magazine was emptied, which only took a few seconds. While he was firing, his copilot started turning the helicopter, breaking to the right. As he did so, Chitwood's submachine gun fire traced an arc across the Zodiac. The AH-6 pulled away, and Chitwood quickly reloaded his weapon.

The helicopter came back around and again approached the boat. There was no sign of the Iranian sailor. He must have concealed himself by lying down in the water filling the boat when he first saw the AH-6 coming in close. The inflatable boat had taken multiple hits from Chitwood's submachine gunfire. It had now folded up in the middle and was beginning to sink.

Back at the *Iran Ajr*, the other AH-6 now hovered in close with its infrared landing light on. Smoke from the fire burning aboard made it difficult to see. However, through their night vision goggles, the crew could make out bulky cylindrical objects on deck. At first, these appeared to be trashcans, but then the pilots saw spikes sticking out of the rounded tops. They looked just like the sea mines in the pictures the Navy had shown to the helicopter crews. The TF-160 pilots notified the skipper of the *Jarrett* that a positive identification of mines had been made. The helicopters remained over the Iranian ship throughout the night as it and its surviving crewmen, now in life rafts, drifted in the Gulf.

Middle East Force ships now converged on the scene. The flagship *LaSalle*, along with the warships *Reeves*, *Kidd* and *Flatley*, steamed toward the *Iran Ajr*'s location. The helicopter carrier *Guadalcanal*, escorted by the *Standley*, headed over from the area around Farsi Island. The *Guadalcanal* was transporting Navy SEAL commandos who would be used to board and capture the Iranian ship. While there were nine mines sitting on the ramp of the abandoned vessel, seven more of the deadly devices had already been dropped into the water. Therefore, the arriving ships had to be careful in approaching the area.

It was still dark when the Middle East Force ships arrived at the *Iran Ajr*'s location around 4:00 A.M. The SEALs on the *Guadalcanal* were concerned that there were still some Iranians remaining on the ship. They wanted to get over to the *Iran Ajr* using rubber boats at night. They would then use caving ladders to scale the sides of the ship. The plan was to secure the main deck, and then bring in a Marine reconnaissance team by fast-rope from a helicopter to help conduct a thorough search of the ship. A decision on whether to board immediately or wait until daylight was bucked all the way up the chain of command to President Reagan. He decided to wait until daylight. There was the threat of the mines just laid in the vicinity. There was also the possibility that, if the ship was still partially manned and offered resistance, the SEALs might take casualties. Daylight would allow accurate covering fire from helicopters and other ships.

Admiral Bernsen briefly discussed the seizure of the ship with the SEAL task unit commander, who interpreted his remarks to mean that the SEALs should be careful not to shoot indiscriminately while searching the vessel. After the Admiral left, with the safety of his men paramount in his mind, the task unit commander gave somewhat different instructions to the platoon: "You see a guy on that ship and he's not physically involved in the act of surrendering, shoot him! Don't put it in your mind that there is anything on that ship worth losing your life over. This is not, 'Hey, guys, come on out. We're here, were going to take care of you.' Shoot them if they're not surrendering."[5]

The plan to board and capture the *Iran Ajr* called for the large U.S. warships to stay safely outside the mined area and to use shallow draft landing craft from the *LaSalle* to board and secure the Iranian ship. The *Guadalcanal* had arrived carrying the SEALs, a Marine Reconnaissance team, and an Explosive Ordnance Disposal (EOD) team. These units were transferred by CH-46 helicopter to the *LaSalle*. From there, an LCM-8 landing craft would carry the SEALs to board the *Iran Ajr*. Another landing craft from the *LaSalle* would carry the EOD team, the Marine Recon team, a doctor, a corpsman, and a photographer. A Farsi speaker from the Middle East Force staff on the *LaSalle* joined the SEALs on the LCM-8. The Marine Reconnaissance team would serve as a ready reserve force. Two Marine Cobra helicopter gunships from the *Guadalcanal* would be aloft with two more on alert. After the *Iran Ajr* was secured, the plan was for the LCM-8 to tow it out of the mined area, at which point the *Jarrett* would take over towing duties.

At 5:40 A.M., almost seven hours after the attack, the Navy SEALs approached the *Iran Ajr* in their landing craft. The two Cobras covered them. One of the SEALs later described the tense ten-minute approach to the ship: "So as we got closer, we hunkered down behind the gunwales. The coxswain was inexperienced, and it took him five minutes to get us in position before we could board. One grenade lobbed into the well deck of the Mike-8 boat, and we all would have been history."[6] They circled around the *Iran Ajr* to see if they could spot anyone aboard. They then pulled alongside with their weapons aimed up at the Iranian vessel's deck, which loomed well above the landing craft. The hovering helicopters were observing the ship for any sign of activity. The fires started by the attack seemed to be out. The *Iran Ajr* was dead in the water.

Several men climbed up and onboard the ship under the cover of the guns of the remaining SEAL's. The boarding party saw no live Iranians, but they did see nine of the bulky black mines standing on the abandoned ship's deck. The SEALs split into four elements to clear the ship. The hull was riddled with bullet holes. Windows in the bridge were shattered. Debris associated with arming mines (horn clips, etc.) was lying on the deck. As the SEALs went through the ship, they discovered personal belongings strewn about the living quarters. Some documents aboard the ship had been shredded or ripped to pieces in the lower deck area prior to the crew abandoning ship. Teletypes were still running and radios had been left on.

The only Iranians found on board were three dead crewmen. They, and the wounded, who had gone overboard, had left blood trails in passageways aboard the ship. Two .50 caliber machine guns were located on each of the bridge wings. A dead Iranian sailor at one of the guns was found literally blown out of his boots, which remained standing some five feet away from his sprawled body.

The Middle East Force warships had secured the area. However, poor communications and incompatible radios among the various small U.S. forces on the scene led to some near "friendly fire" incidents. In Bahrain, Special Boat Unit 20 Commander Paul Evancoe had been told only that an Iranian "landing craft" was located at certain map coordinates and that he was to "take it down," i.e., board and seize it. Evancoe went in one patrol boat, with his Executive Officer, Pete Wikul, in another boat. There was a dense fog in the Bahrain channel that night, and the boats had to use their radars to grope their way from navigation buoy to navigation buoy. The fog was so dense that they had to creep up to the buoy locations and shine search lights on them to verify their presence. The two patrol boats didn't arrive at the *Iran Ajr*'s location until around 8:00 A.M.

Incredibly, Evancoe had been told nothing about the TF-160 attack on the boat. Not about the fact that it had been abandoned and not that it had now been boarded by the SEALs. He had no communications at that point. All he knew was that his boats were to take down a hostile ship. Seeing the *Iran Ajr* for the first time, the patrol boat crews were surprised by the size of the vessel. They had thought the landing craft they had been sent after was a relatively small, open-deck, ship-to-shore type. As the two patrol boats moved slowly and warily toward the Iranian minelayer, they trained their formidable combined armament on it. Evancoe told his men, "If we take any fire at all, sink it."

Suddenly, the patrol boats' radars picked up a contact closing fast. Still unaware that the *Iran Ajr* was under American control, Evancoe feared that it was a boatload of Iranians. When the approaching contact was spotted visually from the patrol boats, they could see it was filled with armed men. This didn't look good. Evancoe ordered the patrol boats to train their powerful 40mm Bofors guns on the approaching boat. As he recalled it:

> Here comes this little white boat right at us! I'm looking at it with binoculars . . . and all I see is a bunch of heads sticking out and guns—men in the boat! And I think, Jesus Christ, this has got to be a boat load of Iranians off that damn thing [*Iran Ajr*] and I'm trying to get radio comms with the flagship. Nobody is talking. By God, we turned one boat [a PB], bear down on this thing, and everybody has got their finger on the trigger—the safes are on—and fire discipline . . . They got closer and closer. And here is an LCPL full of damned Marines coming from the flagship who are going over to support the SEALs. You talk about screwups! Nobody is telling us these guys are bearing down on our sterns. We could have blown them out of the water . . . I'll tell you my heart was in my throat about that point. So we realized they were friendly.[7]

For their part, the SEALs on the *Iran Ajr* were unsure if Evancoe's patrol boats were American or Iranian. They ran to the bridge wings and manned the ship's .50 caliber machine guns just in case. One of the SEALs remembered, "There was absolutely no deconfliction whatsoever and still no communications." Turning back to look at the *Iran Ajr*, Evancoe could see unidentified figures moving around on its upper deck. Finally, as the patrol boats circled the Iranian ship, they saw the U.S. LCM-8 landing craft tied up alongside. At last, the patrol boats got some idea of what was actually going on. The boats went in and tied up alongside the landing craft and Evancoe crossed over to the *Iran Ajr* to get more information on just what was happening. He was able to obtain a hand-held radio, which finally gave him some communications capability. He returned to his boat and set out to search for the Iranian crewmen who had earlier abandoned ship.

The Explosive Ordnance Disposal (EOD) team boarded the *Iran Ajr* after it had been secured. They searched it for hidden explosive devices. Some of the mines on deck had been armed in anticipation of their being laid, and at least one had been damaged in the helicopter attack. The EOD team had to perform a "hand entry" procedure on that mine to render it safe. The undamaged mines were also disarmed. One mine's exploder had been pulled out and left dangling by its connecting wires. It was fortunate that one of the mines had not detonated in the attack, setting off the others like a string of gigantic firecrackers. That would have certainly blown the ship apart. The *Iran Ajr* had been equipped with a simple rig for dropping the mines: makeshift dollies that allowed the 1,000-lb. mines to be rolled down a narrow ramp made of steel and rough timbers lashed together with ropes.

Shortly after the Iranian minelayer was declared safe for boarding, an eight-man prize crew from the *LaSalle* went over to inspect the ship. Electrician's Mate 2nd Class Howard Lewis was instructed to assess the extent of electrical and engineering space damage and report the feasibility of using the minelayer's cranes to offload mines. He discovered that the ship's electrical plant wouldn't "light off." Neither would the main or auxiliary machinery. Evidence of why the ship's systems were out was visible all around him. "There was only one place on that ship that didn't have bullet holes," said Lewis. "That was in a head in the middle of the ship."[8]

Actually, the TF-160 pilots had been more discriminating in the attack than that comment suggests. The SEAL boarding party commander recalled:

That's one thing I'd have to say because I've heard of these 160th pilots before. . . . I've always heard how good they were, and I was real impressed with the way they actually hit the ship. Once it was actually secured, I walked around the ship looking for a lot of bullet holes and places where I could actually see where the ship had been hit. Except for the bridge of the ship and certain sections of the ship, they were very selective about where they shot, and they did a real good job. I mean they didn't just rake the ship with gunfire. It was very selective. Of course, I'm sure that if they did [raked the ship with gunfire] it would have blown up those mines, too. They were real good.[9]

The helicopters had used their mini-guns and flechette warhead rockets to suppress deck movement, including the mining activity and attempts to man the .50-caliber machine guns. The flechette warhead rockets had been less effective than the mini-guns because the rockets had to be fired 700–1,000 yards away from the ship in order for the warheads to arm. At that range, with the poor visibility, the helicopters had trouble even seeing the target with their Night Vision Goggles. The high-explosive warhead rockets had been fired at the hull. Three of the rockets had penetrated the hull near the stern, and their 17-pound warheads had disabled the engine room, steering, and electrical systems. Rocket hits in the bow area had damaged oil tanks at the water line.

The *Guadalcanal* had been designated the search and rescue command ship on the scene. Its helicopter gunships also provided air cover against possible Iranian naval interference. Commander Evancoe's patrol boats began searching the area for the Iranians who had abandoned ship. The patrol boats found a large inflatable raft which had 10 *Iran Ajr* crewmen on board, four of whom were injured.

Efforts to recover the Iranians were hampered by the presence of a large Marine Corps CH-46 helicopter, which persisted in hovering directly over the patrol boats, despite Evancoe's attempts to shoo it away. The helicopter was carrying photographers who were busily snapping pictures of the scene. However, the ear splitting din made by the chopper, along with the jetting sprays of water whipped by the down draft from its rotor blades, made it virtually impossible for the patrol boat crews to even communicate with each other.

This was a potentially dangerous situation if any of the Iranians were armed and chose to resist capture. Rather than have the patrol boats pull alongside the Iranian lifeboat, Evancoe decided he wanted to have the Iranians swim to the boats. Swimming in the water would make it difficult for any of the Iranians to take a shot at the Americans, if they wanted to try something like that. It would also make it difficult to conceal and carry over weapons or explosives. The Iranian crewmen were made to swim over to the swim platform located on the patrol boats sterns. Evancoe's concerns soon proved justified. As the Iranians swam to the boats, some could be seen jettisoning objects, possibly weapons, in the water. As they came aboard, they were searched and then transferred onto the deck, where they were searched again and tied up.

A corpsman treated the wounded. Empty sandbags were put on their heads so they could not see the weapons and equipment carried by patrol boats. Some of the Iranians were quite belligerent and cursed their American captors. As they were cuffed, they had the sandbags placed over their heads and were laid out on the decks. The Executive Officer of the *Iran Ajr*, dressed in a khaki uniform, was taken aboard Evancoe's boat. He was unscratched but outraged at his capture. He could speak English and demanded, "Why you hurt us? We are good friends." Evancoe offered the officer a drink of water and took him aside to explain the facts of life. "You were trying to lay mines to hurt us," Evancoe told him. "Tell your people to behave or I'll take it out on you!" The threat worked. The Iranian officer said something to his fellow prisoners. The unruly sailors suddenly became better behaved.

The patrol boats departed the scene for Bahrain. Because they wanted to keep their presence in the area discrete, Commander Evancoe told the boats' crews to dismount their weapons and to put on the civilian clothes they always carried with them. Flags, like those usually seen on fishing boats in the area, were run up. The disguises apparently worked. News helicopters flying over the boats paid them no mind. The Iranians told their captors that six mines had been deployed to float at a depth of twelve feet before the attack. A floating mine was spotted and the U.S. patrol boats moved cautiously in the area.

A helicopter under the control of the *Jarrett* spotted twelve additional Iranian personnel in the water. A boat from the *LaSalle* picked them up. Eventually, a total of 16 crewmen were plucked individually from the Gulf, the last around 11:00 A.M. The prisoners reported that the ship had carried a crew of thirty-one at the start of the mission. Twenty-six had been recovered. Three dead lay on the *Iran Ajr*, and two were unaccounted for.

Interrogation revealed that all of the prisoners, including the highest ranking officer, Lt. Commander Mohammad Farchain, were regular Iranian Navy personnel. The Iranian commanding officer expressed concern for his men and also for his expensive Rolex watch. Two seriously wounded Iranians got life-saving first aid from a Navy hospital corpsman. The two naval mine technicians who had supervised the mining were among those killed or missing.

The Iranian commercial tug *Horriyat* now sailed into the area, claiming to be on a search and rescue mission. It was directed to remain clear of the U.S. operations, which it did. A second tug, the *Khayyam*, also arrived in the vicinity. Later one of the tugs said it was there to recover Iranian government property and wanted to take the *Iran Ajr* under tow. In the face of persistent requests to do so, the Iranians were told that they would be taken under fire if they tried it. An unarmed Iranian SH-3 helicopter showed up next and requested a search and rescue (SAR) assignment from the U.S. forces. It was assigned an SAR area on the periphery of the U.S. SAR area. The helicopter was relieved by another one later. The U.S. forces passed on information detailing the area to be searched and indicated that two Iranian personnel were not accounted for.

The scene unfolding around the *Iran Ajr* illustrated the peculiar nature of the whole U.S. Gulf operation, falling as it did in an undefined region between peace and war. An Iranian ship laying mines in a transit area to sink tankers or U.S. warships had been attacked and seized. Iranian crewmen had been killed and others captured. Now U.S. and Iranian forces were, to some extent, coordinating their search and rescue operations for missing crewmen. The SAR operations ended at sunset. The two missing Iranian crewmen were not found and were presumed lost.

The Iranian prisoners or "detainees" were taken to the USS *LaSalle*, where they were examined and given navy clothes. Having been attacked, forced into the water for over eight hours, and finally made prisoner by the "great Satan," most of the Iranians were by now reasonably docile. But not all of them. Three of the prisoners appeared to be "hard core" types whose eyes blazed utter hatred at their captors. Observing these men, one of the SEALs thought to himself that, if their roles were reversed, he would be in very serious trouble indeed. Most of the injured had shrapnel wounds, though Lieutenant Commander Farchain had a bullet wound in his hand. The dead were preserved in caskets on dry ice.

The American flag was run up the *Iran Ajr*'s mast and the vessel taken under tow by the LCM-8 to rendezvous with the *Jarrett* and the *LaSalle*. The *Jarrett* was to take over from the LCM, and tow the ship to a position in international waters about three nautical miles north of a navigational point known as the "Bahrain Bell," and anchor it there.

By the early afternoon on the 22nd, the Iranian navy had arrived in the form of an armed, British-built hovercraft, which skimmed over the waves at high speed on an air cushion trapped in a flexible "skirt" underneath the craft. The hovercraft approached at the high speed of 30–35 knots. Ignoring warnings radioed over channel 16, it closed to within one nautical mile of the *Jarrett*, which then fired warning shots. The hovercraft got the message and turned away, taking a position about 2,200 yards from the *Jarrett* and the *Iran Ajr*. The hovercraft cruised near the Jarret and *LaSalle* for about an hour and then departed for Lavan Island.

Navy intelligence personnel searched the *Iran Ajr* and discovered a mine plot chart which showed where it had dropped the mines. Documents included a mining war plan and instructions from Iran's First Naval District at Bandar Abbas. Iran was clearly implicated in the mining of international sea lanes. The intelligence documents weren't the only things brought off the ship. Many of the Americans who went aboard came back with body lice. The Iranian ship was dirty and in poor condition. Sanitary facilities consisted of square holes below deck, which led to chutes over the side. The food looked to be of very poor quality. The Captain of the ship seemed to subsist off of a pile of tuna fish cans stored under his bunk.

The capture of the *Iran Ajr* was a clear military and political victory for the U.S. It came at a good time, too: right on the eve of Iranian President Ali Khamenei's appearance before the U.N. General Assembly. Clearly embarrassed by the incident but nevertheless assuming the mantle of outraged innocence, Khamenei hotly denied the U.S. allegations, calling them a "pack of lies." To cries of "Allahu Akbar" from supporters in the Assembly Gallery, he accused the U.S. of attacking a merchant ship and murdering crewmen in an "abominable act of aggression." He added—as the U.S. delegation walked out in protest—that

Iran's response "shall not be restricted to the Persian Gulf." Khamenei later told reporters: "Today it is we who receive the dead bodies of our sons. But if, God forbid, the day comes when you receive the bodies of your sons, people will say, 'Why didn't you stop it?'"[10]

Tehran radio claimed that the ship was carrying food supplies to an Iranian port. Parliamentary speaker Al Akbar Hashemi Rafsanjani joined in the vituperation and threats, pledging that the U.S. would soon regret its attack on the Iranian vessel. However, no amount of rhetoric could obscure the incontrovertible evidence of Iranian minelaying in the Gulf. In one area, however, the U.S. came up short: a connecting cable had come loose and videotape shot through the MH-6 helicopter's FLIR came up blank, denying the use of pictures showing Iranians in the act of dumping the mines over the side.

It was a big disappointment to the Pentagon, even though, no doubt, Iran would have dismissed the tape as a "Hollywood production." Still, nothing could dim the luster of the successful capture. Admiral William Crowe, Chairman of the Joint Chiefs of Staff, sent a message to Central Command, asking it to convey his personal "Well done" to all participants. Admiral Crowe noted that the operation "is viewed with a great deal of pride and pleasure at the highest levels of government."

Not viewed so well was a lurid news report that a "half-naked boy" trying to flee the *Iran Ajr* had been run down and machine-gunned by a U.S. helicopter. This was obviously the incident involving the Iranian sailor on the Zodiac. Although the newspaper report had only a glancing connection with the facts, it was enough to get Chitwood in hot water. The Army's Criminal Investigation Division questioned him numerous times over a period of two years. He was asked "a million times" if the Iranian sailor had brandished a gun. Chitwood told them that he couldn't honestly say if the Iranian had a gun or not. He could only say that he wasn't putting his co-pilot, his machine, and himself in jeopardy by waiting for the guy to start shooting in order to prove that he had a gun. Chitwood told the investigators that he didn't give a damn what the Iranian sailor had. The second he saw him, "he was out!"

Chitwood was also questioned repeatedly on why he had fired his entire magazine. "Couldn't you have just shot him a few times?" he was asked. "Why did you have to empty the whole magazine at him?" Chitwood told them that his weapon had been set to full automatic and he wanted to make sure the guy was dead. His plan had been to come back, drop his caving ladder, hook the Zodiac and tow it over to the *Iran Ajr*. There it could be searched for the papers he had spotted washing around inside it. Those papers had ended up being lost when the boat sank.

Aside from the newspaper story, the incident may have generated a high profile due to Chitwood's use of his floor mike at the time. While he had been firing his submachine gun, his hands had not been free. He used his foot-activated floor mike to talk to his copilot. Unfortunately, that mike was hooked into the SATCOM (satellite radio) system. His calls, along with the gunfire in the background, had gone out to "CIA guys, to the Navy, to the whole world." Some of those listeners may have gotten the misimpression that the Zodiac was a life raft and made uninformed comments to a reporter. In any case, the fallout from the incident did not prevent Chitwood from being awarded the Distinguished Flying Cross for his part in the action. However, he felt that it ultimately cost him a promotion he otherwise would have gotten.

The Iranian ship was towed to the anchorage near Bahrain where it was put on display with the Department of Defense media pool invited on board. After the captured *Iran Ajr* had been fully exploited for its propaganda value, the U.S. was left with a pair of questions: What did it want to do with the ship, and what did it want to do with its crew?

As to the ship, Admiral William Crowe, Chairman of the Joint Chiefs of Staff preferred to keep it. As far as he was concerned, a captured warship was a captured warship. Further, the ship might be of use one day, possibly in a deception operation of some sort. In contrast, Defense Secretary Caspar Weinberger wanted to just get rid of the ship, preferably by blowing it up rather than quietly scuttling it. The idea was to show Iran that the U.S. was not intimidated by its sulphurous rhetoric. The ship had been fully exploited for any intelligence value, reasoned Weinberger, and had no further use. Some muted criticisms came from U.S. sources, who thought sinking it was unnecessarily provocative and even, absurdly, that the minelaying ship should be returned to Iran.

The *Iran Ajr* was taken under tow from its anchorage by the USS *Hawes* on the evening of September 25. In order to prevent Iranian interference, the USS *Kidd* and three MK III patrol boats escorted the *Hawes*. Navy helicopters were in the air for surveillance, as were TF-160 SEABATs based on the *Hawes*. While under tow, an EOD team was on board the Iranian ship placing explosive charges. If they didn't do the job, the *Hawes* and *Kidd* would finish it off with gunfire. As the group of ships proceeded at about four knots to the planned location for the sinking, they were trailed by the Iranian tug *Harirud*. The tug even contacted the U.S. ships over the radio and asked where they were headed. Captain David Yonkers, who had commanded the first Earnest Will convoy, was in charge of the scuttling operation. He replied that the Iranian ship should keep away at a safe distance. He declined to reveal the purpose of the operation. The Iranian captain was not belligerent at all and actually sounded rather friendly, if overly inquisitive.

The *Iran Ajr* was towed to a location about 40 miles off Qatar where the water depth was 240 feet and a sunken hull would not constitute a hazard to navigation. The EOD team left the *Iran Ajr* on a patrol boat, which moved to a safe distance. At 1:30 A.M. on the 26th, the explosive charges placed in the hull were detonated by remote control. The fireball was visible for miles. The vessel's keel was broken. It doubled up and sank within 12 minutes. The Iranian tug observed the proceedings and called up Yonkers and asked if the operation was over. Yonkers replied, "Yes, I do believe that's it." The Iranian tug said, "I understand." It then left the area. The director of Iran's war publicity office called the sinking of the ship an "act of piracy." Iran claimed that the U.S. sank the ship to get rid of the evidence that it was carrying nonmilitary cargo.

The Iranian prisoners or "detainees" were another matter. There was a debate over their disposition. Sources said that senior State Department officials had even wanted to release the captured Iranians to the Iranian tugboat at the scene of the attack. In strong contrast, the U.S. Ambassador to Bahrain, Sam. H. Zakhem, wanted to retain them.

After due consideration, the decision was made to repatriate the prisoners to Iran through the Sultanate of Oman. This probably was the best course of action. The quick return of the prisoners made the U.S. look fairly magnanimous and did not prolong the incident. Retaining the prisoners would have opened up the U.S. to the charge of hostage-taking, something it had vehemently denounced. To argue instead that the Iranians were prisoners of war would have exposed the administration's flank to critics who argued that the War Powers Act applied to Gulf operations. It would have been difficult to claim that the U.S. actions did not constitute war, when at the same time the U.S. was holding what it characterized as prisoners of war taken in those same actions.

The capture of the *Iran Ajr* revived America's military reputation in the Gulf, which had probably reached its nadir after the *Bridgeton* fiasco. Americans love winners, and polls showed that the successful attack drew the support of over 75 percent of the public. Overall approval for the policy of having the U.S. Navy escort foreign-owned tankers in the Gulf stood at 60 percent. Likely as a result of the prolonged U.S. Embassy hostage crisis, there was a deep reservoir of anti-Iranian sentiment to draw on. Polls showed 78 percent of Americans had unfavorable feelings toward Iran, with a mere two percent having a favorable view.

The seizure of the Iranian minelayer bolstered the confidence of friendly Arab states as well, and was universally cheered in private by Arab leaders. Meanwhile, Iran had unquestionably been dealt a major setback. Bewildered by the U.S. interception of the *Iran Ajr*, the Iranians appeared to be spooked and unsure of U.S. capabilities. It is a measure of the deterrent effect of the *Iran Ajr*'s capture that no new mines appear to have been planted in the Gulf from October 1987 until April 1988, when Iran would try again.

CHAPTER 9

FORT APACHE—THE GULF

The resumption of Iraqi anti-shipping strikes and the inevitable tit-for-tat Iranian response both posed threats to U.S. forces and the re-flagged tankers. In the Iraqi case, it was the threat of accidental attack. In the Iranian case, so far, it didn't look as if they wanted to risk a direct confrontation with the U.S. That left the mines. These had worked well in the northern Gulf with the *Bridgeton* strike. However, the mine weapon had proved to be a double-edged sword. Their use outside the Strait of Hormuz had proved to be a fiasco, prompting foreign naval intervention in the region. Iran's not-so-invisible hand in the minings had also given it a black eye in world opinion.

Given the results of its mining operations to date, the northern portion of the Gulf looked like the area Iran would probably target for new minings. By concentrating on the upper reaches of the Gulf, Iran would avoid hitting ships bound for more southerly destinations, including the ports of Gulf States, which maintained reasonably friendly relations with Iran. That strategy would also avoid the kind of international outrage that had been directed against Iran when it had mined the anchorages in the Gulf of Oman. As Iran's likely target, the northern Gulf was also the logical place for U.S. forces to try to suppress the Iranian mine-laying activity. There was, however, a serious problem.

The Middle East Force needed to station U.S. forces in the northern Gulf for extended periods of time. The occasional presence of U.S. warships, escorting convoys and making return runs down the Gulf, was not going to do the job. Considering their own vulnerability to mines, using relatively deep-draft warships to constantly patrol the area was not a wise idea. The frigate-based helicopters of TF-160 had demonstrated their effectiveness in the capture of the *Iran Ajr*. However, the particular operation had been pinpointed as a result of superb intelligence, something that could not always be counted on. The Army helicopters also could not be permanently based on Navy ships, which lacked the space for spare parts, ammunition, and other equipment. The Navy Special Boat Units had now arrived in the Gulf, and they too needed bases that could support their operations.

Possible base locations included Saudi Arabia and Kuwait. Both countries turned the U.S. down flat. It was frustrating to a Reagan administration trying to sell its Gulf policy to Congress and the public. However, the concerns of the two countries over possible domestic political problems resulting from the stationing of foreign forces on their soil were legitimate. Those kinds of problems were to be expected in an operation taking place in a delicate political situation. Even small Saudi islands in the Gulf, which might have been ideal, were ruled out.

The innovative solution MEF Commander Admiral Bernsen finally came up with was to use two oil field support barges, designated as "Mobile Sea Bases" (MSB's). The bases would be anchored in international waters in the northern Gulf. If the U.S. forces couldn't go to a convenient shore base, in effect, the base would come to them. The U.S. had used so-called Sea Float, barge-type, waterborne platforms during the Vietnam War to support maritime surveillance and anti-infiltration operations on inland rivers. Unlike the Vietnam facilities, though, any bases employed in the Gulf would have to combine the robust sea keeping ability needed to withstand harsh Gulf conditions with the mobility needed to make frequent moves for security purposes and to support operations in different locations. The bases would also have to maintain a low political profile so as not to provoke Iran.

The MEF took a look at the civilian oil service barge market, where many of the vessels were sitting idle because of the slowdown in drilling and production activity precipitated by the steep decline in oil prices being experienced at the time. Brown and Root had two suitable barges sitting idle in port in Bahrain. Following MEF inquiries, that company made a proposal to lease both barges for $21,000 per day. The proposal was for a comprehensive contract, which included provisions for supplying water, fuel, and for housekeeping services (i.e. feeding, laundry, cleaning, maintenance) which were to be provided by an embarked civilian contract crew. On September 1, 1987, the President of Kuwait Oil Tanker Company generously agreed to bear the charges for leasing the two Brown and Root barges. By September 5, contracts for six-month periods had been signed.

The Mobile Sea Bases would function as floating islands in the Gulf from which air and sea patrols would originate. A "sea surveillance area" about 100 miles long was set up within which Iranian activity would be monitored to prevent minelaying and small boat attacks against re-flagged tanker convoys. The area extended north from latitude 27 degrees, 30 minutes, up to the Mina Al Ahmadi deep-water channel and west from the Iranian exclusion zone. Iran's Farsi Island, a base for Revolutionary Guard Corps speedboats, was right in the middle of the surveillance area.

Two barges would be deployed in the Mobile Sea Base role, the "Hercules" and the "Wimbrown VII." The Hercules would house an Atlantic Fleet Naval Special Warfare Task Unit. The Wimbrown VII would house one from the Pacific Fleet. The Hercules was the larger of the two. It had a length of 400 feet, a width of 140 feet, and a 25-foot draft. The Wimbrown VII was a jack up barge with the jacks removed. It was 250 feet long, 70 feet wide, and had a draft of 13 feet. A huge derrick crane that was 150 feet high and 250 feet long, mounted in a revolving turret, visually dominated the Hercules. Designed for offshore oil field construction, the crane had a truly immense lifting capacity of 1,600 tons, which inspired the barge's name.

Commander Paul Evancoe, who had taken Special Boat Unit 20 to the Gulf, was called in by the Naval Special Warfare Task Group commander, Dick Flannigan, and told he was being given a new job: command one of the floating sea bases. Both Flannigan and Evancoe had served on Sea Floats in Vietnam. Evancoe toured both barges pier side in Bahrain. The Hercules had been inactive for only four months and looked seaworthy. However, its football field-sized deck was cluttered with a jumble of oilfield equipment. The Wimbrown VII had been idle for a year and a half. It reeked and looked to be in poor shape. Evancoe chose the Hercules.

He was given carte blanche to lay out the platform. For their role as mobile sea bases, the barges had to be modified to house the Navy patrol boats and the Army helicopters. The Hercules had an elevated landing pad, which was adequate for helicopters making runs to and from the base. However, the TF-160 helicopters were going to be permanently based on the barge. They would have to be sheltered in deck-level hangars and needed a flight pad they could conveniently be rolled out to and from. Evancoe looked at the rotor swaths of the helicopters that could be expected to land on the base, including larger Army Blackhawks and Navy SH-60's. He had a flight deck laid out which was large enough to accommodate them. Also laid out were the hangars, which would have to be built to accommodate the Little Birds. Onboard cranes would lift patrol boats and minesweeping boats stationed on the base in and out of the water. The locations for skids to store the boats on deck were also marked out.

Central Command was anxious to get the bases in operation as soon as possible. Ross Perot, the highly successful businessman who would eventually become better known as a somewhat erratic presidential candidate, owned an interest in Brown and Root. Perot had long been a great friend of the U.S. Special Operations community. To his credit, he has always kept his role out of the glare of the media spotlight. Reportedly, the patriotic Perot said to give the U.S. forces whatever they needed. The first priority was to clear all the oilfield equipment off of the Hercules' large deck. It took two days. That done, the new construction and modifications necessary to convert the commercial oilfield facility into a military base took place at a frenzied rate. Shifts of twenty-eight welders worked around the clock.

A reporter would dub the Hercules "Fort Apache." The name suggested an isolated outpost in the middle of nowhere, with hostiles lurking nearby. It was an accurate picture. However, when the U.S. military pictured a base in the Middle East, there was one thought that ran through a lot of minds: the Marine barracks in Beirut, Lebanon. A suicide driver in an explosive-filled vehicle; a blinding flash; a tremendous thunderclap. Hundreds of dead and wounded U.S. servicemen. Suppose an explosive-laden suicide boat did the same thing to a mobile Sea Base? The Marines in particular seemed to be haunted by that nightmare scenario.

Secretary of the Navy James Webb, a former Marine (and now a U.S. Senator from Virginia), inspected both barges on September 11, 1987, and came away gravely worried about their vulnerability to Iranian attack. A Marine staff captain wrote a widely circulated paper likening the barge concept to the Beirut barracks. Concerns about the bases reverberated through the Navy's Atlantic Command, which opposed their use. The concept did have powerful supporters in the form of JCS Chairman Admiral William Crowe and Defense Secretary Caspar Weinberger. The CENTCOM Commander, Marine General

George Crist, initially supported the concept, but then seemed to waiver in the face of a deluge of opposition from fellow Marine officers.

Given their high level support and their utility, the bases were able to go forward. Still, as one senior officer later put it, General Christ "was absolutely paranoid" about a sea-base being sunk in a nautical replay of Beirut. General Christ did approve the "commissioning" of the bases; however, in a seeming attempt to assuage his gnawing worries, he poured in defensive equipment. A 30-man Marine self-defense force was added to each barge. Marine detachments equipped with Stinger anti-aircraft missiles were also brought in. At one point, there was even talk of plunking down a heavily armored tank turret, with a high-velocity 105-mm gun. The idea was dropped when it was realized that the heavy turret and its mounting would have made the base top-heavy.[1] Ditto a HAWK anti-aircraft missile battery. General Christ never stopped trying. When proponents of the bases pointed out that they would move every few days and be difficult for the Iranians to locate and target for an attack, General Christ replied, "I don't care, I want every bit of defensive equipment we can get on those bases."

In fact, the bases would hardly resemble the Marines' Beirut barracks, with its unblocked access roads and its sentries standing around with unloaded weapons. They were under the radar coverage of orbiting Saudi-based U.S. AWACS, which could alert them to potentially hostile air or surface contacts. Saudi-based Navy P3-C Orion patrol aircraft could also provide early warnings. At first the bases were deployed alone.

Later, a Navy frigate, called the Guard Ship, or "Gulf Sierra," was continuously assigned area air defense duties for the Mobile Sea Bases. The frigate had its air search radar, naval data link capabilities, Combat Information Center (CIC) to monitor events, and, if needed, its long-range anti-aircraft missiles. One frigate, which served in the guard ship role, "babysitting" the Mobile Sea Bases, would have a T-shirt made up showing the Hercules and the frigate. Printed below were the words, "Don't f--- with the babysitter!" The bases operated under blackout conditions and were moved randomly, sometimes every two or three days, among small islands in the area by Kuwaiti tugs.

The bases employed a "layered" defensive concept. A three-mile zone was established around each base to provide a buffer in which no other units were allowed without specific permission. Any surface craft trying to get through would have to get past radar equipped patrol boats with a surveillance range of 20 nautical miles and the SEABAT helicopter patrols with a coverage radius of around 50 nautical miles. A patrol boat, dubbed a "pouncer," was also kept on ready alert in the water. Close-in defense was provided by the Marine security platoon manning weapons on the base itself.

The Mobile Sea Bases had weapons stations ("gun tubs") running around their perimeters. These were low towers, set some 10 feet above deck height to keep water out during rough seas. Some of these positions were manned 24 hours a day by Marines. Armaments included .50 caliber heavy machine guns, breech-loaded 81mm mortars, and later, MK19 40mm automatic grenade launchers. Each base also mounted a TOW II wire-guided anti-tank missile launcher, which could be used against small craft. Weapons positions had double walls of steel plates with sandbags between them. A naval officer who went aboard the Hercules said he felt like he was stepping into a film clip of a Vietnam firebase. On the Mobile Sea Base Wimbrown VII, the patrol boats on board were mounted on skids, one behind another. This allowed their heavy armament to join in the defense of the base by firing over the side. Even the boats' large 40mm Bofors guns had lines run out to their generators so they could be started, allowing the weapon to be used from the Mobile Sea Base. Sandbags and steel plates also protected vital equipment and ammunition.

While it was important to have reasonably secure platforms, the whole point of the mobile sea bases was not to passively defend against possible Iranian attacks but to support operations "leaning forwards," in the words of Admiral Crowe. The Hercules was the first of the bases to come into service. It underwent a shakedown cruise off Bahrain on September 21, stuffed with two minesweeping boats (MSBs), four patrol boats (PBs), two Seafoxes and a SEABAT helicopter team. The Iran Ajr had been tied up alongside the Hercules before it was towed away and sunk. In fact, the two .50 caliber machine-guns on that vessel had been dismounted and added to the Hercules' defensive armament.

On October 6, 1987, the base was moved north to begin surveillance operations some 24 nautical miles west of Iran's Farsi Island. The Wimbrown VII became operational during the first week in October 1987. It embarked two PBs, two PBRs, two Seafoxes, and a SEABAT team. However, by then, the Joint Task Force Middle East under Admiral Dennis Brooks had come into existence, and Admiral Brooks had developed his own reservations about deploying the MSBs. Admiral

Bernsen had been able to persuade him to deploy the Hercules. However, a battle between Hercules-based U.S. forces and Iranian boats on October 8, 1987 (see next chapter), along with other incidents, revived Admiral Brooks' concerns. He refused to let the Wimbrown VII deploy north. JCS Chairman Admiral Crowe had to give a direct order to Brooks to deploy the Wimbrown.[2] Finally, in November 1987, the MSB moved out of Bahraini territorial waters and took up an operational station near Saudi Arabia's Karen Island.

The merchant ships they were trying to protect turned out to be an unexpected threat to the MSB's. A collision with one might utterly wreck or even sink a base. The problem was aggravated by the fact that one or both bases ended up being frequently stationed in or near commercial shipping routes. Unescorted ships coming out of Kuwait often used the cover of darkness and bolted down the Gulf at their highest speeds, which sometimes ran to over 20 knots. The guard ship frigate would try to run interference for the sea bases. As a frigate captain put it, "This often resulted in the absurd situation where a 4,000-ton ship would race in under the bow of a quarter-million-ton tanker to force her away." The frigate would try to get the attention of bridge personnel on the merchant ship, and have them alter course 10 or 15 degrees to pass around the sea bases. Frequently, bridge crews failed to respond to radio hails. In those cases, the frigate would pull up alongside at a distance of 400 to 500 feet, flashing lights with their night filters off and blowing its whistle. Sometimes the frigates would hail the ship on a loudspeaker or fire flares to get its attention.

There might be one or two of these shoulder-asides per night, but sometimes as many as four or five. One frigate captain complained that they always seemed to occur between midnight and 5:00 A.M. He called it "a conspiracy to keep me from getting my sleep." One night, a Russian commercial freighter heading right for the Hercules refused to turn aside. General Quarters sounded and TF-160 pilots ran to their helos in shorts and flip-flops in order to get airborne before the looming collision. The ship was finally persuaded to change course when an 81mm mortar illumination round fired from the base almost landed on its foc'sle.

As the Mobile Sea Bases (MSBs) successively came on line, the SEABAT teams' missions changed from escorting Earnest Will convoys the length of the Gulf to patrolling in the area of responsibility of the MSB on which they were now based. Although many of the helicopter crews felt that being stationed on the escort frigates brought them closer to the action, the MSB's did offer the advantages of larger hangar space, improved quarters, exercise facilities, and better food. The makeshift berthing arrangements on a frigate didn't help the army pilots get the good day's sleep they needed for nighttime operations. Two Army detachments of two aircraft each did continue to ride on frigates escorting convoys. In November 1987, two larger TF-160 Blackhawks were added to the MH-6/AH-6 "Little Bird" force in the Gulf. Painted gray to match navy colors, the UH-60 "Grayhawks" were stationed on the Hercules. They were equipped with FLIR viewing systems and armed with two mini-guns each.

Shakeout operations by the Hercules revealed problems with the base's detection and target vectoring systems. The off-the-shelf commercial Furuno surface search radar which equipped the base had only limited capabilities. The radar was only able to track and detect boats at a range of 12 nautical miles. Air coverage was all but useless, with the systems only able to pick up contacts at a range of a few miles. The barges had come supplied with commercial communication and navigation systems, which were supplemented by the equipment of the naval special warfare task units, the Army TF-160 teams, and the Marine Radio Recon detachment. Some of these were actually handheld units that had to be plugged into adaptors so they could use the base power supply instead of batteries.

The piecemeal installation of antennas, cables and radios caused grounding problems and interference between circuits and nets. These systems were unreliable and unable to handle the high volume of message traffic. The huge crane on the Hercules, nicknamed "Clyde," was found to interfere with the radio antennas of the ad hoc communications equipment first put aboard the base, making contact with the escort frigate and other units difficult. Naval special warfare mobile communications (C3) vans were eventually put aboard the bases, allowing them to communicate more reliably with units around the Gulf.

In the end, the mobile sea bases simply lacked a true command and control facility, such as those found on Navy ships. That kind of facility would have integrated the various surveillance and communication systems. When patrol boats identified an Iranian target and relayed the data back to the base, operations personnel then had to perform the difficult and time-consuming task of converting the data for target intercept by the SEABAT helicopters. One mobile sea base commander described his facility as "back in the Dark Ages in terms of communications and in terms of processing all the data that comes in." These inadequacies helped lead to the decision to keep a Navy frigate on station with the mobile sea bases, providing a sophisticated command and control facility.

Patrols from the bases crisscrossed sea-lanes looking for Iranian minelaying or small boat attacks. The PBR's conducted close-in patrols for sea base security. Of the various small boats sent to the Gulf, the Mark III PB (patrol boat) turned out to be the best choice for the mission. The boats had been built in the mid-1970's, and were crewed by one officer and nine enlisted men. The craft were heavily armed with a 40mm cannon forward, a 20mm cannon on the stern, another 20-mm in a port side position, three .50-caliber machine guns, a Mark 19 automatic grenade launcher, and an 81mm mortar on the port side. The 65-foot craft were capable of 30 knots and had a range of 450 nautical miles. The boats were listed at around 40 tons displacement but ran closer to 60 tons. The boats had decent sea-keeping qualities in moderate seas and were equipped with a Furuno surface radar along with secure communications equipment.

Small boat patrols consisting of two MK III patrol boats, one in the lead for scouting and the other running 200 meters in trail, went out each night from each Mobile Sea Base. A third officer served as a two-boat mission commander. The ten-man crews allowed two five-man watch sections on long patrols. The boats went out during the same early or late periods that the SEABATs were airborne. The patrol boats were much slower but had much greater endurance than the helicopters. They went out for from four to twelve hours at a time. The boats used the same checkpoints and routes as the helicopters, checking in with the on-station frigate at the start of their patrols, which ranged a maximum of 16 nautical miles from their Mobile Sea Base. The Seabats would fly over checkpoints to be sure that no ambush awaited the boats. The patrolling craft were monitored on radar by the frigate and the sea base and made periodic radio checks. The boats carried infrared strobes for identification by the U.S. helicopters.

There was another type of boat that was proposed for use from the mobile sea bases. This was a dhow obtained by the CIA and which the agency planned to operate for intelligence gathering purposes in the area. Commander Evancoe thought this was a really poor idea and summarily rejected it. He thought it was nonsensical to use a boat like that up where it had no business going. The dhow would have needed escorts for protection, and these would have blown its cover. Unescorted, it would have been extremely vulnerable.

The Navy patrol boats did support the CIA's "Eager Glacier" aerial surveillance operation by going to certain positions at certain times in case one of the planes ditched. The CIA aircraft apparently drew Iranian fire on more than one occasion. A patrol boat officer recalled seeing heavy Iranian aircraft fire being directed at something near Farsi when he was sent out to support the CIA aircraft. He thought it wasn't difficult to put two and two together and figure out who the Iranians were shooting at.

Living conditions on the Mobile Sea Bases were essentially similar to those onboard a ship. Men were bunked eight to ten per room. Each had a large drawer and a rack (bed). It was claimed that the civilian cooks did a good job, providing a varied menu that was better than what was available aboard ships. Filipino, Indian and Pakistani-type dishes were offered as well as standard American fare. The food service was very flexible and could provide a meal when requested by men who had been out on an operation. One Special Boat Unit officer said that if a sailor didn't care for the meal being offered, "They could say, 'Cook me a steak,' and they would cook you a steak. So the food was quite good."

Ironically, some of the food products served onboard came from Iran and Libya. One other amenity available on the Mobile Sea Bases was beer. Crewmen were allowed to buy two beers several times a week. Alcohol was forbidden on Navy ships. For some reason, the foreign cooks were unable to provide a good-tasting version of an American staple: pizza. At least one frigate cut a deal with the Hercules. The Mobile Sea Base's crew came aboard for some tasty pizza, and the frigate crew went aboard the base for beer.

The bulk of Special Operations forces deployed to the Gulf (Navy SEALs, Army TF-160, and Navy Special Boat Squadrons), were stationed on the Mobile Sea Bases, a fact that lent them a distinct atmosphere. While dedicated to their missions and skilled with their high technology equipment, the SpecOps Forces were allowed a bit of liberty with their dress. A Navy visitor to MSB Hercules reported that "they all work out with weights, they all have, sometimes, a bandana of two. Just something—it's a little bit like the old west." An officer stationed on one of the mobile sea bases said, "As far as I'm concerned, you're out in the field. You wear what's functional and what's comfortable for you as long as it works." Typical warm weather attire might include tennis shoes, khaki swim trunks, and an olive green tee shirt. In cooler weather, men might wear sweat suits. As might be expected, some didn't quite know where to draw the line. An officer observed, "It would get a little ludicrous sometimes. Always you had one or two guys who want to do something a little weird, so we'd say, 'Don't do that.'" There were some who thought the first Hercules commanding officer, Commander Evancoe, had gotten a bit weird himself.

When the Hercules deployed, it carried a large contingent of foreign contracters doing service work. Many were from Third World countries; some were Arabs. Commander Evancoe had no idea where these men's loyalties lay. There had been no security screening of the workers. It was possible that some were Shitte Arabs with pro-Iranian sympathies. Evancoe had a conscious decision to impress these workers with just who was in charge on the seabase. He had the U.S. servicemen wear holstered pistols at all times, an action that gained Evancoe some notoriety. It was said by some that he had "gone cowboy," with his men being armed all the time, even on the mess deck.

The charge seems unfair. As Evancoe would later recall, his men weren't acting at all like "macho idiots." Not any more than U.S. cops going into a doughnut shop wearing their pistols. Weapons were holstered and never drawn. There were no accidental discharges. On Sea Float, in Vietnam, men had gone about armed. The MEF commander, Admiral Bernsen, visited the sea base several times and observed the men under arms without an objection.

Adding to what some perceived as Evancoe's maverick image was the occasion when he was ordered to move the Hercules 12 miles to the south for a visit from the Chief of Naval Operations. Admiral Bernsen had previously told Evancoe, "Unless you hear from me, don't change your position." On this occasion, Admiral Bernsen was dining with the U.S. Ambassador to Kuwait and was unavailable to approve the move. Evancoe refused to move the base. When Admiral Bernsen later backed him up, Evancoe said to him, "I guess I'm not fired." Admiral Bernsen replied, "No, you did the right thing." Unfortunately, that was a private exchange, whereas Evancoe's refusal to move the base had been heard by every ship listening in on the command net.

Command squabbles, vulnerability concerns, and shakedown problems aside, the Mobile Sea Bases would prove to be a real success. It would take a nasty battle, but the Iranians were quickly convinced that the bases meant business. Their presence in the northern Gulf virtually shut down Iranian attempts to lay mines or attack shipping with small boats based on Farsi. "It's quite clear by now that Farsi Island has been completely neutralized," said a Western ambassador in the Gulf region in November 1987. "The Iranians are still there at Farsi, but they are never alone."[3]

CHAPTER 10

"TURN AND ENGAGE"

The Mobile Sea Base Hercules deployed operationally for the first time at a location some 25 nautical miles away from Iran's Farsi Island. The base was under the command of Navy Commander Paul Evancoe, the SEAL officer who had taken Special Boat Unit 20 to the Gulf and who had overseen the fitting out of the commercial oilfield barge for its military role. Evancoe's deputy was another SEAL officer, Pete Wikul.

The Army TF-160 SEABAT helicopters and the Navy Mark III Patrol Boats based on the Hercules immediately began conducting surveillance on the Iranian forces operating out of Farsi. It took only two nights of patrolling to determine the operating patterns of the Revolutionary Guard speedboats. These small craft obviously had very limited navigational capabilities. It looked like they had to go from buoy to buoy to reach a given destination. The boats were also spotted tying up to platforms and navigational aids near Farsi in order to avoid detection and to ride out rough seas. The gunboats would launch from their tie-up points to attack shipping.

The Iranians on Farsi Island did not take kindly to the arrival of a floating U.S. military base in their vicinity. They would call the Americans on bridge–to–bridge radio channel 16. In heavily accented English they would say things like, "American mudderfucker. Fuck you!" The Americans on the Hercules thought the radio antics were good for a laugh.

Not so funny were some other Iranian actions. In addition to greeting the arrival of the Hercules with radioed endearments, the Iranians immediately began harassing the base by making high-speed nighttime boat runs at it. What looked like incoming attack runs sent the base to

137

battle stations with all weapons manned. However, the speeding Iranian boats didn't open fire, so the base defensive positions held their fire as well. On the first two nights, patrol boats from the Hercules had aggressively moved out and intercepted the Revolutionary Guard speedboats. On both occasions, the Iranians had retreated at high speed to the northeast. Commander Evancoe got a map of the area and plotted the nightly contacts. Looking at the plots, it was obvious that the Iranians were using a lighted navigational aid, known as Middle Shoals Buoy, as the launching point for their runs at the base.

The Iranians may not have actually attacked the base, but tension seemed to be building. On October 8, 1987, Pete Wikul walked into Paul Evancoe's office and said that he "had a gut feeling that something was going to happen that night." Evancoe replied, "That's funny, I was just on my way to find you and tell you the same thing. What do you think we should do?" Wikul answered, "We are in a bind and not getting any intel up here. How about a listening post op at Middle Shoals Light and we'll tighten up the watch tonight." Evancoe looked amazed. "This is weird," he said, "We must be on the same wavelength because I was just thinking the same thing. Tell John the concept; have him put together the details and brief us in two hours; and get a test fire on all the weapons tonight."[1]

The planned operation would use forces from three services to monitor and maybe discourage the Iranian speedboat activity originating around the buoy. A standard Army SEABAT team of one MH-6 and two AH-6's would go on patrol, scouting a string of navigational aids and island checkpoints. A Navy LAMPS helicopter based on the frigate USS *Thatch* (FFG-43) would vector the SEABATS. That ship was keeping a protective eye on the new base from a position not too far away.

One of the SEABAT checkpoints was Middle Shoals Buoy, which was located about eight nautical miles from the Hercules. The plan was for the MH-6 to use its FLIR system to conduct a sweep of the buoy and its vicinity to make sure that no Iranian boats were around. While the SEABATS were in the air, two blacked-out patrol boats would be towing a smaller Seafox craft to drop off at the buoy. The Seafox would have a Marine radio reconnaissance team with a Farsi speaker onboard, and would be able to monitor Iranian radio transmissions. The Seafox hull was constructed of fiberglass and sat low in the water, making it almost invisible to radar. The Iranians on Farsi would see only a single "blip" on their radar screens for the three outbound craft, and for the two returning patrol boats. They would also see only a single radar blip for the buoy, even after the Seafox had been dropped off there. The idea was not to engage the Iranians, but rather to intimidate them and to push them back from their departure point at the buoy. Things, however, did not work out as planned.

At 9:50 P.M., the LAMPS helicopter flying off of the *Thatch* picked up a radar contact north of the buoy. The Navy helicopter was about 15 nautical miles southwest of the buoy at the time. The helicopter vectored the patrolling SEABATS in to investigate. The three TF-160 helicopters closed to within two or three nautical miles of the buoy. The MH-6 equipped with the FLIR flew out ahead to check on the radar contact. The two AH-6's maintained over-watch positions several hundred meters behind the MH-6.

The two MH-6 pilots were using their night vision goggles to fly the copter. There was pretty good natural illumination that night, but they couldn't discern anything at that range through the goggles. About two miles out, they began using the FLIR system. Looking at the FLIR display screen, they could just make out some kind of vessel on the water. "Okay," one said, "we've got an object."[2] As the helicopter flew closer, its crew could now make out several boats. They were in a group about 300 to 400 meters to the side of Middle Shoals Buoy. The TF-160 pilots assumed they were looking at the two U.S. Navy patrol boats and the Seafox, which had gone out for the scheduled operation that night. At least one of the boats they could see had a low freeboard. The helicopter pilots figured that was the Seafox, which they knew sat low in the water. One of the pilots said, "OK, we've got what looks like our friendly patrol boats here."[3] They didn't.

The U.S. patrol boats were actually some four nautical miles away, still heading to the buoy. They had been delayed about an hour due to mechanical problems with the Seafox. It was finally decided to leave the ailing Seafox behind and just take the patrol boats out. Led by the MH-6, the SEABAT team continued inbound toward the group of boats. The pilots were still sure that what they had in sight were "friendlies." The pilots may have been "fat, dumb, and happy" as one of them later put it, but they strictly followed their procedure. They treated the contacts as hostile unless confirmed otherwise. As they continued to close, the MH-6 pilot was calling out information on the contacts: "Okay," he said, "we've got some vessels dead in the water at 12 o'clock, approximately one-half mile, no movement, no hostile intent at this time."[4]

The MH-6 was skimming over the Gulf at 80 knots, heading directly toward the boats. As it closed to within one hundred meters, the pilot looked down again at his FLIR display. He could now see that one of the boats had a heavy machine gun mounted high on a tripod. The adrenalin started flowing. U.S. patrol boats didn't have those kinds of weapon mounts, but Iranian boats did. "Boghammers! Boghammers! Boghammers!" the pilot shouted as he broke hard left. He could see startled Iranian sailors on the boats looking up as he swept over them. Below, he could see one Boghammer and two "Boston whaler"-type boats behind it.

As the MH-6 turned away, the pilot could see an Iranian sailor jump up and get behind the heavy machine gun. Bright muzzle flashes lit the air and reflected off the dark surface of the water as he opened fire. The MH-6 continued to turn sharply to the left, climbing slightly, as a glowing string of deadly tracer fire rose toward it. A second string of tracers now arced up. At least two heavy machine guns were firing at the helicopter. "We're taking fire!" the pilot excitedly called out. The tracers streamed dangerously close by, only about ten feet away from the helicopter's canopy. Fortunately, the Iranians couldn't track the helicopter in the dark, and the tracer fire drifted away as it continued to climb and turn.

As the MH-6 climbed safely away, the Boghammer started its engines and began maneuvering in the area. The AH-6 gunships had seen the tracers arcing up toward the MH-6 and had heard the radio call that it was taking fire. There was no hesitation. The first AH-6 flew in toward the Iranian boats. It was difficult to judge the range over the featureless water. Both pilots were trying hard to estimate the distance to the cluster of boats. They figured it was about 800 meters. The lead pilot armed his 2.75-inch rockets and fired two of them. Both of the rockets mounted flechette warheads. The rocket warheads detonated downrange and sprayed hundreds of the lethal darts right into the area occupied by the Iranian boats. The range estimate had been just about perfect. The AH-6 pressed the attack, firing more rockets and opening up with its minigun. The 4,000-round-per-minute gun was deadly effective. One of the pilots said, "The gun ate up everything in that cluster."[5]

The AH-6 broke right after its first pass. Its attack run had done a lot of damage. One of the Boston Whaler-type boats was broken in half and burning. Flames were also visible on the second Whaler-type. The Boghammer was the largest, fastest, and most heavily armed of the three

Iranian craft. Apparently, it had escaped taking any serious damage in the attack, and now seemed to be moving to get into position to engage the helicopters.

With the first AH-6 on its outbound leg, the second AH-6 now attacked with minigun fire and rockets. The AH-6 fired two 2.75-inch high explosive rockets. One of them hit the burning Whaler-type boat and started a second fire on it. The Boghammer could be seen moving through the smoke of the burning boats, trying to pull some of their crews out of the water. Gasoline from the boats that had been hit was burning on the surface of the water, and garish flames lit the area. When the second AH-6 ended its run and turned outbound, the first AH-6 went back in, aiming its rockets and minigun fire at the Boghammer. This time, the Boghammer fought back. As the AH-6 closed, there was a spurt of fire on the Boghammer and a rocket came streaking off the boat. The rocket did not fly true, but instead went corkscrewing low to the water. The pilot saw it spiral past his right door, smack the surface of the water and bounce up a few times. It then crashed.

It was unclear if the Boghammer had launched a heat-seeking anti-aircraft missile which had failed to lock on the helicopter, or if it had fired its bow-mounted multiple rocket launcher up into the night sky. The latter fired unguided free-flight rockets, which had only the slimmest chance of hitting one of the U.S. helicopters. However, a chance hit by one of the heavy 107mm artillery rockets would have virtually disintegrated a flimsy "Little Bird" and its crew.

The first AH-6 pulled out and the other AH-6 came in for its second run. The Boghammmer had gone around in a big circle and come back into the area of the two burning Boston Whaler-types. The smoke from the burning boats and the burning gasoline on the water was making it difficult for the helicopter pilots to target the largest of the Iranian boats. However, the Boghammer made the mistake of coming around in front of the fires, where it was silhouetted and easier to spot. As the AH-6 flew in to engage, the Iranian boat commander may have realized his mistake. The boat squirted around to the backside of the burning area, where it would be more difficult to hit.

The first AH-6 now flew in for its third run. With the Boghammer moving around to keep the fire and smoke between it and the helicopters, the pilot decided it was time to change tactics. Instead of staying on the north-south circuit the AH-6's had been making their runs on, he broke away at a 90 degree angle. He told the other AH-6 to hold a bit, while he came in on an east-to-west run. That way, the helicopters would be coming in on runs at 90 degrees to each other, making it difficult for the Boghammer to anticipate the direction of their attacks and to stay behind the obscuring fires and smoke. It seemed to be a good tactic, but the attack run didn't produce much of a result.

After the first AH-6 expended its ammunition on its third pass, the MH-6 equipped with the FLIR joined the fray, firing at the Boghammar with a minigun that had recently been installed on the surveillance helicopter. The MH-6 pilot fired a few bursts. He said, "The rounds were on it, but the thing was still underway."[6]

The Boghammar was proving hard to finish off. The second AH-6 had one 2.75-inch flechette rocket and some 7.62mm minigun ammunition left. The pilot of the first AH-6 believed that the gunships were too far from the Boghammar to get good hits and told the other AH-6 to get in really close this time. The AH-6 pilot was determined to sink the Boghammer with his last rocket. Firing at a long enough distance for the flechette warhead to arm and detonate would probably hit the boat with another spray of darts, but was not likely to sink it. Instead, the pilot decided to use the last rocket as a kind of harpoon to puncture the ship's hull. He deliberately brought his AH-6 in too close for the warhead to detonate, and fired the rocket at the Iranian craft. The rocket flew true and punched into the gunboat amidships, directly below the cabin. The Boghammer quickly began to sink as water poured in through the large hole torn in its aluminum hull.

Two of the three helicopters continuously kept station over the surviving Iranians in the water, freeing one at a time to go back to the Hercules to rearm and refuel. Back on the Hercules, the aircrew had to reassure a very concerned Commander Evancoe that they had not just attacked the two U.S. Navy patrol boats in a confused "blue-on-blue" engagement—his worst nightmare. Those two MK III patrol boats were from Special Boat Unit 20 and were commanded by Lt. Jonathan Roark. He was a surface warfare officer who had previously served on a frigate and a cruiser in the engineering sections. He had volunteered for a Special Boat Unit tour even though it was considered outside the mainstream of a surface warfare officer's career track. Roark figured it wouldn't hurt his career, plus he just wanted to do it. He had been excited about going to the Gulf. When he got there, and the reality of the situation sank in, he found himself a little less excited.

The patrol boats had started late for the buoy after leaving the

Seafox behind with its mechanical troubles. When they were about a mile from the buoy, Roark had been talking to the sailor at the bow on mine watch. Suddenly, he was startled to see Soviet-type green-colored tracers arcing into the night sky toward the U.S. helicopters. The Iranian machine gun bursts seemed to be answered almost instantly by red-colored tracer fire from the TF-160 helicopters. To Roark, the 4,000-round-per-minute minigun return fire from the AH-6's was so heavy that it looked like water spraying out of a garden hose. Roark got on the radio to the Hercules and alerted the base that, "Something is going on. Looks like we have a firefight up here." The two patrol boats went to battle stations and headed toward the action at full throttle. The patrol boats closed to within range of their onboard weapons, but held off firing on the Iranian boats. They were afraid that ricocheting rounds might smack off the surface and fly into the air, endangering the low-flying Army helicopters.

Lt. Roark did see the tongue of flame from the Iranian rocket launch. There was no doubt in his mind that a hand-held surface-to-air missile had been fired at the helicopters. He had seen U.S. Stingers fired before, and this one looked just the same. The missile didn't follow a ballistic trajectory like an artillery rocket would have, but instead, tumbled in the air with its exhaust spiraling out behind it. Roark later figured that, in his haste to launch the missile, the Iranian sailor had been in such a hurry that he had failed to un-cage the gyroscope, which would have stabilized it in flight.

The fighting was all over by the time the two patrol boats arrived in the immediate vicinity. The boats throttled back and nosed into the area around 10:30 P.M. The flickering flames of burning gasoline illuminated a hellish scene. The debris of battle was everywhere. Equipment, pieces of destroyed boats, and Iranian bodies floated in a jumble on the water. The air was heavy with the mingled stench of gasoline and burned flesh.

One of the Boston Whaler-type boats had been chopped in half by minigun fire. Its stern, which mounted two Yamaha outboard engines, was still afloat. The boat hulls were constructed of buoyant material and chewed-up pieces of it floated all around. Roark saw the last of the larger Boghammar slipping beneath the waves as the patrol boats threaded their way through the area. Iranian survivors were swimming in the water. Two Iranians could be seen paddling and supporting a third, who was floating face up and who looked to be in bad shape. The

U.S. sailors had the Iranians swim over to the boats if they could. They were pulled up onto the swimmer's platform, low on the stern of the boats, and searched for documents and weapons. They were then taken up to the deck of the patrol boat where their hands were cuffed and they were given first aid.

At least some of the Iranians weren't ready to fully submit. A SEAL on one of the patrol boats said, "As the flames died down, the boats moved in and started pulling prisoners out of the water. We had several cases where the prisoners were pulled out of the water armed. One petty officer actually wrestled a guy for his gun—I mean actually wrestled him on the deck for his gun. The gun went over the side."[7]

The patrol boats picked up five survivors. Two of the Iranians were severely wounded. A veteran SEAL said, "I've been in Vietnam and Lebanon and this, and I've never seen people live with that many holes in them, with that many burns over their body—and still be alive!"[8] Several of the Iranians were so badly wounded that they couldn't swim over to the patrol boats, which had to go and pick them up. One Iranian with a severe head wound had to be retrieved by a U.S. sailor who jumped into the water. Another Iranian survivor was spotted clinging to Middle Shoals Buoy itself. Lt. Roark's patrol boat went over to pick him up. The badly burned Iranian sailor held out his arms to be taken aboard. When a U.S. sailor tried to pull him in, the flesh peeled off of the poor man's arms like the skin off a sausage.

The captured Iranians were checked for wounds so that first aid could be administered. Using only a flashlight with a red lens filter made it difficult to determine he extent of their injuries, so the prisoners were physically examined from the head on down. Lt. Roark checked the Iranian who had been supported by two others in the water. When he first put his hands on the man's head, one finger sank into a hole all the way up to his knuckle. The U.S. sailors found it almost impossible to stop the bleeding from the Iranian sailors' wounds. Some of them even speculated later that the material in which the 2.75-inch rocket flechette darts were packed had anti-coagulant properties. If so, it was certainly not by design. The wounded Iranians were placed in one boat and were sent to the Hercules for additional medical attention. Lt. Roark remained at the scene with the other boat.

The Iranians now began reacting to the battle. The Navy LAMPS helicopter had picked up indications on its radar that the Iranians were massing small boats in the Fereidoon oil field, where they were based on various platforms, and were launching them south toward Farsi Island. In the Tactical Operations Center on the Hercules, the radar screen suddenly showed nearly 40 blips. The Iranian gunboats were coming in at speed. They were "CBDR," constant bearing, decreasing range. In addition to the swarm of speedboats, there was a much larger Iranian corvette-sized warship coming on. A second U.S. patrol boat headed out to reinforce Lt. Roark. The Middle East Force Command immediately dispatched the frigate *Thatch* and the amphibious ship *Raleigh* to reinforce the menaced base. The Hercules went to general quarters, bracing for an attack. Crews frantically began re-arming the Hercules SEABAT team's helicopters. Marines on the base began throwing hand grenades over the side in case Iranian swimmers were trying to attack the Mobile Sea Base.[9]

In his lone boat at Middle Shoals Buoy, Lt. Roark couldn't believe the number of Iranian gunboats headed in his direction. On his radar screen, the white blips looked like a snowstorm. Dozens of gunboats were pouring out of Farsi Island and the nearby platforms in Fereidoon field, and they were now heading directly toward his location. Roark called Commander Evancoe on the Hercules and asked, "What are your orders?" Commander Evancoe told him, "Turn and engage." Lt. Roark replied, "Aye, aye, sir." As Commander Evancoe later put it: "We weren't going to run from these suckers because if they would have come through [the first patrol boat]—that was my first line of defense—and then through [second patrol boat] they would have had my barge with all the helos on it."[10]

Lt. Roark's patrol boat had three screws, but one of them had become fouled while churning through the battle debris at the buoy. He was now facing up to 40-to-1 odds while reduced to running on two screws. He remembered reading accounts of the North Korean capture of the intelligence gathering ship USS *Pueblo* in 1968. He remembered the criticism visited on that ship's Captain, Lloyd Bucher, for surrendering while his vessel still had power. Lt. Roark knew he couldn't win, but he figured he'd take as many of those bastards as possible with him. Grimly, he turned his boat toward the oncoming flotilla. Roark told himself that, no matter what the condition of his patrol boat, as long as he could still move, he'd ram an Iranian boat. Less defiantly, he also hoped that, when he and his men were tied up and laid out as prisoners on the deck of an Iranian ship, they would be treated as well as the U.S. crews had just treated their Iranian prisoners.

Lt. Roark had complete confidence in Commander Evancoe, who was an experienced combat veteran and a charismatic leader. He figured Evancoe would not leave him hanging out there. He was right. The USS *Raleigh*, located some 90 miles to the south of the Hercules, and closing, had launched an AH-6 and an MH-6 to reinforce the SEABATS stationed on the Mobile Sea Base. Those had returned from the battle and been refueled and rearmed. Now, five of the deadly helicopters were in the air. Lt. Roark thought the helicopters would make the odds a lot better. They certainly would help. However, any battle would have almost certainly lasted through the fast approaching daylight, stripping the helicopters of the protective cloak of darkness. At least some of the TF-160 pilots were not looking forward to becoming clearly visible targets for dozens of gunboats.

The frigate USS *Thatch*, which had been some 20 miles away, was also steaming to the scene. The Iranians must have seen the reinforcements on radar. With their lead boats about a mile and a half from Lt. Roark's patrol boat, they abruptly turned back. Evancoe figured that either the Iranians had been monitoring U.S. radio transmissions, or had spotted the incoming reinforcements with radars located on Farsi Island or in Freridoon field.

The wounded Iranian sailors who had received first aid at the scene of the action were taken to the Hercules, which had only a single SEAL corpsman and limited medical facilities. Shortly before midnight, the USS *Raleigh* sent a doctor and a corpsman to the Hercules by CH-46 helicopter. Two of the Iranians had severe head wounds, and these men died in the early morning hours of October 8, one in the triage room and the other while being carried on a litter to the helicopter. The medical personnel were able to save one Iranian who had very serious burns and wounds. That morning, the CH-46 flew the four survivors to the *Raleigh* for further treatment and eventual repatriation to Iran through the offices of the Red Crescent Society. As in the case of the Iranians captured on the *Iran Ajr*, the "detainees" were swiftly transferred to Dhahran, Saudi Arabia and returned to Iran within less than two weeks.

While they were on the Hercules, Marine interpreters from the radio recon unit questioned the Iranian prisoners. They were asked how many people had been on board the boats, so that searchers could be sure that none had been overlooked. As one of the Iranian prisoners was being questioned, a corpsman was trying to insert an IV needle into his ankle, the only unburned part of his body able to receive it. As the corpsmen futilely tried to jab the large needle into the burned sailor's ankle, the Iranian was being asked questions about the gunboat's mission. The poor Iranian sailor may have thought he was being tortured into giving the answers. The prisoners did reveal that the two Boston Whaler-type boats had departed Busher for Farsi on the morning of October 8. Each boat had a three-man crew. The Boghammer had a crew of six and the operation's commanding officer was aboard it. The Boghammer had departed Busher four hours after the other boats. The three boats had rendezvoused at Farsi Island where the commanding officer had briefed a patrol operation in the vicinity of Middle Shoals Buoy.

The three Iranian craft had departed from Farsi Island in the early evening of October 8. The crews had actually been bedded down for the night at Middle Shoals Buoy when they heard the approaching U.S. helicopters. They had opened up with two .51-caliber heavy machine guns, precipitating the battle. One of the Boston Whaler-types had been chopped apart with just its aft section remaining. The other had been set on fire. The Boghammar had tried to hide behind the smoke and fire, but had been riddled with 7.62mm fire. The rocket hit on the crew compartment, which killed several men, had finished it off. Among them, was the Iranian patrol's commanding officer. Seven of the original 13 crewmen had been killed and six survived.

Orange flames, leaping against the night sky from the burning Iranian boats, could be seen from the Hercules. Word of the battle and the arrival of badly burned and profusely bleeding Iranian casualties was a severe jolt to the Hercules' civilian crew. The report that large numbers of Iranian boats were heading to attack the Mobile Sea base made things worse. Many of these men had probably not quite realized what they had gotten into when they signed on to work on the base. A U.S. officer later said that the events of October 8 had "scared the shit out of them . . . they said, 'we're outta here.'"[11] It took some heavy duty talking by their boss and an extra $110 per month in imminent danger pay (the same amount received by U.S. servicemen) to keep the civilian crew on board. The U.S. Middle East Force itself grew more concerned about the potential vulnerability of the Mobile Sea Bases. It was after the Middle Shoals incident that a frigate was usually assigned as guard ship for the bases.

The action at Middle Shoals Buoy produced unwelcome evidence that the Iranians had somehow gotten their hands on U.S.-made Stinger man-portable, heat-seeking anti-aircraft missiles. Amid the wreckage at

the scene of the battle, one of the SEALs had spotted two Stinger battery systems floating in the water in their Styrofoam containers. Despite
four- to six-foot seas, he dove in and retrieved them. The Iranian prisoners revealed that the Boston Whaler-types had each carried a Stinger
missile.

Iran seemed to flaunt the fact that it had equipped some of its boats
with U.S.-made Stinger missiles. One Iranian source even claimed that
U.S. National Security Adviser Robert C. McFarlane had delivered the
missiles as part of the secret arms deal negotiated in 1986. McFarlane
denied the charge.[12] U.S. authorities confirmed that equipment which
"appeared to be associated with the Stinger system"[13] had been found
aboard one of the bullet-riddled Boston Whaler-type boats recovered
after the brief nighttime battle. The material included packaging and
batteries, but not the missiles themselves. The discovery led to widespread speculation that the Afghan rebels, who had been receiving the
missiles from the CIA, had sold or traded some of the missiles to Iran.
In fact, the serial numbers on the batteries were sent to the Defense
Intelligence Agency, which identified them as having been furnished to
the Afghan resistance.

The surprising discovery of the Stinger equipment on the Iranian
boat opened up a can of worms for the Reagan administration. The
Stingers had been supplied to the Afghan Mujahadeen starting in mid-
1986 and had immediately begun taking a heavy toll of Soviet helicopters and aircraft on the battlefield. The introduction of the man-
portable, shoulder-fired missiles was credited with seriously eroding the
Soviet position in Afghanistan, and possibly even creating the turning
point of the war. However, there had always been concern on the part
of the CIA (with the exception of its head, William Casey) and the Joint
Chiefs of Staff that the missiles might end up in the hands of terrorists
or Iran and be used against American interests. Now, with the possible
Iranian use of Stingers against the SEABAT helicopters of Army Task
Force 160 in the Gulf, those fears had been realized.

Exactly how Iran came by the Stingers was a matter of speculation,
and calls mounted in the U.S. for an investigation. There were reports
that Iranian Revolutionary Guards had seized some of the missiles from
an Afghan rebel truck when it broke down close to the border in April
1987 and help was sought in an Iranian village. Other reports claimed
that pro-Iranian rebels operating around the city of Herat in western
Afghanistan had sold the missiles to Iran, and that the truck convoy

breakdown had been staged to make it appear that the Iranians had forcibly confiscated the weapons. The London *Sunday Times* reported that the Younis Khalis Islamic Party, a rebel faction with ties to Iran, had sold at least 16 Stingers out of its stockpile of 32 for $1 million. It was later reported by other sources that Stingers had been put on display during Iran's "war week" parades in late September.[14]

By whatever method, the fact was that Iranians had gotten their hands on some U.S.-made Stingers. The question was how much of a threat did they pose to U.S. forces in the Gulf? The missile was designed to home in on the infrared emissions from the hot exhausts of aircraft or helicopter engines. The AH-6 and MH-6 helicopters of TF-160 had been equipped with exhaust suppressors, which greatly reduced their infrared "signatures," making it difficult for the missiles to track them.

While relatively straightforward in use, the Stinger still required a reasonable level of training to operate effectively. Tracking aircraft was not easy, and gunners needed hours of practice to acquire and maintain the skill. Without proper training, a gunner might fire the missile at an aircraft without knowing that its seeker was aimed at something else. The Stinger is called a "fire and forget" weapon, but several steps had to be taken before the gunner could fire. An inexperienced gunner might discharge the battery-charging unit (which super cools the guidance section) and never get a launch. The Iranians may have gotten some second-hand training from Afghan sources, but their overall ability to effectively operate the system had to be questionable.

Iran also had no assured supply of replacement components, such as batteries, to keep the system in operation. The Iranians definitely did not possess night sights for their Stinger launchers, a critical drawback in the nighttime environment preferred by the U.S. Special Operations helicopters. Overall, given their limited numbers of Stingers and the limited expertise with which they could be employed, Iran's possession of the missiles was probably not a significant threat to U.S. forces. Still, TF-160 was understandably concerned about the weapons' presence in the Gulf. In the U.S., TF-160 crews ran tests against the missiles. The Army's best Stinger gunners were pitted against the TF-160 Little Birds. The Stinger gunners never could get a shot at the helicopters. At night, they found it impossible to acquire and lock-on to the quiet, low-flying, helicopters before they were inside the anti-aircraft missile's minimum range. It also wouldn't help Iranian Stinger gunners that they would be operating from the unstable platform of a small boat, which was usually rocking in the water. Another problem with the Stinger was that, when it was ejected from its launch canister by a CO_2 cartridge, it dropped several feet before its rocket motor kicked in. The TF-160 pilots were told that, if they stayed below 30 feet in altitude, a Stinger gunner would have to aim so low that the missile would drop into the water before its rocket motor could ignite.

Some three months after the incident at Middle Shoals, on January 5, 1988, U.S. forces were able to raise and salvage the Iranian Boghammar. A Navy dive team, working off a tugboat, had located the sunken gunboat in around 130 feet of water. To recover it, the Hercules itself was towed to the location and one of its cranes was used to lift the Iranian craft from the sea bottom. The boat was placed on skids mounted on the deck of the Mobile Sea Base. One source claims that bodies of several Iranian sailors were found aboard the ship, including one holding a damage control wedge he apparently had tried to use to plug the hole blown in the ship's side. A pitifully futile attempt since the hole was much larger than the plug. Allegedly, the divers were told not to bring up the bodies, whose discovery was denied. Only the ship was officially recovered.

On board the Boghammar were a radio, night vision goggles (which Naval Intelligence had claimed the Iranians did not employ in the northern Gulf), and a Stinger missile container. Eventually, the Iranian craft was restored to full operating condition and brought to the U.S. It was later spotted zipping around San Diego harbor.

CHAPTER 11

"WE WILL COMMENCE FIRING"

Near dawn on Friday, October 17, 1987, the 81,283-ton tanker *Sea Isle City* slowly maneuvered to enter Kuwait's Shuaiba oil loading terminal. Flying the Stars and Stripes from its mast, the re-flagged ship (formerly the *Umm Al Maradex*) had arrived at the Kuwaiti oil port of Mina at al-Ahmadi on Tuesday, in the company of three other tankers. The four ships had made the 550-mile Gulf run in an Earnest Will convoy protected by U.S. Navy warships, which had dropped off the their charges in international waters at the entrance to Kuwait's ship channel.

Some 50 miles away on the Faw Peninsula, Iraqi territory occupied by Iran since its capture in 1986, a Revolutionary Guard crew from the 26th Missile Brigade made final preparations to launch one of the big Chinese-made Silkworm anti-ship missiles. The Silkworm had been towed on its wheeled launcher from its support and storage depot in Iranian territory, across the Shatt al Arab waterway. It had been rolled into position a few hours before dawn and had been set up under the cover of darkness. The launch site was at the extreme southern tip of the peninsula, which put Kuwait barely in range. The gyros in the missile's autopilot were aligned. An operator manually inputted ballistic data to the launch system's computer, which then calculated a firing solution and fed it to the missile.

The Revolutionary Guard crew moved away from the launcher and got behind cover. Even in the partial light of a breaking dawn, the launch site was lit up by the brilliant flash of the Silkworm's rocket exhausts as its engines ignited. Blasted off the launch ramp by its under slung solid fuel booster, as well as its liquid fuel main engine, the heavy missile leaped nearly a thousand feet into the brightening sky. As the booster exhausted itself and fell away, the main engine sustained the missile in flight. The Silkworm glided down to its 300-foot cruising altitude as it streaked across the Gulf toward Kuwait.

Peering into their radar screens, Kuwaiti air defense operators started when they saw the blip of the incoming missile appear on their displays. They had seen this before and they knew what it meant. Grimly, they sounded the alarm. Kuwaiti troops stationed in positions along the missile's flight path were alerted. Some of them were equipped with Russian-made SA-7 Strella hand-held anti-aircraft missiles. When the Iranian missile flew within visual range, they hoisted the SA-7 launchers to their shoulders. The Kuwaiti soldiers centered the Silkworm in their launchers' optical sights and pressed the firing triggers. The smoky trails of SA-7's streaked skyward, but none connected with the oncoming Silkworm.

Undisturbed, the Iranian missile flew deeper into Kuwaiti territory. The Silkworm's nose-mounted radar was now "painting" the specific target it had selected. Aboard the Sea Isle City, a crewman on deck saw the missile fly past two other ships. Ominously, it swung around in a turn toward them. Another crewman, looking out a bridge window, saw what looked at a distance to him like a flying oxygen cylinder coming straight at the ship. He shouted a warning to the Captain, "Look!"[1] It was too late.

The big missile roared over the tanker's deck and smashed into the raised superstructure near the stern, at a point just below the bridge. The missile tore a gaping hole in the superstructure of the ship and exploded. The detonation of the thousand-pound warhead sent a tremendous fireball racing through the crew areas and up through companionways to the bridge and navigation deck. A thundering boom rolled across the water, waking nearby residents from their sleep. A tower of black smoke rose from the ship. The Sea Isle City's American Captain, John Hunt, 50, was on the bridge when the missile hit. Flying glass from bridge windows blown out by the explosion sprayed him like shrapnel. Captain Hunt recalled:

> The last thing I remember was hearing a metal on metal sound. It was the missile striking us. Then all went black. When I regained consciousness, I was lying flat. I could smell smoke and knew the ship was on fire. I tried to open my eyes, but nothing happened. I reached my right hand to my right eye and felt

blood . . . I could not speak, I could not move and I could not see. I thought I was dead.[2]

The badly wounded captain was evacuated and underwent eight hours of emergency surgery before being placed in intensive care. The ship's wheelhouse was left blood-spattered and strewn with debris. The missile explosion ignited a fire onboard the ship, which took several hours to put out. Eighteen crewmen, including the captain and the American radio operator, were injured. Captain Hunt survived but would never command a tanker again—his injuries left him permanently blinded. Unaware of his condition, Captain Hunt told a hospital visitor that he couldn't wait to have the bandages removed because the darkness was terrible.[3]

A "heroic deed," Ayahtollah Khomeni called it, sending his personal congratulations to the Iranian Revolutionary Guards. The attack was a cause for celebration in Iran. President Ali Khamenei broke the news of the attack at a Friday prayer service at Tehran University, saying, "The Western media are silent, but I can tell you that a missile has hit an oil tanker over which the American flag was fluttering." Khamenei added with a smile, "Where the missile came from, the Almighty knows best." The crowd of thousands burst into laughter.[4] After the prayer session, the crowd paraded through the city, chanting slogans urging Iran to fight Iraq and the United States. Teenagers in military uniforms passed out candy to passers-by to celebrate what they called a victory over America.

The U.S. quickly condemned the attack as an act of aggression against Kuwait. However, the attack on the *Sea Isle City* did raise the question of U.S. retaliation. Strictly speaking, the U.S. escort mission had ended when the ship arrived in Kuwaiti waters, where Kuwait assumed responsibility for its defense. Some early statements from Washington seemed to indicate that there might not be any U.S. response at all. White House spokesman Marlin Fitzwater said of the attack that, "Although it was a U.S.-flagged ship, it did not involve U.S. military personnel in any way or U.S. Navy ships."[5]

The logic behind this line of reasoning was pretty thin. The *Sea Isle City* was flying the Stars and Stripes when attacked. It was, thus, an American ship. The fact that an American ship was not under actual escort by the Navy at the time it was struck did not seem to be a particularly good reason to let the attacker off the hook, in the Gulf or anywhere else. A re-flagging opponent, Sen. Lowell Weicker (R-Conn.), twitted the administration, saying the attack was "the same as if that missile had hit the Capitol of the United States."[6]

If the U.S. failed to respond, it would certainly raise doubts about the seriousness of its commitment to the escort mission and, by extension, its Gulf allies. Kuwait, Saudi Arabia and other Gulf states were coming under increasing Iranian pressure and needed firm U.S. support to resist it. The Iranian game was becoming fairly clear: slide around direct confrontation with the U.S., where retaliation would be almost certain. Instead, strike in "gray areas" where the U.S. commitment was not clearly delineated. The day before the Sea Isle City had been hit; the Iranians had fired a Silkworm that struck the 276,000-ton Liberian-flagged supertanker Sungari, also anchored in Kuwaiti waters. There were reports that the Sea Isle City had detoured to a location about one-half mile from the Sungari, where the missile had struck it, so that its officers could photograph the damaged tanker.

Moderate Arab states were emphatic about the need for the U.S. to act. The Kuwaiti government was putting intense pressure on the U.S. to strike at the launch sites from which the Silkworms were being fired at their country. Secretary of State George Schultz met with Saudi King Fahd, who made clear his outrage at the latest Iranian actions. In the Saudi view, "almost nothing" the U.S. did to retaliate against Iran would be excessive, according to a senior State Department official accompanying Schultz.[7] President Reagan met to review possible U.S. responses with his top national Security advisors, including Caspar Weinberger, George Schultz, and Colin Powell. Options presented to the President ranged from diplomatic protests to various military strikes. President Reagan told his advisors that the U.S. had to decisively demonstrate its political will to retaliate, but the attack should be directed only at military targets and must be "proportional and measured."

Military options considered by administration working groups included strikes against the Silkworm launching sites in the Faw Peninsula or at the Strait of Hormuz and an attack on Farsi Island, a base for Iranian raiding craft. Aircrews from both the Pacific and Atlantic fleets were practicing to attack Silkworm sites in what some of them dubbed the "Orkin Patrol," a reference to the pest extermination company. Aside from the political considerations, a strike against the Faw launching sites presented serious operational problems. Attack aircraft would have to stage out of the carrier USS Ranger in the Gulf of

Oman, some 600 miles away. The long round trip up and down the full length of the Gulf would require in-air refueling. Further, the Silkworm sites were not very profitable targets. The missiles were mounted on mobile launchers, which were set up during the night, fired near dawn, and then removed. There was no guarantee that the missiles would be in place to hit. "All we'd do there," said Joint-Chiefs Chairman Admiral William Crowe, "is kill a lot of date trees."[8]

Even worse, the area was well defended by anti-aircraft guns and missiles, raising the prospect that one or more planes might be shot down and captured pilots paraded through the streets of Tehran. U.S. aircraft flying the length of the Gulf would very likely be picked up by Iranian radar, giving them plenty of warning of the incoming strike and allowing them to have their anti-aircraft defenses ready and waiting. The Silkworm launch sites at Hormuz presented somewhat similar problems, with the exception of the long Gulf round trip. However, those missiles had not as yet been fired at an American flagged ship, making them less appropriate targets. An attack on Farsi Island would probably cause heavy Iranian casualties, contrary to the limited "send a message" approach the President had decided on.

In the end, the President accepted a "consensus" recommendation from his advisors to attack an Iranian oil platform that was being used as a radar station monitoring ship movements and as a resupply base for small raiding craft. The platform presented an easy target for warships with little risk of loss of life on either side. Adding to its attractiveness as a target, the platform was located in international waters, not Iranian territory.

The retaliatory attack was dubbed Operation "Nimble Archer." The target chosen was the "Rashadat" oil platform, which was actually a platform complex originally consisting of three separate platforms linked by walkways. The platform was located about 120 miles east of Bahrain in Rostam oilfield. A 1986 Iraqi air attack had destroyed the central platform. The remaining two platforms were large three-level steel and concrete structures rising above the Gulf surface on tubular steel legs emplaced on the seabed. They were reportedly manned by between 20 and 30 Iranian Navy and Revolutionary Guard Corps personnel and were armed with 23mm automatic anti-aircraft cannon and .50-caliber heavy machine guns.

The decision had been made to use naval gunfire to destroy the platforms. However, only one ship currently in the Gulf, the destroyer *Kidd*

(DDG-993), had the 5-inch guns needed for the job. Ironically, the *Kidd* had been under construction for the Iranian navy of the Shah as the *Kouroosh* at the time of the Iranian revolution. Halfway completed, the *Kidd* had been taken over by the U.S. Navy. One of four such ships, some jokingly referred to the type in U.S. service as belonging to the "Ayatollah class." In order to get additional firepower in the Gulf, three destroyers armed with 5-inch guns were sent in from the North Arabian Sea. The ships were the USS *Hoel* (DDG-13), USS *Leftwhich* (DD-984), and USS *John Young* (DD-973).

The Commander of the Joint Task force Middle East, Admiral Dennis Brooks, had personally briefed the captains of the *Leftwhich*, *Hoel*, and *Young* on board USS *Long Beach* on October 18. The three destroyers, along with the *Kidd*, would form a "Surface Action Group" under the command of the Commander Destroyer Squadron 35, Capt. "Izzy" Larguier, who was also present at the meeting. The briefing had been succinct and to the point. The mission of the Surface Action Group was to totally destroy the Rashadat oil platform using naval gunfire and, if necessary Navy SEALs. Capt. Larguier was embarked onboard the *Leftwhich* and designated the four ships under his command as Surface Action Group "Alfa" (SAG "A").

The anti-aircraft cruiser USS *William H. Standly* (CG-32) and the frigate USS *Thatch* (FFG-43) would also support the action. The frigate was serving as a floating base for SEAL commandos, and would rendezvous with the Surface Action Group early on the morning of the attack. Air cover would be provided by two F-14A fighters and an E-2C Hawkeye airborne radar surveillance aircraft which would fly into and up the Gulf from the carrier USS *Ranger* in the North Arabian Sea.

The Commanding Officer of USS *Hoel* was Commander Gary Bier. A 29-year Navy veteran, Bier was a "Mustang" who had been commissioned some seven years after he had enlisted in 1958. He had served several tours on the "gun-line" off Vietnam's coast during that war, so he had plenty of experience with naval bombardment missions. The *Hoel* had been performing plane guard duty for the carrier *Ranger* when Bier heard the Battle Group command staff querying various ships on the status of their gun systems over the radio command net. *Hoel* had already turned in a CASREP (casualty report) on one of its two 5-inch guns, indicating that it was not operable. However, the crew had managed to improvise a repair seal to put it back in working condition. Bier was anxious not to miss out on the upcoming action. When the *Hoel*'s turn came, he told the Battle Group staff that, despite the earlier report, his gun systems were now up and capable in all mission areas.

There was still another problem that Bier worried might keep the *Hoel* out of the Gulf. The destroyer was not equipped with a Phalanx close-in anti-missile gun system. Ships that did not mount Phalanx systems were not being allowed into the Gulf. The *Hoel* did have a Standard anti-aircraft missile mount, which could be used for missile defense. It would be reasonably effective against Silkworms. To Bier's delight, the decision was for the *Hoel* to come into the Gulf and join the planned operation. Bier thought that the Battle Group might have wanted his ship for the action because it was equipped with a MK-68 fire control system, which had a good ability to lock-on to a shore bombardment-type "hard target." Ironically, the more modem and more automated MK-86 systems on the other ships were considered less capable for that task.

Commander Bier had gone to the cruiser *Long Beach* for the briefing by Admiral Brooks, his former CO on USS *Kansas City*. Admiral Brooks had asked Bier if he thought the ships could knock down the platforms by shooting out their legs. Bier told him he thought that would be a difficult proposition since the 5-inch guns were really area target weapons, not point target ones. Nevertheless, he would give it a try. After the briefing, Commander Bier had gone back to the *Hoel* and told his crew about the upcoming mission. He warned them that, based on his experience, once the guns began firing at the target, it would be obscured by smoke and it would become easy to be confused about what was happening. He told them that continuing to fire blindly into the smoke and dust of the target area might look neat, but usually resulted in few, if any, hits. Instead, they would fire short bursts and let the smoke clear between them so they could assess the damage they were doing.

To prepare for the mission, *Hoel* crewmen studied target folders, which included an intelligence photo of a 26-foot motor whaleboat tied up at the target structure. In order to get that structure's height above the surface, a pair of dividers was set to the known length of the whaleboat and then used to determine the relative length of the platform's height in the picture. That height was then manually inputted into the destroyer's fire control system.

The *Hoel* sailed through the Strait of Hormuz using deceptive lighting techniques in order to mimic a civilian vessel. For the look of a tanker, with its aft accommodation section rising above an otherwise flat deck, *Hoel* put out its forward lights and showed plenty of light aft. To give the narrow-hulled warship the appearance of a wide-beam tanker, 2-foot by 4-foot boards with lights on the ends projected out from the bridge wings. The *Hoel* waited for a civilian ship to enter the strait and then fell in a distance behind it for the run.

Passing through the Silkworm envelope on the way in, there were some cocky crewmen who actually hoped the Iranians would fire one of the missiles at them. The crew was confident that, even without a Phalanx CIWS or Stinger hand-held anti-aircraft missiles aboard, the ships could knock down a Silkworm. The *Hoel* had been successful in anti-missile training exercises using its standard anti-aircraft missiles and its 5-inch guns firing VT (variable time fuse) fragmentation rounds. Some of the exercises had employed drone targets, others synthetic radar targets. For the radar exercise, Commander Bier had doubled the speed of the simulated incoming missiles. He told the men that, if they had to really deal with one in the Gulf, a missile coming in at its true speed would seem like it was moving in slow motion after their speeded up exercises.

The exercises in preparation for the *Hoel*'s Gulf deployment hadn't all been defensive. The ship had also practiced destroying dummy Silkworm launch sites, which had been built on San Clemente Island. The destroyer would make a high speed head-on run to the missile site. Bow-on, it presented its smallest aspect as a target. When it got within range for its 5-inch guns, it would swing broadside, allowing both guns to bombard the site. The ship would then turn directly away, "ass to blast," again presenting the smallest target aspect for a high-speed run out.

When the *Hoel* went through the Silkworm envelope, Bier had ordered that two standard anti-aircraft missiles be mounted on the launch rails. The locations of the Iranian launch sites were known and had been mapped. As the ship passed from one to another, it kept its fire control radars turned off, but pointed at the closest site. The men had been told that a nighttime Silkworm launch would have a tremendous visual signature, with a huge exhaust plume being generated by the missile engine and its rocket booster. If one was spotted, the fire-control radars could be quickly activated and get on target. Fortunately, there were no Silkworm launches.

Inside the Gulf, the U.S. ships proceeded toward the targeted platform in a column formation with an interval of 1,000 yards between them. The Iranians were known to have a search radar operating in Rostam oil field, the location of the targeted platform. The Iranian radar had the ability to detect U.S. ships at a range of around 24 nautical miles. At the rate the warships were closing on the area, they would be within radar detection range for nearly 2-1/2 hours before opening fire on the target.

A column of ships heading directly for their platform would give the Iranians a pretty good idea that trouble was coming. They would also have a fair amount of time to react. Accordingly, Captain Larguier ordered his ships to take an offset approach, so that they would not look like they were heading directly toward the platform. Prior to the ships' approach, it had been estimated that the group would be picked up on Iranian radar around 11:20 A.M. The estimate was pretty close to the mark: at 11:35 A.M. the *Hoel* reported picking up signals from a possible Decca 68 search radar in the vicinity of Rostam oil field.

The Surface Action Group had sailed to within about eight nautical miles south of the target by about forty-five minutes past noon. The ships now turned and headed directly towards the platform. When they got close enough, the group spotted two ships: a small cargo vessel of the inter-island supply type, moored to the target platform, and a small tug about 3,500 yards off another (non-targeted) platform to the north. Both ships flew Iranian flags. The situation in the area of the target platform had not been clear to the U.S. ships until they approached within visual range. There had been no pre-strike aerial reconnaissance because of a possible hand-held surface-to-air missile threat from platforms in the area.

On the *Hoel*, Commander Bier had been worried about the possibility of there being an Iranian helicopter equipped with small air-to-surface missiles on the platform when the Surface Action Group arrived. The Iranians were known to have launched helicopter attacks on shipping from the structure. A helicopter coming at the ships from the platform as they approached it would probably already be inside the minimum range of the *Hoel's* Standard anti-aircraft missiles, so those wouldn't be any help. Accordingly, Bier had ordered that variable time fuse (VT) airburst rounds be loaded in the 5-inch guns and placed as the first rounds in the reload trays. These, he was confident, could knock down any Iranian helicopters they encountered. The crew had asked if they should download the VT rounds and replace them with high explosive

(HE) for the platform attack if no helicopters were encountered. Bier told them no, they would "unload at the muzzle," firing the initial VT rounds at the structure. Bier figured that the airburst fragmentation rounds would take out any defenders on the platforms, or at least make them keep their heads down and prevent them from returning fire.

Various accounts, particularly contemporary news accounts, reflect some confusion over the platforms involved in the subsequent action. The target of the attack was the Rashadat "platform," which actually was a platform complex originally consisting of three separate, but closely spaced and connected platforms, each self-supporting on it own pilings. The middle platform had been destroyed in an Iraqi air attack, leaving the remaining two platforms about 130 meters apart. Also located in Rostam field, around 3,500 yards to the north, was another Iranian oil platform, which was not targeted for attack. News reports would blur the two targeted platforms with the non-targeted platform to the north. Confusion over the actual targets of the attack would extend to the Iranians as well, with some unintended consequences.

The Surface Action Group received information from radio intercepts that an Iranian platform was reporting the ships' position. Throughout the operation, communications intercepts would give the American ships near real-time information on Iranian reactions. When the situation at the platforms was reported to him, Admiral Bernsen, the Commander of the Middle East Force, gave the Surface Action Group Commander the latitude to delay commencing fire if it appeared that there was a reasonable attempt underway to abandon the targeted platforms. However, Captain Larguier said he was going to open fire on schedule, even if the supply boat tied up there had not left. The *Thatch* began broadcasting warnings in both Farsi and English over Bridge-to-Bridge Channe16, UHF Military Air Distress and International Distress frequencies. "Rashadat, Rashadat," was the warning call. "This is the U.S. Navy. We will commence firing on your position at 1400 hours [2:00 P.M.]. You have twenty minutes to evacuate the platform."

Following the warning, the U.S ships picked up mayday signals on Bridge-to-Bridge UHF. The *Leftwhich* issued warnings to the Iranian supply vessel and to the tugboat, to clear the area. The supply ship claimed that it had engine problems and requested a delay. The request was answered by repeating the original warning. This may have provided the incentive for the supply vessel to get its engines started, which it did within about four or five minutes, and began clearing the area. All of the Iranians visible on the target platforms appeared to have boarded the supply ship for evacuation. The Iranian ship requested a heading and was told to steer north, which it promptly did.

The plan was for the warships to run a north-south racetrack pattern, firing to the west. The idea was to leave the Iranian oil platform located to the north, and a United Arab Emirates platform, located to the south, out of the line of fire. Apparently, the non-targeted Iranian platform thought the warning was meant for them as well. Iranian personnel on it could be seen manning Russian-made 23mm ZSU-23-2 twin automatic anti-aircraft guns and training them in the direction of the U.S. ships. News accounts of the time made it sound like the guns were on the targeted platforms. The tugboat closed on the non-targeted platform and began to take on personnel.

At precisely 2:00 PM Gulf time, the four U.S. destroyers opened fire with their 5-inch guns. The *Kidd* and the *Leftwhich* took the northernmost structure. The *Hoel* and the *John Young* took the southernmost. As the firing commenced, some, but not all, Iranian personnel on the non-targeted platform rapidly evacuated to the tug, which then proceeded to the north. The U.S. warships steamed by in column and made their first firing pass at a range of 6,000 yards. "It was exciting and scary," recalled Brent Harris, the *Kidd*'s chief engineman. "The adrenaline started flowing. I thought everything was going to break loose." Harris heard excited sailors shouting when their ship opened fire. "When the Captain came on and said 'Direct Hit,' everyone cheered harder," he recalled.[9]

The *Hoel* used its visual director to align the target in azimuth and used its radar for range. The *Hoel* then aimed "center of mass" on the southernmost structure. The first burst of 5-inch rounds was exactly on target. Exploding rounds hit on or around the living quarters and caused a secondary explosion from what was probably generator fuel stored on the platform. Several of the VT rounds, which had been fired first, detonated before reaching the structure. A few men thought the airbursts were return fire. With the first burst, Commander Bier figured they'd destroyed what they wanted to. It had taken 21 seconds. The *Hoel* went to a greatly reduced rate of fire as it began to aim at the platform legs.

The four U.S. ships made three more firing runs at decreasing ranges of 5,000 yards, 4,200 yards, and finally 2,300 yards. Nearly 400 rounds were fired in each of the first two passes, 224 on the third and 84 on the fourth. The large volume of fire made spotting difficult, and not all of the rounds hit their targets. On its third pass, the *Hoel*'s initial salvo fell short. Apparently, its fire control radar saw the water plume from that salvo as the target and directed some additional rounds to that location. The *Hoel* quickly adjusted to get back on the real target. At close range, the *Leftwich* experienced "jumping/jitter" on its radar because of the large target return. A manual joystick was used to direct fire on target. The *Young* reduced its rate of fire to get spot on; it then went to rapid continuous fire until its ammunition was depleted. The *Kidd* used slow fire with varied elevations to spread rounds vertically through the different deck levels of the targets.

As the ships were preparing to commence their final firing run, the *John Young* reported that an Iranian tug was requesting permission to close on the area and pick up any remaining Iranians. The platform to the north of the two under attack had been partly evacuated after the warning broadcast, under the misimpression that it was going to be a target. The Iranians who had remained aboard were now in a small boat or raft near the platform. Captain Larquier apparently had an idea at this point and, not wanting to confirm that the northern platform was not a target, advised the tug that it could pick up personnel in the small boat but to stay away from the platforms under fire. The tug thanked the U.S. Navy for giving him permission to rescue the personnel in the small boat near the northern platform, apparently still under the impression that it would be hit next.

The gunfire attack had set the northernmost of the two target platforms burning out of control. Safety devices used to shut wells connected to the platform were apparently ruptured, and the wells fed a furious fire which sent a plume of smoke hundreds of feet into the air. The flames could be seen for miles and would continue to burn until August 1988, occasionally giving rise to reports that a ship was on fire in the Gulf. Secretary of Defense Caspar Weinberger's staff would later refer to it as "The Ayatollah's 'eternal flame.'"

With the northern platform ablaze, the ships had attempted to knock down the southern platform by shooting away its legs. The spindly legs proved to be a tough target, although hits were seen on them. From the *Hoel*'s bridge, Commander Bier could see 5-inch rounds from his ship's guns hit three of the four platform legs. However, the ship couldn't seem to get the right angle to hit the fourth. Apparently, some of the rounds that did hit passed right though without detonating.

In the end, only one leg was completely knocked down. The Surface Action Group Commander even attributed that knock down to "lady luck." The platform sagged noticeably but remained in place.

Around 3:30 P.M., the U.S. ships ceased firing. They had poured out a total of 1,065 high explosive and armor piercing rounds. Some of the guns had fired so rapidly that the paint on their barrels had melted. Piping in the gun mounts had gotten so hot it could not be touched. Gun house doors had to be opened to help dissipate the heat and gas generated by the heavy firing. The guns had performed reliably, though two had fouled bores (i.e., un-fired rounds stuck in the guns) by the time firing ceased. The guns were cleared shortly afterward.

The *Thatch* had been positioned 10 nautical miles north of the target platforms and had performed a battle damage assessment during a pause in the action. With the gunfire attack now over, the *Thatch* closed on the target structures to conduct search and rescue operations as well as another battle damage assessment. The northern target was an inferno and in no way usable by the Iranians. The southern target was charred and smoldering. The entire three-level structure was tilting at an angle because of the missing leg. No Iranian casualties or survivors were to be seen. The Iranians had probably completely evacuated the platforms before they were hit. After making their last firing runs, the ships of the Surface Action Group departed to the southeast, heading for a passage through the Strait of Hormuz to rejoin the battle group in the Arabian Sea.

The SEALs on the *Thatch* were from SEAL Team Two, 4th Platoon. They had been embarked on the USS *Guadalcanal*, and had been flown by helicopter to the *Thatch* shortly after sunset on the day before the attack. They were there to board and search the platforms in Rostam field following the naval gunfire bombardment. The SEALs' mission was to gather intelligence, take any Iranians still on board as prisoners, and destroy the remaining structure. For the destruction job, the SEAL commander had requested and gotten an Explosive Ordnance Disposal (EOD) detachment, which would have demolition expertise. It turned out that the EOD detachment had some appropriate experience to draw on: one member had previously worked on the demolition of an oil platform in the Gulf of Mexico.

When the SEALs cross-decked to the *Thatch*, they brought four Combat Rubber Raiding Craft (CRRCs), motors, gasoline, weapons, ammo, and other equipment with them. Because they did not know the extent of the planned naval gunfire bombardment, they took all of the C-4 explosive they could get their hands on: over 1,500 pounds.

In their planning to board the platforms, the SEALs were concerned about the lengthy climb up from the sea level landing to the platform deck in broad daylight. They could be exposed to hostile fire the whole way. They were also worried about structural instability in the platform after the bombardment, making it too hazardous to board. It was also possible that fire or heat would make the metal surfaces too hot to plant explosive charges. Three CRRCs carrying the SEAL platoon shoved off towards the southern platform as the oil-fed fires engulfed the northern one. Each of the three CRRCs carried a M-60 machine gun and light antitank (LAW) rockets. If Iranian resistance was encountered, the plan was for the SEALs to engage the Iranians while the EOD team planted the charges. The boats would then withdraw. At a safe distance, the charges would then be detonated, dropping the platform into the Gulf.

The SEALs made it over to the southern platform a little before 5:00 P.M. in their CRRC craft. The SEALs could see flames from the fires raging on the northern platform shooting up hundreds of feet into the air. Even at a distance, they could feel the intense heat being put out by the burning platform. Oil floating on the surface of the water was also burning in an area extending about 200 feet out from that platform.

The SEALs carefully steered their rubber boats loaded with explosives away from the burning oil. Up close to the southern platform, they could see that the naval guns had reduced its decks to twisted masses of charred metal. Taking no chances, the SEALs fired three LAW rockets into potential Iranian hiding spots on the structure. The exploding rocket warheads drew no response from the silent and apparently abandoned structure. The SEALs could clearly see that the sagging platform was too unstable to climb and search without running a serious risk of it collapsing. The SEAL task unit commander recalled:

So then we got underneath it and got on board the bottom level of the platform. It was all shot up. One of the legs was totally severed, two of the other legs were cut real bad near the waterline where we wanted to put explosives, and one leg was still whole. I asked the platoon commander, "Do you want to take a chance on going up there?" Because it was really smashed up. He said, "No, if we don't have to, no need to take a chance on really getting somebody hurt up there."[10]

The EOD detachment came over in a boat from the *Thatch*, carrying a load of 500 pounds of C-4 explosive. The EOD detachment and the SEALs packed the inside of one of the legs, which had been sliced open by the naval gunfire, with haversacks filled with C-4. Another damaged leg and two supporting cross members were rigged on the outside with charges. Time was getting critical because the operation was supposed to end at 5:48 P.M. More urgently, the oil burning on the water was starting to drift toward the platform the SEALs and the EOD detachment were working on from their boats.

While the SEALs and the EOD team were busy placing their charges, the *Thatch* queried higher authority about approaching the non-targeted platform located to the north of the original target complex. That platform seemed to have been abandoned by its crew under the impression that the U.S. warning broadcasts had been directed at them as well as the targeted platforms. They must have thought that they were going to be shelled next. By radio, the *Thatch*'s commanding officer discussed approaching the non-target platform with the SEAL task unit commander. That platform had two ZSU-23 twin 23mm automatic anti-aircraft cannon mounts on it. The SEAL officer thought that the guns could probably even reach them at their present location if they were manned and the Iranians wanted to. The 23mm rounds could quickly shred the rubber boats and the men on them. The SEAL officer figured that, if they got close enough to the non-target platform, they would get under the lowest level to which the 23mm gun barrels could be depressed. Under the guns' "downtrain," they would be safe from their fire.

The discussion went back and forth for some time. The SEAL officer did say that, "If we're going to get that close, though, I want to board it. I don't want to just get close to it to take a look. I want to board it."[11] The JTFME finally approved the SEALs trying to board the platform. However, they were told that, if they encountered any resistance at all during their approach, they were to turn back immediately.

A little after 5:00 P.M., led by Lieutenant Dave Jones, the 16-man SEAL platoon left the EOD detachment to finish the demolition of the sagging platform and headed over in their rubber boats to the one which had not been originally targeted. USS *Standley* moved in to cover the SEAL team's approach. Forty-five minutes later, the EOD detachment detonated its charges on the southern platform, which buckled and toppled into the Gulf. Only the remnants of its support legs were left visible above the surface of the water. The adjacent platform continued to burn furiously, preventing it from being finished off in the same way. A few minutes later, the SEALs made it to the northern platform. When the SEALs arrived, they decided to recon by fire in case any Iranians were still lurking around. Tracer bursts from M-60 machine-guns arced into the darkened upper levels and ricocheted around, but drew no response.

The SEALs decided to go ahead and board. They landed at a docking area on the base of the platform and began climbing up the ladders to the main deck. That was where the multi-level buildings housing the living quarters and work areas were located. There were several stairways leading up to the main deck The SEALs moved up the stairs methodically, with squads taking turns providing cover and leapfrogging forward.

The squad that made it to the main deck, at first, just stopped and looked around. Then, realizing that they could be taken under fire by any Iranian stay behinds, they hurriedly took cover. They doped out a plan to methodically clear the buildings they could see on that level. The SEALs had flashlights mounted on their M16 rifles and used their close-quarters battle drills to enter and clear rooms. The four-man assault teams moved through the rooms, calling out to each other as they did so. The team moving up to the electrical control room could hear voices inside. Maybe there were some Iranian diehards still onboard.

A SEAL crept alongside the doorway, pulled the pin on a hand grenade, and tossed it into the room. Immediately on the heels of the explosion, the men charged into the room to clear it. There was nobody there. In the room, they did discover the source of the voices they had heard: a radio that had been left on by the Iranians who had earlier fled the facility. The communication spaces for the complex were located on the third level of the building. Chief Petty Officer Douglas Bracca led one of the four four-man assault teams. When he got to the radio room, a telephone was ringing. Braca wondered, if he picked up the receiver, who would he find on the other end of the line—the Ayatollah?

The room-clearing operation didn't turn up any Iranians still aboard. The platform was declared secure. Looking around the structure, the SEALs noticed that the living conditions on it were very poor. The SEALs requested permission to go ahead and destroy the platform, but were turned down. They were told to collect anything of possible intelligence value, destroy or confiscate weapons, and to put any radar or communications equipment out of commission. Intelligence collection was to be their first priority. When the SEALs went through the communications area, they spotted a Teletype machine still printing out messages in Farsi. The SEALs collected equipment and numerous documents, which might yield valuable intelligence. The Teletype machine was disconnected and carried off. Reportedly, U.S. forces later operated it to pick up Iranian messages. The Seals went through a safe and took documents, which included Iranian coastal defense plans. Twelve West German-designed 7.62mm G-3 rifles, radios and cryptographic encoding devices were also seized.

The SEALs broke into teams to set explosive charges on the Iranian equipment they had not been able to remove. The men were carrying small C-4 charges for door breaching purposes. These charges weighed less than a pound. To increase the charges' explosive effect for demolition work, the SEALs placed them on top of hand grenades. The SEALs placed those charges on the Decca radar, both ZSU 23-2 AA guns and on communication antennas.

After they had placed their charges, most of the SEALs gathered at a mid-level area to wait for the men who were putting charges on the anti-aircraft guns. The SEALs grew increasingly anxious as they waited for what seemed like a long time for those charges to be detonated and for the men to rejoin them. When they finally did, it turned out that they had been delayed by some extra-curricular activities. As one of the waiting SEALs later put it, "The knuckleheads had been busy rigging booby traps." The SEALs finally pushed off in their boats and headed back to the *Thatch*. The idea had been to inflict minimal damage on the facility they had boarded, but it didn't work out that way. The charge placed on the radar console had ignited wood paneling in that room and the fire was now growing and spreading.

As the SEALs headed to the *Thatch*, they could look back and see parts of the platform now burning furiously in the twilight. In fact, the structure looked to be burning almost as badly as the one set ablaze earlier by naval gunfire. The amount of damage done to the boarded platform either never made it all the way up the chain of command or was publicly downplayed. Around 10:30 P.M., the SEALs rejoined the EOD detachment back on the *Thatch*. The SEALs had barely gotten on board the ship's flight deck when they were surprised to hear over one of the men's portable radios a BBC announcement that U.S. Navy SEALs had demolished an Iranian platform and returned safely without loss. Along with the *Standley*, the *Thatch* headed to the vicinity of Bahrain. The next morning, the SEALs and EOD detachment returned to the *Guadalcanal*.

When the Surface Action Group had completed its firing mission, it had departed the area and headed for the Strait of Hormuz. There were serious worries that the Iranians might mount a revenge strike against the ships that had destroyed their platforms. Still, it was thought that the group would be able to reach the Strait and sail out of the Gulf before the Iranians could decide to act and to organize an action against the ships.

At 11:00 P.M., USS *Kidd* peeled away and USS *Rentz*, a "gate-guard" at the Strait of Hormuz, joined the group to provide anti-aircraft missile coverage for the gun-heavy ships. At 3:00 A.M. on April 20th, the group entered the Silkworm envelope. They took formation with the *Rentz* in the lead. It had a bow-mounted anti-aircraft missile launcher. The *Hoel*, with its stern mounted launcher, took up the rear. Passing near Bandar Abbas, the ships could see no Iranian activity. The ships did not restrict their electronic emissions (radar, etc.) in an effort to make a covert passage, since it was assumed that they would be detected anyway. The *Hoel* did dim its lighting, which didn't seem to make much difference. One contact, claiming to be a Soviet ship, flashed the *Hoel* with a bright signal lamp, possibly silhouetting it for identification. The *Hoel* believed that the contact was actually an Iranian *Hengam*-class LST.

Concerned about mines during the outbound transit of the Strait, the *Hoel* had evacuated the forward end of the ship except for the gun mount. The ship was at general quarters and had damage control crewmen standing by with fire hoses, and dewatering gear near the ship's forward area. A large portion of USS *Ranger*'s air wing, including fighters and strike aircraft, launched from the carrier and flew up to the northern part of the Arabian Sea to provide air cover for the ships' transit of the Strait. The ships came streaming through at 22 knots. The Iranian "Scanarpa" target acquisition radar at Kuhestak radiated intermittently during the transit, but was jammed by an EA-6B Prowler electronic warfare aircraft flying off of USS *Ranger*. The battleship USS *Missouri* (BB 63) and the USS *Bunker Hill* came up to meet the ships as they exited the Strait without incident. The crews were tired and, no doubt, many breathed a deep sigh of relief.

The U.S. forces had certainly lived up the operation's code name by nimbly taking advantage of Iranian confusion and boarding the non-target northern platform. That platform actually appeared to be the center of Iranian military activity in the area, mounting as it did the Decca search radar, military communications facilities, and anti-aircraft guns. While there had certainly been Iranian military activity on the two targeted structures, at least up until Iraq's 1986 air strike, it is not clear that much, if any, military activity was taking place on them at the time the U.S. struck, making their selection a curious choice, even for a symbolic attack. In the event, the opportunistic boarding of the northern platform redeemed any mistake in the original target selection.

Reporters back in the U.S. criticized the seemingly large number of shells fired at the facilities. It was estimated that the 1,065 shells fired had cost between $200,000 and $1 million. At a news briefing held by Defense Department Spokesman Fred S. Hoffman immediately after the attack, reporters needled him about using a thousand rounds to hit a "stable target." In all fairness to the Navy ships, they were actually shooting at two self-supporting target structures, not one. They also destroyed the actual facilities very quickly. If there were any criticism to be made, it would be over the continued firing in an attempt to knock the platforms down by shooting at their legs. That idea had proved to be a mistake because the small diameter of the legs made them a poor target for naval gunfire.

Reaction to the U.S. attack was mixed. Many in the region saw an attack on a platform, considered something of a wreck after the Iraqi attack two years before, as an anticlimax to all the speculation about a major blow to be delivered against Iran. "It's more just for show, rather than actually doing any real harm," a Gulf shipping agent said. "It's purely symbolic." Nonetheless, there was a definite increase in tension in the region. A diplomat cautioned, "I suspect the Iranians will do something back." A Gulf tug owner also worried that the Iranians would strike: "I hope whatever happens, it isn't aimed at us."[12] Rates for war-risk insurance to some destinations in the Gulf doubled to 1.5 percent of the ship's value. Shippers took the increase philosophically. "It's business as usual—just more expensive business," one agent said.[13]

In Kuwait, the government issued a mild endorsement of the American bombardment, calling it "a calculated action against the continuing Iranian practices of putting hurdles in the way of navigation."[14] In fact, the Kuwaitis were disappointed with what they considered a relatively weak U.S. response to the Iranian attacks. Kuwaiti doubts about U.S. steadfastness had not been assuaged.

In the U.S., President Reagan downplayed the possibility of an escalating conflict with Iran. "We're not going to war with Iran," he said.
"They're not that stupid."[15] Congressional reaction was generally sup-
portive of the President. An overwhelming majority of Americans supported the attack. A *Washington Post*/ABC poll showed that 76 percent
of those interviewed approved of the action against the Rashadat platform. Any public and Congressional concerns over the Gulf were quickly pushed into the background when the stock market took a breath-
taking 500-point (25%) plunge on "Black Monday," October 20, 1987.
Financial shockwaves reverberated around the world.

The Iranian Silkworm attacks in October had been preceded by similar missile firings in January–February and in September. Iran appeared
to be firing the missiles at sporadic intervals, but in a pattern: clusters
of three with similar launch times. The January/February missiles had
all been launched in the evening. The September missiles had been
launched between 3:00 A.M. and 5:00 A.M. So far, the October pattern
featured an early morning launch time. The other aspect of the October
pattern was that these missiles, unlike the earlier ones, were doing serious damage to Kuwaiti targets. If the pattern held, one more missile was
due and the result was likely to be ugly. It was.

Kuwait's "Sea Island" export terminal is an artificial platform of
concrete and steel pipes located about 10 miles off the Al Ahmadi oil
port, to which it is connected by a system of underwater pipelines. It is
Kuwait's main facility for loading supertankers, which have too deep a
draft to go into Al Ahmadi. At the time, Sea Island was handling about
one-third of Kuwait's crude oil exports.

On the morning of October 22, less than 72 hours after the
American bombardment of the Rashadat platform, another Chinese-
made Silkworm missile streaked into Kuwaiti waters. No ships were in
the vicinity of Sea Island, which stood out as a strong radar target
against the water because of its 100-foot height. The Silkworm missile
homed in on the terminal and dived into it. The blast could be heard in
Kuwait City, more than 25 miles away. The explosion ignited crude oil
which had overflowed into "slop" tanks. The fires sent a 300-foot column of dense black smoke rising over the facility. Shrapnel from the
exploding missile warhead shredded the complicated network of pipes,
pumps, and valves used in loading operations. Three workers were
injured. Firefighting tugs were summoned from Shuaiba Port, but they
had trouble getting close to the blaze because of the dense smoke

whipped around the facility by the wind. They were finally able to pour enough sea water on the fire to extinguish it by early afternoon.

The control center for Sea Island operations had been destroyed. The facility had to be closed down for repairs, which were expected to last over a month. Kuwait would be able to maintain a reasonable level of crude oil exports by using alternative facilities, including a mooring buoy loading-point for large vessels. However, the attack on the Sea Island terminal posed a direct threat to Kuwait's capability to continue exporting petroleum.

Once again, Iran had managed to slip past the areas where a strong U.S. retaliatory response was clearly called for, and was able to land a solid blow against Kuwait. In its campaign to intimidate Kuwait and Saudi Arabia into ending their support for Iraq's war effort, and to indirectly pressure Iraq into ending its anti-shipping campaign, Iran had first struck at the tankers carrying Kuwaiti exports in the Gulf. Blocked there by U.S. intervention, Iran next struck at a re-flagged tanker in Kuwaiti waters, ostensibly outside the scope of U.S. protection. Blocked again by the prospect of U.S. retaliation, such as had just occurred at Rashadat, Iran appears to have carefully considered its targets and struck at Kuwait's tanker loading facilities. "Now Kuwait itself had become the target," said a Western diplomat in the Gulf. "It's exactly the reverse of the outcome the Kuwaitis wanted."[16]

It also presented the Reagan administration with a nice dilemma. To retaliate for the Sea Island attack would involve a substantial expansion of the U.S. commitment. Failure to do so would highlight the limited nature of the protection being offered by the U.S., and might cause the already jittery Gulf States to further question just how much they could count on the U.S. for support in the crunch. It seems clear that the threatened Gulf States viewed the American presence as rather more than a tanker escort operation.

"The Americans cannot say that they do not have to retaliate because the attack was not directed against them," said an Arab diplomat. "They are not here merely to protect a handful of Kuwaiti tankers." "To argue otherwise," said another Arab diplomat "would mean that the Iranians would have a free hand to hit at the heart of the Arabian oil industry in return for a U.S. pledge to protect the mere arteries."[17]

However, in the end, the U.S. chose not to retaliate for the Sea Island attack, but it did respond with defensive measures to buttress Kuwait. The day after the attack, Kuwaiti Improved-HAWK anti-air-

craft missiles were moved from the mainland to Failaka Island, directly
under the flight path of the Silkworms being launched from the Faw
Peninsula. In an unpublicized move, U.S. personnel manned an air
defense operations center to help coordinate Kuwaiti defenses.[18] The
Naval Research Lab was given the job of developing defenses against
future Silkworm attacks. Their efforts resulted in the deployment of
about 10 small Kuwaiti-funded barges equipped with metal grid radar
reflectors. These were designed to decoy the radar guided Silkworms
away from the ships and facilities which were their real targets.

The Silkworm was a "smart" weapon, but not too smart. A U.S.
Navy officer described the missile as "a weapon you launch along a line
of bearing and it will bump into the first iron object it finds."[19] Iran had
deployed somewhat similar barges at Kharg and at other locations to
decoy Iraqi Exocets. The fact that the U.S. had not retaliated for the
attack on Sea Island may have encouraged the Iranians to try again. The
Sea Island facility resumed partial operation in late November. The
Iranians must have been watching and waiting. Ten days later, on
December 7, they fired another Silkworm at it.

Roaring in at 7:53 A.M., the missile picked up the strong radar
return from a reflector barge moored about half a nautical mile southeast of the Sea Island terminal. The Kuwaitis had anchored eight of the
barges in the vicinity of the Sea Island mooring buoy and at a neighboring anchorage. The Silkworm homed in on a barge and slammed
into the three radar reflectors on it. The reflectors were too flimsy to
detonate the warhead, so the big missile sheared them off as it scoured
a path across the barge deck. The Silkworm even managed to fly on a
way before it plunged into the water and exploded.

Kuwaiti troops on Bubiyan Island had again tried to shoot down the
Iranian missile with an SA-7 Strella, and had again missed. The decoy
barges had worked well, but the improvements to Kuwait's active
defenses had failed dismally. For some reason, the radar for the
Improved Hawk anti-aircraft missile systems installed on Failaka Island
had not even picked up the Silkworm launch. A different radar, used for
the Kuwaitis' Tigercat anti-aircraft missile system, had also failed to
pick it up.

One U.S. response to the Iranian attacks was to continue to pressure
China to stop selling the Silkworms to Iran. Plans that would have made
it easier for China to purchase certain U.S. high-technology products
were shelved. China had repeatedly refused to acknowledge that it was

even selling weapons to Iran. Looking for more help, Kuwait secured Egyptian military assistance in a deal involving a $20 billion financial aid package. Egyptian military advisors and technicians were sent to Kuwait. Reportedly, Egyptian air force units were on short notice to be dispatched to Kuwait, if needed. Egyptian President Mubarak saw his country's support of the threatened Arab Gulf states as a means of getting accepted back into the Arab community. Egypt had been ostracized after signing its 1979 peace treaty with Israel. Debt-plagued Egypt could not afford any major new military commitment without Gulf money. Kuwait, with Saudi assistance, provided it.

Cash in hand, Egyptian President Mubarak had said of the Iranian attack on Sea Island: "We cannot accept or ignore this action. Egypt is ready to carry out its Arab duty to its brothers in Kuwait."[20]

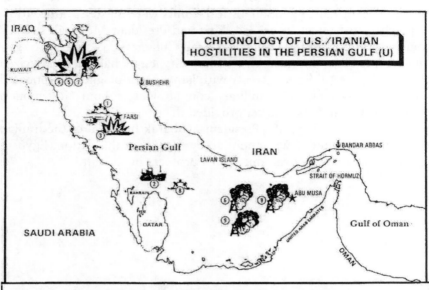

CHRONOLOGY OF U.S./IRANIAN HOSTILITIES IN THE PERSIAN GULF (U)

21 JUL 87	U.S. COMMENCES ESCORT OF REFLAGGED KUWAITI MERTANKERS.
24 JUL 87	SS BRIDGETON, REFLAGGED KUWAITI TANKER, HITS MINE NEAR FARSI ISLAND (1).
21 SEP 87	IRANIAN LSM IRAN AJR CAPTURED WHILE LAYING MINES NEAR BAHRAIN (2).
08 OCT 87	U.S. AH-6 SEABATS ENGAGE AND SINK SEVERAL BOGHAMMER WPB'S AND SMALL BOATS IN DEFENSE OF U.S. BARGES NEAR FARSI ISLAND (3).
15 OCT 87	IRANIAN SILKWORM LAUNCHED FROM AL FAW HITS PANAMANIAN FLAGGED, U.S. OWNED TANKER "SUNGARI" IN KUWAITI WATERS (4).
16 OCT 87	IRANIAN SILKWORM HITS U.S. FLAGGED TANKER SEA ISLE CITY IN KUWAITI WATERS (5).
19 OCT 87	U.S. DESTROYS RASHADAT OIL PLATFORM (6).
22 OCT 87	IRANIAN SILKWORM HITS KUWAIT'S SEA ISLE OIL TERMINAL (7).
14 APR 88	USS SAMUEL B. ROBERTS HITS IRANIAN MINE NEAR ROSTAM OIL FIELD (8).
18 APR 88	USN FORCES DESTROY SIRRI AND SASSAN OIL PLATFORMS (9). IRAN ATTACKS THE UAE'S MUBARAK OIL PLATFORM AND U.S. MERTUG. USN SHIPS AND PLANES SINK KAMAN PTG, SAAM FFG, ONE TO THREE BOGHAMMERS AND DAMAGE ANOTHER SAAM FFG. ONE U.S. SEA COBRA HELO IS LOST.

CHAPTER 12

"WE ARE THE BIG WINNERS IN THE GULF NOW"

Since the *Bridgeton* had struck the Iranian mine in July 1987, things were going much smoother for the re-flagged Kuwaiti tankers. Not a single ship under escort by the U.S. Navy or, for that matter, other Western navies, had been attacked by Iran through early 1988. The capture of the *Iran Ajr* seemed to have cooled Iranian enthusiasm for mining. In testimony before the House Appropriations subcommittee in February 1988, Central Command's General Crist said:

> I think when the *Stark* was hit they expected us to leave the Gulf. When *Bridgeton* got hit, it was not really a big thing, but it became a big thing to the United States. I don't think anyone in the Arab world thought we would stay the course. I think they wanted us to, but I don't think they were completely convinced we would do so. As a result, we are the big winners now in the Gulf.[1]

The U.S. did take the opportunity to revise its Gulf command structure, replacing Rear Admiral Dennis M. Brooks, Commander of the Joint Task Force Middle East (JTFME) and Rear Admiral Harold Bernsen, Commander of the Middle East Force (MEF), with one officer; Rear Admiral Anthony Less. He became JTFME commander with the "dual hat" collateral duty as Commander, Middle East Force. Admiral Bernsen had commanded Navy forces in the Gulf itself and reported to Admiral Brooks, who also commanded the battleship and aircraft carrier groups in the Arabian Sea, as well as non-Navy forces in the Gulf. The Joint Task Force Middle East had been established in September

1987 when the Gulf command had first been reorganized. Now, by replacing two commanders with one, a layer in the chain of command running to the Gulf had been removed. There were other reasons for the change. Joint Chiefs Chairman Admiral Crowe would later note what he felt was the excessive rigidity being imposed on the MEF's Gulf Operations by the JTFME:

> The carrier group admiral gave us a very hard time. He wanted strict schedules; he wanted to know six weeks ahead of time where every ship would be, where the convoys would meet, and how they would get to where they were going. Exactly the kind of predictability I did not want. In addition, he formulated a series of instructions to make sure the convoying ships did not get into trouble with the Iranians. If they behaved we would not bother them, but if they challenged us we were not going to back down.[2]

Admiral Brooks had his other critics. As one of them later put it, "It was hard to judge the motivation behind Brooks' actions. He seemed to have one compelling idea, and it didn't mater what the mission was: he was going to subject U.S. forces to as little danger as possible." In one example, the Kuwaitis had offered to fill a U.S. tanker once a month with 30,000 tons of bunker fuel, gratis. Admiral Brooks didn't want to take advantage of the Kuwaiti offer since he saw the ship going up to Kuwait as just another potential target for the Iranians.

Some thought that Brooks had a "blue water" mentality, and saw the Gulf mission as a bad deal for the Navy. Admiral Brooks had become extremely upset at the October 1987 battle with Iranian gunboats at Middle Shoals Buoy. His approach seemed to be that the U.S. should bend over backwards to avoid any such confrontations. His concerns apparently led to his foot dragging on the deployment of the second mobile sea base, the Wimbrown VII. It had finally taken a direct order from an exasperated Admiral Crowe to get the base deployed operationally.

Things appear to have come to a head in early 1988 when Admiral Crowe called Admiral Bernsen, the MEF Commander. The Chairman of the U.S. Joint Chiefs of Staff was not happy. He ticked off a list of items he had expected action on, but which remained undone. "Am I going to have to fire you?" he ominously asked Admiral Bernsen. "I have been directed not to do these things by Admiral Brooks," was Bernsen's reply. The Gulf was a long way from Washington D.C., but Admiral Bernsen could almost feel the heat and hear the crackle of flames coming through his telephone receiver. Two days later, an Admiral from the Joint Staff arrived in the Gulf. He visited with both Admiral Bernsen and Admiral Brooks before returning to Washington. Following his report, Admiral Crowe seems to have completely lost confidence in Admiral Brooks, and to have sacked him.

Admiral Brooks officially requested relief from his assignment, which was a face-saving gesture allowing him to cover his removal. Admiral Bernsen's normal tour as MEF commander would end on February 27, 1988. The new JTFME commander, Rear Admiral Anthony Less, would run his command from inside the Gulf itself, rather than hundreds of miles away in the Arabian Sea. The changeover took place on February 15 with the MEF and JTFME staffs consolidating aboard USS *LaSalle* in the Gulf.

The re-flagged ships under U.S. escort hadn't had to dodge any Silkworms yet. Neither had any other re-flagged tankers under U.S. escort. Still, the missiles were extremely worrisome to U.S. authorities. At one point, in January 1988, administration officials had seriously considered intercepting a shipment of Silkworm missiles bound for Iran. Contingency plans to intercept missiles in transit had been drawn up following the Silkworm attacks on Kuwait in October and December 1987.

That month, in North Korea, an Iranian merchant ship had taken on a load of Silkworms, including versions that could be launched from ships. The ship may also have loaded different and more advanced Chinese anti-ship missile types. It was making the long voyage to the Iranian port of Bandar Abbas while national security officials weighed their options. U.S. forces were stalking the ship, named the *Iran Bayan*. The frigate USS *John A. Moore* had been heading to the Gulf of Oman from Columbo, Sri Lanka when it was ordered by the Seventh Fleet to return to Columbo to take on fuel and then to maintain covert surveillance on the *Iran Bayan*. A P-3 Orion maritime patrol aircraft directed the *Moore* to a patrol area where, on January 2, its helicopter spotted the ship. The helicopter took photographs and videotaped the *Iran Bayan*. While officials in Washington debated a course of action, the Moore maintained contact on the missile-laden ship. Finally, the proposed interception was rejected as probably illegal and diplomatically unwise.

Saddam Hussein's Iraq continued its attacks on Iranian shuttle run tankers. In spite of the Iraqi attacks, Iran had managed to increase its export of crude through 1987. However, the extra costs to Iran of running the tanker shuttle and of importing refined products were estimated to be running at $420 million a year by 1988.[3] The Iranian shuttle run pretty much remained an Iraqi shooting gallery. One tanker making the run, the *Khark 4*, had been hit four times previously and would be hit a fifth time in 1988. The *Dena* was hit five times in less than a year. The *Fortuneship L* was hit three times in two days.[4]

The Iraqi air activity may have been damaging the Iranians, but it was also causing major headaches for U.S. forces. Iraqi jets were often flying in a pattern dubbed the "Farsi hook." They would hug the Saudi coast going down the Gulf, then, when they got abreast of the Mobile Sea Bases; they would cut across to the Iranian exclusion zone for their attacks. The Iraqis seemed to be using the U.S. bases as convenient navigational reference points and as safety buffers. The Iraqis must have figured that the Iranians would not come out after them in the vicinity of the sea bases, where they risked being engaged by U.S. forces.

On one occasion, the Hercules was moved five miles south in the middle of the night. The next day, Iraqi jets came down the Gulf on a mission to bomb Farsi Island. The Iraqis must have thought that the Mobile Sea Base was still in its previous position. Using it for their navigational checkpoint, they flew on and proceeded to bomb a small Saudi island by mistake. The Mobile Sea Bases were sometimes stationed close enough to Farsi Island that guards manning defensive posts could see the glow of fire and tracers rising into the sky during Iraqi air raids. Dogfights between Iraqi and Iranian jets could occasionally be glimpsed from the Hercules. Sometimes, with an Iraqi strike underway, Hercules crewmen would put out lawn chairs on deck so they could sit back and watch the show.

U.S. forces considered the northern Gulf to be "Indian country." However, as one officer, who commanded a warship that spent a fair amount of time there, observed:

> The old mindset of not putting a white missile (a real one) on the rail and not speaking harshly or forcefully on radio circuits for fear of "offending" either the Iranians or Iraqis still existed out there among some of the CO's. . . . This is exactly what got us into trouble with the USS *Stark*. . . . I never hesitated to load

up a white missile and have pre launch checks completed and the bird ready to fire at a moment's notice if I perceived a threat developing.

During de-conflictions with the Iraqi Air Force, we were very aggressive in directing them by radio to fly a directed course away from USN units. More than once I threatened to shoot someone out of the sky in very harsh tones if they didn't comply. Typically, the Iraqi fighters would mark on top of me and my TACAN to confirm my position while I was talking to them at altitudes between 100–200 feet and they would see my white missile on the launcher. That left an impression with them as well as their indicator light in the cockpit that told them they were being illuminated by my fire control radar. We illuminated them as soon as we established voice communications so they could identify us. There was no room for misunderstanding our intentions.[5]

De-confliction could be a demanding business. One ship's captain remembered that he slept in "khaki pajamas" while his ship had anti-air warfare coordination duty in the northern Gulf. At least some of the Destroyer Squadron commanders made a point out of only sending what they considered to be their sharpest ships under the best captains to the northern Gulf. Less highly thought of captains were mostly kept in the southern Gulf.

In 1987, USS *Kidd* had come within five seconds of firing its missiles at an oncoming aircraft. The *Kidd*'s CO, Daniel I. Murphy, and Destroyer Squadron 14 Commander, David Yonkers, had stood side by side in the *Kidd*'s darkened CIC as the decision was made to shoot down the Iraqi jet. The missiles were on their launch rails when, literally a few seconds before the warship fired, the Iraqi pilot turned away. Another commanding officer noted that de-confliction wasn't too difficult as long as the Iraqi pilots listened to his directions. Sometimes, however, they got stubborn. On one occasion, an Iraqi pilot would not turn away from the U.S. ship as requested. The captain mounted anti-aircraft missiles on the rails and locked his fire control radar on the Iraqi jet. It was daylight, and the Iraqi pilot nervously asked if those were missiles mounted on the launcher. Told they were, he asked that he not be locked on by the ship's radar. The captain told him he would always lock on when his directions were ignored. The Iraqi pilot turned away.

Some U.S. officers thought that many of the Iraqi pilots were not well-trained and were scared stiff at the prospect of being shot down by Iranian interceptors or air defenses. The possibility of being shot down by U.S. warships only added to their fears. To some, the Iraqis seemed to want to get down the Gulf flying as low and as fast as possible, swing around, dump their missiles at the first target they saw, without the faintest idea of its identity, and run for home. However, the Iraqi pilots were clearly under pressure from their government to avoid incidents with U.S. forces, and appeared to be genuinely trying to do so. When contacted by a U.S. ship for de-confliction, the Iraqi pilots would sometimes respond in broken English, "Help me. I don't want to hit your ships." Following warnings by U.S. warships, Iraqi pilots could sometimes be heard nervously stammering on the radio and would usually react quickly, but not always.

On February 11, Earnest Will convoy 88013 headed north toward Kuwait. It consisted of four re-flagged tankers escorted by two U.S. destroyers: USS *Chandler* and USS *Reuben James*. As the convoy proceeded north on the night of February 12, the *Chandler* detected an Iraqi TU-16 "Badger" bomber flying an attack profile and headed toward the convoy. The Badger was armed with two Chinese-made C-601 missiles, which were air-launched versions of the Silkworm. The *Chandler*'s commanding officer, Commander Steve Smith, called his crew to general quarters. The *Chandler* attempted to alert the Iraqi pilot by radio, but he did not seem to understand English—the international language of aviation. The problem may actually have been the poor-quality Chinese radios that equipped the Badgers. While the radios on the French-made Mirages had good sound quality, voice transmissions from the Chinese-made Badgers was frequently unintelligible.

When the radio attempt to divert the inbound Iraqi bomber failed, the *Chandler* fired two illumination rounds (flares suspended from parachutes) from its 5-inch guns to warn off the aircraft. Less than a minute later, the Iraqi plane changed course, banking away from the convoy. However, it then proceeded to launch its two Silkworm missiles. What the Iraqi pilot was aiming at was not clear since the *Chandler*'s radar showed no potential shipping targets in the area where the missiles seemed to have been aimed.

The *Chandler* stood ready to try to shoot down the missiles as one disappeared over the horizon toward Sirri Island. The missile either hit the island and exploded or flew into the water nearby. The other

Silkworm appeared to be passing well astern of the convoy when it made an abrupt turn and streaked down the *Chandler*'s side at a distance of several miles and exploded. Commander Smith was clearly upset by the close call and urged a Pentagon investigation of the incident. He contrasted the Iranians, who seemed to be fairly careful as to the ships they targeted, with the Iraqis, who, he said, "Come down and they shoot at radar blips."[6]

General George Crist, commander of Central Command, was livid about the indiscriminate Iraqi targeting procedures. General Crist sent a strongly worded message to Baghdad, telling the Iraqis to "knock off," in the words of a military official, their dangerous actions in the Gulf.[7] The Chief of Staff of the Middle East Force met with an Iraqi delegation in the United Arab Emirates. A four-man team flew to Baghdad. The frustrated Americans re-emphasized warning procedures and reminded the Iraqis that U.S. ship commanders had the authority to shoot down Iraqi aircraft approaching U.S. ships. Senior Navy officials made it clear that in the cases of the *Chandler* and the *James*, the ships' captains would have been "perfectly within their rights" to shoot down the offending Iraqi planes.[8] The Iraqis were informed that Washington would back up naval commanders if they had to fire on Iraqi aircraft. The Iraqis took the U.S. warnings seriously enough to suspend air strikes on shipping targets in the Gulf for a time.

U.S. officers working on de-confliction with the Iraqis in Baghdad found themselves hosted in the best hotels. One Air Force officer recalled, "We were afforded preferential, often deferential treatment. We were chauffeured everywhere in Mercedes sedans—traffic was halted by police officers to give us the right-of-way—and we dined at the best restaurants."[9] The Iraqis were sometimes described as "quasi-allies." U.S. officers who worked with them on the de-confliction problem, however, had few illusions about who they were dealing with. A Navy Commander, who was the Air Operations Officer for the JTFME and who had been to Iraq several times, recounted that:

> We talked to Iraqi Air Force individuals—yes—but there is always their "section six" people that are always there—and they escort us around and make sure that we are taken care of. . . . Their M6 people basically are their intelligence folks. . . . Every time I've ever been there- we've been met and greeted by a certain general who speaks excellent English, French, you

name it—and he is always our escort—he is always with us. His room is right across the room from ours in the hotel, etc. So we do face-to-face discussions-what the problems are—how we can iron them out. . . . They're extremely friendly to us and they take great care of us—but my personal view is that they are still a bunch of thugs. They really are. They're going to get whatever they can get and whatever they have to do. It's by no means democratic; it's an autocratic situation up there. The pilots are good—the military people are good. They've got a lot of experts. Again, they're very smiling—very forward- up front—but I do not trust them.[10]

While the level of confrontation with the Iranians had scaled way back, there were still incidents. On February 3, an inexperienced watch officer on the Hercules looked at the base's search radar display and saw multiple contacts inbound. Shouting, "Emergency! They're coming in!" he sounded the alarm and scrambled TF-160 helicopters aloft to intercept the Iranian boats. The frigate serving as guard ship for the sea bases couldn't see anything on its much superior search radar, but, because the Hercules was closer to the presumed threat, it didn't interfere. The Hercules, using its Furano surface search radar, tried to vector the TF-160 helicopters toward the contacts. Those contacts were actually false radar returns, or "ghosts."

The Hercules also managed to lose the precise location of the helicopters it had launched. By the time it was all sorted out, the helicopters had flown over Iranian waters, barely five miles from Farsi Island. Chasing ghosts, the SEABAT team was confused as to exactly who was vectoring them: the Hercules, the frigate, or it's aloft LAMPS helicopter. They returned to the Mobile Sea Base without incident. A few days later, U.S. intelligence revealed that the Iranians had been tracking the helicopters on radar and had prepared an anti-aircraft ambush for them if they had continued deeper into Iranian territory.

Less than a month later, there was another helicopter incident. USS *Simpson*, under the command of Captain James McTigue, was carrying a TF-160 SEABAT team of one MH-6 and one AH-6. The *Simpson* was entering the Gulf through the Strait on the night of March 5/6 and had launched the "Little Birds" and its own LAMPS helicopter on a surveillance mission. The launch of those aircraft was complicated because media pool reporters were onboard the *Simpson*. The ship had to hide the presence of the SEABAT team from the reporters, so they were invited to watch the nighttime launch of the ship's LAMPS helicopter. After the reporters left the flight deck, unknown to them, the Little Birds were now quietly rolled out and launched.

As the SEABATS patrolled ahead of the *Simpson*, they called the LAMPS Seahawk and reported that, while all the other oil platforms in the area were brightly lit, one particular platform was completely dark. The Army helos said they'd check it out on the way back from their patrol. The SEABATS turned back after about a half-hour and flew close toward the darkened platform, and smack into an Iranian ambush. On the platform, at least two twin 23mn ZSU 23-2 anti-aircraft cannon opened up on the little birds. Two Iranian boats were also blacked out and anchored in the area.

They opened up with heavy machine guns, catching the helicopters in a deadly crossfire. The Iranian craft were not the small speedboats but rather larger tugboat or supply vessel size. Sheets of anti-aircraft fire poured toward the Army helicopters, which began wildly jinking to avoid the fire. The TF-160 pilots gave no thought to returning fire but only frantically tried to escape the kill-zone as dozens of bright tracers flashed close past their cockpits, nearly blinding them. The two copters made it out unscathed and were darned lucky to have done so. It was later estimated that the Iranians had fired over 1,000 rounds in a span of less than three minutes. Three of the four warrant officer pilots had flown in Vietnam and none of them had ever encountered the kind of intense ground fire they experienced that night in the Gulf. They were amazed that they came out whole. Neither copter had a scratch.

The Iranians were probably equipped with night vision goggles and had spotted the SEABAT team on its outbound run, allowing them to set up the ambush on the return flight. Iran claimed that "warning shots" had been fired at the U.S. helicopters after they ignored radioed warnings that they were approaching an Iranian zone. The Iranians claimed anti-aircraft fire from their naval forces had forced the U.S. helicopters to flee.[11]

Captain McTigue did inform the media pool about the shooting, but finessed the awkward situation by saying only that a helicopter flying from the ship had been fired on. He didn't say which one. Most of the reporters assumed it was the only helicopter they knew about: the LAMPS Seahawk, although some may have suspected the presence of the Little Birds. McTigue had timed his announcement to coincide with the arrival of a "Desert Duck" helicopter scheduled to pick up the pool representatives. No sooner had he made his statement than a crewman came in and announced that the helicopter was there. The reporters were on their way before any awkward follow-up questions could be asked. The incident showed that, while the Gulf hadn't exploded into the feared major confrontation with Iran, there was still plenty of potential for lower-level military action.

With those possibilities in mind, the Mobile Sea Bases were upgraded in 1988 with vertical barriers against small arms fire, overhead cover from indirect fire, and a stand-off protection against the rocket-propelled grenades commonly fired from Iranian speedboats. For their part, the Iranians tried to keep an eye on the Mobile Sea Bases. A Navy Special Warfare Task Unit officer noted, "We're constantly aware of small boats up in the shipping lanes that are suspicious in nature, that hide behind larger ships. As they come close, they have antennas and other equipment on board that normally wouldn't be on board an average fishing vessel or a vessel of whatever type."[12]

Periodically, unidentified helicopters, possibly out of the oil fields, would fly close to the bases and suddenly go back. A Mobile Sea Base commander said, "I see signal deception taking place. I see what I think is intelligence collection taking place, with unusual units."[13] The Iranians operated one special dhow out of Farsi that was almost certainly used for intelligence gathering purposes. The Iranian craft was equipped with extremely powerful engines. On several occasions, U.S. patrol boats tried to intercept it in order to take photographs, but the speedy craft was always able to outrun them.

The 10 AH/MH-6 helicopters of Army Task Force 160, mostly stationed on the Mobile Sea Bases, were starting to be replaced with a similar number of modified AH-58D Kiowa helicopters, which equipped a unit known as TF-118. The Little Birds had been ideal for the nighttime armed surveillance role in the gulf and had chalked up notable successes such as the Iran Ajr capture and the battle at Middle Shoals Buoy. However, it was not considered desirable to tie down some of the limited number of U.S. Special Forces helicopter elements to an open-ended commitment in the Gulf.

The Army had looked at the AH-64 Apache as a potential replacement for the AH/MH-6's, but decided that it was too big to operate from ships. Accordingly, the Joint Chiefs of Staff directed the Army to replace TF-160 with OH-58D's modified for the Gulf role. The OH-

58D's were deployed to the Gulf under what was dubbed Operation "Prime Chance II." The first helicopters were modified and delivered by Bell Helicopter in November 1987, less than 100 days after getting the go-ahead to proceed. A total of 15 aircraft were modified, and the last one was delivered in April 1988.[14]

The AH-58D Kiowa scout helicopters had originally been modified under the Army Helicopter Improvement Program (AHIP) with the addition of a ball-shaped targeting system mounted above the mast, and with the associated cockpit control systems. The targeting system, which one Mobile Sea Base commander called the "million dollar beach ball," included a 12-power TV camera, a thermal imaging sensor, a laser range-finder, and designator. As one TF-118 member put it, "The sight was very critical for us because this whole bird is all about the sight." The AH-58D combined the FLIR surveillance capability of the MH-6 with armament that exceeded that of the AH-6 gunship. The AH-58D could carry Hellfire laser-guided heavy antitank missiles, Stinger anti-aircraft missiles, and unguided 2.75-inch rockets. It could also be equipped with a .50 caliber machine gun and 500 rounds of ammunition. Given that expected opposition in the Gulf was from fairly small-sized Iranian speedboats, the normal load was a seven-round Hydra-70 rocket pod on the right with a .50 caliber machine gun pod on the left.

Although the unit was originally classified, the members of TF-118 were not formally considered to be "special forces." Given the caliber of their pilots, their equipment, and the fact that they took on a mission performed by the 160th, TF-118 might have qualified by some definitions. As a TF-118 member put it: "Basically we are a non-special ops unit that operates totally special ops missions profile, which makes for a pretty screwed up lifestyle, pretty screwed up situation. Nobody else in the Army does what we do except 160th, which are a special ops unit. So we have been told we are a unique unit, but we are not a special unit, which leads to all kinds of confusion. We're told we're not classified, yet we are classified, yet we can't talk about it. It's really confusing. We don't know what we are. All we know is we're not special, but we're doing a special mission."[15] One naval officer who worked with both units thought that the TF-160 pilots did have more of a "can do" attitude than the regular Army pilots of TF-118.

Not surprisingly, there were different opinions on the merits of the two helicopter types. A TF-160 pilot found the AH-58D Kiowas did not measure up to their Little Birds: "I flew with the AHIPs. I helped them do their initial testing. . . . Our aircraft [MH/AH-6] is smaller. It is lighter. It is actually more powerful. I think their FLIR system, now that they have improved it, is better than ours. The 58-type aircraft rotor is better. But capability-wise, I would take ours any day."[16]

On the other hand, a commander of the Wimbrown VII would recall, "Our barge had TF-118's AH-58 Warrior helos, the tiny gunships with the mast-mounted sight. They were wonderful birds, with superb pilots, and they didn't get the credit they deserved from the guys on the Hercules, who had helicopters and crews from Task Force 160 Night Stalkers. There was a lot of contention back and forth about just who had the best helicopter operation, but the AH-58s seemed to fly a lot of times when the AH-6s and MH-6s from TF-160 wouldn't fly."[17]

The Iranians sometimes harassed the Mobile Sea Bases by sending out radio messages indicating that the bases were going to be attacked. When intercepted, the messages could put the bases on alert. Occasionally, things got dicier. Shortly after midnight on March 5, the guided missile frigate *John A. Moore* detected radar blips, thought to be two high-speed boats, making a run at Mobile Sea Base Wimbrown VII. The *Moore* fired a warning shot off its port bow with its 76mm cannon, but then went to firing rapidly and in earnest, engaging one contact then the other. The *Moore* reported it heard firing in the distance to port, with one of the contacts approaching as close as six miles before it began pulling away. The *Moore* pumped out nearly 100 76mm cannon rounds at the contacts in a little over twenty minutes. It was an extremely dark night with fog and dust making visibility poor, and there never was any visual contact. Apparently the Iranian boats withdrew. It was unknown if any were hit.

Such incidents helped U.S. forces stay on the alert. Electronic and visual surveillance, along with cryptography, painted a pretty clear picture of ongoing Gulf activity. The Iranians had not tried any new mining since the *Iran Ajr* capture, but were still being closely watched. "Nothing Iranian can move on the Gulf without us knowing about it,"[18] a U.S. official said in late February. He would shortly be proved wrong.

Barge crewmen load a Mark III Patrol Boat into the water from the Mobile Sea Base Hercules. (Courtesy of USSOCOM)

TF-160 pilots aboard MSB Wimbrown VII with passing tanker in background. (Author's collecton)

Two AH-6 "Little Birds" of Army 160th SOAR attack a remote control target boat in practice for their deployment to the Gulf. (Author's collection)

Another shot of a practice run against small vessels. Once deployed to the Gulf, TF-160 pilots only flew at night in order to reduce their vulnerability. (Author's collection)

A glum JCS Chairman Admiral William J. Crowe with Defense Secretary
Frank J. Carlucci at a news conference following USS *Vincennes'*
shoot down of Iran Air Flight 655 on July 3, 1988.
(8/19/88. JOSN Oscar Sosa)

Dusk picture of US frigate guard ship near MSB Wimbrown VII.
(Author's collection)

CHAPTER 13

"NO HIGHER HONOR"

The two Iranian warships were trying to "scissor" USS *Samuel Roberts*. The navy frigate had been escorting a seven-ship Earnest Will convoy when the Iranian warships appeared. Now, they were charging at the *Roberts* from different directions. One of the Iranian ships was a modern *Saam*-class frigate; the other was an older U.S.-built *Sumner*-class destroyer. Commander Paul X. Rinn, the *Roberts'* CO, ordered general quarters sounded. One of the closing Iranian warships now locked its fire-control radar onto the *Roberts*. At best, the Iranians were playing a dangerous harassment game. Maybe it was worse than that. Commander Rinn didn't know. One thing he did know was that he wasn't going to passively sit there and cede the initiative to the Iranians. He had a missile mounted on the frigate's launcher. He ordered flank speed and began to maneuver his ship for a possible fight.

Rinn radioed to the Iranian warships and gave them an ultimatum: they had five minutes to back off or he would engage them. As the clock wound down, Rinn ordered more missiles warmed up for use. His first priority was his most dangerous potential opponent: the *Saam*-class frigate. Rinn planned to pump four missiles into it, and then quickly turn to the older destroyer and put four missiles into it as well.

The Iranians came up on the radio and protested that they were in international waters. The Iranian protests cut no ice with Commander Rinn. The Iranian warships were hardly sailing by peaceably in the international sea lanes. What they were doing was engaging in highly threatening behavior toward his ship. He simply ignored the protests and repeated his warning. The seconds ticked by until finally, in the high seas, high stakes game of "chicken," the Iranians backed down. With one minute to go, the two warships turned away and left the area.

The *Roberts* had deployed to the Gulf in February 1988, under Commander Paul X. Rinn, 40. The Bronx-born Rinn had joined the Navy in 1968 and had served on the "gun line," giving fire support off of Vietnam. He later returned to Southeast Asia as an in-country advisor in Laos and Cambodia. He was involved in activities at the time that he still cannot talk about. In 1984, the Bronx-born Rinn had traveled several hundred miles by car to the Bath Iron works in Bath, Maine, to watch the *Roberts'* keel being laid. "It was," he said, "a very emotional experience, not unlike having a child."[1] Rising rapidly through the ranks, he became the youngest ship commander in the Navy at the time he took over the *Roberts'* pre-commissioning unit.

Under the publicly announced rules of engagement in effect at the time, U.S. ships like the *Roberts* were not allowed to protect non-U.S. flag vessels from attack. They were allowed to render humanitarian assistance, but only after the attacker had finished with his victim. Despite the public U. S. position, senior officers in the Gulf were encouraging at least some ship captains to try to break up Iranian attacks on neutral shipping when they thought they could do so without excessive risk. Captains were told to use their own judgment but not to start a war. The CO's of U.S. warships were obviously left a lot of discretion in just how far they could go in trying to disrupt Iranian attacks on neutral shipping. In command of the *Samuel Roberts*, Paul Rinn was prepared to go a ways.

On several occasions the *Samuel Roberts* had intervened and aggressively broken up Iranian attacks on neutral ships. Once, the *Roberts* had closed on an Iranian frigate at 31 knots, steaming past within an intimidating 50 yards of the Iranian warship. The *Roberts* had threateningly mounted a guided missile on its launcher. The two warships then got into a kind of swirling dogfight as they circled one another. The Iranian frigate ultimately gave up and left the area.

One way the *Roberts* crew kept up morale during their Gulf tour was by making a "Persian Excursion" videotape to send to families back home. Set to music, including some from the movie "Top Gun," the tape featured shots of the crewmen going about their tasks along with a one-minute interview with each sailor. Another morale booster was a hilariously non-professional nightly news show broadcast over the ship's closed circuit TV system. The featured announcer was Senior Chief Petty Officer Earl "Silver Tongue" Crosby, whose on-air wardrobe included a T-shirt with the words "These Colors Don't Run" on the back, and a "Jack Daniels Lynchburg Lemonade" hat. "The crew likes to see the mistakes we make," observed Crosby. "I get tongue-tied, they slap me on the back—spontaneous—that's the way we like it."[2]

The afternoon of Thursday, April 14 found the *Roberts* was steaming toward the southern Gulf. The frigate had completed a mission escorting the 46,732-ton, re-flagged liquid gas carrier *Gas Queen*, formerly the *Gas Kuwait*, through the Gulf up to Kuwait. For the *Roberts*, it had been its ninth Earnest Will convoy, and it's sixth as convoy commander. The *Roberts* was headed for a rendezvous with the combat stores ship USS *San Jose* and a scheduled replenishment. After it was re-supplied, the *Roberts* would head back north for further operations.

The ship was transiting a busy shipping lane in the central Gulf, about 55 miles northeast of Qatar, when the bow lookout spotted three objects in the water, about half a mile off the starboard bow. The three objects looked to him like dolphins, a common enough sight in the Gulf. However, as the lookout continued to observe them, he noticed that these "dolphins" were not bobbing in and out of the water. Suspicious, the lookout picked up his binoculars and focused them in. Rounded floating objects with projecting spikes appeared in his view. He immediately rang the bridge.

Commander Rinn was in his cabin with the chief cook, discussing plans for a special meal to celebrate the halfway point of the *Roberts'* cruise. Another subject of discussion was spinach, which, in Commander Rinn's considered opinion, was making all-too-frequent appearances on the ship's monthly menu. The officer of the deck, Lieutenant Robert Firehammer, called Commander Rinn and began to tell him about the suspicious objects which had been sighted. He continued to describe the objects but he was already speaking to a dangling phone. Commander Rinn had dropped the receiver at his end and was hurrying to the bridge. Rinn figured it was probably the usual floating junk, but when he looked at the three objects through his binoculars, he thought, "Damn, those look just like mines."[3] He ordered the ship to full stop. Rather than sound General Quarters, he got on the loudspeaker and announced to the crew that they were now in a minefield. He then verbally ordered the men to go to their stations. If the ship hit a mine, the blast would be at or below the waterline. As a precaution, he ordered the men in the lower levels to get out of those spaces and move up to their damage control stations on deck.

Rinn then radioed Admiral Anthony A. Less, the Joint Task Force Middle East commander, and told him what he was facing. Admiral Less directed Rinn to send his helicopter aloft to mark the mines with smoke floats. He was also told to try to keep the ship at least 300 meters away from them. Good advice, but the *Roberts* was already closer than that to the mines. The best chance for the frigate to get out unharmed from the minefield it had sailed into was to reverse its propeller and back down its own wake, That way; it would be following the path it had "cleared" by sailing to its current position. To try to hold a straight path as it reversed course, the *Roberts* lowered two pods from the forward hull. These contained auxiliary electrical propulsion systems. Running one of those would help stabilize the ship by counteracting a tendency to swing that was induced by the reversed main propeller.

As the *Roberts'* helicopter prepared to go aloft, the 453-foot long ship began gingerly backing away from the mines at minimum speed. The ship had been backing up for about ten minutes when its luck ran out. At about 5:00 P.M., the *Roberts'* hull swiped one of the horns projecting from an Iranian mine floating invisibly below the surface. Two hundred and fifty pounds of TNT detonated within a few feet of the frigate's underside.

The underwater explosion generated a powerful "bubble" of expanding gas which punched a gaping 20-foot hole in the port side aft hull of the *Roberts*, venting most its explosive force inside the ship. The blast violently jerked the stern of the ship upward some 10 to 15 feet. Most of the crew were slammed to the deck or thrown against overheads and bulkheads. The ship's two LM-2500 gas turbine main engines were knocked off of their mounts. Some heavy engine room equipment went flying up into the overhead like projectiles. The mine had detonated directly under the port engine, which had been running at the time.

Two 10,000-gallon fuel tanks and the main reduction gear oil sump were ruptured. Fuel spewed up into the hot turbine engine, where it ignited and exploded. A fireball roared up the main exhaust stack and shot 150 feet into the air. Flaming debris rained back down onto the ship. Seawater gushed into the main engineering room through the hole punched in the hull. The surging seawater ruptured a bulkhead and poured into an auxiliary engineering space located aft. The onrush of water quickly flooded both rooms to within a foot of their upper level deck plates. Fuel-fed fires flashed through the main engine room, and it began to fill with choking smoke. The ship's lights flickered and died.

EW2 Fernando Cruz was topside when the mine exploded. "My initial reaction was shock—none of us could believe what we were seeing. There was flaming lagging and debris everywhere. I thought the helo might have blown up. We took cover under the SLQ-32 antenna and, as soon as the debris had all come down, I shouted, 'Let's go!' then hit the deck and started hauling hose down to the stack area where the flames were."[4] Crewmen on deck started stamping out small fires caused by the burning debris, which had fallen back on the ship.

Commander Rinn was on the bridge, some 100 feet forward of the location of the mine explosion. Still, the shock transmitted through the ship slammed his foot hard into some unyielding structure. He exclaimed, "Oh Jesus, that hurts!" He would later find out that he had actually broken his left foot. On the fantail, Boatswain's Mate Kim Sandle was preparing to launch the ship's helicopter. Chocks and chains were removed and the copter's rotor blades were spinning when the mine blew. The helicopter was locked into the trap on the pad, so it was carried violently up and down with it when the blast shook the ship. The helicopter's spinning blades flapped wildly up and then down to within 4 or 5 feet of the flight deck. Sandle was hurled into the air towards the whirling blades. If he fell into them, he would be instantly sliced to pieces. Horrified, he sailed in the air towards the spinning blades . . . and landed a couple of feet shy of them. He fell to the deck stunned and bruised—but still in one piece. He said a short prayer of thanks.[5]

Working in the main engine room, Chief Technician Alex Perez, 38, had heard the announcement over the PA system that the *Roberts* was now in a minefield. He had dispatched some men to their damage control stations. The engine room was low in the ship. Perez knew it was extremely vulnerable to a mine strike. Taking no chances, he ordered all of the remaining men to climb to an upper level deck within the room. It was a lifesaving move, The mine explosion, followed by flooding and fire, almost certainly would have claimed the lives of many of the men if they had stayed in the lower level of the room. Perez had made it to the upper level himself, but it wasn't good enough. The mine explosion violently whipped the ship and threw Perez down into the water that gushed into the lower level of the engine room.[6] He hit his head and badly injured his neck in the fall. He later recalled that, "It happened so quickly. . . . I thought I was lost. It was all dark and all I could see was the fire from the burning engine. I was in water . . . I thought I was going to drown."[7]

Fortunately, he didn't, but he was now trapped under the upper level deck grating with only about a foot of clearance for his head between the surface of the water and the deck above. Shipmates, standing right above his head on the grating, worked feverishly to get a section loose so Perez could climb up and out of the water. However, they couldn't loosen any of the segments. There was an opening in the grating some twenty feet away. For Perez to reach it, he would have to swim for it. One of the men turned on a battle lantern and held it underwater to guide Perez to the opening. Perez looked at the black water, which was covered with fuel oil, took a deep breath, and dove under it to reach the light, he had to swim through an obstacle course of submerged, mangled equipment. He made it to the light and surfaced in the open area.[8] He was finally able to climb out of the flooded lower level and onto the upper deck. Perez was evacuated to the triage area, a makeshift battle dressing station set up on the signal bridge. He was later found to have suffered three fractured lumbar vertebrae when he had been hurled from the upper deck level by the mine blast.

The auxiliary engineering room immediately aft of the main room was manned when the mine exploded. Engineman 1st Class Mark Dejno was standing in the middle of the upper level of the room when the mine blast and fuel explosion hurled a rippling wall of flame at him, badly burning his face and one arm. Dejno climbed up an escape "trunk" or vertical passageway as the onrushing water flooded the lower level. Once out, on deck, Dejno dressed his burned arm. He then looked around and saw a friend, Gas Systems Technician Larry Welch, who was burned far worse than he. Welch had charred skin hanging in flaps from his badly burned arms and hands. Dejno tried cutting away Welch's clothes with a knife but couldn't cut through the soaked cloth. He got some scissors from a first aid kit and was finally able to cut away the clothes. He also used the scissors to cut off the dangling skin. Dejno wiped the fuel oil staining Welch's face, wrapped him in a clean white sheet, and headed him to the triage area.[9]

The *Samuel Roberts'* electrical power had faltered when the mine exploded, with the lights dimming and then coming back on. The shock of the explosion had stopped a generator in auxiliary machine room one (AMR1), located forward in the ship. That space should have been evacuated completely when Commander Rinn had given the order, but one young sailor was still in it. Fireman Mike Tilley had figured that he might be needed there, so he had deliberately stayed behind. When the mine exploded, the blast had wrecked the ladder that was his only exit from the compartment. Tilley was now trapped.

Since joining the ship's company Tilley's behavior had constantly been landing him in trouble. It was never anything major, but there had been a series of lesser infractions, such as using a fake ID card to buy beer. On one occasion, local police had nabbed Tilley during a liberty call in Nassau. The patrons at a nice open-air restaurant there had found that their dining experience was not enhanced by their view of a drunken seaman Tilley blissfully relieving himself in some nearby bushes. These antics had garnered him two appearances before non-judicial Captain's Masts. Some Senior Chiefs were so unhappy with him that they wanted him kicked out of the Navy. The Chiefs thought the young sailor was unsalvageable. Rinn disagreed. Nevertheless, he had told Tilley that, one more incident, and he was out. The young sailor did seem irrepressible. While working a watch rotation in the fully enclosed engineering spaces, he did not get to see much daylight. Unhappy with his dim, gray environment, he had put a cheeky proposal in the ship's suggestion box for the Captain: "Can we add some portholes down here?"

Tilley was now trapped "down here." With part of its generating capacity offline, the ship's electrical output was marginal. Lights were flickering and the fire mains were inoperative. The main engines were in a flooded compartment topped with burning fuel. The auxiliary propulsion units were electrically powered and were the only way the *Roberts* could move under its own power and escape the mined area.

There was a way to get the diesel generator restarted, but it was a dangerous way. It would require him to use a long screwdriver to hand crank the engine. The problem was, the restarted engine would quickly spool up to thousands of revolutions per second. It might just rip his arm off if he didn't get it away in time. This restart method was appropriately known as a "suicide start." Tilley was determined to give it a try. He mounted the engine, like a cowboy astride a horse, inserted the screwdriver, and cranked the engine. It started and Tilley instantly jumped away with his screwdriver . . . and his arm. With the additional power on line, the ship's lights steadied.

Commander Rinn was in radio contact with Admiral Less. Rinn summarized the ship's condition and his general situation. It looked pretty bad to both men. "Considering your situation," asked Admiral Less, "What do you think about remaining with the ship?" The Admiral was holding the door open for Commander Rinn to say he thought his crew should abandon ship. "I haven't thought about it at all," replied Rinn. "I have no desire to leave the ship. We'll stay with the ship and fight it. Right now, I think we can win this thing. We have no other choice." A little less positively, he added, "In a nutshell, we're in trouble." Admiral Less asked, "Do you have anything else to pass?" "Roger," Rinn responded, "No higher honor." He had signed off, as he usually did, with the *Samuel Roberts*' motto.

The water pouring through the hole in the *Roberts*' hull had immediately flooded some compartments and was threatening others. The battle to stop the flooding centered on the number two auxiliary machine room (AMR2), located forward and adjacent to the flooded main engine room. The number three auxiliary machine room (AMR3), located immediately aft of the main engine room had already flooded. It was absolutely critical to keep AMR2 from flooding. Located there were two more of the diesel generators powering the ship's electrical system. Commander Rinn thought that the efforts to keep the ship afloat would be hopeless if the engineering space was submerged and lost. AMR2 was separated from the flooded main engine room by a bulkhead that had been buckled forward and weakened by the mine explosion. The bulkhead had sprung leaks, and water was steadily rising in the room. The physical integrity of the bulkhead had to be maintained to hold back the water pressing against it from the adjacent flooded engine room.

About an hour and a half after the blast, Commander Rinn made his way through the ship to take a firsthand look at the damage and repair efforts in AMR2. A bizarre scene met him. As he entered the lower level of the space, three men, two of whom had been put on a special program to lose weight, ran past him wearing only their underwear. Rinn's astonished reaction was "What the hell is this?" There was a good explanation.

It turned out that the men had been taking off items of clothing and using them to stuff into leaks. The bulkhead in AMR2 had four sizeable holes in it, and the seam in the middle was splitting. Rinn inspected the weakened bulkhead and then addressed the men. He gave it to them straight: "This is not a very good situation, but the situation is this: We must save the space or the ship is lost. If you don't save the bulkhead and we lose this space, this ship will go quickly and you will not get out of here alive."

Chief Kevin Ford, the repair team leader, responded, "It's no big deal, Captain. We can hold the bulkhead and save the space."[10] Actually, as both men recognized, the bulkhead could collapse in an instant, drowning Chief Ford and his crew. The men were equally determined and confident that they could prevail. One told Rinn, "We can win this one, Captain." Another sailor seconded the first, "We can do it." A third sailor said: "Don't worry, Captain, we got this one in hand. In fact, this is nothing; you should see the next space."

Commander Rinn had two attractive teenage daughters and had taken some ribbing from the men. They had warned him that, one night, he would come home and find them parked with guys in the driveway. A tape with romantic songs by the group Journey would be playing in the background. As Rinn was leaving the area, one of the sailors pulled out a boom box and put in a Journey tape. With the earlier ribbing in mind, Rinn stopped and joked with the sailor. He told him, "I don't appreciate your taste in music." The battle to save AMR2 continued in earnest.

The men in AMR2 used steel and wood shoring or supports to strengthen the threatened bulkhead. They wedged blankets, pillows, and, even their clothing into leaks to plug them. Water in the room rose to a depth of several feet, knee-high. It got within a foot of the main diesels needed to power the ship's auxiliary propulsion system, but no higher. The men managed to stop it at that point. The desperately needed diesels and generators never shut down. After winning their battle with the flooding in AMR2, the men reported to Commander Rinn: "We're done with that job, Captain, where do you want us to go now?"[11] There was still plenty to do.

The fuel-fed fires, which had ignited in the main engine area, were blazing above the flooded lower level and spreading upward. There was a Halon-gas fire extinguishing system in the main engine room. However, its power supply had been knocked out by the blast, so it hadn't automatically released its fire quenching gas. There was a manual backup, but it was in the flooded compartment and unreachable. Fire-main pressure had been lost due to damage amidships, so jumper hoses were connected to restore operation. However, water pressure was much lower than it would have been if the line had remained fully intact. The fire was proving difficult to fight because compartments adjacent to it were flooded or secured to prevent flooding. Flames were licking out of the starboard exhaust stack, which ran down to the engine room, but damage control teams could not see the actual source of the fire. A hose-man was stationed on top of the stack and water and fire-fighting foam were poured directly down it. The fire fighting efforts reduced the intensity of the fires but didn't seem to be able to extinguish them.

The *Roberts*' 76mm automatic gun and its below-deck magazine were located in the vicinity of and above the fires. As in the case of the *Stark*, the ship's own weapons presented the threat of a disastrous explosion. The bulkheads within the ammunition magazine were too hot to touch, being roasted by the heat radiating up from the fires below. The magazine had lost pressure for its sprinkler system, so hose teams cooled the bulkheads while crewmen began to remove over 500 rounds of 76mm ammunition. At first, some of the ammo was simply pitched overboard. However, a human chain moved most of the 50-pound shells to the forecastle of the ship, where they were stacked away from the dangerous heat.

The water being used for firefighting inside the ship was a more serious problem. So much was accumulating inside the ship that it was creating its own danger, just as it had on the *Stark*. Water from fire hoses was pouring across topside decks and flowing down into already flooded spaces. So much water was running across the main deck that it filled crewmen's shoes when they walked along it. Operating on slippery, wet decks was becoming such a problem that damage control teams had to lay down blankets on the slick surfaces for traction.

The *Roberts* was sinking at the rate of about two feet every 30 minutes. BM2 Sandle had been sent to the fantail by Commander Rinn in order to give status reports on the remaining freeboard. When asked where the Gulf waters were relative to the name "Samuel B. Roberts" painted on the ship's stem, Sandle said he couldn't see the name anymore. It was already beneath the water.[12] In fact, Sandle informed Rinn over the sound-powered phone that, if he got down on his knees at the aft end of the ship, he could reach down and touch the surface of the Gulf. The ship's freeboard was rapidly disappearing.

Commander Rinn now had a decision to make. It was two hours into the mine explosion. Fires were still burning, with flames shooting out of the stacks above the ship. The *Roberts* was also sinking. Rinn had to choose between fighting fires, and stopping the ship from sinking. He felt like he really had no choice in the matter. He had to order the crew to stop fighting the fires and to put all their efforts into dewatering the ship. He would be deviating from the damage control doctrine he was supposed to observe. Still, he figured that there wasn't much point in the crew continuing their fire fighting efforts at that point anyway. At the rate the *Roberts* was sinking, the fires would be extinguished in about half an hour—by the Gulf.

Lieutenant Commander Timothy Matthews and Lieutenant Steven Blaisdell had been at the controls of the *Roberts'* SH-60B helicopter, preparing to launch in about two minutes, when the ship hit the mine. The helicopter was locked onto the landing pad but the severe jolt from the mine explosion had caused a total loss of aircraft electrical power. For a moment following the blast, Matthews and Blaisdell had sat frozen in their harnesses, staring open mouthed at each other. The pilots quickly recovered themselves and had executed an emergency shutdown to prevent any further damage.

With darkness fast approaching, the pilots volunteered to fly the damaged helicopter in order to evacuate the injured and bring in damage control supplies. The flight deck personnel and the helicopter crew rapidly pre-flighted the aircraft and got it running again. Amazingly, it had no apparent damage, although the nearby hanger had been uprooted and cracked by the blast. After the quick inspection of the copter, Blaisdell and Matthews launched from the *Roberts.* They carried the most seriously burned crewman to USS *Trenton,* some 72 nautical miles away, where medical facilities were available.[13] They returned with additional damage control gear. In spite of darkness and smoke, the helicopter made repeated round trips to the ship, landing on the partially debris-covered and smoke-obscured flight deck to deliver the critical damage control supplies.

Commander Rinn remained in communication with Admiral Less, who still seemed to be thinking about abandoning ship. After getting an updated status report, Admiral Less said, "It doesn't sound like it's getting any better. What are your considerations for remaining aboard?" Rinn was not about to abandon his ship. He replied, "We are determined to save the ship. That is our intention. We can save our ship. Intend to stay here and do just that." Other ships, including the *San Jose, Trenton,* and *Wainwright,* were standing by to go to the *Roberts'* assistance, but Commander Rinn had scotched that idea in the conversation with Admiral Less, "We never saw the mine that hit us.

Recommend you establish a mine danger zone and don't send other ships. We'll get out on our own."[14]

After the CH-46 had lifted off with the injured crewmen, Commander Rinn made his way to the flight deck aft. When he got there, he spotted a smoke float in the water to starboard. A young Lieutenant (jg) told him that he had thrown it in to mark a 200-gallon fuel bladder, which had been jettisoned by the evacuation helicopter to make more room aboard it. Commander Rinn's ship was on fire. It was partly flooded from the jagged hole torn in its side. Its keel was broken and it was threatening to break in half. Rinn now contemplated the fuel bladder so helpfully marked by the young Lieutenant: 200 gallons of JP5 aviation fuel floating near intensely burning magnesium flare ignition source. He turned away and glanced over to the port side of the ship: jettisoned containers of live 76mm rounds bobbed in the water nearby. It was not, he thought, his best day in the Navy.

Rinn came to another decision. He had to get his ship out of there. He returned to the bridge, strode purposely to the chart table, took up a pair of dividers and plotted a course. He told the officer of the deck to start the auxiliary power units and to get underway. "Come to course 137 and stay on it unless I tell you to deviate," he determinedly told the officer. Staying on that course, the *Roberts* slowly extricated itself from the mined area. Later, his Navy superiors would question Rinn on how he came up with that heading. The officers were incredulous when he told them that he had no recollection at all of how or why he came up with it.

As night fell, the ship slowly made its way out of the area. Its searchlights swept the water as lookouts kept a tense watch for any additional mines. Quartermaster 2nd Class Dan Nicholson manned the starboard aft searchlight. As he studied the waters illuminated by his light, it looked to him like some kind of family reunion of all the lethal sealife in the area was taking place that night. All he saw were sea snakes and sharks. He was damn glad they weren't abandoning ship.[15]

As the *Roberts* limped along, the crew was gradually prevailing in its battle with the flooding which had threatened to sink the ship. They were even able to refocus some of their efforts on the fires, which continued to rage onboard. Still, the efforts of the damage control teams had been exhausting. The ship's supply of fresh water had been used up in fighting the fires. Nobody was putting coins into the soft drink machines. Men broke into them to get the drinks they needed. It was at this point that Rinn took a good look around at his men and realized that they were starting to run out of gas. He had seen repeated courageous acts by his officers and men as they fought to save the ship. At one point, a spraying, high-pressure fire hose had come loose and was whipping wildly about, threatening to seriously injure someone with its heavy nozzle. Lieutenant David Llewellyn had dived on it to hold it down. As he grabbed the hose, the whipping nozzle had struck him a heavy blow on the head. He lay motionless on the deck. At first, Commander Rinn was afraid that the officer might have been killed. To his great relief, he saw him get up.

Seaman Carr, who fought the fires as a hose-man on top of the stacks, had stayed at his position until the heat had melted his shoes from his feet. Rinn felt that every man had been giving one thousand percent, but he estimated that many had only 45 minutes or so of effort left to give.

The *Roberts'* Chief Engineer, Lieutenant Gordan Van Hook, had been leading a team trying to find the source of the fire, which was raging somewhere down in the engine modules and flooded intake trunks. The fires were fed by the burning fuel, which was floating in a layer about two feet deep atop the water in the flooded compartments. The intense heat generated by the fires onboard the USS *Stark* had mostly stayed contained within the hull of that ship and had roasted the compartments located above it. Luckily for the *Roberts*, much of the heat generated by the fires on board was being vented upward and out of the ship through the stack and even through cracks in its structure caused by the whiplash of the mine explosion. The temperature of the fires in the *Roberts* never reached anywhere near what they did on the *Stark*.

With nightfall, the team led by Van Hook made an important discovery. Through a crack, which had developed in the superstructure, they could look down into one of the main engine intake trunks and see the flames at the source of the fire. Earlier, in daylight, the men had not been able to pinpoint the fire burning below.[16] If they could remove an access plate, they thought the crew could get to the fuel oil fire. However, Rinn was concerned that removal of the 10 x 10 foot steel port would create a "chimney effect," causing the fire to intensify. Given the exhausted state of the crew, the fire might even spread out of control and cause the loss of the ship.

It was decision time again. Convinced that the wrong call would lose the ship, Rinn debated the merits of opening the hatch with

Lieutenant Van Hook for about four minutes. Rinn decided to remove the hatch. Van Hook agreed, telling him, "It's the right decision." Commander Rinn and Van Hook stood by and watched as the bolts were removed and the plate was pried away. Suddenly, a sheet of flame ripped 15 feet up into the air through the open hatch. Maintaining a sense of humor in the otherwise grim circumstances, Van Hook turned to Commander Rinn and said, "Maybe this wasn't such a good idea. Maybe we should have waited until tomorrow." Firefighters moved in and stuck four nozzles into the hatchway. Foam poured down into the source of the fire. Within a minute the flames receded, and the rising smoke changed color from black to white. It had taken about five hours, but the fires were being licked at last.[17]

The *Roberts* had beaten the flooding and the fires, but it still faced another potentially lethal problem: the ship was threatening to break in half. Aside from punching the huge hole in the *Roberts*'s hull, the underwater mine blast had caused a violent whipping motion in the ship's structure, all but tearing it in two. The *Roberts*'s keel was broken, and large cracks ran up and through decks and the superstructure. In fact, the only thing really holding the aft end to the rest of the ship was the main deck itself.

Once more, the crew rose to the occasion. Senior Chief Boatswain's Mate George " Jack" Frost came up with the ingenious idea of using steel cables to lace the ship together. The cables were strung across the huge cracks on deck, pulled tight, and then secured fore and aft. Crewmen also welded large aluminum "doubler plates" over the cracks in the superstructure to try to maintain the integrity of the ship. During the night, the dewatering efforts had allowed the ship to stabilize at the point where she was down about four feet at the fore end and seven feet at the stern, with her pumps continuing to discharge water over the sides. Off-duty crewmen were sleeping on cots topside or simply lay sprawled in exhaustion on deck.

By daybreak, the *Roberts* had gotten well clear of the danger area and rendezvoused with USS *San Jose* and USS *Wainwright*. The *San Jose* sent over additional welders who joined in the work of patching and repairing the hull. The crippled ship was taken under tow at a plodding 5-1/2 knots about midday on the 15th by the Kuwaiti Oil Company tug *Hunter*, which had been dispatched from Bahrain. The Gulf waters had been calm when the *Roberts* struck the mine; however, they were getting rougher and rougher by the time it was taken under tow. A strong wind churned the five-foot seas into a dark froth. The *Roberts'* pumps were managing to hold their own against the water flooding in through the large hole in the underside of the hull. However, the heavy seas were pounding the damaged hull and superstructure. With its keel broken, the ship was flexing alarmingly up and down in the turbulent seas.

As the ship flexed up and down, it made an eerie hollow metallic cranking sound. It seemed to Commander Rinn like a greatly amplified version of the sound you got if you took an empty beer can, bent it in the middle, and then pulled the ends up and down. Do that enough to a beer can and it will tear in half. In the hands of rough Gulf seas, the *Roberts* was facing the same thing on a much larger scale. The ship was definitely not out of the woods yet. Lieutenant (j.g.) Michael Valliere, the auxiliaries' officer, told Rinn that they had to do more shoring if they wanted to hold the ship together. He oversaw the additional efforts, as "X" and "H"-types of bracing were installed at critical spots. Commander Rinn thought that Lieutenant Velierie's quick action probably prevented the ship from breaking up as it was tossed around in the rough seas while being towed.

Finally, flying signal flags spelling out "We are OK," the *Roberts* was brought into the Emirates port of Dubai, where it was dry-docked. It was estimated that the frigate, normally 3,700 tons displacement, was up to 5,000 gross tons because of all the water it had taken on. When engineers were able to get a good look at the ship in dry dock, they saw that it was so badly damaged that it wasn't practical to repair in Dubai. Some temporary repairs were made and the ship was loaded aboard the Dutch commercial heavy lift ship *Mighty Servant II* and carried home to its birthplace at the Bath Iron Works. A caretaker crew of 30 remained on board for the trip, while the rest of the crew flew home. Repairs would take 18 months and cost $96 million. The mine it hit was estimated to have cost $1,500.

While in Dubai, Senior Chief Frost, who was unaware of Fireman Tilley's critical restart of the forward generator, angrily walked up to Commander Rinn with another suggestion sheet from Tilley. With his previous cheeky request for additional portholes down below in mind, and seeing the large hole blasted in the ship by the mine, Tilley wrote, "Captain, with regard to my last request, you've exceeded my expectations!" Rinn just laughed. The Chief may have been irritated, but when Rinn found out about what Tilley had done, he felt vindicated in his decision to keep him.

Much later, while on duty in Washington, D.C., Commander Rinn
met a researcher at the David Taylor Model Basin, part of the Applied
Physics Lab at John Hopkins University. The researcher told Rinn that
they had carefully modeled the *Roberts*' situation after the mine strike,
putting the correct scale amounts of fuel and water that had flooded the
engine compartment into an exact scale model of the frigate. Every time
they ran the simulation, the model ship sank within 14 minutes. The
model didn't gradually settle into the water, either. It made a *Titanic*-like
sternward plunge, that, had it occurred on the real ship, would have
taken most of the crew with it.

The officers and men of the *Roberts* had done an outstanding job
saving their ship when it probably should have gone to the bottom in
two pieces. Commander Rinn described the incident as "the story of a
ship that refused to die, of a crew that is well trained and disciplined
and that has tremendous spirit and pride." Rinn later judged that, with
one exception, the crew had reacted to the crisis in an "incredibly
unafraid manner." He said his men had looked death in the face and
said, "Not today!"

Crewmen credited the intense, realistic damage control training they
had received for their performance. Some crewmembers said they felt
that they were probably one of the best-trained crews in the fleet
because they drilled and trained to fight until it became second nature
to them. Boatswain's Mate 1st Class Dick Fridley noted that, "Every
guy I saw, from the newest to the older guys never stopped to think.
They just reacted right. A good crew with a lot of training—that's what
saved the ship."[18] A technical observer who had spent a few days
aboard ship the previous September said, "It didn't surprise me one bit
when I read the *Roberts* had hit a mine and that the crew had saved the
ship. The morale was tremendous and the crew was well trained. If anyone could save a ship, those were the ones who could do it."[19]

During its pre-deployment training in Guantanamo Bay, Cuba, the
crew had gone through various damage control scenarios to prepare
them for what they might face in the Gulf. When the *Samuel Roberts*
completed the intensive training, it received the highest score available.
In transit to the Gulf, personnel from the Fleet Training Unit (FTU) had
drilled the crew in a final "cram course." Trainers had come aboard
with smoke generators, percussion grenades, and systems that could
flood ship spaces. According to Lieutenant Gordon Van Hook, "Two of
the major drills FTU put us through were almost identical to what hap-

pened when the mine hit. It was all very familiar to us. While recalling the whole incident, I even heard some guys say that it was almost like deja vu."[20]

The Navy had learned from the *Stark*. Damage control training had been increased significantly. The *Roberts* carried double the number of Oxygen Breathing Devices and canisters previously allotted. A thermal imager was aboard as was three times the firefighting foam previously carried. Equipment aside, there was no doubt as to whom the real credit was due. The day after the *Roberts* docked, President Reagan telephoned Commander Rinn and congratulated him on the great job he and his crew had done. The President told him that the nation was indebted to them. Shortly after the incident, the Superintendent of the Naval Academy stated that the outstanding damage control by the *Roberts'* crew would become an element of the curriculum of damage control taught at the Academy.

Later that week, Commander Rinn sent a message to Rear Admiral Less: "We have stood up to the test. We will restore the ship to fighting trim. Morale is higher than ever. We saved her; we will fix her and will fight her again. No Higher Honor."

CHAPTER 14

"A ONE-DAY WAR"

One day after the *Samuel Roberts* mining, President Reagan met with his top national security advisors in Washington to review his options for retaliatory strikes. In the Gulf, within hours of the near-loss of the *Roberts*, a crisis action team had met with the Commander of the Joint Task Force Middle East (JTFME), Admiral Less, to review contingency plans for possible strikes against Iran. Intelligence personnel began gathering imagery and other information on potential targets, while maintaining an up-to-date plot on the locations of Iranian forces. Recommendations for strikes against Iran were sent to the U.S. Central Command on April 15. However, no decision on retaliatory action had been made at the President's initial meeting because proof of the mine's origin was not yet available.

It was not long in coming. On that same April 15, 1988, Marine helicopters from the USS *Trenton* found an M-08 type mine in the vicinity of the Shah Alum Shoals, where the *Roberts* was hit. Guided by smoke markers dropped by Marine CH-46 helicopters, Explosive Ordnance Disposal (EOD) personnel took intelligence photographs of them, showing their serial numbers. Lot numbers on these mines indicated that they were from the same series found aboard the Iran Ajr when that ship had been seized in September 1987. Clearly, they had been laid by Iran.

President Reagan again met with his top advisors. It was felt that failure to take action would only encourage Iran to commit further provocations. The State Department wanted any action to be "proportionate" and related to the provocation. The Pentagon was more interested in striking at targets that had real military significance, particularly ones whose destruction would reduce Iran's ability to hurt U.S. forces in the Gulf. Those kinds of targets included Iranian minelaying ships and mine storage depots. The JTFME's first choice was to hit those targets with cruise missiles and air strikes. However, limiting collateral damage was an important consideration. That ruled out the Iranian naval headquarters at Bandar Abbas, which was located right next door to a hospital. In the end, the President again elected to refrain from hitting Iranian territory and chose to go after platforms in the Gulf. The Pentagon was also able to obtain approval to sink an Iranian warship. The idea was that an Iranian mine had seriously damaged and nearly claimed a U.S. warship, and now Iran would pay in kind. "They got one of our frigates, and we wanted one of theirs," an official later said.[1]

There was one particular Iranian ship that the U.S. Navy was hoping to get a shot at: the frigate *Sabalan*. It was a 1,540-ton, Vosper Mark V-class frigate built in Britain for the navy of the Shah. Over the last few years it had earned a bloody reputation for its attacks on neutral ships, in which it would viciously concentrate its fire against the civilian crew quarters. On several occasions the *Sabalan* had stopped ships in the Strait of Hormuz and boarded them to inquire about their destinations and cargoes. An Iranian naval officer would politely thank the ship's master for his cooperation, wish him "bon voyage and a good trip" before returning to the frigate, and then the Iranian ship would cut loose at the hapless victim with guns or missiles.

The *Sabalan*'s sister ship, the *Sahand*, was almost as bad. The area off Dubai, UAE was used as a convenient stopping point by many ships headed north. Wary of traveling at night, the ships would anchor together, taking some comfort in the relative safety of their numbers. Iranian frigates would go right in among the ships and boldly choose a victim, like "a famished wolf quietly stalking through a field of sleeping sheep."[2]

The frigate USS *Gary* (FFG 51), under the command of Commander Dallas Bethea, had shadowed the *Sahand* in March 1988, and had heard a heated VHF bridge-to-bridge exchange between the *Sahand* and the Singapore ammonium-nitrate tanker *Havglimt*. The tanker was anchored 12 nautical miles off Dubai. The master of the *Havglimt* had given the requested information once he realized an Iranian warship was interrogating him. The *Sahand* thanked him for his cooperation and told him to have a nice day. The Iranian ship backed off 4,000 yards and opened fire with its big 4.5-inch gun. Two IRGC speedboats joined in the attack, which hit the *Havglimt* 100 times, killing two crewmen. During the radio exchange that preceded the attack, the *Gary* had been about 17,000 yards away, just outside of visual range. When the attack began, the *Gary* edged out of its normal patrol area and approached to within visual range of the action. In closer, it was obvious that the Iranian frigate and gunboats were murderously concentrating their fire on the crew quarters.

As the Iranian fire ripped into the tanker, a strong odor of ammonia filled the Gulf air. Over Channel 16, the *Gary* could hear the crew of the *Havglimt* pleading for help as explosions erupted in the background. Commander Bethea felt that he could no longer passively stand by and called the JTFME, requesting permission to close and engage the Iranian ships. Permission was denied. Seething with frustration, Commander Bethea wrote a lengthy, detailed narrative report on the incident, emphasizing the brutality of the Iranian attack. The report was eventually sent up all the way to the Joint Chiefs of Staff. Capt. Bethea later mused that his report may have had some influence on the decision to sink an Iranian frigate during the upcoming operation. He hoped so.

On April 16, the JTFME received both its warning and alert orders describing the courses of action chosen by Washington. Major commanders, including the Marine task force commander and the leaders of two SEAL platoons, were brought into the planning process onboard the flagship USS *Coronado*. Planning was completed by midnight on April 17. The JTFME issued the order for what was dubbed "Operation Praying Mantis" late on the 17th.

Three surface action groups (SAGs) of Navy ships were formed for the strikes. Surface action group "Bravo" was given the job of "neutralizing" the Sasson oil platform, i.e., destroying its military capability. They were to follow up the strike on Sassan with a strike against the Rakesh platform. Rakesh Oil Field was located to the north of and fairly close to Sassan. Surface action group "Charlie" targeted the Sirri platform. Surface action group "Delta" was to sink the Iranian warship *Sabalan* or whatever other Iranian frigate was its on-station replacement in the Strait of Hormuz. JCS Chairman Admiral William Crowe had told Admiral Less over the telephone to "Sink the *Sabalan*, put it on the bottom."[3]

Originally, SAG "Delta" had been tasked with the duty of being prepared to neutralize the Rakish oil platform. Prior to H-hour, this task was shifted to SAG "Bravo," after it completed its Sassan mission. SAG

"Delta's" alternate tasking was changed so the group could remain in the Strait of Hormuz and concentrate on its primary mission of sinking an Iranian warship. "H-hour" was set for 8:00 A.M. Gulf time (0500 "Zulu" time), April 18. (There are actually several different times used in the Gulf. To give a consistent representative local time, this account will use Zulu plus three.) The goal was to simultaneously hit the two platforms and the *Sabalan*.

Battle Group Foxtrot, composed of the nuclear powered aircraft carrier USS *Enterprise* and its escorting warships, would remain outside the Gulf, in the North Arabian Sea. The *Enterprise* would launch aircraft in support of the operation. Several of the *Enterprise*'s escorts had entered the Gulf on the 17th to bolster the surface action groups. USS *Gary* would serve, in American football jargon, as a "free safety" in the northern Gulf, with the responsibility of protecting the Mobile Sea Bases against Iranian counterstrikes. The U.S. Air Force would operate its large Saudi-based KC-10 tankers to refuel Navy aircraft over the Gulf. Its E-3A Sentry AWACS aircraft would provide radar surveillance.

Planning for air operations aboard the USS *Enterprise* had gone late into the night. After a few hours of restless sleep, aircrews arrived in their ready rooms for formal briefings at 4:30 A.M. on April 18th. The air plan called for a surface combat air patrol (SUCAP) with two A-6E Intruder attack bombers armed with a mix of anti-ship weapons, including Harpoon missiles, laser-guided bombs, and Walleye TV-guided glide bombs. Combat air patrol (CAP) consisted of four F-14 Tomcat fighters. The combined aircraft, along with two EA-6B Prowler electronic warfare aircraft, were known as the SUCAP Group. A backup "war-at-sea" strike group of A-7 Corsair light attack aircraft was kept on deck alert on the *Enterprise*.

The first SUCAP Group was launched at 7:00 A.M. so it could arrive on station at the Strait of Hormuz at 7:45. The first group was scheduled for six and one-half hours of flight time. Expecting the most action, it included senior aircrew. Rear Admiral Raymond G. Zeller, who commanded the carrier battle group, later noted that the group's air cover "initially was set up as a ruse. Our activities were designed to look like just another Earnest Will escort operation . . . so if someone were looking, they'd think it was just another Earnest Will convoy coming through the Straits."[4] The warships from the battle group used the same radio frequencies as normal convoys and were supported by the same "package" of aircraft.

The SUCAP Group took station near the entrance to the Strait of Hormuz at the scheduled time. The Strait was expected to be the scene of the planned attack on the Iranian frigate. The group was positioned over international waters in the vicinity of the UAE port of Khor Fakkan, which was southwest of the major Iranian air and naval base at Bandar Abbas. The Air Force stationed a large KC-10 tanker aircraft, flying out of Dhahran, Saudi Arabia, in the vicinity of the Strait of Hormuz. A Navy E2-C Hawkeye radar early warning aircraft from the *Enterprise* was positioned about 50 miles to the southeast of the SUCAP Group, where its Surveillance radar could sweep the Straight of Hormuz and the southern Gulf.

Surface action group (SAG) "Bravo" consisted of two destroyers: the 7,810-ton USS *Merrill* (DD-976) and the 4,500-ton USS *Lynde McCormick* (DDG-8), as well as the 17,000-ton amphibious transport USS *Trenton* (LPD-14). The 27-year old *McCormick* was armed with anti-aircraft guided missiles and had been brought into the Gulf from the battle group sailing in the North Arabian Sea. The *Trenton* carried the Marines of Contingency Marine Air Ground Task Force 2-88. An LPD-class ship like the *Trenton* would normally have deployed with only two helicopters. However, for its Gulf mission, the *Trenton* had been packed with eight helicopters from Marine Squadron HML/A-167: four AH-IT Cobra gunships, two UH-IN utility transports, and two much larger CH-46E transports. For Operation Praying Mantis, yet another aircraft, the SH-60 Lamps III helicopter, normally flown from the mine-damaged USS *Roberts*, was squeezed on board. A Navy SH-2F helicopter was based on the *Merrill*.

The commander of Destroyer Squadron Nine, Captain James B. Perkins, had been responsible for planning and executing the platform attacks. A 1964 Naval Academy graduate who had spent most of his career to date on destroyers and frigates, Capt. Perkins was serving on the *Enterprise* in the dual roles of anti-surface warfare coordinator and anti-submarine warfare coordinator for the carrier battle group. He had been directed to fly from the *Enterprise* into the Gulf to Bahrain on a carrier-based S-3 aircraft. He was to personally command one of the three SAG's, and would plan the platform attacks. He was told to take a small planning staff along with him. Perkins took only one man, Lieutenant Mark Kosnik, whom he described as his "micro staff."

In Bahrain, Perkins had met with Admiral Less and had been given the parameters within which he was to come up with an operational plan. Intelligence photos of the targets were made available for planning purposes. The Rules of Engagement under which the operation would take place specified that warnings were to be issued in both Farsi and in English before engaging Iranian targets. Perkins was not particularly happy with that requirement and said so. However, it stood. Another constraint he had to operate under was that U.S. forces were to avoid or minimize environmental damage in the platform attacks. Perkins, bemused, thought of the numerous and extensive oil slicks he had seen floating from one end of the Gulf to the other and wondered to himself, "What was the point?"

Perkins and Kosnik put together a very short, simple plan, which featured mission-type orders for the surface action groups. Units were allotted to each of the groups, and radio frequencies were assigned. Late on the 17th, Perkins and Kosnik made an extremely long and tiring helicopter flight down the Gulf to USS *Wainwright* to deliver the plan for SAG "C". Then it was on to USS *Merrill*, where Perkins would serve as on-scene commander for SAG "B" during the operation. The mission of that group was to destroy the Sassan gas-oil separation platform. That facility had been completely refitted by the Revolutionary Guards as a replacement surveillance platform following the destruction of the Iranian platforms during Operation Nimble Archer in September the previous year. The plan was to neutralize the facility with gunfire from the destroyers, and then land a Marine force to seize the platform, gather intelligence information, and set explosive charges.

The Nimble Archer operation in September the previous year had made it clear that trying to knock platforms off of their legs with naval gunfire was a losing proposition. The relatively small diameter of the legs and their ability to take hits made them poor targets for a gunfire attack. Therefore, Sassan would be destroyed with explosive charges. As Perkins boarded the S-3 to fly from the *Enterprise* to Bahrain, the battle group commander, Rear Admiral Zeller, had told him half-jokingly, "No thousand rounds this time."

Landing on a platform, as the SEALs had done in Nimble Archer, also had the advantage of allowing potentially useful intelligence information to be seized. The Sassan complex actually consisted of seven separate platforms connected by a spidery network of catwalks. The platform was also being used as an Iranian communications and control facility, an observation platform, and a launch point for small boat attacks against Gulf merchant shipping. A mixed Iranian military and civilian crew apparently manned it. At least three Russian made ZSU 23-2 twin 23mm automatic anti-aircraft cannon (often called "ZOO 23's") were mounted on it, along with other crew-served weapons. It was these guns, which had fired on the two TF-160 SEABAT helicopters flying from the *Simpson* on the night of March 5/6.

As dawn broke over the Gulf on April 18, SAG "Bravo" drew near Sasson, which seemed unaware of its approaching fate. The *Merrill*, under Commander Craig Covington, and the *Lynde McCormick*, under Commander Terrance T. Etnyre, took station some 4,000 yards to the east of the platform, following a north-south "race-track" pattern. The destroyers' line of fire was limited by the UAE's Abu Al-Bukush oil field, located some three miles to the south, and the presence of a large hydrogen sulfide (H2S) tank on the seventh platform at the northern end of the complex. The lethal hydrogen sulfide gas had killed people on Gulf platforms. Standard U.S. issue gas masks did not offer any protection against it. The gas was heavier than air and, if released, would tend to settle to the surface of the Gulf.

As the U.S. ships closed on the platform, the Iranians appear to have noticed them at last. Activity on the structure increased. The *Trenton*, under Capt. Robert M. Nutwell, took position about ten nautical miles to the southeast. The SH-60B from the *Roberts* conducted a pre-strike reconnaissance of the platform and surrounding area. The *Trenton* also launched a LCM-8 landing craft and a Marine Corps Avon "Searider" for search and rescue.

From the *Merrill*, warnings to evacuate the platform were broadcast at 7:55 A.M. in Arabic, Farsi, and English over military and civilian air distress frequencies and over the Gulf commercial ship-to-ship circuit. The Navy employed a native Iranian linguist for the warnings, which bluntly stated, "Attention Sassan oil platform. This is U.S. warship. This is your warning. You have five minutes to clear the platform before we commence fire." The platform responded that the warnings were understood. The warning time was short, but as Captain Perkins dryly observed, "If you're highly motivated, you can do a lot in five minutes."

The warnings stirred a variety of actions on the platform. One group of Iranians milled about on the roof of the living quarters. Some were running around with small arms. Others manned a 23mm gun and aimed it at the *Merrill*. Around 30 of the Iranians headed for a small tug and an offshore workboat, which were conveniently tied up in the vicinity of the platform. The tug got underway immediately and the other boat followed soon after, departing to the west. The remaining Iranians got on the radio and began simultaneously screaming in Farsi to their naval headquarters and calling in English to the American ships, pleading for more time. They were granted a few more minutes.

At 8:08, they were told their time was up and the destroyers opened fire with their 5-inch guns. The ships aimed their airburst shells at the southern platform area, away from the Iranians who were visible, in an effort to spur the evacuation of remaining personnel. They also continued to issue multiple warnings for the personnel still on the platform to clear it and get in the water immediately. Some of the Iranians were not ready to abandon the platform without a fight. They opened fire with one of the 23mm guns, aiming at the *Merrill* and at two Marine Cobra helicopters hovering just north of the ship. The ships and helicopters were theoretically within the maximum range of the Iranian gun, but outside of what was considered their effective range. The Iranian rounds fell short.

"I guess they're bad shots, and I don't think they had a lot of time to devote to targeting. We spoiled their aim," Captain Perkins later observed. Muzzle flashes from the Iranian gun were clearly visible, as were the splashes of rounds impacting in front of the *Merrill*. That ship now aimed its fire at the gun emplacement, and almost immediately knocked it out with five 5-inch airburst rounds. Following the initial barrage of naval gunfire, a group of Iranians could now be seen gathered on the northern part of the platform, apparently seeking to evacuate. Captain Perkins later described these Iranians as "converted martyrs."[5]

The U.S. ships were in radio communication with the Iranian tugs, and ceased fire to allow one to return and pick up the Iranians trying to leave. The tug then cleared the area, and two minutes later the *Merrill* and the *McCormick* resumed fire. The ships now alternated in firing shells over the entire complex, with the exception of the Hydrogen Sulfide tank platform. The ships fired time-fused shells set to burst in the air so they would avoid blasting holes in platform surfaces, which might be used by the helicopters landing the Marines.

The second phase of the operation would involve landing a Marine assault force on the platform. The Marines on board the *Trenton* were from Contingency Marine Air-Ground Task Force (MAGTF) 2-88, which had been activated in November 1987 under the command of Colonel William M. Rakow. Captain Perkins had him co-locate on the bridge of the *Merrill* for the operation. Perkins felt that there had been pressure from General Crist, himself a Marine, to be sure Marines were employed in the action. He intended to do so, but he wanted to be sure that it was safe for the Marines to land on the platform when the time came. That was one of the main reasons he wanted the Marine commander standing next to him on the bridge of the *Merrill*. That way, they could talk face-to-face without any potential "I thought you said this" problems resulting from misunderstood radio communication.

Now two CH-46's and a UH-1 carrying the Marine raiding force were holding at their initial point, awaiting the signal to commence the assault. Cobra gunships would provide fire support, with another UH-1 being used for command and control. Shortly after 9:00 A.M., a coordinated naval gunfire and Cobra preparatory attack began. Two minutes later, the assault helicopters departed the initial point and began their low-level run to the platform. The ships checked their fire and the Cobras maneuvered to deliver close-in suppressive fire with TOW anti-tank missiles and their 20-mm cannon.

The approaching helicopters thought they were taking antiaircraft fire, and the suspected position was taken out by fire from the Cobras. The helicopter gunships hit anything that looked like a gun emplacement. At one point, they identified "possible Harpoons," i.e. anti-ship missiles, on the platform and shot up that part of the installation. The Cobras poured 20mm cannon fire into the living quarters, igniting intensely burning fires.

The raid force mission commander, Major Clyde Brinkley, had been circling in the command and control UH-1 helicopter. He could see the fires burning on the complex and the explosions of ammunition "cooking off." Considering the fires and the possibility of booby-trapped landing pads, he decided to revise the landing plan so that the assault elements would fast rope into alternate landing points. The changes were radioed to the transport helicopters and their assault teams. As they flew in, the Marines in the helicopters received an intelligence report that three to six Iranian marines on the platform had vowed to fight to the death.

Making things seem even dicier, what looked like muzzle flashes were now erupting from different areas of the platform. The *Merrill* and the *McCormick* closed in on the structure to provide naval gunfire support if needed. From the *Merrill*'s bridge, Capt. Perkins could distinctly hear the pop-pop of rounds going off on the Iranian platform. He thought, "Oh my God, somebody had remained onboard and was resisting the Marine assault."

Now at the complex, the transport helicopters flew through the smoke from the fires and dodged exploding Iranian ammunition in order to get into position to insert the raiding force. The hovering helicopters dropped suspended ropes to the platform decks and the assaulting Marines began to slide down. As they did so, one of the support boats saw an Iranian dive into the water from the platform. He was never seen again.

The assault force was commanded by Captain Thomas Hastings, and consisted of two assault teams and a command group. Assault Team 2 fast-roped onto a platform that mounted one of the 23mm guns. Fires ignited by the pre-assault bombardment were causing 23mm ammunition stored at the position to explode. Flammable liquids were also leaking into the site. The team quickly moved out of the dangerous area before proceeding with its mission of clearing a portion of the complex.

The assault element command group landed moments after the assault teams. The team set up a security perimeter and positioned a sniper at the highest point to cover the movement of the two assault teams. The exploding Iranian ammunition caused the Marines to think that a firefight had broken out. They opened up with their weapons, laying down a base of fire as the assault teams began to systematically clear the seven linked platforms using close-quarter battle tactics.

The search teams were mostly equipped with MP5 9mm submachine guns, "flash-bang" grenades to stun and blind room occupants prior to entering, and radios with throat mikes which left their hands free. However, within barely 15 minutes of landing, the fires, secondary explosions, fuel spills and fumes had gotten to the point that Capt. Hastings put the clearing operations on hold and alerted the *Merrill* for a possible emergency extraction. The living quarters in particular were wreathed in billowing flames. Fortunately, things on the platform began to settle down somewhat, and Capt. Hastings ordered the operation to resume. The fires in the living quarters apparently consumed all the flammable materials located there and burned themselves out.

The assault squads had to be careful in using their grenades, out of fear of setting off further secondary explosions and fires. They had to pick their way through an obstacle course of holes in the platform floors, twisted wreckage, and sagging catwalks. The threat of possible stay-behind Iranian snipers was also on the minds of team members. The first assault squad cleared four of the seven platforms. Every time the assault teams cleared a room on the structure, they would hurl in a "flash-bang" or a percussion grenade prior to entering it. The metal platform structure had apparently accumulated a lot of rust in the maritime environment, and the Iranians seem to have had a casual attitude toward maintenance. The grenade explosions kicked up thick, swirling clouds of rust particles in the rooms. The Marines could only check them out with the aid of the powerful flashlights attached to their weapons.

Structures were cleared working from the top level down. No Iranians were found on the facility. Slightly after 10:00 A.M., the objective was declared secured, and a few minutes later, intelligence, photo, and explosive ordnance disposal (EOD) teams were lifted over. Because of the destruction caused by the fires, the Marines found little intelligence material. Captured weapons, including one of the ZSU 23-2 guns, a tripod-mounted 12.7mm heavy machine gun, and two SA-7 hand held anti-aircraft missile launchers, were loaded aboard or slung under helicopters and carried off. Two other ZSU 23-2's were blown up in place.

Two pallets of explosives were then lifted onto the platform and the Marine EOD team placed them at key locations on the platform. They used satchel charges, cratering charges, and sticks of dynamite. A total of 1,300 pounds of explosives were strung together with 2,500 feet of detonating cord. Like the assault element that preceded it, the EOD team had to carefully work its way around twisted wreckage, fires, and exploding ammunition as the men laid and primed their charges.

At 1:03 P.M., all of the Marines had been withdrawn from the platform. Seven minutes later the explosives detonated with a deafening blast. A cloud of fire and smoke rose 500 feet into the air. Captain Perkins dryly described it as a "reasonably impressive bang." Sailors and Marines on the three ships cheered and applauded. As the heavy black smoke settled and the numerous secondary explosions tapered off, Cobra attack helicopters went back in with TOW missiles to destroy any targets remaining intact on the complex.

Despite all of the destruction, there were no oil or gas leaks presenting environmental hazards. The northern (seventh) platform, with its hydrogen sulfide tank, was left undamaged. Fires could be seen burning on the helicopter pad, in the living quarters again, as well as other platform areas. The work area was not burning but was heavily damaged. The target was considered effectively neutralized. The *Merrill* had fired 103 rounds, the *McCormick* 30.

Several commercial tugs had come into the area, probably hoping to get salvage work. By 1:40 P.M., the Marine staff was planning for an attack on the Rakesh platform as the surface action group headed north toward it. The plan for Rakesh was similar to the one just executed at Sasson: neutralize the platform with naval gunfire and Cobra attack helicopters, then land a Marine raiding force if feasible.

A somewhat ludicrous but potentially dangerous incident took place when a surface contact was detected closing at an alarming 25 knots from the northeast. A Marine Cobra helicopter identified it as a warship, possibly an Iranian *Saam*-class frigate. The U.S. ships prepared to engage. Harpoon anti-ship missiles and Standard missiles being used in the surface-to-surface mode were readied to launch. Fire control solutions were developed and fire control radars locked on the closing warship. However, Captain Perkins wanted an absolutely positive identification on the ship before shooting. He knew that some officers rather wanted the ship to be an Iranian frigate so that they could take it out. A Navy LAMPS helicopter joined the Marine Cobra in observing the suspect ship. There was a surface haze, which limited visibility.

Perkins got on the radio with the helicopter pilots and patiently walked them through a description of the warship they were looking at. "Tell me exactly what you see," he said. "Start at the bow. Is there a missile launcher?" He also asked for the hull number of the ship. It was a warship all right, but not a *Saam*-class Iranian frigate. It was actually a *Sovremenny*-class Soviet Navy destroyer. When asked his intentions, the Soviet captain replied that he had just come to take a look. In heavily accented English he said, "I vant to take peectures for heestory."[6] He was fortunate he didn't make history as the commander of the first Soviet Navy ship sunk by the U.S. Navy during the Cold War.

In mid-afternoon, the order came down canceling the Rakesh operation. The surface action group was now instructed to proceed to the eastern Gulf. While they could not have known it, at least some of the Iranian evacuees from Sassan had been spared a repeat of their unpleasant experience that morning. They had been taken to Rakesh following the destruction of Sassan.

In parallel with SAG "Bravo's" attack on the Sasson platform, SAG "Charlie" was to destroy the Sirri platform, located some 19 nautical miles southwest of Sirri Island. The platform was actively producing oil at the time. The surface action group consisted of three ships: the 8,200-ton guided missile cruiser USS *Wainwright* (CG-28) and the frigates USS *Simpson* (FFG-56) and *Bagley* (FF-1069). Captain James F. Chandler, commanding officer of the *Wainwright*, was the group's commander. Instead of the Marines employed in the Sasson attack, SAG "Charlie" would use a Navy SEAL commando platoon from the Pacific Fleet, which had been transferred to the *Simpson* from Mobile Sea Base Wimbrown VII by an Army Task Force 160 UH-60 helicopter. The Army helicopter remained aboard, and would be used to insert the SEALs onto the platform. The *Bagley* embarked a LAMPS MK I SH-2F helicopter; the *Simpson* embarked a LAMPS MK III SH-60B in addition to the Army TF-160 UH-60B.

The three ships had rendezvoused on April 17th to form the surface action group. Capt. Chandler held a 1:00 A.M. briefing on the *Wainwright* for the planned attack. The ship commanders and Commander Tom Richards, the Naval Special Warfare Task Unit Commander in charge of the SEALS, were all present. Two hours later, the weary commanders returned to their ships, which steamed southeast toward their target. Captain Chandler had told them to try to get a couple of hours sleep; they were going to have a busy day.

James McTigue, a Boston native, commanded the USS *Simpson*. He had graduated from the Harvard University Naval ROTC program in 1969. Anti-Vietnam war sentiment was strong on campus in that turbulent year, but NROTC students at Harvard found little antagonism directed at them personally. However, during his senior year, they had prudently backed off from wearing their uniforms around the campus. McTigue's degree was in International Relations. He had wanted to be a naval aviator but was disqualified because of an astigmatism that affected his vision. With aviation blocked, he chose surface warfare as a career field. He went on to serve a year in Vietnam as a naval intelligence liaison officer attached to the U.S. Army, and ironically, ended by flying missions on Army surveillance aircraft. Some of these flights took ground-fire and McTigue was awarded two air medals. He was now a surface warfare officer whose uniform somehow sported air medals. Later, Naval aviators, who themselves had not earned air medals, would cast questioning glances at him. It was as if they were saying, "Are you sure you're wearing the right thing there, son?"

When the *Roberts* hit the Iranian mine, *Simpson* had been outside the Gulf tied up to the tender *Samuel Gompers* at Masirah Island,

Oman. A drifting and abandoned Iranian speedboat, grabbed by the USS *Reuben James*, had been taken to the *Gompers* and put on deck. It made for interesting viewing, but crewmen aboard the *Simpson* were more interested in catching glimpses of the female sailors on the *Gompers*, one of the first ships deployed with a mixed crew. Following the *Roberts* mining, McTigue knew something was going to happen in the Gulf, and he was worried that he and his ship weren't going to be in on it. Finally, on Saturday night (April 16), he got orders to proceed through the Strait and into the Gulf. On its run through the Strait, the *Simpson* passed a patrolling Iranian warship: it was the *Sabalan*. McTigue knew by then that this particular ship had been targeted for destruction by U.S. forces. No one else onboard (except his chief radio operator) was aware of the U.S. plans at that point. It was an eerie feeling watching the *Sabalan* sail by. With grim humor, McTigue thought, "I know something you don't know."

The Navy LAMPS helicopters from the *Bagley* and *Simpson*, along with the Army UH-60 Blackhawk, were launched for surveillance and to assess battle damage. The ships of the surface action group approached Sirri platform from two different directions so they wouldn't reveal their intentions. *Wainwright* approached from the west, *Bagley* and *Simpson* from the south. In accordance with the Praying Mantis operational plan, the *Wainwright* issued a warning twice in English and Farsi over the bridge-to-bridge channel 16: "Sirri gas and oil separation platform, this is U.S. Navy warship. You have five minutes to evacuate your platform. Any actions other than evacuation will result in immediate destruction. Have a nice day."

The warning was issued at 7:55 A.M., with plans to open fire at 8:00 A.M. A tug standing off the platform radioed that it needed more time to evacuate the personnel. The *Wainwright* responded by repeating its initial warning. However, with less than a minute to go before opening fire, the American ships could see a line of Iranians on the lower level of the platform awaiting evacuation by the approaching tug. Capt. Chandler relented and ordered the group to hold its fire until the evacuees' boat was clear of the platform. That took around 20 minutes. Some personnel remained on the platform and activity could be seen at the ZSU-23mm gun positions. When the tug had cleared by 2,000 yards, the three U.S. ships opened fire. The *Bagley* and *Wainwright*, which had 5-inch guns, were some five miles away from the platform. The *Simpson* was located four miles away, which was the optimum range for its smaller-caliber 76mm gun. Captain Chandler had positioned the ships so that they were outside the range of the Iranian ZSU-23mm guns. However, the platform was still well within range of their own guns.

The *Wainwright* passed the message "weapons free" to both the *Bagley* and the *Simpson*, and all three ships opened fire. The *Bagley's* 5-inch gun malfunctioned after three rounds and went out of action with a round jammed in the lower gun carriage. The first salvo consisted of eight 5-inch variable time fuse rounds and 29 point-detonating 76mm rounds. At least one of the Iranian ZSU-23mm guns returned fire, but its shots splashed harmlessly short of the U.S. ships.

The U.S. shells did a lot more damage. The first airburst salvo hit the platform in the vicinity of a ZSU gun located near a helicopter pad. Several of the Iranians manning the gun position were blown off the platform. Small figures could be seen falling several levels down into the water. The helicopters went in for an initial battle damage assessment and reported moderate shrapnel damage to the platform. They could also see Iranian personnel still moving around on the structure. In fact, it looked like the ZSU 23mm gun mount was being re-manned. After several more minutes of bombardment, the U.S. ships checked fire to allow any Iranians who had changed their minds the opportunity to leave. Some did just that and jumped into the water. These and the ones last observed on the platform were wearing olive drab military utility uniforms.

It had been rumored that the Iranian military personnel who had evacuated their platforms before coming under U.S. fire during Operation Nimble Archer in October 1987 had been executed upon return to Iran. Whatever the truth to that story, on both Sassan and Sirri, Iranian military personnel did not at first evacuate with civilian workers, but stayed at least until the U.S. ships opened fire.

The attack plan called for the SEALs to be inserted onto the platform by the single Army MH-60 helicopter. The interior of the Special Forces transport copter had been stripped of almost everything except spare ammo cans to accommodate the nearly 20 Seals crammed into it. The plan was for the Navy commandos to fast rope onto the platform from the hovering helicopter. The SEALs had duffle bags of extra ammunition they would kick out the door as they landed. Once the platform was secured, some 800 pounds of explosives would be ferried over to demolish it.

The TF-160 pilots had thought that the plan was for them to land "in the smoke" of the first salvos from the U.S. warships. Instead, for reasons that were not clear to them, the insertion was delayed. The helicopter conducting battle damage assessment could not confirm that all personnel movement on the platform had ceased. As the TF–160 helicopter commenced its assault run; it began taking heavy Iranian anti-aircraft fire. Rounds could be seen impacting in the water around the helicopter. The SEAL team leader was in communication with Captain Chandler over a secure voice channel, and it was decided not to try to insert the SEALs at that time. The helicopter aborted its run and turned back.

Instead, the ships reengaged with their guns. Shells could be seen impacting the communication and office areas. One round from the *Wainwright* hit a compressed gas tank, which exploded, setting the entire central section of the platform ablaze. When the shelling stopped, the TF-160 Blackhawk, with the SEALs onboard, made its second run at the platform. Flying at 135–140 knots, the MH-60 came in low, below the level of the upper platform decks, in order to minimize the threat of hand-held anti-aircraft missiles. The helicopter flew within 200 yards of the burning platform. The TF-160 crew shot at the Iranians remaining on the structure with the helicopter's minigun until it jammed. The Iranians on the structure were carrying small arms. The Navy SEALs then stood in the open doorway, firing at the Iranians with their M-16's and an M-60 machine-gun borrowed from the *Simpson*.

A major fire was now raging on the center platform; secondary explosions from ammunition were sending tracer rounds flying crazily in all directions. The landing of the Navy SEALs on the platform was called off. With the intense fires and secondary explosions, it just looked too risky. The SEALs were left fuming. They thought that it had been unnecessary to resume fire. They figured that they should have been allowed to assault the platform after the ships initially checked fire. The frustration of the keyed-up SEALs was understandable, but they lacked the close support of the attack helicopters available to the Marines at Sasson. Iranian anti-aircraft gun positions had remained active after the brief first bombardment lifted, making it a dicey proposition for the SEALs to assault the platform in broad daylight on a single helicopter with no backup aircraft. It made sense to thoroughly clear the platform using naval gunfire prior to any attempt at seizing it. It was a stroke of bad luck that one of the shells had hit the compressed gas tank.

An SH-60 LAMPS helicopter from the *Simpson* closed on the now furiously burning platform to photograph it for intelligence purposes. The helicopter spotted six Iranians in the water, wearing life jackets over their fatigues. Some of the men were waving their arms, indicating surrender. Several were obviously wounded. The U.S. forces did not attempt to rescue these men because of the dangers presented by the heavy flames and secondary explosions. The Army MH-60 dropped its life raft to the men, and five of them were seen climbing aboard it. A sixth floated in the water, showing no signs of life. The U.S. helicopter also dropped a first aid kit to the Iranians.

A Belgian-flag tug came into the area and requested permission to recover survivors and fight fires. It was granted permission to recover the survivors but was told it could not combat the raging fires. A ruptured pipe on the lowest level was spraying oil, which helped fuel a spectacular fire. Flames were leaping 300 to 500 feet above the center platform, with smoke billowing some 2,000 feet into the air. The center platform was totally destroyed by the fire. The northern platform was located only thirty meters away from the central platform, and looked to have been rendered structurally unsound and unusable by the tremendous heat radiating from the fires. A little before 11:00 A.M., the surface action group departed the vicinity of the Sirri platform. Aside from the Belgian-flag tug carrying survivors, two other tugs or small boats were sighted closing on the platform, probably to fight the fires.

When the United States had destroyed the Rashadat platform in October 1987, Iranian air and naval forces had not intervened. Now, two more platforms were burning in the Gulf, and this time the Iranians came out to fight. An officer later described it as a "one-day war."

CHAPTER 15

"STOP, ABANDON SHIP, I INTEND TO SINK YOU"

Toward midday on April 18, the Iranians began reacting to the American attacks by launching their own attacks against oil and gas facilities in the southern Gulf that had some U.S. ownership association. "We are under fire!" shouted scared oil field workers over the radio. Iranian boats rampaged around offshore oil and gas facilities, firing rocket-propelled grenades and machine guns. "It was a non-stop bloody scenario," said an executive of a Texas-based marine service company operating in the area. A helicopter pilot flying over the oil fields reported, "They are firing at anything and everything that moves."[1]

The Iranian attack began around 11:00 A.M. when three Revolutionary Guard gunboats sortied from Abu Musa Island and approached the oil storage tanker *York Marine*, which was anchored in nearby Mubarak field. The field was located to the southeast of Abu Musa, between that island and the United Arab Emirates. When the tanker crewmen first saw the Iranian gunboats, they weren't particularly worried since they assumed the craft were out on a training exercise.

They soon found out otherwise. One of the boats sailed to within 100 feet of the tanker's portside and stopped opposite the aft accommodation section. Revolutionary Guard sailors on the boat stood up, hoisted shoulder-mounted rocket-propelled grenade (RPG) launchers and began firing anti-tank rockets at the ship. At such close range, it was hard to miss. Rockets streaked across the water and exploded on the aft deck and in the engine room. Two of the ships' oil storage tanks were punctured. A rocket that hit the engine room ignited a fire.

Another Revolutionary Guard gunboat sailed leisurely alongside the tanker, firing rockets into the forward section. About 45 minutes after the attack started, the gunboats broke off and headed back in the direction of Abu Musa. With the Iranian boats at least temporarily gone, the battered *York Marine*'s workers were able to transfer to crew boats, which had been summoned from the U.A.E.

The U.S.-based Crescent Petroleum Company operated Mubarak field. Concerned with the possibility that the Iranians might make further attacks, Crescent's Field Superintendent ordered that the company's "A" platform, located not far from the *York Marine*, be shut down and evacuated. Workers began bleeding off and flaring gas stored in production pressure vessels prior to abandoning the platform. It was too late. While the work was going on, the Iranian gunboats returned. This time, some of them headed for the "A" platform. They began firing shoulder-launched rockets at the structure. Initially, their aim was off. Three rockets splashed into the water in front of the platform. Then, raising their sights, the Iranians sent a rocket sailing over the structure's top. When the evacuation helicopter flew into the vicinity the Iranians greeted it, too, with a rocket. Fortunately, it missed.

It was at this time that the Iranians broadcast an ominous message in English over Channel 16: "Evacuate the field because we are going to destroy it." The gunboats broke off their attack and sailed about halfway back to Abu Musa, where they met a supply boat and took on a fresh load of ammunition. There were now seven IRGC gunboats in the area. Four of these could be seen heading back toward the "A" platform. The workers hurriedly jumped into a boat and pulled away before the Iranians returned to the structure.

The four IRGC boats subjected the now-deserted platform to another rocket barrage. This time, their aim was better. They were able to score some hits, with one rocket igniting a fire near the platform's control room. Two crew boats, loaded with tanker and platform workers, headed toward Sharjah. As they cleared the field, they could see the Iranian gunboats swirling around in the area, continuously firing rockets and machine-guns at the facilities. One gunboat loosed a warning burst after the departing crew boats.

The American-flagged *Willi Tide* was a 180-foot long, 283-ton, towing supply vessel working in the field for Crescent Petroleum. It had received the distress call from the *York Marine* and the New Orleans-based *Willi Tide* now headed to the assistance of the storage tanker. By then, the Iranian boats, ripping through the area at 30 to 40 knots, had also hit the "A" platform and started the fire. The *Willi Tide* changed course and headed to the platform to try to fight the fire. The *Willi Tide* held off while the Iranians continued to attack the rig, but went in when they departed. The Iranian boats later returned for another visit, this time firing rockets at the *Willi Tide* itself. The Iranian fire missed the vessel, but came close enough for Captain Robert Bavle, the only American on the ship, who said, "We fought the fire at the complex and ran like hell."[2] The *Willi Tide* had requested help from American warships. However, none was forthcoming since U.S. ships or aircraft were not in a position to respond at the time. Luckily, no one aboard the oil-field craft was hurt in the attack.

Shortly after noon, the IRGC boats again attacked in Mubarak field. This time the target was the *Scan Bay*, a Panamanian-flag jack-up barge rig with six Americans among her 70-man crew. Bob Jackson, a 55 year-old Odessa, Texas man who worked as a consultant to the UAE's government-owned petroleum company, was aboard the *Scan Bay*. He had earlier witnessed the Iranian gunboat attack on the *York Marine*. The boats then left the area, departing in the direction of their Abu Musa Island base located about 10 miles away. On their way out, one of the IRGC boats had fired two shots at the *Scan Bay*, but missed. The threat was obvious, and workers were issued life jackets. Some were told to go to the helipad area to wait for eventual evacuation. Several men on the rig were using their binoculars to keep an anxious lookout for the Iranian boats. "I kept scanning over the horizon and looking that none came back before we went back to work," Jackson said. "We're out there trying to make a living, that's all."[3]

Then he saw a white wake coming over the horizon and knew it was the gunboats coming back. Workers were told to come down from the helipad and to try to hide out of sight on the rig. The Iranian boats looked like they were en route to hit the storage tanker again, but they made an abrupt 90 degree turn and headed for the rig. One boat came to a stop about 200 meters away and, for a while, just sat and observed the *Scan Bay*. Then it slowly swung around, pointing a bow-mounted multiple rocket launcher at the rig rising some 80 feet above the water. "Boy, this is it," said Jackson.[4]

Unlike the American Navy, which had warned the Iranian dual-use (civilian/military) platforms of their pending attacks, and had allowed time for evacuation of personnel, the IRGC went straight into the attack against what they had to know were purely civilian facilities. Some of the IRGC boats fired rockets into the galley area on the rig. Another

American who was present said, "The attack was a deliberate attempt to inflict the heaviest possible casualties. . . . They knew where the galley was and the timing. If we had not gone to general quarters, we would have had a galley full of people."

The Iranian boat with the multiple rocket launcher fired 10 or 12 large artillery rockets, mostly aiming at the rig's legs in an apparent effort to topple it. They didn't have any better luck with rockets than the American warships had had with their cannon during operation Nimble Archer. Still, fired at very close range, six to ten of the rockets hit the moveable three-legged rig. "When they hit the rig, it bounced me off the floor about two feet," said Jackson.[5] One rocket flew high and went spiraling away after it deflected off the derrick structure. Fortunately, the rig was solidly built and none of the legs failed. Unfortunately, the Iranians weren't about to call it quits.

The gunboats now circled the rig, opening fire with their heavy machine guns. "They would rake the deck trying to kill people," said Jackson. The Iranians and the rig workers played a potentially deadly game of cat and mouse. Whenever a worker exposed himself, the Iranians tried to machine-gun him. As the boats fired on the platform, some crewmen would run to the opposite side as the boats circled, trying to keep equipment and structures as shields between themselves and the gunfire.

"I think they were trying to kill all of us," said Jackson. "They were going to kill anything that moved."[6] At one point, a gunboat stationed itself directly under the rig and fired straight up at it. The rig crew was shocked by the unexpected and violent attack. However, most managed to maintain their composure in the face of the Iranian fire. Two men panicked, but the others helped get them under control. A workboat chartered by Crescent tried to evacuate the rig earlier but had been driven off by rockets and machine-gun fire. The only other method was by helicopter. Crescent chartered four helicopters from Aerogulf and dispatched them to the rig. When the helicopters first arrived to evacuate the rig crew, the Iranian fire seemed to lighten. "They were having fun, like children," observed Jackson. "But when they saw the helicopters there, they let up."[7]

Two small helicopters each pulled out four workers. Next in was a larger helicopter capable of taking off fifteen personnel. As the larger helicopter came in, the Iranians resumed heavy firing. Some of the machine-gun fire was aimed at the helicopter itself. Ignoring the bullets, the commercial pilot courageously put the aircraft down on the landing pad and shouted for the passengers to board. Men scrambled on and the copter lifted off under continuous fire from the gunboats. For several hours, the four choppers would make round trips to the rig, evacuating its workers. The patter of bullets striking their hulls could be distinctly heard. When the last load of evacuees lifted off, the Iranians were still shooting at the helicopter. One American on the rig observed, "I must say that Aerogulf conducted themselves magnificently, and I feel that personnel aboard the *Scan Bay* owed their lives to the pilots."[8]

The Iranian choice of targets for their retaliatory attack was distinctly odd. Mubarak field was run by the U.S. Crescent Petroleum Corporation, but on behalf of the Arab Emirate of Sharjah, described by some as the closest thing to a friend Iran had in the Gulf. The field was closer to Abu Musa Island than the UAE, and actually lay within the Iranian exclusion zone. The Shah had seized the island from Sharjah in the early 1970s. Iran owned an interest in and shared in revenues from the field. Until the previous year, the field's operating headquarters was actually on Abu Musa. Iran was even obligated by its agreement with Sharjah to pay one-half of the cost of repairing the damage inflicted on the rig by its own gunboats. The Iranian attack on the facilities in the field caused as much puzzlement as anger and seemed to confirm the widely held local opinion that the IRGC were crazies. In any case, the Iranian tear through the oil fields was about to come to an abrupt end.

U.S. Navy aircraft from the carrier *Enterprise* had flown into the Gulf proper and had arrived overhead. The *Enterprise* had been keeping the groups of surface combat air patrol and combat air patrol aircraft operating continuously near the Strait of Hormuz from about 8:45 A.M. on. To stay aloft for extended periods, the aircraft were refueling from Navy KA-6 tankers and A-7E strike aircraft carrying "buddy" refueling pods. A large Air Force KC-10 tanker was in turn, refueling these. The KC-10 also refueled some Navy aircraft directly.

The planes that responded to the IRGC attack included two A-6E Intruder attack bombers and an F-14 fighter. Lieutenant Commander Jim Engler piloted the lead A-6E; his bombardier/navigator was Lieutenant Commander Joe Nortz. Paul Webb piloted the other A-6. Each of the strike aircraft carried a single Harpoon anti-ship missile, a MK-82 500-pound laser-guided bomb, and five Rockeye cluster bombs. The aircraft had not been on station outside the Gulf long before they were contacted by the Navy E-2C Hawkeye, call sign "Banger," and directed to fly inside the Gulf to search for an Iranian *Hengham*-class LST thought to be in the vicinity of Abu Musa Island.

So far that day, U.S. strike aircraft had not flown into the Gulf, and Commander Engler thought to himself, "Holy cow, something big is up." Flying at 14,000 feet, the two A-6E's and the F-14 proceeded down the middle of the Strait of Hormuz and into the Gulf. The F-14 was escorting the strike aircraft to protect them from Iranian fighters. The E-2C was putting out continuous reports of Iranian fighters lifting off from Bandar Abbas. Many of these reports turned out to be false, but there were some Iranian F-4's in the air. The Navy jets were approaching the vicinity of Abu Musa from the southeast when the E-2C called and told Commander Engler that Americans on an oil platform near the island were under Iranian attack. The E-2C was stationed outside the Gulf, but was working with the Air Force AWACS orbiting over the UAE, and relaying reports from it.

The sun was behind them and visibility was good as the jets flew into the area. Commander Engler could look down and pick out the platform under attack without much difficulty. The curling white wakes of the Iranian speedboats were easy to see against the blue water, and the wakes were clearly converging on one of the structures below. Commander Engler called the E-2C and asked, "Please confirm cleared to engage Boghammers."

The request was relayed to the *Enterprise*. Upon receipt of the request, the commander on the *Enterprise* picked up a red scrambler phone and called in the request to Admiral Less, the Commander of the Joint Task Force Middle East on USS *Coronado*. Admiral Less relayed the request by satellite to the U.S. Central Command in Florida. From there, Lieutenant General George Crist sent it to the National Command Center in the Pentagon, where Admiral Crowe, Chairman of the Joint Chiefs of Staff, received it. Admiral Crowe handed it off to Defense Secretary Frank Carlucci, who queried President Reagan. The president gave his OK.[9] The E-2C responded to Commander Engler, "Roger that, cleared to engage." Despite the seemingly cumbersome process, the President's permission to attack was relayed to the A-6's less than three minutes after their initial request to the *Enterprise*. The President had to be consulted because no American ships or facilities were under immediate threat of attack at the time of the request.

The F-14 "held high" to provide air cover while the A-6's went in to engage the Boghammers. The small, very fast Iranian craft were not the easiest targets for aircraft. However, the *Enterprise*'s air wing had worked up for its Gulf deployment by practicing on high-speed surface targets at the Navy's Pacific Missile Test Center. Commander Engler picked the boat closest to the platform as his target. He figured it was the most immediate threat to the men on the structure, and hitting it would send a "keep away" warning to the other boats.

Commander Engler dropped to a little below 500 feet for a low level run with Rockeye cluster bombs. He selected two Rockeyes for release as he swooped in at 450 knots air speed. He did a manual bomb release and turned to watch the impact of the bomblets, which looked much like a large handful of pebbles thrown into the water when they hit. The bomblet pattern actually covered a football field-sized area. The Boghammer he had aimed at was clearly in the pattern. However, the bomblets were relatively small, and the speedboat did not sink or even appear to be heavily damaged. The boat may have been hit though, because it immediately broke off the attack, turned 180 degrees, and headed back toward Abu Musa.

Engler then cleared his wingman for a run. The other A-6E came in with its laser-guided 500-pound bomb. The laser-guided free-fall weapons could be very accurate when used against stationary or slow moving targets. However, they had limited maneuverability once released. The one dropped by the other A-6E was unable to follow the fast moving Boghammer it had targeted, and missed. Engler then made a second run using two more Rockeyes, but was unable to get any hits on the twisting boats.

The Iranian craft were proving to be difficult targets, more difficult than the remote-control target boats used at the Navy's Pacific Missile Center. The workup there had been useful, but the Boghammers now skittering around the platform were moving nearly twice as fast as the "high speed" surface targets the aircrews had practiced on. The other A-6 made its second run using three Rockeyes. This time, the pilot correctly anticipated the course of a Boghammer and was able to put his bombs in the area the boat turned into. The Boghammer took multiple hits, slowed, and lost heading control. It finally stopped dead in the water and began to sink.

This was too much for the surviving Boghammers, and they sped away in a panicky retreat toward Abu Musa. Commander Engler followed them back, flying overhead. The intelligence briefings he had received had painted in his mind the image of fanatical Iranians bent on martyrdom. Now, instead, he was watching them "run like rats." The three U.S. jets flew towards Abu Musa and saw three of the boats reach the island. Apparently frantic to escape their aerial pursuers, they just kept on going, beaching themselves hard on the eastern shore. One boat stayed in the water and sought refuge in the Abu Musa port facility. The U.S. jets flew around the island, attracting heavy anti-aircraft fire from Iranian 23mm and maybe also 37mm guns.

The jets made a left-angle turn at an altitude of 3,500 feet and a range of more than three miles. As they circled, they could see the muzzle flashes of Iranian anti-aircraft sites light up in sequence as the jets flew opposite them. Commander Engler didn't feel particularly threatened since they appeared to be out of range of the Iranian guns. After the run around the island, he called the E-2C and told it the strike group was egressing. The aircraft flew over the UAE and returned to station outside the Gulf.

While the IRGC were hitting the oil fields, the regular Iranian Navy and Air Force made their appearances. After it had completed its action against the Sirri platform, Surface Action Group "C" was ordered to withdraw to the west and await instructions. The ships steamed away from the burning platform in column formation. The ships were proceeding slowly in a northwesterly direction when the JTFME called and reported it had picked up an Iranian navy surface combatant heading their way. The *Wainwright* had a great deal of electronic intelligence equipment onboard and was itself picking up the same information through radio intercepts. The surface action group was instructed to locate the Iranian ship.

Captain Chandler ordered the group to spread out line abreast with a 6,000-yard spacing between ships. This gave a broad baseline for using their electronic support measures (ESM) systems to cross-fix the approaching Iranian ship for over-the-horizon targeting. The idea was that if a single ship picked up a radar signal from the Iranian warship, it would have a bearing on the signal's source but not its position or range along that bearing. If another ship picked up the signal, it could provide a different bearing. When the bearings were laid across each other, their point of intersection would mark the location of the source of the radar signal. Moving the U.S. ships farther apart for the search allowed them to obtain more distinct bearings and hence a more accurate cross-fix on the target. In effect, the Surface Action Group had cast a 12,000-yard-wide electronic net to catch and locate the source of radar emissions from the reported Iranian warship.

As the group swept toward the Iranian ship at 25 knots, it was preceded by the *Bagley*'s SH-2F LAMPS Mk I and the *Simpson*'s SH-60B LAMPS Mk III helicopters, which were searching ahead of the ships. A surface haze forced the helicopters to approach contacts a little closer than was desirable to visually identify them. The Army Blackhawk, which had two high rate of fire machine guns, flew along to escort the Navy choppers, which only had one door-mounted M-60 machine-gun each. At 11:13 A.M., the *Bagley*'s helicopter, call sign "Magus 42," reported that it was taking small arms fire from the trail Boghammer in a group of three of the Iranian speedboats. The Army MH-60 was in the air at the time and could clearly see the Iranians firing at the Navy chopper. The TF-160 pilots were amazed to see that, even while taking enemy fire, the Navy helicopter still had its bright anti-collision lights on. That helicopter was able to dodge out of the area without taking any hits. The *Wainwright* was ordered to take any Boghammers in the area under fire. At the time, the U.S. ships were about 13 nautical miles from the Iranian small boats.

After the helicopter had been fired on, with the Surface Action Group en route to intercept the Boghammers, the *Wainwright* picked up and held an ESM reading for what was described as a "Mk 92 Fire Control System Radar." This was the U.S. designation for the Dutch Signaal radar system employed both by certain U.S. ships and the sought-after Iranian missile boat. The *Wainwright* got an ESM cross-fix from the other ships and then directed the *Bagley*'s SH-2F Seasprite to the indicated location of the Iranian ship. The *Bagley*'s helicopter initially reported that the contact was "a frigate-sized Iranian warship with a mast and a radar amidships. It has two missiles astern of the mast." However the helicopter crew was able to use gyro-stabilized binoculars to visually identify the ship; it was not a frigate, but the smaller Iranian missile patrol boat *Joshan*. The ship was a French-built 275-ton Combattante-II patrol boat, known as the "Kaman" class in Iranian service.

The missile boat had completed escorting an Iranian tanker convoy from Kharg Island to Lavan Island and had been ordered into the southern Gulf to try to determine exactly what was going on in the vicinity of the Sirri platform. The helicopter crew hadn't initially been sure of the ship's identity, but the *Wainwright* already knew, thanks to its communication intercepts. The *Wainwright* not only knew the ship's name, but Captain Chandler even had a photograph of its captain in his intelligence file. The JTFME also warned the U.S. ships that the Iranian ship might possess a lethal sting. They were told that, if the Iranians retained any operational U.S.-made Harpoon anti-ship missiles in their inventory, this particular warship had them. After identifying the *Joshan*, the Seasprite helicopter cleared to the west to get out of the line of fire between the Surface Action Group and the Iranian warship.

The U.S. ships were in a line of bearing formation, with three nautical mile spacing between ships. The *Wainwright* was to the west, the *Bagley* in the center, and the *Simpson* to the east. The *Wainwright* was located about 24 nautical miles southwest of Sirri Island and about 13.5 nautical miles from the *Joshan*. At this point, the U.S. surface action group only intended to keep the Iranian ship away from the area. They did not intend to engage it, but were taking no chances. Captain Chandler had the ships take a weaving course as they closed on the *Joshan*, sometimes running directly toward it, sometimes running parallel. The idea was to make it more difficult for the Iranian ship to arrive at a fire control solution for targeting the U.S. ships.

The JTFME told Captain Chandler to "warn away" the Iranian missile boat. As the *Joshan* neared the American ships, the *Wainwright* got on VHF Bridge to Bridge Channel 16 and warned the Iranian ship that it was standing into danger and advised it to change course and depart the area. Warnings were also made on the Military Air Distress Channel. A Farsi linguist on the *Wainwright* delivered some of the warnings; others were made in English by Captain Chandler. The *Wainwright*'s initial warning was acknowledged by the *Joshan*, which replied that it would not commit any provocative actions and requested that the *Wainwright* not lock its fire control system on it. The *Joshan* claimed that it was conducting a routine passage and that it had no hostile intentions. The *Wainwright* issued another warning to stop or the *Joshan* would be standing into danger. The *Joshan* kept coming.

At 12:09 P.M., the Iranian ship still had not heeded the request to stop. The *Wainwright*, *Bagley*, and *Simpson* all locked their fire control radars on the *Joshan*. On board the *Simpson*, Lieutenant Commander Richard Rush, the Executive Officer, used the ship's "big eyes" observation binoculars to peer through the Gulf haze and visually confirm the approaching Iranian missile boat, now only around 9–10 miles from the *Simpson*. Rush caught a brief glimpse of *Joshan* before it disappeared into the haze. On its stern, he saw two Harpoon missile canisters.

Lieutenant Commander Rush told Captain McTigue, who passed the word to Captain Chandler.

The U.S. ships had approached the *Joshan* bow-on. There were around 25 or so dhows in the area, and the Iranian warship appeared to be deliberately using them for cover, moving in and out among them. The Iranian ship still refused to change course. Its captain determinedly told Captain Chandler, "I'm carrying out my mission." Chandler now had no choice. The *Wainwright* issued a third warning to stop, not proceed further or "I will sink you." There was no response. Finally, around 12:13 P.M., the *Wainwright* issued its fourth and final warning: "Stop, abandon ship, I intend to sink you." There was no radio response from the *Joshan*, but a reply came in another form: the patrol boat locked its fire control radar on the *Wainwright*.

Captain Chandler had been ordering course changes for the Surface Action Group and even issuing his warnings to the *Joshan* in a very calm voice. That voice stayed amazingly calm as he radioed, "*Simpson*, this is *Wainwright*. I am presently launching chaff. I am being locked-on with fire control radar. . . . You have batteries released." *Simpson* had a Standard SM-1 missile mounted on its launcher and was ready to go. McTigue turned to his Tactical Action Officer (TAO) and said, "Shoot!" The TAO turned to the weapons control officer and said, "Shoot!" That officer in turn relayed the order to the petty officer operating the weapons control console. The Standard missile streaked into the sky within three seconds of McTigue receiving the "batteries released" order. One of the U.S. helicopters reported seeing the white smoke of a suspected missile launch from the *Joshan* and radar operators on the *Simpson* and the *Wainwright* were able to see the separation of a missile from the Iranian ship on their radar video displays. In the air, the Army MH-60 pilots could see the Harpoon fired by *Joshan* skimming across the surface of the Gulf toward the U.S. ships. Iranian and U.S. missiles were now both in the air heading for their intended targets.

The U.S.-made Harpoon fired by the Iranian ship was flying a low, sea-skimming attack profile. The Standard missile fired by the *Simpson* was launched on a trajectory that took it up at a high angle before screaming down toward its target. The Standard missile was about three times as fast as the Harpoon. It had a relatively small (65-lb) proximity fused warhead, which would detonate in the near vicinity of a target, shredding it with fragments. The Harpoon had a much larger (500-lb), high explosive warhead, which would detonate either on contact or after penetrating a ship's hull. The supersonic Standard anti-aircraft missile launched by the *Simpson* did not slowly fly off the ship, majestically gathering speed like a space shuttle launch. Instead, the rocket's booster motor ignited with a terrific explosion, which hurtled the Mach-2.5 missile into the air. The U.S. ships had been taking a weaving approach to the *Joshan*. At the time the action commenced, *Simpson* had turned to the northwest, so its target lay to starboard and behind it. The *Simpson*'s launcher was thus turned for an "over the right shoulder" shot, over the starboard bridge wing where Lt. Commander Rush and around nine other men were stationed.

There was no time to warn the exposed men on the bridge wing, so the shattering blast of the launch took them completely by surprise. Spitting flame and smoke, the Standard missile was launched at a steep angle right over the men, slamming them with the concussion of its booster ignition and gagging them with thick exhaust fumes. Lieutenant Commander Rush later told McTigue that the men's reaction to the unexpected missile launch did prove that ten guys could fit through one door at the same time.

The *Wainwright*'s missile fire control system had been put in the surface engagement mode to fire on the Iranian ship, and might have been used to try to shoot down the incoming Harpoon. However, it was unable to lock-on to the aerial target presented by the missile in time to attempt to shoot it down. The problem was that the *Wainwright* had been equipped with an experimental automatic target designation system. It started automatically designating targets all right. Only they were the radar "blooms" of the decoy chaff the *Wainwright* itself was firing, and not the Iranian warship or the Harpoon.

The *Wainwright* was now in a real pickle. The *Joshan* had targeted it, and a Harpoon missile was in the air. Although its launcher was pointed right at the Iranian ship, the *Wainwright* couldn't fire its own missiles at either the *Joshan* or at the incoming Harpoon. Captain Chandler had positioned *Wainwright* almost bow-on toward *Joshan*. Given the wind conditions, that position provided for optimum chaff coverage. *Wainwright* had both rear-mounted and forward-mounted Phalanx gun systems. The latter was mounted off the centerline of the ship. Unfortunately, the Harpoon launched by the Iranian missile boat was coming in on the wrong side of the ship. The guns were set to the anti-aircraft automatic mode, but both were masked and neither could fire without seeing a target.

All of the American ships launched chaff and activated their electronic warfare systems to jam the Iranian missile. On board the *Simpson*, when McTigue had ordered chaff fired, the electronic warfare technician immediately fired all twelve tubes, putting up a huge cloud of chaff in the air. As far as McTigue was concerned, that was the right decision. Navy chaff doctrine, however, called for sequenced firing of chaff tubes in order to maintain continuous coverage against incoming missiles. Later, when curious officers asked McTigue about the chaff doctrine he had employed during the engagement with the *Joshan*, he told them: "All of it, all at once!" The incoming Harpoon was sighted by the signal bridge and starboard lookout on the *Wainwright* as it streaked by, forward to aft, 100 feet off the starboard side of the ship. Anxious crewmen on the ship heard the missile loudly roar by. The missile then landed downrange, falling harmlessly into the water.

Meanwhile, McTigue and his CIC crew had been following the flight of *Simpson*'s SM-1 to its target on their radarscopes. McTigue wasn't sure if it had actually hit the *Joshan*. The proximity-fused missiles did not usually strike their targets with "skin to skin" contact, but rather detonated near to them. McTigue called Chandler and requested permission to fire another missile. Chandler's response was, "Well, all I can tell you is that his radar doesn't work anymore. Something happened, but go ahead and fire another one. "

The *Simpson* followed up its first missile shot with a second SM-1. Both of the supersonic SM-1 anti-aircraft missiles fired from the *Simpson* exploded close to the *Joshan*. The helicopters confirmed that the missiles were "hits." Fragments from the first Standard's warhead detonation had probably shredded the *Joshan*'s fire control radar. One of the U.S. helicopters reported seeing smoke on the horizon. The *Simpson* fired a third SM-1 missile for insurance and recorded another hit. The *Wainwright* was finally able to fire a single Standard SM-1 ER (extended range) missile which also recorded a hit on the Iranian ship.

The U.S. ships were firing the SM-1 anti-aircraft missiles, which could be used in a surface-to-surface mode, in preference to their Harpoon anti-ship missiles because of other boat contacts in the vicinity of the targeted *Joshan*. Harpoon missiles, once launched would have used their own radars to automatically lock on and hit a target. The Harpoons might have been distracted away from the *Joshan* by the nearby presence of dhows, and perhaps hit some of them instead. In contrast, the SM-1 anti-aircraft missiles were directed all the way to their target by the fire control radars on the launching ships, making sure that they would hit only the targeted ship. The high speed of the missile, which quickly knocked out the *Joshan*, was also appreciated. Iranian F-4 fighters were orbiting around 35 miles away to the north, so the ships had had the Standards already mounted on their launcher rails as a precaution.

There was some speculation that the Iranian missile's seeker had not activated because it was fired at such close range to the American ship. However, the *Wainwright*'s AN/SLQ-32 (V13) electronic countermeasures system had identified the Harpoon by its radar signal, indicating that the seeker was active at launch. The seeker, which intelligence indicated had received no maintenance since 1979, failed about a mile from the *Wainwright*. The missile appears to have then followed a ballistic trajectory close alongside the cruiser. The combination of chaff and electronic countermeasures may have distracted the Iranian missile while the seeker was active. A seaman reloading chaff launchers topside on the *Wainwright* said he saw the missile fly past the ship and into a chaff cloud, which may have been the last thing the seeker saw before it failed. In contrast, the *Joshan* does not appear to have made any effort to deflect the U.S. missiles by firing chaff or taking other defensive actions. "We got chaff from Britain four years ago, but they are not on board ships now," said a former Iranian naval officer. "The crews don't know how to use them tactically. They don't train with them."[10]

The *Joshan* was dead in the water and not believed to be combat-capable. The two U.S. helicopters were now observing the Iranian missile boat and providing real time battle damage assessment. They reported no damage to the ship's forward gun or to its hull, but that the superstructure had suffered extensive damage from the bridge to the aft end of the ship and was burning. The U.S. missiles had apparently homed in on and detonated near the highest part of the ship, its superstructure. A life raft was in the water, but no one was in it or in the water. No activity could be seen topside on the stricken ship. By this time, the *Joshan* had drifted into the midst of numerous dhows and would have been hard to engage because of the risk of hitting the smaller boats. Only after the missile exchange did Captain Chandler have the opportunity to catch his breath and to tell Admiral Less what had occurred.

The JTFME ordered the U.S. ships to break off the engagement. The JTFME still apparently wanted to sink the targeted *Sabalan* in preference to the smaller *Joshan*. Range from the U.S. ships to the *Joshan* was about 14 nautical miles at that point. The Surface Action Group broke off the engagement and opened the distance between themselves and the damaged Iranian ship as they commenced searching for the boats that had earlier fired on the *Bagley*'s Seasprite helicopter.

Three Iranian Air Force F-4 Phantom jet fighters in the air had launched earlier from Bandar Abbas. Flying in formation, the Iranian jets had initially been picked up by the AWACS aircraft. The jets were orbiting some 30 to 35 miles north of the area in which Surface Action Group "Charlie" had engaged the *Joshan*. From 30 miles away, the supersonic F-4's could sweep down upon the U.S. warships in virtually no time. Captain Chandler decided to drive them away. He called up McTigue on the *Simpson*, which was the closest ship to the Iranians, and asked him if he wanted to take an anti-aircraft missile shot. McTigue advised Chandler that the Iranian fighters were outside the engagement envelope of his roughly 25-mile range SM-1 missiles. The *Wainwright* carried longer-range SM-2ER missiles, which could easily reach the Iranian jets. The *Wainwright* warned the LAMPS helicopter "Magus 42" to clear out of the way. The helicopter dove for the deck as the *Wainwright* prepared to engage the Iranian jets.

At 12:50 P.M., the *Wainwright* fired two SM-2ER anti-aircraft missiles at one of the fighters. The first missile detonated near the Iranian fighter. A debris cloud was evident on air search and missile fire control radars. The F-4 went from 500 knots airspeed to 200 knots and rapidly lost altitude. The stricken Iranian jet initiated an emergency IFF squawk as it ducked low over Kish Island. With something like ten feet of its right wing missing, the fighter limped back to Bandar Abbas suffering from, in the words of a Navy report, "a mild dose of continuous rod" (a reference to the type of warhead on the anti-aircraft missile). By the time the second missile arrived, however, the stricken Iranian fighter had dived below its engageability envelope and it missed. The other two F-4's lit their afterburners and went supersonic as they fled back over land. Ironically, the Iranian F-4 pilot, a Major, had been trained in the U.S. and had employed the missile avoidance tactics that had been taught to him.

After the anti-air engagement, the Surface Action Group ceased hunting for the small boats that had fired on the helicopter, and was ordered by the JTFME to head back to the *Joshan* and finish her off. Captain Chandler replied "Wilco" to Admiral Less. He intended to do a high-speed run-in at 25 knots and sink the missile boat with guns. This was a logical plan, as long as the *Joshan* was dead in the water and not combat capable. However, *Wainwright* reported that it was detecting electronic emissions from the vicinity of the *Joshan*. Captain McTigue radioed the observation that, if the missile boat could jam, "then it could get a round out of its gun." Taking no chances with the Iranian ship Captain Chandler radioed, "I intend to take down his fire control system and finish [him] off with guns."

Captain Chandler ordered McTigue to fire another Standard missile at *Joshan*. McTigue thought the target was pretty much reduced to a hulk and was skeptical about it being the source of the electronic emissions. In any case, at 1:52 P.M., the *Simpson* fired the fourth SM-1 missile of the day. Unlike the other Standards that had been fired, this one actually hit the *Joshan*. The exploding warhead and the tremendous wallop of kinetic energy delivered by the impact of the Mach 2.5 missile ripped off the remaining superstructure on the Iranian ship, which was now about 13 nautical miles away. Radar video showed debris flying off the ship opposite the side of the missile impact. Based on information provided to him by observers on *Simpson*'s bridge, McTigue called Captain Chandler and told him that the *Joshan* was:

> On fire. Has fires burning onboard. All fires appear to be top-side. There does not appear to be any damage to his hull integrity. Does not appear to be any danger of sinking. Superstructure from bridge area aft has taken most of the damage. We can see his Oto Melara 76mm gun on the foc'sle. At least at long distance, it does not appear to have been hit.

Six minutes later, the *Bagley* was cleared to fire a Harpoon anti-ship missile, which it did. The version of the Harpoon being fired by the *Bagley* had a selectable flight profile as it neared its target. It could be programmed to pop up and dive down onto it. It could pop up in a shallower maneuver and dive onto the target, or it could fly in at a sea-skimming height. The pop up maneuvers made the missile more vulnerable to close-in defenses. However, the *Joshan* was hardly capable of defending itself at this point, so the *Bagley* selected a pop-up terminal maneuver for its Harpoon.

Unfortunately, the *Bagley*'s fire control system had not been modified to accommodate the latest version of the Harpoon, so the *Bagley* was trying to exercise a terminal maneuver option it really didn't have.

The default terminal flight maneuver for the missile was a sea-skimming run-in and that is what the *Bagley* got.

The Harpoon flew straight in toward its target and then right over it. Apparently the missile skimmed over the settling, burning hulk and landed in the water down range. If the missile had done a pop-up maneuver, it probably would have dived into the wrecked ship. The *Bagley*'s SH-2F Seasprite had followed the flight of the Harpoon in and now provided an updated battle damage assessment. Everything aft of the *Joshan*'s gun mount was burned to the water line. Life rafts were in the water, but no one could be seen in them. No one could be seen topside.

The three U.S. warships now closed to a range of 10,000 yards and turned broadside to the wrecked Iranian ship to deliver the coup de grace with guns. Captain Chandler radioed, "*Simpson, Bagley*, this is *Wainwright*. Immediate execute. Turn starboard one three zero at speed one two . . . stand by . . . execute. You have batteries released." At 2:21 P.M., the *Simpson* opened fire. During the gunfire attack on the Sirri platform, Commander McTigue had carefully controlled his 76mm gun, specifying how many rounds it could fire in each salvo. When the gunfire attack on the *Joshan* was commenced, McTigue was up on the bridge and had not specified how many rounds were to be fired. As soon as they got "batteries released," the gun control crew ripped out 49 rounds before he could stop them. McTigue had actually wanted about 20 rounds fired. The *Simpson* and *Bagley* helicopters saw the rounds impacting on the *Joshan* and saw secondary explosions. The *Bagley* and *Wainwright* joined in, also scoring direct hits. The last 5-inch salvo fired by the *Wainwright* hit forward on the *Joshan* and caused a violent explosion. A shell had probably detonated the magazine for the Iranian ship's own 76mm gun.

The U.S. ships broke off the engagement after ten minutes of gunfire. The *Bagley* and *Wainwright* had fired 49 5-inch rounds, the *Simpson* a total of 74 76mm rounds. The *Joshan* sank quickly, leaving an oil slick but not much debris. The ship's egg-shaped plastic radome remained bobbing on the surface, a temporary marker over its watery grave. The helicopters reported two injured Iranians wearing orange life jackets floating in the water. The bodies of three dead crewmen were also observed floating in the water. The Iranian ship would normally have carried a crew of around 31. It seems likely that the dhows sailing nearby during the battle were able to pick up the survivors; especially if any had abandoned ship during the one-hour respite the U.S. surface action group had given them.

It is difficult to see what the *Joshan's* captain had been up to. He could have launched his Harpoon missile from a much longer range if he had simply intended to attack the American ships. He had received numerous clear warnings, which were acknowledged. Nevertheless, he continued to defiantly close on the American ships. Perhaps, up until the fourth and final warning, he was not convinced that he would be fired on and thought he could just bluff his way through. Prior to that day, the U.S. Navy had not engaged regular Iranian Navy warships. The *Iran Ajr* had a regular navy crew but was under commercial registry. The other various actions which had taken place were against IRGC speed-boats. Certainly there had been several tense encounters between the U.S. and Iranian warships, but they had not actually come to blows until the *Joshan* engagement.

As to the final U.S. warning, legitimate questions were later raised about the wisdom of alerting an armed warship to your intention to sink him, particularly when within range of his weapons. The U.S. procedure, which had apparently come down from Washington, had allowed the *Joshan* to get off the first shot, was probably not the best idea, regardless of how it had turned out. The need for some preliminary warning was clear; however, giving a ship's captain the choice of abandoning his ship or going down fighting is really no choice at all. What captain could possibly present himself to his superiors after abandoning his warship to be sunk or seized without a fight? Duty aside, rational calculation would be for him to take even the slimmest chances of fighting as opposed to the certainty of a court-martial leading to imprisonment or execution. Without much difficulty, one can guess at the fate of such an officer under the revolutionary regime of Iran, which was already extremely distrustful of its regular military officers.

CHAPTER 16

"NONE OF THESE LADIES HAS A SCRATCH ON HER"

Surface Action Group "Delta" was composed of the USS *Jack Williams* (FFG 24), USS *Joseph Strauss* (DDG 16), and USS *O'Brien* (DD 975). The latter ship carried Pacific Fleet SEAL Commandos and an Army TF-160 UH-60B helicopter, in addition to its own two SH-2F's. The *Jack Williams* also carried a SH-2F. The SEALs were aboard in case the opportunity came to "take down," or board, an Iranian ship. Captain Donald Dyer, Commander, Destroyer Squadron 22, who was embarked on the *Jack Williams*, commanded the group. Also onboard the *Jack Williams* were reporters from the DoD media pool. The ship's Captain, Commander Edward Mann, had earlier entertained the reporters by shooting sea snakes swimming near the ship with a pistol.

Surface Action Group D's tasking had been to sink the Iranian frigate *Sabalan*, or its on-station replacement, at H-hour. It hadn't happened. U.S. forces had been unable to locate either the *Sabalan* or a suitable replacement frigate target. One of the Iranian ships was usually operating in or near the Strait of Hormuz. The *Sabalan* had been there the day before, when the *Simpson* and the *Bagley* had passed through into the Gulf to participate in Operation Praying Mantis. In fact, the *Sabalan* had locked its fire control radar on the *Bagley*'s helicopter, which was aloft at the time. All intelligence sources were being used to try to locate the ship.

At 5:30 A.M. on the morning of April 18th, it had been tracked to a point 15 nautical miles southeast of Larak Island. However, as "H" hour passed, surface combat air patrol aircraft were unable to locate the ship. Instead, 8:00 A.M. found the surface action group proceeding toward the Strait of Hormuz while awaiting the results of the air search for its primary target. As the three U.S. warships entered the Silkworm missile envelope, battle ensigns rose on their masts and snapped in the Gulf breeze. In calm seas and under clear skies, the U.S. warships transited eastward through the Strait. On their way through, the column passed the Gulf-bound Danish supertanker *Katrina Maersk* and the Pakistani tanker *Jokar*, both previous victims of Iranian attacks. Less than an hour later, the group entered the traffic separation scheme at the entrance to the Strait.

The group exited the Strait and remained for a period in the vicinity of its eastern end. There followed a frustrating hunt for their quarry. Indications now came in that the *Sabalan* was located in the vicinity of the northern Strait of Hormuz traffic separation scheme. SAG "D" immediately proceeded at best speed to that area. The *Jack Williams* launched its SH-2F LAMPS helicopter to check out two contacts which correlated to ESM bearings (i.e. radar signals) for a *Saam*-class frigate. However, both contacts were identified as commercial ships. Various U.S. aircraft were searching for the frigate, but were not turning up anything. As they were finishing up their unavailing search, indications were received that the *Sabalan* was preparing to enter port at Bandar Abbas. "Nobody wants to come out and play," said a disappointed Captain Dyer.[1] As part of the search for another warship target, SUCAP aircraft were vectored to check out a contact of interest near Abu Musa Island inside the Gulf. It was these aircraft that went on to attack the Boghammers shooting up Mubarak Oil Field.

With their primary mission on hold, the U.S. warships proceeded through the Strait of Hormuz and back into the Gulf. Media pool reporters onboard the *Jack Williams* were only told that the American ships were "exercising the right of transit" through the Strait. And so they were, in the course of hunting for the *Sabalan* so they could attack it and sink it.

Surface Action Group "Delta" had returned to the Gulf and was steaming toward Abu Musa Island at a swift 25 knots when indications were received that an Iranian *Saam*-class frigate had gotten underway from Bandar Abbas and was enroute towards Saleh Oil Field, not far from the current position of the U.S. ships. A helicopter based on USS *Reasoner* (FF 1063), which was escorting the carrier *Enterprise* in the Gulf of Oman, used radar and electronic sensors to fix the position of an Iranian ship identified as a *Saam*-class frigate. Those ships were armed with Italian-made Sea Killer anti-ship missiles and normally carried a crew of 135. The frigate had steamed out of Bandar Abbas and was speeding southwest at 25 knots in the direction of the Mubarak and Saleh oil fields, which were then being shot-up by the IRGC Boghammers. Reportedly, the ship had been ordered to join in the attacks on the UAE platforms.

At about 1:00 P.M., the *Strauss* correlated ESM and radar to locate the oncoming Iranian frigate. The *Strauss* then requested "weapons free," i.e. permission to open fire on the targeted ship when it got within range. However, the JTFME Commander denied the request, perhaps because of identification concerns and possible uncertainty about going after a second ship following the *Joshan* engagement. The SUCAP aircraft were ordered turned over from the E-2C Hawkeye to the control of the *Strauss*. Finally, at 1:28 P.M., Admiral Less contacted Captain Dyer and gave him the order: "Take her." At 2:15, Captain Dyer, the SAG "D" commander, issued his battle plan. The U.S. warships dispersed in a ten nautical mile line perpendicular to the Iranian exclusion zone line, with the *Jack Williams* the northernmost ship. The plan was for the group was to use helicopters to visually identify the target at a range of 30 nautical miles. With visual confirmation of its identity, it would be attacked with Harpoon anti-ship missiles at a range of 20 nautical miles. The surface group thought they had the primary mission of sinking the Iranian warship. However, this was not the understanding of the aircrews.

An A-6E attack aircraft, piloted by the "war-at-sea" strike leader, along with two F-14 fighters as escorts, had been following vectors provided by EA-6B's and the E-2C searching for the Iranian ship. The EA-6B's were providing line of bearing "cuts" on possible frigate radar signals. The A-6E strike aircraft would then be vectored to check out and positively identify the contacts. At around 2:40 P.M., a contact, which appeared to be a *Saam*-class frigate moving at about 25 knots through the Strait toward the southwestern Gulf, was located. Bud Langston, the Deputy Carrier Air Group (CAG) Commander, piloted the A-6E attack aircraft. The bombardier/navigator was Lieutenant Bob "Pappy" Papadakis. A highly experienced A-6 pilot, Langston had flown 272 combat missions over Vietnam in A-6's. Langston was aloft on a search mission to try to locate the target. However, his A-6 carried a full strike load of ordnance. This meant that, if he had to return to the carrier without locating and attacking the ship, he would have to jettison some of his load before landing.

Reports later stated that Captain Dyer, the surface action group commander, ordered the SUCAP aircraft not to engage the Iranian ship without his permission. However, Langston never got any such message. In fact, the carrier air group had planned on the anti-shipping strike as their mission. They had received an alert order from Admiral Less two days previously, which they understood assigned them the mission of sinking the *Sabalan*. The air group planners never received any JCS-approved plan placing them in a back-up role. As far as they were concerned, they were the "primary go" on sinking the Iranian frigate. Sunrise on April 18 had found the strike group planes sitting on the deck of the *Enterprise*, armed and ready to launch as soon as the target was located. How this planning disconnect occurred is not clear. In any case, as far as Langston knew, he was still under the control of the E-2C Hawkeye, not the *Strauss*.

The A-6E strike aircraft was backed up by the EA-6B Prowler electronic warfare aircraft, which began jamming the Iranian ship's air search radar and its communications. The SUCAP aircraft used the forward looking infrared (FLIR) sensor on the A-6 as well as high-magnification television cameras on the F-14's to give them a 90 percent confidence factor in identifying the contact as an Iranian warship. Electronic warfare readings also indicated that it was an Iranian frigate. Flying at 15,000 feet, Langston thought the ship definitely looked like the targeted frigate. However, he felt there were too many neutral and allied ships (possibly including British Royal Navy ships of the same type) in the area to take even small chances.

Langston felt that it was absolutely imperative that a 100 percent positive visual identification be made. Accordingly, after taking on fuel from a tanker, Langston decided to take the risk of making a close fly-by. Langston decided to make his pass down the port side of the ship. He kidded Lieutenant "Pappy" Papadakis, sitting in the right seat, that he needed the "185-pounds of flak protection" the bombardier/navigator would provide him. About three miles behind the ship and flying above 20,000 feet, Langston put the A-6 into a steep dive and leveled off at 500 knots-plus at an indicated 50 feet on his radar altimeter.

Approaching stern-on, he saw the muzzle flashes of anti-aircraft fire aimed at him from the ship. He passed alongside within a couple of hundred feet, maybe even as close as 150 feet. He could clearly see Iranian sailors on deck. He could also see tracers from 23mm and 35mm anti-aircraft guns streaking toward him. Langston had gotten so low because he figured it would be harder for anti-aircraft gunners to target his plane if he flew below the visual horizon, that is, if he was not silhouetted against the sky. He also figured it would be difficult for the Iranians to depress the barrels of their weapons low enough to hit him. It seemed to work. The A-6 did not take any hits as it flashed by the ship. The Iranians also fired several hand-held anti-aircraft missiles, probably SA-7's at the Navy jet. The bombardier/navigator had set decoy flares to be released automatically, while Langston punched out more manually. The A-6 broke sharply, and the heat-seeking missiles rising after it were successfully decoyed away.

It turned out that Langston had not found the notorious *Sabalan* but its sister ship, the *Sahand*. But because the frigate had fired guns and missiles at the U.S. aircraft, under the rules of engagement, Langston was now authorized to retaliate. He decided to do so. He radioed the E-2C and told it he was taking defensive action. He also told it to launch the "war-at-sea" strike from the *Enterprise*. Langston figured he would give the Iranians below a warning so they could save themselves from the impending attack if they chose to. He came up on the guard frequency and told the frigate, "I'm going to sink you in five minutes." There was no reply, and no evacuation appears to have taken place. Langston set up a Harpoon anti-ship missile shot. On the first attempt, the Harpoon wouldn't release. Langston swung around for another try. He didn't think it was a "switchology" problem, but Papadakis went through their checklist and reset all switches for the second run. This time, the anti-ship missile launched "as advertised." The following conversation was then reported between Langston's A-6 ("Green lizard 500") and its controller:

A-6: "I've found the *Sahand*."
Controller: "Are you sure?"
A-6: "Yes, I'm sure."
Controller: "How do you know?"
A-6: "I just flew by her starboard side and saw her."
Controller: "How close did you come?"
A-6: "Oh, maybe a quarter or half mile."
Controller: "What was your altitude?"
A-6: "About a couple of hundred feet."
Controller: "What are your intentions?"
A-6: "Well, he shot at me. I'm now twelve miles out and I just launched a Harpoon missile. I'm waiting for it to hit."[2]

It did. The missile hit amidships and exploded. A shock wave slapped the water and raced out in a circle from the impact point. The *Sahand* went dead in the water with fires burning. The A-6 had fired the Harpoon from a 7,000-foot altitude and at a range of 10 nautical miles. The plane followed up with a self-designated MK.82 laser guided 500-pound bomb, which also scored a hit.

The U.S. had only targeted one Iranian ship for sinking, and the *Joshan* had satisfied that tasking. Official reports later claimed that Captain Dyer had authorized the Harpoon launch at the *Sahand* as an immediate response to the ship's firing on the A-6, and that additional attacks by the SUCAP aircraft were denied until a battle damage assessment could be undertaken. In fact, Langston was not in radio contact with the *Strauss* until after he had dropped the laser-guided bomb. His initial attacks left the Iranian ship burning and dead in the water. However, even more trouble for the *Sahand* was on the way. Langston passed the *Sahand*'s coordinates to the other strike aircraft that had been launched and to the surface action group. He reported that the *Sahand* was sinking but still capable of taking action. SAG "Delta" was also now closing on the Iranian frigate's location at high speed. The *Enterprise* had launched a "war-at-sea" strike of six A-7E Corsair light attack aircraft and another A-6.

Lieutenant Papadakis quickly armed the two remaining 1,000-pound, laser-guided, rocket powered "Skippers" as Langston yanked the A-6E around for another attack run. Papadakis illuminated the ship with the aircraft's laser designator. When the display symbology was right, Langston squeezed the trigger. One of the "Skippers" hit directly under the bridge, causing a major explosion. However, the other failed to guide and fell into the water. By this time, the *Sahand* was burning fiercely and smoke may have caused the bomb to lose acquisition of its laser-illuminated target spot. After launching the two Skipper rockets at the *Sahand*, Langston had "gone Winchester," i.e., expended all of his ordnance. However, as "war-at sea" strike leader, he decided to stay around to coordinate the incoming strike and to get battle damage assessment (BDA). Langston cleared the strike aircraft "hot" on the Iranian ship. He was warned about the Iranian F-4 Phantom fighters airborne at the time, and he kept close track of what the E-2C and the F-14 fighters were saying about them.

Lieutenant Commander Mark Needler piloted the "war-at-sea" A-6E. The bombardier and aircraft commander was Commander John

Schork, who was also the squadron Executive Officer. The A-6 crews had been briefed on the upcoming operation the day before and had decided to employ Harpoon missiles for the anti-ship mission. They had taken the missiles under wing when flying on the 17th in order to verify their performance using built-in test equipment. The missiles had checked out fine. When he had been briefed, Commander Schork had felt a bit of trepidation but had reminded himself that this was what he had trained for. In the end, his biggest concern was that he successfully carry out his assigned mission. The "war-at-sea" strike aircraft had been pre-flighted and were ready to launch at dawn on the 18th. However, the morning and early afternoon events had proved anticlimactic. While U.S. forces scrambled to locate the targeted Iranian warship, most aircrews ended up sitting around twiddling their thumbs. Finally, around 3:00 P.M., the word came: "We've found it!"

The "war-at-sea" strike aircraft were ordered to launch. Aircrews did a "LeMans Start," running out to their waiting aircraft like drivers commencing the famous 24-hour road race. In his A-6 cockpit, Commander Schork proceeded to obtain an inertial alignment for his navigation/attack system from the carrier. Normally this was done via a RF (radio frequency) signal, but now, of all times, the RF was not working. Schork was forced to use a cable back-up system, which had a much slower data transfer rate. Increasingly anxious about being left behind as the data slowly loaded, Schork decided that there was no way he was going to miss the show. He pulled out before his inertial system was fully aligned. What the heck, he figured, it's a clear day and he knew the Gulf like the back of his hand. He was damn glad to finally get going.

Once the A-6 had launched and was underway, Schork contacted the carrier-based E-2C Hawkeye airborne radar aircraft and requested the target co-ordinates. Schork was already talking to the E-2C over a voice-scrambled radio. However, the controller on the Hawkeye wanted to further protect the target coordinates by using a cumbersome numerical "AKAC" encryption system. Schork didn't see any need to use the numerical encryption for the target location and told the controller, "He [the Iranian ship] already knows where he is." The controller relented and passed the longitude and latitude over the voice scrambled radio. Schork inputted the data into his navigation system. From over 40 miles away, he got a strong radar return from that location.

Piloted by Commander Needler, the A-6 headed directly for the Iranian warship. There was no circling or forming up with the A-7's.

Normally, the carrier aircraft were careful to thread the needle through the Strait of Hormuz, flying down the middle in international airspace. This time, the A-6 made a beeline straight to the target, even cutting across the UAE on its run. Although a column of brown smoke rising from the damaged *Sahand* could be seen at quite a distance, Commander Schork realized he was very shortly going to be firing a radar guided Harpoon missile into an area normally transited by numerous other vessels. The thought got him a bit uptight, and he contacted Bud Langston, pilot of "Green Lizard 500," and asked him to verify the target, which he did.

Closing fast, Schork began his attack run about 16 miles out from the *Sahand*. The A-6 was flying at 5,000 feet. Schork wanted to fire the missile from in close. He had studied the Falklands war and was aware of the damage done by even an unexploded missile which had plenty of fuel still aboard. He wanted to fire the Harpoon so close that it retained lots of fuel, maximizing the potential damage it would inflict on the frigate. Also, the closer he got, the better the missile seeker's target discrimination, making it much less likely to hit an innocent ship.

Schork set his system for an attack run. He selected the under-wing station carrying the Harpoon, which then started "talking" to the plane's computer. He turned on the fusing circuits and then the master arm switch. The computer checked the system. There was no reselect light, so he was good to go. He pushed the red "Attack" button. All of the symbology on his 11-inch FLIR (Forward Looking Infrared) view screen was now attack related. The pilot was getting symbology directing him to a point in space, which fell within the weapon launch parameters of the weapon he had selected. When the computer signaled that it was able to launch, Lt. Commander Needler pulled the commit trigger. Two seconds later, at a range of about 11 miles, the computer fired the missile. The plane bobbed slightly as the heavy missile fell away. About twenty feet below the aircraft, the Harpoon engine ignited, and it sped away toward the *Sahand*.

Surface Action Group "Delta" was also now within range of the Iranian ship. An SH-2J helicopter from the *Jack Williams* closed with the *Sahand* in order to confirm the Surface Action Group's targeting solution. The *Joseph Strauss* then launched its own Harpoon at the *Sahand*. Later, an official gloss on the action would state that the *Joseph Strauss* and the A-6 had coordinated their Harpoon launches to arrive on target simultaneously. There was no such coordination. In fact, during the A-6's run-in to the target, the *Joseph Strauss* had tried to get the aircraft to abort its launch. John Schork told the *Strauss* that it was too late; they were already committed. Another A-6 pilot later cynically observed of the purported coordinated attack, "We probably would have screwed it up if we had planned it."

As the white Harpoon missile roared skyward off the *Joseph Strauss* in a cloud of smoke and streaked over the horizon, the men on the *Jack Williams'* bridge cheered: "Yeah! Yeah! Yeah!" The *Joseph Strauss* was about 15 nautical miles away from the *Sahand* when it fired its Harpoon. The *Williams* was two nautical miles to the northwest of the *Strauss* and the *O'Brien* was seven nautical miles to the southeast. The *Joseph Strauss'* Harpoon hit the *Sahand*'s bridge. If the ship had any remaining combat capability, it wouldn't be getting any central direction. From the *Jack Williams*, the missile's impact was seen as a flash and a puff of smoke.

The Harpoon fired by the A-6 also hit the *Sahand*, this time amidships. The exploding warhead ignited the load of fuel still carried aboard the missile. John Schork was too busy to notice. Instead of following the flight of the Harpoon on his FLIR screen, he was pre-occupied in setting up a follow-on attack using the aircraft's two laser-guided, rocket-powered Skippers. Those weapons had launch parameters that differed from those of the just-fired Harpoon. Schork had to reset ten different switches to put his attack system in the Skipper delivery mode. Pilot Mark Needler was very familiar with the Skipper, having worked with it extensively while in the Navy's weapons trials unit. Once inside the Skipper delivery envelope, his preference was to get a bit higher and a bit closer for optimum hit probability.

The Skipper homed in on the laser energy reflected off a target when the A-6's laser designator was aimed at a spot and activated, illuminating it. Schork would use a small joystick to manually place a cursor for the laser designator on the target as seen through his FLIR view screen. To keep the daylight shining into his cockpit from washing out his views screen, Schork had his head under a leather hood over the screen. The FLIR could be set for "white hot" or "black hot," with the switch sometimes revealing details otherwise missed.

As his A-6 commenced its next run, on his screen Schork could see smoke pouring out of the *Sahand* where the Harpoons and bomb had earlier hit it. He aimed his laser designator toward the undamaged stern of the ship. Because the Skippers homed in on the reflected laser energy, the target had to be kept continuously illuminated until they hit.

Needler had to fly the A-6 so that the laser designator stayed aimed on target the whole time. If the plane turned the wrong way, the designator couldn't be kept on target and the missiles would go awry. Laser guided weapons also had a tendency to "porpoise" very slightly in the air, rising and falling a bit along their trajectory as their control fins made small adjustments in their flight path to keep them on target. In order to avoid the possibility of one of the missiles passing just over the ship during a small rise in its flight, Schork "aimed down" by placing the cursor for his laser designator slightly lower on the *Sahand* than his desired impact point.

At a range of about five miles and an altitude of 3,000 feet, the A-6 launched two Skippers in rapid succession. Some 40 seconds after it was fired, the first Skipper impacted toward the aft end of the *Sahand* and exploded. Watching on his FLIR screen. Schork was stunned by the violence of the blast. "Holy shit!" he exclaimed, as pieces of the ship's stem were hurled into the air. The A-6 swung away to allow the crew to catch their breath. The two attack runs had lasted a total of about 10 minutes.

There was no break for the *Sahand*, as the A-7E's now took their turn and joined in the attack. The first section of four A-7E's came in to launch two Walleye II TV-guided glide bombs, one of which failed to guide. The A-7Es then pressed in high dive-bombing runs and dropped 18 unguided Mk 83 thousand pound "iron" bombs, at least five of which hit the ship. One of these blew up the ship's Seakiller missile mount with a direct hit. Finally, an A-7E dropped three more Mk 83 bombs on the hapless ship.

As the attack proceeded, the SH-2F helicopter from the *Jack Williams* flew within anti-aircraft range of the *Sahand*, recording data from its FLIR system and relaying tactical information to the U.S. ships. Despite the extensive damage inflicted on it, the *Sahand* was evaluated as possibly retaining some combat systems capability. The A-7's then went in to finish off the ship, scoring hits with Skippers, a Walleye, and several 1,000 pound bombs and cluster bombs. The *Sahand* still had some teeth. Initially, at least, it fought back, firing anti-aircraft guns and surface-to-air missiles at its tormenters. The defensive efforts proved futile and the ship took an incredible pounding, being hit by just about every type of air-to-ground and anti-ship weapon in the American inventory.

The *Sahand* now presented a scene of utter destruction. The Sea-Killer mount, used to fire missiles at tankers, had been obliterated. The large and heavy 4.5- inch gun turret, which had so often fired on the crews' quarters of innocent ships, had been blown off its mount and lay askew on the foredeck. Thick smoke poured out of almost every part of the ship. The superstructure was crumpled. The rear half of the ship had massive chunks blown out of it and was completely engulfed in fire and smoke. The ghostly image on the helicopter's FLIR revealed intense fires burning deep inside the ship, running along the waterline from the leading edge of the deckhouse aft to the funnel. Two life rafts were in the water alongside the ship, but no crewmen could be seen.

John Schork's A-6E had flown away from the *Sahand* for a while after its two attack runs. The aircraft then reversed course and flew back toward the Iranian frigate. The A-6E still carried one 500-pound laser-guided bomb under its wing. When the A-6E returned to the ship's location, the A-7E's had finished their runs. It would have been easy to put the A-6E's remaining 500-pound bomb into the ship. There was, however, Schork thought, a difference between combat and simply pummeling the now helpless ship. The *Sahand* was clearly in a sinking condition. He figured the survivors were probably trying to aid and evacuate the injured. Schork decided not to drop his last bomb. The A-6E did hang around a while, taking on fuel from a tanker. The crew of the attack aircraft then heard a radio warning that Iranian F-4 fighters were airborne from Bandar Abbas. They decided that discretion was the better part of valor and flew back over the UAE out to where U.S. fighters could be quickly called in by the E-2C if needed.

Meanwhile, large secondary explosions wracked the *Sahand*. The *Jack Williams* vibrated in the shock waves as they rolled across the Gulf. Nevertheless, the wreck of the frigate was still stubbornly afloat as the sun set, much to the frustration of Bud Langston. Flying overhead, he had watched the A-7E's make their bombing runs on the ship. They had been briefed to make a quick strike at altitude to reduce the threat of anti-aircraft fire. Langston saw the A-7's score hits but also saw near misses raising splashes in the water. He thought the A-7's should have come in lower with their unguided "iron bombs" toward the end, since the *Sahand* appeared unable to defend itself at that point.

Langston had the "knife between his teeth" and was anxious to accomplish his assigned mission of sinking the Iranian warship. He was actually starting to worry that the ship might not be sunk. By late in the day, the strike group had expended all of its ordnance and the frigate was still afloat, if completely wrecked. Langston had seen target hulks hit in a similar fashion without being sunk. He had been told then that they hadn't sunk because they did not carry the fuel and ammunition that ships in active service would have. Well, the *Sahand* obviously had fuel and ammunition aboard, but it wasn't sinking either.

The size of the bombs used by the strike aircraft was a sore spot with Langston. In planning for the anti-shipping mission, he had decided to employ 2,000-pound, laser-guided bombs. The Strike Operations officer refused to release them. He wanted to retain the bombs in case the carrier had to execute pre-planned contingency strikes against Iran. Langston argued strenuously that the 500-pound bombs he was being forced to use were like "firecrackers" in the anti-ship role. Based on his Vietnam experience, Langston was convinced that bigger was better. As for the possibility of exhausting the supply of 2,000-pounders, Langston figured that that's what the logistics re-supply pipeline was for.

Langston tried to get the support of the Carrier Air Group (CAG) commander. However, the CAG was reluctant to challenge the Strike Ops officer and the Operations officer on the issue. A briefing on the war-at-sea strike plans had been held on the evening of the 17th for the battle group commander, Admiral Guy Zeller. The CAG told Langston not to mention his concerns about the planned size of the bombs during the briefing. Langston made his presentation and didn't mention the bombs. He thought that Admiral Zeller might have sensed he was holding back something because he then gave the officers a last chance to raise any objections to the plans. Langston wasn't sure if Admiral Zeller's inquiry reached past the more senior officers to his level, but he could contain himself no longer. "If this includes me," he spoke up, "this stinks!" Langston went on to give his objections to the planned ordnance load. However, the other officers present continued to voice support for the original plan. In the end, based on their recommendations, Admiral Zeller accepted that plan.

Langston wasn't the only one concerned that the frigate had not been sunk. Sometime after John Schork returned to the *Enterprise*, he heard that the Iranian ship was still above the water. He began to wonder about his decision not to drop his last bomb. Later that evening, with the *Sahand* still afloat, Bud Langston and the officers who had derided the need for the 2,000-pound bombs were called to Admiral Zeller's office. The Admiral told Langston that his opinion on the need for the large bombs had been vindicated. The 500-pounders had indeed been "firecrackers" when used against the warship. Langston was dismissed and the officers who had argued in favor of the smaller weapons remained for further discussions with the Admiral.

The two A-6E's and the F-14 under Lieutenant Commander Engler, which had earlier engaged the Boghammers near Abu Musa, had returned to their station outside the Gulf. The three aircraft were low on fuel, and the *Enterprise* told them to "RTB" (return to base—the carrier) and land. Jim Engler still had a 500-pound LGB and a Harpoon. His wingman had a Harpoon and a Rockeye. Engler contacted the *Enterprise* and asked for permission to remain on station. The carrier gave the OK, so the three aircraft filled up from an Air Force KC-10 tanker. The F-14 fighter had the lowest fuel state, so it went first. After all three had taken on fuel, the group had stayed together with the A-6E's using their radars to search for the Iranian frigate, as the hunt for the *Sabalan* had proceeded. The radar screens were painting numerous surface contacts, nearly 50 of them, so it had proved impossible to pick out the frigate using the search radars only.

Commander Engler was contacted by the USS *Joseph Strauss*, call sign "Yankee 8," and vectored to investigate a contact on a specific range and bearing from the U.S. ship. The contact was a possible *Saam*-class frigate in the vicinity of Larak Island. Arriving in the area, the A-6E's actually saw two contacts. The first one turned out to be a civilian tanker. The second looked more interesting. Commander Engler could click a switch on his stick and bring up the FLIR image (what the bombardier was seeing) on his Altitude Display Indicator (ADI), a CRT-display screen, which normally showed an artificial horizon.

He approached the contact at an altitude of 15,000 feet. At a range of about eight nautical miles, he looked at the FLIR image on his ADI display and then down at an intelligence photograph of the *Sabalan* attached to his kneeboard. It was an eerie feeling looking from the intelligence photo to the virtually identical live FLIR image being displayed in front of him. There was little doubt that the contact was a *Saam*-class frigate. On the FLIR display, he could also see the muzzle flashes of anti-aircraft cannon firing at him from the ship. The other A-6 spotted three hand-held SAM's being fired from the Iranian frigate. The crew of the ship may have been a bit panicky at this point. The SA-7's didn't guide, possibly because they hadn't been properly locked on before being fired. The A-6's didn't even bother to employ chaff or flares to distract the missiles. The anti-aircraft gunfire was also ineffective. For the frigate crew, with reports of other Iranian ships being sunk and menacing aircraft swooping overhead, it was not quite the same experience as leisurely shooting up the crew quarters of an unarmed merchant ship.

Commander Engler couldn't see a hull number on the ship. The other Iranian frigate, which had been attacked and devastated, had been identified as the *Sahand*. Engler figured this was probably the long sought-after *Sabalan*, and reported back to the E-2C. Having been fired at, Commander Engler decided to retaliate with his 500-pound laser-guided bomb. As he made his bombing run, he had to be mindful of his aircraft's possible exposure to Iranian anti-aircraft missiles located at Bandar Abbas. These were the dangerous American-made Improved HAWKS (I-HAWKS). The U.S. aircraft were now just outside the edge of the I-HAWK envelope. Commander Engler's planned bombing run would keep him only a mile or so out of that envelope. He also had to ensure that the FLIR turret, with its laser designator, would maintain a clear and uninterrupted track on the target. He used the A-6 pilot's rule of thumb: "If the eye can see it, the FLIR can too."

He rolled in at 17,900 feet and went into a steep 45-degree dive. At an indicated 540 knots, he released the laser-guided bomb. He felt the bomb release and pulled back on the stick, recovering from the dive at 12,000 feet. He kept his left wing down and his eye on the target. The bomb guided true and Commander Engler could see it hit the ship with a puff of dark smoke. The ship immediately went dead in the water. Within a few minutes, a huge oil slick had spread behind the ship. It was widely reported that the bomb went right down the exhaust stack into the engineering spaces, where it exploded. In fact, the bomb penetrated the starboard hull of the ship about a foot and a half above the waterline, before exploding in the engineering spaces.

The A-6's were each still carrying a Harpoon anti-ship missile and Rockeye cluster bombs. They were unable to follow up the laser-guided bomb with a Harpoon attack because the targeted ship was only a quarter mile from land. The radar return from the coast would have interfered with the missile guidance system. The action was obviously taking place in Iranian territorial waters. If the A-6's had reoriented to the northeast to give the missile seekers a clear shot, the aircraft would have to have flown within range of the Iranian I-HAWK anti-aircraft missiles located at Bandar Abbas. The Rockeye cluster bombs the A-6's also carried required a low altitude delivery, which was judged too risky in light of the anti-aircraft fire being put out by the *Sabalan*. Commander Engler received a call from the E-2C to return to the carrier. Another "war-at-sea" strike group had been launched and was on its way to finish off the *Sabalan*. Indications were also being received that yet a third *Saam*-class frigate was getting underway from Bandar Abbas. The U.S. ships had picked up a mayday call from the *Sabalan* after the initial bomb strike.

It was around this time that Surface Action Group "Delta" and the *Jack Williams* in particular, came under Iranian anti-ship missile attack. With the first warning of incoming missiles, crewmen on the *Jack Williams* scrambled across the deck as the ship maneuvered violently to avoid the missiles. None of them hit, apparently being successfully decoyed away from the ships, which did not have to use their Phalanx close-in weapon systems. Four of the missiles reportedly passed too far away from the ships to be seen. The fifth, however, could be seen crossing harmlessly behind the ship. Elated that the ships had avoided being hit, Captain Don Dyer said, "Not one of these ladies has a scratch on her, and the other guys can't say that." Some initial reports claimed that the dreaded Silkworms had been fired at the U.S. ships. However, it was unclear if missiles had been fired by one of the Iranian frigates or even Iranian aircraft. The Pentagon later stated that there was no evidence that Silkworms had been fired at the Navy ships.

During the reported missile attacks, all SUCAP aircraft were ordered out of the area to prevent a "blue on blue" engagement. The *Sabalan* thus had a grace period from further attack, during which it summoned two tugs to its aid. The ship was low at the stern, apparently from flooding, and its oil slick spread out for miles. No fires were visible. One tug rigged a cable to its bow for a tow; the second tug came alongside the port side. The ship was being towed to port at Bandar Abbas when two fresh A-6's, carrying laser-guided bombs and escorted by an F-14 arrived over the scene. The "war-at-sea" strike group also was enroute.

Light was fading fast in the Gulf, but the *Sabalan* was an easy target now. Captain Dyer directed the A-6's to engage it. Admiral Less reportedly preferred to sink her. Defense Secretary Frank Carlucci and Admiral William Crowe, Jr. were sitting in the Pentagon Command Center listening to radio traffic from the Gulf. They called off the attack on the *Sabalan* in the interest of ending the day's sea battles. The JTFME directed the A-6's to perform battle damage assessment but not attack the *Sabalan* unless hostile intent was shown. "We've shed enough blood today," Admiral Crowe told Carlucci.[3] The *Sabalan* was towed, stern down, into Bandar Abbas.

The decision to spare the *Sabalan* led to a certain amount of grousing among U.S. forces in the Gulf, who would have preferred to finish her off. One of the A-6 pilots participating in the strikes that day described his and the other aircrews as "thoroughly pissed" about the decision not to sink the ship. They had received plenty of intelligence reports on the vicious attacks made by the *Sabalan* against unarmed commercial ships, and were eager to have at it. Caught up in the action that day and given that the *Sabalan* was their original target, their feelings are understandable. From the perspective of America's policy interests in the Gulf, however, cold logic does not reveal anything to be gained by sinking the ship. The U.S. had been trying to deliver a measured response to the *Roberts* mining. The Iranians had reacted with unexpected ferocity. As the level of violence rose, there was an increasing possibility that events could get out of hand. It was best to cap the day as soon as possible and let things cool off.

Now nearly over, the day had, in fact, gone very well for American forces, who had not suffered any losses. Unfortunately, it would not end that way. Two of the Marine AH-IT Cobra gunships on the *Trenton* had lifted off from that ship around 6:00 P.M. to deploy to USS *Wainwright*. The Cobras would be used to visually identify potentially hostile contacts in the area. By around 8:30 P.M., the helicopters were preparing to secure for the day. One of them, "Warrior 1-1" had already landed on the *Wainwright* and was being towed off the helicopter landing spot. "Warrior 1-2" was still in the air when it got a call from the *Wainwright*'s Combat Information Center to check out a contact some 18 miles to the east. The commander of Surface Action Group "Delta" believed the ship was the *Larak*—hull number 240T. Army TF-160 SEABATS on the *Jack Williams* were also sent to investigate.

Vectored by radar on the *Wainwright*, "Warrior 1-2" closed on the ship and visually identified it as an Iranian *Hengham*-class LST. There were a lot of other ships in the area and the Iranian LST may have been pulling alongside freighters to shield itself against possible American attack. The Cobra reported being challenged by the ship at about 8:50 P.M. and then reported that it had been "locked-up" by a fire control radar. Radio communication was lost and the copter disappeared from the *Wainwright*'s radar.

The Army MH-60 had been flying in the same area at the time, and the crew chief had started yelling, "Missile! Missile! Missile!" as what looked like a small surface-to-air missile streaked past the helicopter's tail. The MH-60 called the *Wainwright* to ask if they had fired a missile. They had not. By the time the SEABATS based on the *Jack Williams* arrived, the Iranian ship was gone.

An immediate and extensive search was begun for the helicopter and its crew: Marine Captains Kenneth Hill and Stephen Leslie. The commander of Surface Action Group "Delta" initiated a Search and Rescue (SAR) plan for the missing helicopter. Air and sea searchers could find no wreckage or survivors.

Anticipating further spasms of violence in the wake of the U.S.-Iranian clashes, shipping in the southern Gulf came to a virtual standstill the next day. U.S. forces remained vigilant. The three Surface Action Groups continued patrolling, with SAG "Delta" operating southeast of Abu Musa Island and continuing search and rescue operations for the missing Marine helicopter. At 6:52 P.M. on April 19, Operation Praying Mantis was officially terminated.

American leaders had been genuinely taken aback by the strong Iranian response to the platform attacks. The Iranians were greatly overmatched in firepower and they stood to lose heavily in such a battle, as in fact, they did on April 18. Why they were ordered into action was not clear. "It certainly didn't follow the precedent," said U.S. Defense Secretary Frank Carlucci. "I'm not sure it's explainable in terms of Western logic."[4] A Gulf shipping executive said, "Those people across the Gulf seem to be wound up pretty tight, and as you saw last week, when the Americans came in here, they [Iran's navy] came pouring out of Bandar Abbas like bees from a hive."[5]

Iran's official Islamic Republic News Agency claimed that their warships had, in a "heroic clash with the aggressor America's helicopters" shot down the missing Marine helicopter, and that naval units of the Revolutionary Guards had found wreckage belonging to the copter.[6] This claim was only made after the Pentagon announced that a U.S. helicopter was missing. U.S. search efforts for the helicopter were given up, and its two-man crew was declared killed in action by the Department of Defense.

While it was originally thought that the helicopter and the remains of the crew would never be recovered, U.S. forces did in fact locate the wreckage of the Cobra in mid-May. Sonobuoys picked up signals from a saltwater activated mechanical tapping device carried onboard the craft. By midday on the 19th, intermittent signals from the "tapper" were being picked up. Salvage tugs and a floating crane were brought in to lift out the wreckage and the bodies of the pilots. Examination of the aircraft did not reveal any battle damage. Iranian claims to the contrary, it didn't appear that it had been shot down. The helicopter had been challenged shortly before it reported being locked-on by fire control radar; however, the Iranian LST-type ships did not have radar-directed fire control systems, so the radar lock-on report appears questionable.

The Army MH-60 crew had observed what they identified as a surface-to-air missile in the air at the same time and location. This was possibly a handheld SA-7-type missile. Perhaps the helicopter was reporting that it had been "locked-on" by the missile. The Cobra appears to have tried to "break lock" or dodge the missile fired from the *Larak*. The Marine crew, wearing night vision goggles, and fatigued from being in operation since dawn, may have made a violent turning maneuver which resulted in a rotor tip striking the water surface, which was hard to discern in the gathering darkness.

U.S. intelligence projected a severe Iranian reaction to the events of April 18. Accordingly, the Navy stopped the Earnest Will convoys for a few days in an effort to gauge Iranian intentions. Fortunately, fears of a violent Iranian response were not realized, as Iran did not take any action. Perhaps it was distracted by the fact that it was starting to lose its war against Iraq.

If Iran had received a bloody nose at the hands of U.S. forces in the Gulf, it took a punishing body blow from Saddam Hussein's Iraq at the same time. Iraq had secretly concentrated armor and infantry forces opposite the Iranian-held Al-Faw peninsula and launched a surprise attack which hurled the stunned Iranians back across the Shatt al-Arab waterway in a 36-hour blitzkrieg. "Your sons have entered the dear town of Faw, liberating its soil from the filth of the invaders," stated an Iraqi communiqué.[7] Iran accused the U.S. of supporting the Iraqi attack with helicopters, and vowed retaliation against what one spokesman described as the "Baghdad-Kuwait-Washington axis."[8]

The Iraqi and U.S. actions were not coordinated, but their coincidental timing apparently convinced Iran that they were. Iranian parliamentary speaker Rasfsanjani charged that the Iraqi land attack and U.S. sea attack were launched by "anti-Islamic, arrogant powers." Iran fired a Scud missile at a Kuwaiti oil field in revenge. It missed. In the wake of recent Iranian setbacks, Rafsanjani admitted that, "Time is not on our side anymore."⁹

U.S. military and political leaders were highly satisfied with Operation Praying Mantis. A sharp, controlled blow had been successfully delivered to Iran. True, Iranian reaction to the platform attacks had been much stronger than anticipated, but thankfully, events had not escalated out of control. It was particularly important that Iran had not crossed the "Silkworm threshold" as early reports had indicated. The U.S. had publicly stated on a variety of occasions that it would attack the missile launch sites in Iranian territory if Iran so much as locked on to U.S. ships with Silkworm fire control radars.

The U.S. government was clearly hoping that the smoke of battle would blow away. A few days after the Praying Mantis Operation, President Reagan sent a letter to Congress justifying the actions as "the exercise of our inherent right of self-defense." He added, "We have completed these self-defense actions and consider that matter closed." And so it was. However, one aspect of events that day needs to be reopened. Iran had, in fact, attacked U.S. forces at both ends of the Gulf with Silkworm missiles, which fact the Pentagon had covered up.

CHAPTER 17

"MULTIPLE SILKWORMS INBOUND"

On April 18, it had been expected that there would only be a minimal Iranian response in the northern Gulf to the U.S. retaliatory strikes. The frigate USS *Gary*, commanded by Captain W. Dallas Bethea, was serving as the guard ship for the Mobile Sea Bases stationed there. The Atlanta-born Bethea had received his commission in April 1969 through the Naval Reserve Officers Candidate program and attended Cal State, Northridge. He had served as a Beach Master in Vietnam, directing shoreline activity during Marine Corps amphibious operations. Bethea had gone on to serve in positions of increasing responsibility aboard surface ships prior to taking command of the *Gary* in Burnbury, Australia in December 1986.

At its northern location, the *Gary*'s biggest concern was usually errant Iraqi air attacks. Early on the morning of the 18th, in fact, the *Gary* had picked up a flight of Iraqi planes coming down the Gulf. When communications were established, the Iraqis gave the Americans a call sign that indicated the aircraft were on a maritime strike mission. However, this was not going to be a routine de-confliction. The *Gary* ordered the Iraqi pilot to "RTB," i.e. return to base. The pilot's response, in a joking tone of voice, was, "U.S. Navy warship, you have a problem?" With the U.S. combat actions against the Iranians underway that day, the *Gary* wasn't in on the joke. It repeated the "RTB" order. The Iraqi pilot responded with a professional "Roger Out," and the strike formation obligingly turned back to the north. Following the *Gary*'s "RTB" order, no more Iraqi aircraft came out that day.

The *Gary* and the Mobile Sea Bases were positioned about 25 miles south of Iran's Farsi Island. The bases were some five to eight miles apart, with the *Gary* patrolling in between them. The Hercules was the larger of the two and the *Gary* tended to favor it, trying to stay within two miles of the base. Late in the afternoon, *Gary*'s air search radar picked up an Iranian helicopter. The aircraft, thought to be a large American-built Sikorsky H-3, flew out from the mainland and went into an orbit over Farsi Island. The helicopter was flying at an altitude of 8,000 feet. It was also carefully keeping just outside the range of the *Gary*'s anti-aircraft missiles. Obviously, the Iranians were aware of the frigate's roughly 25-nautical mile anti-aircraft missile engagability envelope. From its height, the Iranian helicopter would be able to pinpoint the location of the *Gary* and the Mobile Sea Bases using its search radar or possibly even an ESM system to determine the bearings of the radar emitters on the sea bases and the *Gary*.

Like other CO's, Captain Bethea had attended the Prospective Commanding Officers Course at Newport, Rhode Island prior to taking command of his ship. The Director of the course he attended was Commodore Donald Dyer, who at that very moment was commanding Surface Action Group "Delta" near the Strait of Hormuz. During the course, Commodore Dyer had told the future ship captains that they must have been doing something right to have risen to command rank. He told them to "trust your nerve endings; they have served you well over the years." Captain Bethea's tingling nerve endings now told him that the Iranian helicopter he was watching on his radar screen was targeting his ship and the Mobile Sea Bases.

Captain Bethea picked up the radio and called the Joint Task Force Middle East. He advised them of the situation he was facing and requested permission "to take with birds," i.e., shoot down the helicopter with anti-aircraft missiles. The JTFME approved Captain Bethea's request. The *Gary* mounted an anti-aircraft missile on its launcher, locked fire control radar on the Iranian helicopter, and was ready to fire without warning. However, the Iranian helo's orbit was keeping it tantalizingly just out of range. Captain Bethea even ordered his Tactical Action Officer to try to override the fire control computer and shoot. The launcher was "synched," or aligned with the fire control system, and aimed at the aircraft, but the computer balked at letting the ship fire.

After watching in frustration for about 15 minutes as the helicopter orbited just out of range, one of the *Gary*'s officers came up with a suggestion. If the helicopter was not using a search radar, but only passively reading the ship's electronic emissions in order to locate them, they might shut down their active radar emitters and close at flank speed to get within range for a missile shot. Captain Bethea decided to try that approach, setting what was, in Navy tactical terminology, a "missile trap." That is, get within range of the target without its being aware of the ship's presence, and then suddenly bring the radar systems online for a quick anti-aircraft missile launch.

The *Gary* shut down its systems and steamed at flank speed toward the Iranian helicopter for some 6,000 yards before coming to a halt and setting up a shot. The *Gary* brought up its radar systems and locked its continuous-wave fire control radar on the helicopter. Captain Bethea then ordered, "batteries released." However, just as the *Gary* was about to fire, the Iranian helicopter began plummeting like a stone toward Farsi Island. The helicopter may have been equipped with a radar warning receiver which had sounded an alert when it picked up the continuous-wave illumination from the *Gary*'s fire control radar; or maybe the *Gary* had been seen coiling to strike either by a radar on Farsi or on the helicopter itself.

As he watched the helicopter's plunging descent on radar, Captain Bethea and several other officers in the *Gary*'s Combat Information Center (CIC) thought that it may have gone into autorotation, which is a kind of controlled semi-crash. The technique involves disconnecting the rotor from the power train and allowing it to windmill in the air stream so the airfoil blades can provide enough lift to make a safe landing. Seeing the helicopter abruptly drop, Captain Bethea aborted the missile launch against it.

While it was attempting to engage the helo, the *Gary* received confirmation of Captain Bethea's fears: The Iranian chopper was indeed relaying targeting data on the location of the U.S. ship. The Hercules had a section monitoring Iranian communications, and they had apparently intercepted the Iranian messages. This was an ominous development. Things began to look even worse when a large group of Iranian F-4 Phantom fighters now flew out of Busher on the Iranian coast and went into an orbit about 40 nautical miles away. The seven fighters were an unusually large group, and holding position so close to the U.S. forces was also highly unusual. Something was definitely up, as the *Gary* and the Mobile Sea Bases were about to find out.

Approximately a half hour after the helicopter incident, the JTFME called the *Gary* on a satellite relay and advised that it had picked up indications of Silkworm launches directed at the frigate from the north-east. An entry was made in the *Gary*'s deck log: "Multiple Silkworms inbound this unit."

Almost immediately, the *Gary*'s "Slick 32" (SLQ-32) ESM system picked up emissions from a Silkworm missile seeker, i.e. a signal from the small radar mounted in the nose of the missile. The emissions were on a bearing to the northeast. About 15–20 seconds after detecting the Silkworm emissions, the *Gary*'s AN/SPS-49 air search radar picked up a "bogey," or an unidentified contact at a range of about 40 nautical miles. The bogey was coming in from the northeast and had an exact correlation with the Silkworm signals being picked up on the SLQ-32's. The *Gary*'s CAS or Combined Antenna System radar, located in an egg shaped radome, detected the bogey, as did the ship's dish-shaped STIR radar. The bogey was coming in on a sea-skimming flight path at high speed. At a range of 30 nautical miles, the incoming contact veered a few degrees before holding to a steady course, one that headed directly toward the *Gary* and the Mobile Sea Bases.

Captain Bethea had to very quickly size up his situation. A Silkworm attack at this location didn't make sense. The only known launch sites in the northern Gulf were at the Al-Faw peninsula, located to the northwest, not the northeast. Further, Al-Faw was at a distance from the *Gary* of well over twice the range possessed by the Silkworm. The only other launch sites he knew of were hundreds of miles away along the Strait of Hormuz. The electronic evidence in front of his eyes told a different story. A clear incoming contact was visible on the SPS-49 search radar. The STIR radar and the CAS radar had picked it up as well. The radar contract correlated exactly with the ESM pickup of a Silkworm missile radar seeker. If it wasn't apparent where the missile (or missiles) had come from, it was only too clear where it was headed. The contact was "constant bearing, decreasing range," i.e. headed straight for the frigate and the sea bases.

Captain Bethea ordered both of the *Gary*'s turbine engines on line. The frigate hunkered down at the stern under full power and then came charging out from between the Mobile Sea Bases toward the incoming Silkworm. The *Gary*'s LAMPS helicopter was airborne and Bethea posi-tioned it directly over the ship at an altitude of 8,000 feet. The LAMPS could act as an additional ESM platform since it was equipped with its own radar threat-warning receiver. Its altitude would also keep the heli-copter clear if the *Gary* engaged the Silkworm with its anti-aircraft missiles, its 76mm gun, or, as a last resort, its Phalanx CIWS.

Upon picking up the Silkworm indications, the *Gary* had passed the word that missiles were inbound to the two Mobile Sea Bases. The officer in charge of the Wimbrown VII was Commander Gary Stubblefield, a SEAL officer who was something of a rarity in that he had spent (and would go on to spend) his entire career in Naval Special Warfare. He had been commanding SEAL Team Three when he was called in by his boss and told that somebody who could think operationally was needed to take command of the sea base. The previous commander was administratively solid but considered not up to the mark on the operational end. Stubblefield was exhilarated at the prospect and would consider his tour in the Gulf, along with his service in Vietnam, as the high point of his career. Sadly, only a few weeks after he arrived, Stubblefield was advised that his father had been diagnosed as having terminal cancer and was not expected to survive to the end of his scheduled four-month tenure as CO of the Wimbrown VII. Stubblefield was confronted with a dilemma, tugged between his feelings for his father and the responsibility he felt toward the nearly two hundred men under his command. In the end, he felt that the seriousness of the situation in the Gulf required continuity of command, and he decided to stay. As it turned out, his father would not pass away until several months after he returned from the Gulf.

On board the Wimbrown VII, Commander Stubblefield was at a Stinger anti-aircraft missile platform located high up on the crane when the Silkworm report came in. Stubblefield was with Captain Ted Grabowsky, Commodore of Navy Special Warfare Group I, who happened to be visiting that day. Grabowsky asked, "What do you want me to do?"

"Get in the PB's (patrol boats) and get them away from the barge—standby to pick up survivors!" Commander Stubblefield told him. "If this thing hits us we will have a lot of casualties."[1]

Crewmen were scrambling to their action stations as the sea base went to general quarters. Some men actually ran to the far side of the barge, ready to jump off; some were ducking under tables in the mess deck and bracing for the shock of impact. A Master Chief asked Commander Stubblefield, "What do I do? Should I put on my life preserver and jump over the side?" "No," Stubblefield told him, "nobody jumps; we don't know where it will hit or if it will hit. Nobody jumps until after it hits us!"[2] The patrol boats pulled away from the base. The

Army TF-118 helicopters scrambled into the air in unaccustomed broad daylight so that the high-value aircraft would be saved if the base was hit. They could also assist in possible rescue efforts.

As the Silkworm continued inbound, a Marine Corps Stinger anti-aircraft missile gunner standing next to Commander Stubblefield was shaking and nervously asked what he should do. As Commander Stubblefield recounted:

> My mouth went dry. I was NOT a happy camper at this moment. We were getting the range on the inbound missile from the destroyer: "44 mi . . . 42 mi . . . 40 mi . . .: "Treat this like a training scenario," I told the young Marine. "Try to lock on that thing, and if you do, tell me 'lock on' just the way you were trained. I'll tell you to fire." Like a good Marine, he said, "Yes SIR!"[3]

The *Gary* had now put itself between the incoming Silkworm and the sea bases. Hoping to distract the missile, the frigate began firing chaff rounds and Sea Gnat decoys. Captain Bethea was also hoping to shoot down the Silkworm with one of his anti-aircraft missiles. However, the contact was too low for the *Gary*'s fire control system to establish continuous lock-on, even though the radar could "see" the target, which was bobbing slightly between 30 and 50 feet in altitude as it skimmed across the Gulf surface. Yet another search radar, this time the one in the *Gary*'s Phalanx close-in weapon system (CIWS), now picked up the contact.

As the missile continued to close, the *Gary* was finally able to get a solid radar lock. However, the missile was now inside the ship's Standard anti-aircraft system's minimum range. The *Gary* did have another weapon it could use at that range: its 76mm gun. That weapon could be aimed manually from a visual director. The *Gary*'s gun was loaded with special infrared proximity-fused high-explosive anti-aircraft rounds. As the missile streaked to within the roughly 8–9 nautical mile range of its 76mm gun, the *Gary* cut loose at the weapon's maximum rate of fire.

Looking through his optical gun director, the operator couldn't see far enough into the Gulf haze to spot the missile, so he fired along the line of bearing of the incoming contact. An officer on the bridge saw the first three 76mm rounds splash into the water. The operator then raised his point of aim along the same bearing until shots were flying into the haze. The range and bearing of the incoming contact was passed to the ship's small arms stations, which included machine guns and a 25mm automatic cannon. They were told "batteries released," and the staccato bursts of automatic weapons fire joined the deeper thumping of the 76mm gun. Strings of tracers streaked outward from the ship. Captain Bethea reasoned that, if the light automatic weapons were already shooting when the missile appeared out of the haze, the guns might be able to quickly "walk" their tracer rounds onto the target in the short interval they would have before it reached the ship.

The *Gary* was running at 30 knots on a course that would give the best possible separation between the ship and the chaff/decoys it was firing. Unfortunately, that course took it right past a shoal sticking slightly out of the water on its port side. The frigate had to be careful not to run into it at high speed. Captain Bethea was also very concerned that his 76mm gunfire stay aimed at the inbound contact during the ship's maneuvers, and not end up putting out rounds in the direction of the Mobile Sea Bases, which were within range. Successfully running past the shoal, the *Gary* turned to expose its starboard quarter to the incoming missile. The maneuver unmasked its "last-ditch" defense Phalanx gun. It also presented a smaller radar cross-section of the ship to the missile seeker than if it had turned fully broadside.

The *Gary* continued to fire chaff and launched two more Sea Gnat decoys. It also fired a "Torch" decoy, designed to put out an intense heat signature in case the missile had an infrared seeker. When it had gone to general quarters, the *Gary* had set condition "Zebra," which meant that all watertight hatches and doors had been secured. As the ship fired away its chaff, an officer on the bridge asked the Officer of the Deck (OOD) if the chaff team could break Zebra and reload the launchers. On the only occasion throughout the tense engagement in which that officer would raise his voice, the OOD screamed at them to "just get out there and load the launchers!"

In the darkened CIC below decks, Captain Bethea had watched as the contact came streaking in past the 30-mile range ring on the radar display, then the 25-mile ring, the 20-mile, the 15, and now the 10. He racked his brain, trying to think of something else he could do to defend his ship, but couldn't come up with anything. He knew that the huge warhead on a Silkworm would absolutely lay waste to the *Gary*. He wondered, "What do I want my last thoughts to be?" Captain Bethea got on the PA system and announced to the crew, "We have an inbound missile. All hands, brace for impact!" There was no panic or shouting on the bridge or among the CIC crew as the men quietly went about their assigned tasks. They had drilled intensely prior to their deployment to the Gulf and those workups had prepared them well for the real thing.

Four Stinger hand-held anti-aircraft missile teams were standing by on the Hercules to engage the Silkworm when it got within range. However, because the *Gary* had sailed between the incoming missile and the Mobile Sea Bases, it was blocking their line of fire. The Hercules ordered "weapons tight" to the Stinger teams. From that base, the *Gary* could be seen in the distance firing its 76mm gun and launching chaff. Further out, coming in over the horizon was the glow of a "rocket burn." A Stinger gunner shouted, "I've got lock-on!" Two other Stinger gunners locked-on as well. The *Gary*'s 76mm gun pounded out rounds at the Silkworm. At a range of around seven nautical miles from the ship, the missile splashed into the Gulf. The *Gary*'s search radar lost contact. The ESM indications, the signals being picked up from the missile's seeker, abruptly ceased.

On the *Gary*'s bridge, the Tactical Action Officer (TAO) reported over the sound-powered phone speaker that the missile had missed. There was a quiet sigh of relief from the bridge crew. The *Gary* slowed as the men counted their blessings. Lieutenant (jg) Steve Rehwald had been on the satellite radio MEF execution net during the attack. Known as "iceman" because of his ability to talk on the radio without emotion, Lieutenant Rehwald had been counting down the incoming missile's range as it headed toward the *Gary*.

In addition to the JTFME command center on USS *LaSalle*, his reports were being relayed to the National Military Command Center (NMCC), the Pentagon's war room. Gathered there were high-ranking officers and civilian officials. These listeners last heard that the inbound missile was ten miles from the ship, then there was nothing but silence. The atmosphere was tense as the minutes ticked by. Finally, Lieutenant Rehwald reported that the Silkworm had missed. According to a high-ranking officer who was present, the war room erupted in cheers. It was seen that an object impacted fairly close astern of the frigate at 4:52 P.M. The impact was observed from both the *Gary* and the Mobile Sea Bases. The object did not detonate, although there was smoke, a flash, and fire in the water before it sank.

Shortly after engaging the first missile, the *Gary* picked up ESM readings from the seeker of another inbound Silkworm. This one didn't get anywhere close to the ship and appeared to splash down some 25 nautical miles away. The threat facing the Mobile Sea Bases was starkly obvious, and tugs were summoned in an emergency operation to evacuate them from the vicinity of what now appeared to be a northern Silkworm envelope.

When the first reports of a Silkworm attack on the Mobile Sea Bases came in, hearts must have skipped a beat at the JTFME operations center on USS *Coronado*, at Central Command Headquarters in Tampa, and at the Pentagon's "War Room." It was about to get a lot worse. Several hundred miles away from the *Gary*, as Surface Action Group "Delta" cruised in the western end of the Strait of Hormuz, a Navy surface combat air patrol (SUCAP) aircraft, flying over the Strait under the control of USS *Joseph Strauss*, reported sighting multiple Silkworm missile launches. The plane was an EA-6B Prowler electronic warfare aircraft, and it promptly proceeded to jam the Silkworm missile guidance systems. The EA-6B also reported visually sighting a Silkworm flying inbound from the north toward the U.S. ships. At this time (4:42 P.M.), the USS *Jack Williams* picked up Silkworm readings from the northnortheast. A minute later, the USS *Strauss* also reported picking up Silkworm readings on its ESM receiver.

"Silkworm inbound! Silkworm inbound!" shouted Lieutenant Augustine Ponturier, Officer of the Deck on the *Jack Williams*, "Look astern! Everybody look astern!" he shouted to lookouts and junior officers. "Lookouts! Find that missile!" Shipboard Stinger anti-aircraft missile crews scrambled to their topside firing positions. Lookouts initially reported nothing visible. "Combat Bridge! Where the hell is it? What's the bearing on the Silkworm?" Ponturier shouted into the phone. Bearing zero three four came the reply. Ponturier barked orders to increase speed and to change course. The helmsman sitting at the control console in front of him repeated the orders. The frigate's two gas turbine engines shrieked as the ship rolled sharply to point its stern toward the incoming missiles, presenting them with the smallest target.[4]

The U.S. ships maneuvered vigorously and launched chaff to decoy the missiles. "Fire chaff," ordered Ponturtier. Blam! Blam! Blam! Blam! The chaff launchers fired in rapid sequence. The *Joseph Strauss* launched a "Torch" decoy in case any of the missiles had infrared guidance systems. None of the U.S. warships were hit by the incoming missiles. Ponturier told reporters from the media pool on board the *Jack Williams* that two Silkworms had been launched, but he didn't know what had happened to them.[5] The missiles had apparently been defeated by a combination of jamming, chaff, and ship maneuvers.

The Iranians had gotten precise targeting data on the *Gary* and the Mobile Sea Bases from the helicopter launched out to Farsi. In the Strait of Hormuz, too, the Iranians may have had an airborne observer. At 5:17 P.M., what was identified as an Iranian C-130 aircraft was detected orbiting at 18,000 feet over the Strait at a range of 50,000 yards from the *Joseph Strauss*. The *Strauss* "picked up" the contact on its AN/SPG-511 radar. The *Jack Williams* held it on its N/SPS-49 radar and also had a MK 92 Fire Control System radar contact. The *Jack Williams* was picking up above-normal noise on its radar and thought it was being jammed by the C-130. The Iranians had been using the U.S.-built cargo aircraft, bought during the Shah's reign, for surveillance. This one appeared to be targeting the U.S. warships for attack by the Silkworms.

The C-130 was thought to be relaying the location of warships by giving line of bearings in relation to Tacan international navigation beacons. The Surface Action Group had to put a stop to that, and at 5:20 P.M., the *Joseph Strauss* began firing anti-aircraft missiles at the C-130, launching two SM-1's. Unfortunately, the action against the C-130 came a bit too late. A minute earlier, a U.S. aircraft had reported visually identifying a Silkworm launch and missile flight. Another wave of Silkworms was now inbound to the U.S. warships.

The *Jack Williams* detected Silkworm ESM readings and the cry "Silkworms Inbound!" went up again. All three ships began launching chaff and maneuvering.[6] The USS *O'Brien* launched a "Rubber Duck," a floating, inflatable radar-reflecting decoy. Multiple Silkworms were reported inbound as the ships again took evasive action.

The *Jack Williams* reported it had visually identified a Silkworm flying by at an altitude of 100 feet. Helicopter crewmen and a fire detail on the helicopter deck at the stern of the ship dropped flat but saw one of the missiles, described as a bright orange flame with a white point, as it raced from left to right about a mile behind the ship. A Stinger anti-aircraft missile gunner on the ship was able to lock on the Silkworm. Lookouts on the *Jack Williams* as well as that ship's LAMPS helicopter, airborne at the time, saw the missile fly through a cloud of chaff about 100 feet off the ship and then into the United Arab Emirates' Saleh Oilfield, where it hit the water near an oil rig.

The three U.S. warships began withdrawing to get out of missile range. Under missile attack, and knowing that its action would slow its escape from the Silkworm envelope, the *Joseph Strauss* nevertheless came about in a slow 360-degree turn to again engage the Iranian C-130 targeting the ships. The *Jack Williams* and the *O'Brien* concentrated on Silkworm defense and continued to withdraw. As it reported missiles inbound astern, the *Joseph Strauss* launched two more SM-l (MR) anti-aircraft missiles at the C-130. The two SM-l's were fired at 5:26 P.M.; the first one malfunctioned and snaked into the water within a mile of the ship. Two more were fired four minutes later. The first of this pair turned around during flight, and it had to be destroyed. The *O'Brien* reported a missile inbound. U.S. Army Major Barry Willey, a Central Command Public Affairs Officer, described the view from the bridge of the *Jack Williams* as "both spectacular and frightening—contrails from missiles could be seen in almost every direction."[7]

Once again, the U.S. warships were able to dodge the incoming missiles. Referring to the chaff fired to decoy the missiles, a communications crewman on the bridge of the *Jack Williams* grinned under his steel helmet and observed, "That stuff works, man."[8] At 5:40 P.M., the *Joseph Strauss* detected another Silkworm launch, but no missile was ever spotted.

The Surface Action Group was withdrawing toward the edge of the Qeshem [Island launch site] Silkworm envelope, but it was not out yet. The *Joseph Strauss* had fired a total of six SM-l (MR) anti-aircraft missiles at the C-130 targeting them. None of the missiles hit the Iranian aircraft. Normally, a large, slow and relatively unmaneuverable aircraft like the C-130 would have been an easy target for surface-to-air missiles. However, the C-l30 was flying at the very limit of the missiles' range. The C-130 appeared to be in an orbit that took it to between 35,000 and 45,000 yards of the U.S. warship. Two of the six missiles fired were failures. One had to be destroyed and one had an erratic flight due to what may have been a lost fin. The C-130 may have been able to dodge the remainder by dancing in and out of their maximum range as it flew over the Strait.

Frustrated at being unable to hit the C-130 with its anti-aircraft missiles, the *Strauss* called on combat air patrol F-14 fighters flying off the carrier *Enterprise* and vectored them to shoot down the Iranian plane. At 5:40 P.M. the *Strauss* vectored two F-14's into the Strait and through the engagement area. The F-14's had been on station some 65 nautical miles away from the action. However, it was a clear day with excellent visibility at altitude, and the F-14's had observed the fly-out of anti-aircraft missiles from the *Strauss*. Sweeping through the Strait, the F-14's were not able to pick up the C-130 on their radars or spot it visually. The fighters described the *Strauss*'s vectors as "erratic."

Thirteen minutes later, the *Strauss* tried again, vectoring two more F-14's into the Strait. Again, the fighters could not spot the C-130. The Iranian aircraft had been reported heading north (away from the U.S. ship) for some time. Possibly the reconnaissance aircraft had been alerted to the approaching F-14's by Iranian ground control intercept radar and had withdrawn over Iranian territory. The *Strauss* attempted to vector the F-14's to chase the C-130 within range of Iranian HAWK anti-aircraft missile batteries located at Bandar Abbas. However, lacking their own radar contact and facing the HAWK threat, the F-14's decided against entering the formidable Iranian anti-aircraft missile umbrella at Bandar Abbas.

The *Joseph Strauss* was not the only ship in the surface action group firing anti-aircraft missiles that day. Shortly after 5:30 P.M., the *Jack Williams* detected a low-flying contact headed toward the ship at a slow speed. Nine minutes later, the *Jack Williams* fired two SM-1's at an unidentified helicopter. The first missile was a dud and the second missed, which was just as well, since its target was a U.S. Navy helicopter flying off the USS *O'Brien*. The SH-2F LAMPS helicopter, call sign "Seasnake 22," was flown by Lieutenant Commander Paul D. Berg. When he sighted the contrail of the anti-aircraft missile coming at him, Commander Berg executed a series of violent evasive maneuvers, diving to the wave tops, causing the missile to narrowly miss his aircraft. As one officer later put it, "He dodged the missile by putting his wheels in the water." The *O'Brien* reported its helicopter under fire from the location of the *Strauss* and *O'Brien*.

Taking no chances on another "friendly fire" incident, Commodore Dyer ordered all helicopters to land on their ships. The incident prompted a heated radio exchange between the commanders of the *Jack Williams* and the *O'Brien*. The *Jack Williams* claimed it had not received the proper IFF reply from the helicopter; nor had the helicopter responded to radio challenges. The *Strauss* later reported that it had received the correct IFF signal from the helicopter. The *O'Brien* heard none of the *Jack Williams*'s challenges, while the *Strauss* heard warnings, but not one specifically directed at Sea Snake 22. Commander Berg was later awarded the Navy Commendation Medal for successfully avoiding the *Jack Williams*'s missile.

In the northern Gulf, the Iranians continued to react. Five Iranian F-4 fighters flew directly toward the Wimbrown VII but broke away when USS *Gary* locked its fire control radar on them. By 5:42 P.M. both Mobile Sea Bases had been taken under tow by tugs and were headed south. The *Gary* shepherded the bases out of the danger area. Back in the southern Gulf, at around 6:00 P.M., the U.S. ships began clearing the Queshem Silkworm envelope. Last out was the *Joseph Strauss* at 6:07 P.M. The surface action group then assumed a blocking position in the Strait of Hormuz western patrol area. The two Mobile Sea Bases were eventually repositioned to the southwest of Saudi Arabia's Karen Island at around 10:30 P.M.

The next day, April 19, found the *Gary* still guarding the Mobile Sea Bases. The *Gary* and its LAMPS helicopter detected six high-speed boats at a 40-nautical-mile range closing in on the platforms. Preparing for an attack, the Mobile Sea Bases launched their patrol boats. After the U.S. boats came out, the Iranian headquarters on Farsi Island ordered their craft to return. Commander Stubblefield thought that the fact that the Iranians' boats had turned back right after the U.S. boats were launched indicated that "one of the dhows or something . . . in the area may well have been acting as a tipper operation and telling them what we were doing."

USS *Simpson* was dispatched to the northern Gulf to help the Mobile Sea bases, but only stayed a few days. The *Gary* then remained the only U.S. ship in the area. Captain Bethea felt alone and exposed in those waters. However, with U.S. forces spread thin, there was simply no way to reinforce him. Admiral Less called and told him that he wished he could paint a better picture, but he didn't have anything else available. He did put a verbal arm around Bethea's shoulder, telling him he didn't have anybody with better experience to be up there.

The situation "up there" was still looking dicey. A steady stream of Iranian gunboats began collecting at Farsi Island. The *Gary* stayed at General Quarters for three straight days. On the fourth day, for the first time since April 18, two Iraqi fighters coming down the Gulf were picked up on radar. The *Gary* began normal de-confliction procedures with the Iraqis, who gave the call sign "Zebra" for their mission. This was the code word for an attack on a fixed target, not a maritime one. It was the first time the *Gary* had heard the call sign. The *Gary* watched the Iraqis fly to Farsi, where the ship's radar could even discern weapons separating from the jets as they attacked. On their return the Iraqi flight leader requested a close fly-by because his wing-mate had been hit and might have to eject. The two Iraqi fighters flew within a mile across the *Gary*'s bow. Shortly after they passed by the ship, the Iraqis requested a bearing to Dhahran, Saudi Arabia. Onboard the *Gary*'s bridge, the bearing was calculated and passed to the Iraqis. Possibly hit in the Iraqi attack, the Iranian boats which had been gathering at Farsi returned to the mainland.

With the reported Silkworm missile attacks against U.S. forces, events in the Gulf could have been headed for an ominous turn. The United States had repeatedly and publicly warned Iran that it would not tolerate the use of Silkworm missiles against U.S. warships or the convoys they were escorting. The U.S. had warned Iran that it would strike if the Silkworm fire control radars were even "locked on" U.S. ships, much less the missiles actually fired. Private warnings had been conveyed to Iran through intermediaries. U.S. retaliatory strikes prompted by Silkworm firings would have been directed at least against the launching sites and associated storage facilities. Because the sites were located on Iranian territory, strikes on them would mark a significant escalation of U.S. operations in the Gulf. Previous U.S. attacks had been limited to Iranian platforms and ships located at sea, almost always in international waters.

There were likely to be few good, and many bad, consequences flowing from U.S. attacks on the Silkworm sites. At least some of the missiles and their associated equipment would be destroyed, preventing their future use. It is unlikely, however, that all of the missiles could be destroyed in limited duration attacks. What was very likely was that the hand of the more radical elements in the Iranian leadership would be strengthened by the U.S. action. That leadership would attempt to use the confrontation with the "Great Satan" to re-energize the masses and rally them for renewed efforts in the war with Iraq, possibly prolonging that war. That would be exactly the opposite of the result sought by the United States.

Iranian-inspired terrorist attacks on U.S. targets in other parts of the world were also a distinct possibility. In the Gulf itself, tension would ratchet up to yet higher levels, greatly heightening the possibility of further incidents between American and Iranian forces. In a revenge bid to humiliate the U.S., the Iranians might even use their remaining

Silkworms or other means to mount a high-profile strike against an escorted tanker or U.S. warship.

Those scenarios raised the possibility of a series of tit-for-tat strikes escalating out of control. If events took that course, they stood to reduce the cautious and limited U.S. policy commitment in the Gulf to a shambles. The Reagan administration's Gulf policy had been garnering solid Congressional and public support on the wings of success. However, it might well crash if there was a drastic escalation of the level of violence, the probability of heavy U.S. casualties, and operations continuing for a prolonged period of time with no visible end. Such a situation would erode public support and strengthen Congressional opposition for a War Powers Act vote. In the end, the administration might be faced with the unpalatable alternatives of staging a humiliating withdrawal or continually escalating the commitment of men and material in the Gulf, at an increasingly heavy cost in dollars and lives. In short, it would be a policy disaster if the Iranians launched a Silkworm attack on U.S. forces in the Gulf, or, more precisely, if it were publicly recognized that they had done so.

The Chairman of the Joint Chiefs of Staff, Admiral William Crowe, had a finely tuned set of political antennae and knew well the implications if it were publicly acknowledged that Silkworms had been fired at U.S. ships. Apparently anxious to head off any such conclusion based on the Media Pool reports from the *Jack Williams*, Admiral Crowe stated in a briefing to President Reagan and Republican leaders that there was no evidence to support the news that Silkworms had been fired at the U.S. warships.[9] Public knowledge of the missile attack was limited to the Department of Defense Media Pool reports of the warnings of incoming Silkworms heard on the *Jack Williams* and the accounts of the subsequent maneuvering and chaff firing. The Silkworm attack in the northern Gulf was not reported at all. Even the pool accounts arrived amidst a welter of other reports on the various platform attacks and other actions during Operation Praying Mantis. Thus, what the public knew was limited, and the Silkworm reports did not necessarily stand out to the average person. They were also starting to be obscured by a cloud of artificial fog.

Pentagon officials noted that half a dozen different types of missiles and other weapons were fired by both sides during the action involving the *Williams*, the other ships of the surface action group, U.S. A-6 attack aircraft, and the two Iranian frigates *Sabalan* and *Sahand*. These officials speculated that, in the heat of battle, the *Williams* might have misidentified the missiles. Admiral Crowe said, during a White House briefing, that the *Williams* and the other ships "were operating well within the envelope [range] of the Silkworms. Any ship operating in such a circumstance that gets a track on the scope has to assume a worst case scenario." The official line was that there was no "positive proof" that Silkworms had been used.[10]

There were also questions over the number of missiles actually fired at the ships of the surface action group "Delta." Initial reports indicated there had been as many as five missiles. The group commander, Captain Donald Dyer, said that with the three different ships maneuvering and firing chaff, "It could mean some duplication" in the reports on the number of missiles. "To go back and try to reconstruct it in the fog of war, to put it all together, it's very difficult," said Dyer. "It's only a matter of counting beans . . . but there is no doubt that missiles were fired at these ships."[11]

Pentagon officials suggested that the missiles were probably not Silkworms but instead ship-to-ship missiles fired by Iranian frigates. At an April 21 news conference, Admiral Henry Mustin stated, "We have no confirmation that Silkworms were fired. . . . We have indications that Harpoons were fired at us. . . . The predominant missiles we think fired at us were Seakillers." Admiral Mustin also referred to the confusion involved in identifying the missiles under the circumstances: "When you're on the business end of incoming mail, it's pretty damn difficult to tell whether it's an Exocet or a Harpoon or anything else. Even with peculiar electronic signatures, because many of them are a lot like others. So it's hard for us to tell now exactly what kind of missiles were fired at us."[12]

Senior naval officers in the Gulf were telling a different story, stating that they were unaware of anything in Iran's arsenal that might be easily confused with the Silkworm.[13] Interestingly, when asked for specific numbers on the missiles fired by U.S. ships, Admiral Mustin only mentioned two missiles fired at aircraft. The reference was obviously to the two Standard anti-aircraft missiles publicly reported to have been fired by the *Wainwright* at an Iranian F-4 fighter.[14] No mention was made of the missiles fired at the C-130, or at the U.S. helicopter for that matter.

In late April, Pentagon officials, speaking only on the condition that they not be named, said that Iran had not fired Silkworms at the U.S.

Navy ships. An unnamed source stated, "There were missiles fired, which our ships successfully evaded. But there are strong indicators they weren't Silkworms." The sources claimed that the matter had been "exhaustively investigated."[15] Defense Department officials told the publication *Aviation Week* that Iran may have modified some C-130's to carry Harpoon missiles and that U.S. radars had detected an Iranian C-130 and a P-3.[16]

In early June 1988, General George B. Crist, CENTCOM Commander, stated emphatically that no Chinese-made Silkworms or any other land-based anti-ship missiles had been fired at U.S. warships. "What you had," said General Crist, "was a number of missiles outgoing, a number of laser-guided bombs and missiles coming in from aircraft," and that "what you were getting were hits on the system as they picked up seekers and missiles moving through the air."[17] In other words, U.S. radar sensors had picked up U.S.-directed, as opposed to Iranian-fired, missiles moving through the air. There, the matter pretty much seemed to end.

The Pentagon did do an official Praying Mantis After-Action Report, approximately half of which has been publicly released. The balance was redacted.[18] The report concluded that analysis of the Silkworm indications in the southern Gulf revealed, "no conclusive evidence that Silkworms were launched at U.S. units." While its discussion and analysis of other Praying Mantis engagements are fairly straightforward, the report's treatment of the Silkworm attacks on the ships of Surface Action Group "Delta" and on the *Gary* and the Mobile Sea Bases is disappointingly inaccurate and incomplete. Indeed, the account is so distorted that it looks suspiciously like it was made known to the report's authors that it would be best if some kind of plausible alternative explanations were put forward for those events. Plausible, that is, for those not in possession of the facts.

The most heavily redacted portions of the report deal with the Silkworm attacks on the ships of Surface Action Group "Delta." No explanation is available for the Silkworm ESM readings registered individually by each of the U.S. ships, nor for the aircraft visual sightings of missile launches and of Silkworms inbound to the warships.

As to the Iranian C-130 aircraft flying over the Strait, the report questions its existence, noting that the two flights of F-14's sent to shoot it down never made radar or visual contact with the aircraft. The report does admit that the air contact could not be explained away by "anomalous propagation" of radar signals, and that a Navy E-2C Hawkeye airborne radar surveillance aircraft also picked up a radar contact. The *Strauss* picked it up on its search radar; the *Jack Williams* on a search radar and a fire control system radar. The details are not available, but the report's alternative explanation seems to suggest that the air contact was not a C-130 targeting the U.S. ships, but rather a Fokker F-27 logistics aircraft flying between the Iranian mainland and Qeshem Island.

Whether or not there was a C-130 targeting the U.S. ships remains a good question. It is true that the two fighter sweeps produced no visual sightings. However, the fighter pilots reported that the vectors given them by the *Strauss* were "erratic." Further, as previously noted, a C-130 could well have been warned of the incoming U.S. fighters by Iranian ground radar and quickly withdrawn over the nearby mainland. The official after-action report explanation that it was a Fokker F-27 aircraft flying to Queshem doesn't quite fit the available facts. The radar contact was orbiting in a racetrack pattern at 18,000 feet, which would hardly have been the flight profile of a puddle-jumping logistics flight from the adjacent mainland.

While the report cites the lack of F-14 visual and radar sighting of the aircraft as weighing against the existence of a C-130, the lack of sightings would also seem to weigh against the report's alternative explanation that it was an F-27. It seems possible that a C-130 reconnaissance aircraft orbiting over the Strait would have quickly and easily withdrawn to Iranian territory when warned about the incoming U.S. fighters. The *Jack Williams* thought its radar was being jammed by the C-130. This does not seem likely. The Iranian C-130's were air force transport aircraft that had been pressed into service as maritime patrol aircraft. There is no evidence that these planes had any jamming capability. It seems likely that the interference picked up by the *Jack Williams* had another source, possibly even the U.S. EA-6B's electronic warfare aircraft operating in the area. In the end, the available evidence on the C-130 is ambiguous and inconclusive.

The visual sighting of a Silkworm by the lookouts on the *Jack Williams*, as well as by its LAMPS helicopter, is supposedly correlated with the report of one of the two errant U.S. anti-aircraft missiles that had been fired at the C-130 by the *Joseph Strauss*. This is an interesting conclusion in light of the fact that the report's explanation of the missile sighting does not correlate with its own account of events. The report states that the visual identification of a Silkworm by the *Jack*

Williams occurred at 5:19 P.M. (1419 Z). However, the report also states that the firing of the first of two errant U.S. anti-aircraft missiles by the *Joseph Strauss* took place at 5:26 P.M. (1426 Z). That missile was described as "going snaking into the water about a mile from the ship." Neither in time, description, nor location does the errant anti-aircraft missile fired by the *Strauss* "correlate" to the missile that had streaked past the *Jack Williams* some seven minutes earlier and which then flew through a chaff cloud into Saleh oilfield.

As to the reported attack on the *Gary* and the Mobile Sea Bases, once again, it looks like the idea was to come up with some kind of superficially plausible cover story. The *Gary's* radar contact of an inbound object is dismissed as a "false target," caused by the "anomalous propagation" of signals coming from well beyond the normal radar horizon. The report suggests that the radar signal either came from a Silkworm fired by the Iranians from the Al-Faw Peninsula, or was a "clutter phenomenon." There had been fairly widespread public reports on Iranian missile firings from Al-Faw into Kuwaiti waters—notably, the one that hit the *Sea Isle City* and precipitated U.S. retaliation in Operation Nimble Archer. Possibly it was thought that these firings would lend some credibility to the report's theory. The report even speculated that the Iranians fired the missile because they faced a "use it or lose it" situation when Iraqi forces recaptured the peninsula on April 18. The fact that the missiles were stored on the Iranian side of the Shatt al-Arab, which the Iraqi attack did not reach, and that there were no reports of a missile splashing down anywhere in Kuwaiti territory, the only logical target within range, argue against this theory.

The characterization of what the *Gary* picked up as a "false target" or a "clutter phenomenon" is unconvincing, to say the least. Captain Bethea later observed:

> In retrospect, and all my officers including the pilots [of the *Gary's* helicopter] still—to this day—agree that we had something. First the satellite call-up by CMEF that they had detected a Silkworm being launched against us to the NE; then our almost immediate ESM detection on a specific bearing to the NE; then the SPS-49 long range air search radar detection just seconds later which was an exact correlation to the NE bearing; then detection by the MK-92 fire control system (STIR and CAS) about 15 seconds later followed by a CIWS target detec-

tion. Something caused that and it wasn't false radar detection. Not when four very reliable, independent systems also detect a correlating target. Something had to be there.

Some five months before our "Silkworm" event, we had fired a live missile against a specially Silkworm configured drone off the coast of California in preparation for the upcoming deployment. This "Silkworm" behaved exactly like the target drone—identical to the timeline by sensor detection to engagement sequence. It was a classic textbook engagement.[19]

A Silkworm attack on the *Gary* and the Mobile Sea Bases does raise one obvious question: Where did the missile or missiles come from? At the time of the reported attack, the frigate and the Mobile Sea Bases were located some 120 nautical miles away from the Al-Faw Peninsula to the northwest and some 90 nautical miles away from Iran's coastline to the northeast. The nominal maximum range of the HY-2 Silkworm missile is 95 kilometers, or some 50 nautical miles. Thus, the sea bases were well outside of the missile's range, if fired from either of those coastal locations.

However, the missiles may well have been launched from a location within range of the sea bases. Logical candidates here include Iranian ships and Iranian islands in the vicinity or Iranian oil platforms. The report only addresses the first possibility, stating that a review of tapes from the AWACS radar warning aircraft did not show any ships within missile range. This is a bit odd. It seems that a 50-nautical-mile-long swath of the Gulf, of reasonable width, would have turned up some contacts, especially given the number of fishing boats constantly working the area. The Iranians had reportedly acquired the ship-launched version of the Silkworm as part of the shipment carried by the *Iran Bayan* in early 1988. Still, the islands or platforms seem to be better bets. The platforms were well-established permanent bases with good communications. Given the cranes used to move heavy oilfield equipment onto platforms, it would have been easy to place a couple of missiles on one.

Yet another possibility exists which was not discussed in the report. It seems possible that the Iranians had obtained some HY-4 versions of the Silkworm missiles. As opposed to the HY-2 model, which uses rocket propulsion, the HY-4 uses a turbojet engine to achieve greatly increased range. (The U.S. Harpoon also uses turbojet propulsion.) The

HY-4 has a nominal maximum range of some 81 nautical miles. A radar contact disappearing some seven nautical miles from the USS *Gary* fits rather well with an HY-4 Silkworm fired from the Iranian coast located some 90 miles away and falling short of its intended target, which was located just outside of its maximum range.

It is also possible that the *Gary* shot down the missile. The frigate's 76mm gun crew painted the silhouette of a broken Silkworm on their mount. However, the gun was not locked on the target with the radar fire control system, but rather was only being fired blindly down the bearing of the incoming missile. The special IR-fused rounds might have helped improve the chances of a hit, but overall the odds appear slim.

Not addressed by the unredacted portions of the report is the fact that the JTFME called the *Gary* on a satellite radio relay and advised that it had indications of Silkworm launches to the northeast of the U.S. forces. The source of this warning will not be discussed here in order to protect U.S. capabilities. However, the mere fact of the warning, followed shortly thereafter by an incoming Silkworm-like contact picked up by four different systems on the *Gary*, argues strongly against the "anomalous propagation" theory.

The official After Action Report does appear to have gotten it right in its explanation of visual sightings of an object impacting the water about 400–500 yards astern of the *Gary*. Observers on both the frigate and the Mobile Sea Bases saw the impact. The report concluded that the object was probably the "Torch" decoy round fired by the *Gary*. This explanation seems reasonable. The *Gary*'s radar track and ESM on the missile's seeker both ceased when the missile splashed some seven miles from the ship. The observers didn't have that information and knew only that a missile was incoming. When they saw something hitting astern of the *Gary*, they logically assumed that it was the missile.

Some observers on both the Hercules and the Wimbrown VII sea bases also thought they saw a cylindrical object emerge from the Gulf haze, fly levelly past the bases, and disappear again in the haze. There was some thought that perhaps the *Gary*'s radar contact had consisted of two missiles flying close together, with one splashing down and the other flying through a chaff cloud and past the bases. This does not seem likely. Once the *Gary*'s initial radar track disappeared, the ship held no other track going past the mobile sea bases. ESM from the Silkworm's nose-mounted radar seeker also ceased upon impact of the first track, with no other ESM immediately being held. It seems improbable that two missiles, even if fired simultaneously from different launchers, could have taken flight paths that kept them so close together that they continuously appeared as only one radar "blip."

Based on the evidence, it appears almost certain that Silkworms were fired at U.S. forces during Operation Praying Mantis. U.S. aircraft detected Silkworm missiles being launched. U.S. aircraft visually identified at least two Silkworms inbound toward the ships of Surface Action Group "Delta." According to their deck logs, at least two ships in the group individually identified inbound Silkworms with their ESM systems. The O'Brien's did not state that it had Silkworm ESM, but it did state "Silkworm inbound." Desperate efforts were made to shoot down what was identified as an Iranian C-130 reconnaissance aircraft providing targeting information on the U.S. ships to Silkworm shore batteries. The Gary's radar and ESM data are convincing, and strongly refute the official story.

Further supporting the likelihood of a Silkworm attack was the timing. It hardly seems to be a coincidence that missile launches were detected within two minutes of each other both in the northern Gulf and at the Strait of Hormuz, located hundreds of miles away. This timing strongly suggests that a central command authority gave the order to fire missiles at both ends of the Gulf simultaneously. Some Silkworm batteries were operated by the IRGC, others by the regular Iranian Navy. However, both services shared the Navy's command and control network. Launch orders for all Silkworms came directly from Navy headquarters in Tehran. These, in turn, would have had to be cleared at the highest levels of the Iranian government. Aside from the timing, if there had been a C-130 in the Strait, another common feature of both attacks would have been the use of aerial platforms to obtain over-the-horizon targeting data on the locations of U.S. forces.

Pentagon sources initially suggested that some other kinds of missiles were fired at SAG "Delta. "Sea-Killer" ship-to-ship missiles and Harpoon anti-ship missiles being mentioned as candidates. The Italian-made Sea-Killer missiles equipped Iranian frigates like the Sahand and the Sabalan. Sources claimed these missiles might have been fired at U.S. ships. The Sea Killer was a relatively small, command-guided missile whose range was limited to line of sight, i.e. about 25 nautical miles. Of the two Iranian frigates which could have launched such missiles, the Sahand had been put out of action by numerous missile and bomb hits over an hour before the first wave of Silkworms was reported inbound to U.S. ships at 4:42 P.M. The heavily damaged and burning *Sahand* had been assessed as "no threat" by 3:40 P.M. It was definitely not in any condition to have launched the missiles detected by the U.S. warships. The *Sabalan* was not hit by an A-6's laser-guided bomb until 5:05 P.M. and could have launched missiles around the first time the U.S. ships came under attack, but not the second. However, the *Sabalan* never got within Sea Killer range of the U.S. ships before it was put out of action by the single laser-guided bomb hit.

Another possibility mentioned by Pentagon sources was the U.S.-made Harpoon missile, which had been acquired by pre-revolutionary Iran. These sources said that Iran may have rigged a C-130 to fire Harpoons, and mentioned that U.S. ships had detected a C-130. The same "sources" managed not to mention all the U.S. efforts to shoot down the C-130. Iran had only a very small number of Harpoon missiles left in its inventory, and these were thought to be in a deteriorated condition. It might be recalled that the JTFME had advised Surface Action Group "Charlie" that, if the Iranians had any operational Harpoons, the missile-boat *Joshan* had them. The Iranian ship had two Harpoon canisters on its stern. In fact, the Praying Mantis after action report states that, "The *Joshan* launched the Iranian Navy's only known operational Harpoon missile at the *Wainwright*."

Interestingly, in light of all the speculation on other missile types, the final public Pentagon position, explained by General Crist on June 2, 1988, was not that some other kinds of missiles had been fired, but that there had been no missile attacks at all on the warships of Surface Action Group "Delta." The Silkworms in the northern Gulf had not been disclosed and remained unmentioned, save for an offhand comment that another Silkworm shot from Al-Faw had been picked up. According to General Crist, it turned out that it was all a case of confusion caused by multiple outgoing U.S. missiles fired by the ships, and by missiles and bombs released by U.S. aircraft.

Rubbish. No U.S. missiles of any sort were being fired from the ships of SAG "Delta" at the 4:42 P.M. time the first Silkworm attack was picked up. That first attack was well over at 5:17 P.M. when the Iranian C-130 was detected. The first U.S. anti-aircraft missiles were not fired until a few minutes later at 5:20 P.M. The "second wave" of Silkworms were detected inbound at 5:21 P.M., so here, at least, there was some overlap between outgoing anti-aircraft missiles and incoming anti-ship missiles. Still, given the different types of guidance systems employed by the weapons, it stretches credibility to believe that the U.S. warships' ESM receivers could not distinguish Silkworms from their own anti-aircraft missiles. These had no radars of their own putting out a signal, but only passively homed in on radar energy reflected off of a target illuminated by shipboard radars. The firings of the Standard anti-aircraft missiles at the C-130 by the *Joseph Strauss* were still not made public even though it would seem to have buttressed the Pentagon's "confusion" theory. A decision appears to have been made that any advantage in mentioning the missile firings was outweighed by the disadvantages of revealing the existence of the C-130 possibly targeting the ships for over-the-horizon missile batteries. That is a telling judgment in and of itself.

As to the other weapons being employed against Iranian ships, air- and ship-launched radar-guided Harpoons had been launched at and hit the *Sahand* well before the Silkworm attack on the U.S. ships. At the time of the Iranian missile attack, it was possible that the *Sahand* was being hit by non-radar guided weapons such as laser-guided bombs, unguided "iron bombs," TV or imaging Walleyes, and laser-guided Skipper bombs. A single laser-guided bomb hit the *Sabalan*. Not one of these weapons put out a radar signal and thus could not be picked up by the ESM receivers on the U.S. warships.

The information withheld and the dubious conclusions put forth by the Pentagon all fit nicely together into the classic pattern of a cover-up. The information available to the public had been carefully telescoped down to exclude incidents and facts that might support a conclusion that the Iranians had employed their Silkworms. Indeed, one suspects that if the DoD Media Pool had not been aboard the *Jack Williams* or another ship of SAG "Delta," nothing at all would have been heard about the missile attack on the ships.

When all of the "red herring" speculation on other missile types has been examined, and when the cloud of obfuscation about the U.S. ships misreading U.S. weapons is dispersed, far and away the most likely explanation for the apparent Silkworm attack is that it in actually was a Silkworm attack.

A conjectural, but logical, scenario playing out in Teheran would have had a tug-of-war going on over the proper response to the developing U.S. retaliatory strikes. The speedboat attack on Mubarak oilfield may have been a pre-planned tit-for-tat response to U.S. platform attacks, decided on after the October 1987 destruction of the Rostam platform in Operation Nimble Archer. The missile patrol boat *Joshan* does not appear to have been sent on a mission to attack U.S. ships, but its destruction may have set the stage for a battle between the "confrontationists," who were probably calling for vigorous counterattacks against U.S. forces and the "pragmatists," who were likely advocating a more cautious course. The sinking of the *Joshan* may have prompted the dispatch of the *Sahand* with the intent of striking at U.S. forces. At this point, Tehran had probably not yet decided to cross the "Silkworm threshold." The devastation wreaked on the *Sahand*, however, may have torn it.

Iranian platforms were burning in the Gulf. Iranian warships were being attacked and sunk. U.S. fighters and anti-aircraft missiles were holding Iranian aircraft at bay. The retaliatory attack in Mubarak field had been aborted. The hotheads may have been able to gain at least a temporary ascendancy and lash out with the only effective weapon Iran had left: the Silkworms. A little over an hour after the first hit on the *Sahand*, Silkworms were being launched in the Strait of Hormuz and the northern Gulf as well. The later dispatch of the *Sabalan* on what, but for U.S. restraint, would have been a suicide mission, only shows the intense desire to strike at the Americans regardless of the cost or prospects for success.

Revolutionary Guards Commander Rezai was reportedly the driving force behind the dispatch of the Iranian Navy on counterstrikes. At least on April 18, 1988, the balance of power seems to have shifted in favor of the Revolutionary Guards, which ordered the regular Navy out on missions which its professional leadership had to know could only have one result given the obvious mismatch in forces. "I have no doubt they knew they were inviting suicide," said a former serving officer of the Iranian Navy, Firouz Beheresht.[20] A former captain who sought asylum in England in 1985, Beheresht kept in contact with his former colleagues and was certain that they would not have tried to engage the U.S. Navy unless they absolutely had to. Beheresht noted, "The mullahs have several official and unofficial agents on board ships," and that officers had no choice but to obey their orders or the "mullahs" would retaliate against the men or their families.[21]

In truth, the U.S. had gotten itself into a box on the Iranian use of Silkworm missiles. All the dire warnings of retaliation should the missiles be used were in the context of Iran's periodic threats to close the Strait of Hormuz or the potential threat of attacks on U.S. warships or the tankers they were escorting. Given the national interest at stake in these circumstances, retaliation against Iran was an appropriate response.

The problems started when the U.S. and Iran got tangled in a medium-size naval battle on April 18. In the midst of that battle, with ships and aircraft going at it, Iran's crossing of the "Silkworm threshold" should not have been allowed to trigger U.S. attacks on Iranian territory. It is not easy to draw a rational distinction between Iran's use of Silkworms and Iran's use of other types of missiles during a naval battle. For example, two Harpoon missiles carry the same warhead weight as a single Silkworm, were harder to defend against, and arguably would do more damage to a ship. Does it make any sense to say that if the Iranians fired two Harpoons at a U.S. target during a battle that was fair enough, but if, instead, they had fired one Silkworm then the U.S. would bomb Iran, opening a Pandora's box of consequences?

The problem for the U.S. was that there was no acceptable way out of the box in which it found itself. Admitting that Iran had used Silkworms and either striking back or publicly backing down were both unattractive. The perils of the former have been discussed. The latter would seriously undercut the perception of U.S. resolve, which had been so painstakingly built up in the Gulf. The best solution was to avoid the box altogether by concealing what actually happened. In the immediate aftermath of Praying Mantis, some officers and diplomats in the Gulf said that they believed Washington would play down or even deny the Iranian firing of Silkworms in order to avoid having to retaliate and thereby escalate the conflict in the Gulf. "That's what I think, and that's what a lot of other people think," said a Western diplomat.[22]

At the same time, Iran would hardly be disposed to invite attack by disputing the U.S. conclusion that Silkworms had not been used. It may not have been clear to them what the U.S. Navy knew for certain. The facts known to the public were scarce and hazy enough to facilitate this approach. The cover-up certainly took place at the Pentagon. How far it extended into the political side of the Reagan administration is not clear. Defense Secretary Carlucci was in the Pentagon's command center that day and had to have heard the initial Silkworm reports. Indeed, the Silkworm attacks shed new light on the decision not to sink the *Sabalan*. Sparing that ship may have been a deliberate signal that the U.S. was staying its hand and that it was time for both sides to call it quits that day in the Gulf.

Admiral Crowe provided a clear indication of Pentagon thinking when he visited the Wimbrown VII a few weeks after Operation Praying Mantis. The commander of the Mobile Sea Base, Cmdr. Gary Stubblefield wrote:

> A couple of weeks later we got another lesson on operations in the Persian Gulf. ADM William Crowe, then Chairman of the Joint Chiefs of Staff came out to talk to us about the incident. The admiral, a very gracious gentleman and leader, talked to us about our role in the Gulf. "If those guys attack you," he said, "we will respond with force." Well, the Iranians already HAD used force against us with those Silkworm missile launches; we all saw them, and we knew we'd been attacked. But in the days since the attacks we'd been getting told that—despite what we all saw—the Silkworm attacks were just a false alarm . . . we all imagined them somehow.
>
> [Commander] Tom Richards, never shy about speaking up, asked the admiral, "Sir, could you tell us how these Silkworm missiles we all saw didn't attack us? We have the radar tracks, recordings, and we all saw them."
>
> "No, Commander," I think Admiral Crowe said, "there weren't any Silkworms fired at you guys. You see, if there had been, according to the threats we made to the Iranians, we would have to respond with some serious damage. Well, we aren't quite ready to go in and do that . . . so we don't acknowledge they did anything to merit a response."[23]

In one of the most famous incidents of naval lore, Horatio Nelson ignored orders from his superior to break off a hard-fought action by the British fleet at Copenhagen in 1801. Holding a telescope to his blind eye, Nelson said, "What signal? I don't see any signal!" The Royal Navy went on to win the day. In 1988, for reasons that benefited the U.S., Iran, and just about everybody but the undertakers, the Pentagon held up a blind eye to the video display terminals of the ESM receivers on U.S. warships in the Gulf and said, "Silkworms? We don't see any Silkworms."

In the immediate wake of Praying Mantis, officers in the Gulf appeared to be convinced Silkworms had been fired. "Everything we know says that's what they were," a senior officer said. Another declared angrily, "I know Silkworms were fired just as well as I know my own name."[24] Crewmen composed the "Ballad of the *Jack Williams*," which, in part, read:

> Atheist, agnostic, we don't care,
> With Silkworms inbound, the Lord is there.
> Silkworm on the left, Silkworm on the right,
> Hell, we're just beginning to fight . . . [25]

When Admiral Crowe's early comments were misquoted as denying that the missiles were Silkworms, one officer pointed to the rank on his collar and laughed. "See that?" he said. "Do you think I'm going to argue?"[26] A few hints of official acknowledgement of what happened eventually leaked out around the edges. Commander Samuel K. Anderson, Captain of the *Joseph Strauss*, was awarded the Bronze Star. In the words of the official citation: "While under enemy attack, he fearlessly turned his ship to engage and drive off enemy aircraft conducting targeting and jamming of the SAG despite the fact that this action delayed his own departure from the enemy missile zone." The Executive Officer of the *Jack Williams* was awarded the Navy Commendation Medal for his actions during "The two hour surface engagement of the Iranian frigate *Sahand* and subsequent anti-surface missile attack."

For others, there was frustration. Commodore Dyer sent in a video clip that showed a light burning brighter and brighter as it approached the ship, then seemingly flying past and going out. He was convinced that it showed the Silkworm that had flown past the ship and into Saleh oilfield, where it hit the water. Pentagon analysts told him the video only showed light on a mountain in the background. Visibility in the Gulf surface haze that day was only about 10 miles. The nearest mountains, on the Iranian coast, were at least 25 miles away. Said Commodore Dyer, "If that's a light on a mountain, I'll eat it!"

When an officer on the Hercules got word of the official denial that they had been attacked, he bitingly observed, "Whoever sent that message obviously didn't have a liplock on the deck awaiting impact." He went on to make it something of a personal crusade to get official recognition that the Mobile Sea Base had come under missile attack. Four times he sent in a recommendation that crewmen present on April 18 be awarded the Combat Action Ribbon. Supporting documentation went with the recommendations. Each time, when the package reached a certain level, it disappeared. The official stonewall remained: There had been no missile attacks.

Others knew better. After charging out to put itself between the Mobile Sea Bases and the incoming Silkworm on April 18, the USS *Gary* had maintained station for several days but was beginning to run dangerously low on fuel. It was decided to perform the difficult task of "twisting in" to the Hercules and taking on JP5 fuel from the base. When the *Gary* pulled alongside, crewmen of the Hercules stood on deck in silent salute. When Captain Bethea went onboard the Mobile Sea Base, the crew parted, opening up a passage for him and stood in respectful silence. Bethea thought it was an awesome moment.

One of the officers directly involved in the *Gary*'s engagement later observed:

> In the end, *GARY*'s contribution during Praying Mantis was the most significant action that any of my other ships have ever been involved in. Most significantly, I am convinced that the Iranian plan for the day was to take out *GARY* with the Silkworms and then the F-4s would roll in and finish off the barges. The US casualties would have been in the hundreds and might well have equaled the Iranian casualties of that day. It would have, in a way, been the equivalent of the Iraqi Scud attack on the barracks in Dhahran during the Gulf War. Casualties of that magnitude could easily have impacted US policy in the Gulf, and potentially even our response several years later to the Iraqi invasion of Kuwait. It is always difficult to assign credit or significance to an action that prevented something else from happening, and as such never appeared significant on the world stage. I derive great fulfillment in my career from having taken part in a never-known action that saved American lives.[27]

Not too long after Operation Praying Mantis, "the Word" from the Pentagon on the missile attack had obviously reached the Gulf. A reporter noted that Captain Dyer, the Commander of Surface Action Group "Delta," looked skeptical but wouldn't argue with Washington. "All I know," he said, "is that it was big, it was fast, and it came from Iran."[28]

CHAPTER 18

POLICEMAN OF THE GULF?

For several days after Operation Praying Mantis, the atmosphere in the Persian Gulf remained tense. A marine salvage executive described the Gulf as "ghostly" from lack of shipping.[1] The battered *York Marine* was towed into Sharjah harbor for repairs. Sharjah's ruler, Sheikh Sultan, summoned the Iranian ambassador to the UAE and angrily protested the Mubarak attack. Despite eyewitness evidence to the contrary, the Iranians continued to insist that they were not responsible for it. Iranian sources even had the effrontery to blame the attack on U.S. forces. Offshore oilfield operators well knew who had made the attacks. However, they were extremely critical of the fact that while the U.S. attacks on platform targets had made the U.S.-operated offshore facilities fair game for Iranian retaliatory strikes, no real protection had been provided to them by U.S. forces.

Some accounts of Praying Mantis in the popular press spoke of Iran losing its navy or half of it. Actually, the Iranians had lost about a fifth of their naval units. However, of the four *Saam*-class frigates, the most modern and effective units in their service, half had been lost, with the *Sahand* sunk and the *Sabalan* put out of action indefinitely. For a short period following Praying Mantis, the Iranian Navy ceased patrolling in the Strait of Hormuz. The maritime patrol aircraft stayed home. A U.S. Navy officer later said that for a month, "We didn't see the Iranians sneeze." They then gradually began reestablishing a modest naval presence. Perhaps out of fear that the U.S. was targeting its *Saam*-class frigates, it initially kept its two remaining ships of that type in port at Bandar Abbas, and instead deployed a replenishment oiler and tank landing ships (LSTs) in areas normally patrolled by the frigates.

Having suffered defeats on land and at sea, Iran was clearly on the defensive in the Gulf for the first time in years. Some analysts were calling it a turning point in the war. The renewed spate of mining in the Gulf once again rebounded to Iran's political disadvantage in the international arena. European foreign ministers meeting in the Hague "demanded urgently" that all mining and other acts hostile to free navigation in international waters be halted. Eight Iranian mines were eventually found and neutralized in the Shah Alum Shoals area. Approximately 50 nautical miles to the northwest, eight more were discovered and neutralized in the Rostam Field area.

Just how Iran had managed to plant two minefields in the face of U.S. surveillance is not clear. U.S. intelligence suspected that a small Iranian service tender, used to supply oil platforms, had been used, and that the Iranians had carefully targeted an area used by U.S. warships to rehearse escort missions. U.S. forces may not have been watching for minelaying activity with the same intensity they had at the time of the *Iran Ajr* capture. The JTFME's problem was that it simply lacked a sufficient number of surface and air units to maintain continual surveillance over established "Q-routes." Given the size of the Gulf, the number of dedicated units required to fully perform the task was prohibitive. Admiral Less observed of the Gulf, "that it was very small when you have to fight in it, but when you have to surveil it, it's very large."[2]

The procedures being used by U.S. forces in the Gulf may have made it easy for the Iranians to target them. The escorted convoys, and the warships making solo runs, usually sailed on so-called "Q-routes," which were the designated channels which the JTFME instructed the ships to use whenever possible. One U.S. frigate captain noted that the Iranian Navy very methodically watched the U.S. ships as they traversed

> . . . the same portion of the Gulf each time we transited either to re-position or during the Earnest Will missions. Back and forth, back and forth day and night we went across the same patch of water and the Iranians were not stupid and they sat there and watched us. They studied our tactics in the 1970's when the Shah was in power and many of their mid-grade naval officers attended U.S. Navy training schools (I had eight of them attend Destroyer School with me from 1976–77—a six month curriculum in Newport, RI that prepared us to be department heads aboard surface combatants). They knew we were follow-

ing Q routes, which were infrequently swept, and if they were going to mine anywhere, it should be there. It's my opinion that SS *Roberts* suffered the hit because they were following the Q Route to the letter and the IRGC laid the mines the night before.[3]

Interestingly, this particular captain never believed that the Q-routes were safe and so varied his ship's routes. He would often use a path recently taken by the heavy merchant traffic in the Gulf, feeling that a big tanker would either strike a mine or push it out of the way of following ships with its huge bow wave. Another captain asked if the Q-routes were being swept. Told no, he likewise refused to sail them.

The most recent Gulf mining, along with the success of Operation Praying Mantis, encouraged the U.S. to tighten the screw on Iran. On April 29, Defense Secretary Frank Carlucci announced President Reagan's decision to authorize American forces to protect neutral ships in distress in the Gulf and the Strait of Hormuz under certain circumstances. The aid could only be rendered to neutral ships outside of declared war/exclusion zones. The ships must not be carrying contraband or must not be resisting a legitimate search by a belligerent. Assistance would be rendered if requested and only if a U.S. unit was in the vicinity and its mission permitted it to render the assistance.[4]

The two U.S. Mobile Sea Bases returned to their regular location in the northern Gulf, which remained well outside of the nominal range of the HY2 version of the Silkworm fired from the mainland. However, no doubt due to concerns over another attack by "anomalous propagation," they received anti-missile protection in the form of radar-reflecting decoys deployed on floats. The reflectors were similar to the system used by Kuwait to protect its Sea Island terminal and were deployed around the bases in June. One drawback to the reflectors was that they put out a large radar signature, making the Mobile Sea Bases much easier for the Iranians to locate.

As an additional defensive measure against Silkworm attacks, the Mobile Sea Bases were also put on schedule to receive Tactical Air Defense Alerting Radars (TADARS) and Army 20mm "Vulcan" anti-aircraft guns from the 82nd Airborne Division. The high-rate-of-fire, flat-trajectory Gatling-type guns also promised to be very effective against small boats. The radar reflectors, air defense radars, and anti-aircraft guns made sense in light of the Silkworm threat.

Still, equipment was being sent out to the Mobile Sea Bases without sufficient thought given to the problems of integrating and operating it. The boxed-up TADAR arrived on the Hercules without any personnel to even assemble it. Navy crews puzzled their way through the instructions and managed to put it together. However, they never could seem to get it to work right. Eventually, it was disassembled and put back in the box it had come in.

In early June, radar onboard the Wimbrown VII detected an incoming airborne target. The Mobile Sea Base immediately went to general quarters with crews manning their battle stations. Observers spotted an unidentified missile-armed helicopter about four miles away heading straight for the base. The helicopter ignored radio calls and warning flares as it continued to close. As the helicopter came within range of Stinger anti-aircraft missile teams, they were locked on and ready to fire. One of the teams identified it through its markings as a French Navy Lynx. One of the Marines on the barge security force said the helicopter "came right by, took some pictures, and its just—we had like Pierre up there flagging at us, you know, waving."[5] The helicopter circled the barge at very close range, taking photographs from all angles, and then it departed over the horizon. It had launched from a French warship operating in the area. Commander Stubblefield immediately notified Admiral Less, who had some forceful words with the French senior officer. Admiral Less told the Frenchman that, if an incident like that occurred again, the Mobile Sea Bases would have his permission to shoot down intruding helicopters.[6]

Some thought that, with Gallic cynicism, the French supplied the helicopter photos of the secret American base to Iran as part of a deal to normalize relations between the two countries. On May 4, three French hostages had been released by their Lebanese captors. On June 16, France and Iran restored formal diplomatic relations. France reportedly agreed to repay a $1 billion loan made during the Shah's reign.

Whatever the truth of the supposition about a French deal with the Iranians, relations between U.S. and French forces in the region were excellent. Many U.S. officers had good personal relationships with their French counterparts. Indeed, during Operation Praying Mantis, the French carrier *Clemenceau* actually put fighters in the air near the *Enterprise* to provide additional protection for the U.S. carrier. This action was taken on the personal initiative of the *Clemenceau* battle group commander, Admiral Francois Deramonde. The French Admiral had become personal friends with Admiral Zeller, the *Enterprise* battle group commander.

Following Operation Praying Mantis, Iran expanded its Silkworm launch sites in the Gulf, building new cement launch platforms, storage sheds, and other facilities near the Strait of Hormuz. One particular new launch site, which was especially troubling to the U.S., was at Kuhestak, a coastal town inside the Strait and already the location of several Silkworm launch sites. Now, however, Iran was constructing a permanent underground facility to accommodate four missiles on a bluff overlooking the Strait near Kuhestak.

Modern anti-ship missiles are solid-fueled and can be fired out of their canisters on short notice. In contrast, the Silkworm missile system is based on 1950's technology and requires a cumbersome procedure before it can be fired. This missile is launched by a solid fuel rocket booster, but once underway is sustained by an old-fashioned liquid fuel rocket. The liquid fuel—toxic unsymmetrical dimethalhydrazine and red fuming nitric acid—has to be pumped into the missile's tanks by means of a high-pressure gas. Whereas more modem missiles can be more or less treated as a "round of ammunition" up to the point of being fired, the Silkworm required a fair amount of preparatory work prior to launch. All of this pre-launch activity, if detected by, say, surveillance aircraft, could give a valuable warning of imminent Silkworm launches. The underground site would take away this potential warning advantage. General Crist said that the facility would allow the Iranians to have a missile ready to be fired in five minutes.[7]

Featuring earthen and concrete bunkers, the site would cover the entire Strait and allow Iran to launch missiles within a few minutes, drastically shortening the warning time allowed by the previous requirement to move missiles to launch sites and mount them on above-ground pads, such as those used at Qeshem Island and Abu Musa, which could be monitored much more easily by U.S. surveillance.

The site had been under construction for a year and was expected to be operational by late summer or fall. It was seen as dramatically escalating the military threat in the region. General Crist said the Silkworm bunker site charged the whole equation for shipping in the region. Aside from the inability of U.S forces to detect pre-launch activity at the site, they would have a far more difficult problem in knocking it out as opposed to the open-air sites along the shores of the Gulf and the Strait.[8]

The U.S. response to the emerging Iranian threat was to dispatch an Aegis anti-aircraft cruiser to the Gulf area. The Aegis cruiser had the Navy's most sophisticated radar directed anti-aircraft missile system, and offered the best defense against short-notice anti-ship missile attacks. The ship also offered enhanced capabilities against Iranian aircraft. Increased Iranian fighter activity had been observed in the vicinity of Bandar Abbas, probably in response to recent Iraqi air raids in the southern Gulf.

In the early morning hours of July 2/3, the USS *Elmer Montgomery* (FF-1082) was patrolling near the western end of the Strait when it received a "Mayday" distress call from the Danish supertanker *Karama Maersk*. The tanker was carrying a cargo of Saudi crude oil when it came under attack by three Iranian Revolutionary Guard speedboats about 13 miles south of Abu Musa Island. The speedboats were firing rocket-propelled grenades at the ship.

In response to the distress call, the *Elmer Montgomery* went to general quarters and closed on the scene. The U.S. ship issued standard radio warnings for the gunboats to clear the area. The Iranian craft did not respond, nor did they clear the area. (They may well not have had radios.) Indeed, one of the boats appeared to be commencing a high-speed run toward the *Elmer Montgomery*. The U.S. ship first fired two illumination rounds from its 5-inch gun and finally a warning shot. Suitably encouraged, the Iranian speedboats departed the area. A U.S. warship had come to the aid of a neutral ship in the Gulf for the first time, with a successful result

A few weeks earlier, in late May, the Aegis cruiser, USS *Vincennes*, had arrived in the Gulf. On June 25, Iranian Air Force F-14 fighters had been detected for the first time flying out of Bandar Abbas. On July 2, the U.S. had confronted Iranian boats for the first time in defense of neutral shipping. A confluence of factors was swirling toward a great tragedy.

CHAPTER 19

"UNKNOWN, ASSUMED HOSTILE"

The Iranian expatriate owner of the "Hormuz" supermarket in Dubai, United Arab Emirates, stopped by the nearby Iran Air office on the morning of July 3, 1988 to deliver bottled water and soft drinks. The man had eleven family members, including eight children, due in on a short 20-minute Iran Air flight crossing the Strait of Hormuz from Bandar Abbas. When he got to the Iran Air office, the store owner discovered the staff intently monitoring news of an air crash. The earth suddenly seemed to yawn open beneath his feet, plunging him into an abyss of unbearable horror. A U.S. Navy warship had shot down Iran Air flight 655, the plane carrying his family. All aboard were dead. The wretched man began violently banging his head on a post. Said a witness, "He has lost his mind."[1]

Dawn on Sunday, July 3, had found three U.S. warships in the Strait of Hormuz or its vicinity. The frigate USS *Sides* (FFG 14) was heading into the Strait for an east-to-west transit into the Gulf after completing an outbound escort mission. The frigate USS *Elmer Montgomery* (FF 1082) was patrolling the northern portion of the strait. The Aegis cruiser USS *Vincennes* (CG 49) was proceeding through the Strait en route to Bahrain for the Fourth of July holiday.

At 6:30 A.M., the *Elmer Montgomery* spotted seven Iranian speedboats approaching a Pakistani merchant vessel, the *Sarghoda*. The *Montgomery* could see that the Iranian boat crews had manned their machine gun mounts and their rocket launchers. It looked like they were getting ready to attack the ship. The number of Iranian boats grew to around thirteen before they split into three groups. One of the groups took a position off the *Montgomery*'s port quarter. On board the

Vincennes, Captain Rogers was shaving in his sea cabin when the Combat Information Center (CIC) watch officer buzzed him on the phone and told him, "Skipper, you better come down. It looks like the *Montgomery* has her nose in a beehive."[2] The *Vincennes* immediately cranked up to flank speed. It headed to the area to support the *Montgomery* at 30 knots, then 32 knots. However, the Iranian boats the *Montgomery* was keeping an eye on didn't seem to be taking any kind of aggressive action. The *Montgomery*'s situation did not appear quite as serious as initially thought, and the *Vincennes* slowed to normal speed within a few minutes of starting out to support the frigate.

A little after 7:00 A.M., the *Montgomery* heard the IRGC boats challenging merchant ships over bridge-to-bridge radio. The U.S. ship also heard five to seven explosions to the north. The explosions might have indicated that the IRGC boats were shooting up a merchant ship. However, *Montgomery* didn't pick up any distress calls from a ship reporting it was under attack. The Commander of Destroyer Squadron 25 (DESRON 25), Captain Richard McKenna, was the operational commander for U.S. surface forces in the Gulf. He was monitoring the situation from onboard the USS *John Hancock* (DD 981), some 325 miles away at Sitrah anchorage in Bahrain. Captain McKenna, who had the call sign "Gulf Sierra" (GS), ordered the *Vincennes* to send its helicopter to investigate what was going on with the Iranian boats. He also told *Vincennes* itself to proceed to the general area of the *Montgomery*, but to hold out of the immediate vicinity. The *Vincennes* again cranked up to 30 knots and manned its small arms stations for possible surface action.

The *Vincennes* helicopter, call sign "Oceanlord 25," had been on routine morning patrol since shortly after sunrise. It headed to the area north of the *Montgomery* so it could monitor the activity of the small IRGC gunboats. Captain Rogers said he wanted the helicopter crew not to approach closer than four miles to the Iranian boats. "We didn't want to appear provocative," he later said.[3] When Overlord 25 got to the area, it reported that the gunboats were harassing a German merchant ship, the *Dahulagiri*. The boats were not actually attacking the ship, but were threateningly circling around it. From the *John Hancock*, Captain McKenna ordered the *Vincennes* to have its helicopter keep the Iranian boats under observation. Aside from a possible attack on a merchant ship, Captain McKenna apparently wanted to keep an eye on the Iranian boats in connection with the upcoming transit of the USS *Sides* through the Strait and into the Gulf. Oceanlord 25 carried a surface search radar and could relay its radar picture to other ships over the naval data link, so they could see what its radar saw.

At 8:18 A.M., Captain Rogers sounded General Quarters on the *Vincennes* as the ship continued to head at high speed toward the *Montgomery.* Before the *Vincennes* could get to the frigate's location, an Omani patrol boat appeared and ordered the Iranian boats circling the *Dahulagiri* to clear the area. The Iranians complied, breaking off their harassment of the merchant ship. The Omanis also reprimanded the *Vincennes* for cutting through their territorial waters at high speed, and requested that it leave them. About a half hour later, the *Vincennes* sailed past the German ship, which flashed an "A-OK" signal, and pulled alongside the *Montgomery.*[4]

Captain McKenna had wanted *Vincennes* to keep out of the immediate area, and was now reportedly startled to discover that the cruiser had gone well north of where it was supposed to be. He ordered it back south. Captain Rogers replied, "You want me to do what?" Captain McKenna was reportedly furious and muttered, "Aegis arrogance."[5] The *Vincennes* slowed to 15 knots, and at 8:46 A.M., the cruiser requested, and was granted, the authority to resume its transit to Bahrain.

The *Vincennes'* helicopter, Oceanlord 25, was still observing the Iranian boats. It was orbiting at low speed and at an altitude of 1,200 feet. The U.S. Rules of Engagement prohibited the helicopter from flying closer than four miles to the Iranian boats. Piloted by Lieutenant Mark Collier and commanded by Lieutenant Roger Huff, the chopper nevertheless closed to within two to three miles of the small Iranian craft. Apparently that was too close for the Iranians. At 9:15 A.M., as the helicopter was making a port turn, a burst of tracer bullets whipped by 100 yards in front of it.

Lieutenant Collier radioed to the *Vincennes*, "Trinity Sword, this is Oceanlord two-five. We're taking fire. . . . Executing evasion, clearing!" Captain Rogers asked the helicopter to confirm it had taken hostile fire and if anyone had been hurt. The helicopter reported no injuries and confirmed "eight . . . ten rounds . . . airbursts, returning!"[6] Captain Rogers ordered the helicopter back and told the bridge to close at best speed. He contacted JTFME command, and ordered general quarters sounded. For the third time in less than three hours the *Vincennes* cranked up to full power and charged north at 30 knots.

The *Vincennes* covered at least 10 miles at high speed heading toward the Iranian boats. Now, she could see two groups of them some seven to eight miles away. DESRON 25 Commodore McKenna directed the *Vincennes* to take tactical control of the *Montgomery*. Captain Rogers positioned that ship 8,000 yards off the *Vincennes'* port quarter. Rogers also radioed the aircraft carrier USS *Forrestal*, sailing some two hundred miles away in the deep water of the Arabian Sea, to launch its alert aircraft. A Surface Combat Air Patrol (SUCAP) "package" consisting of two F-14 fighters, one A-7E Corsair II, and one A-6E Intruder strike aircraft began catapulting off of the carrier's flight deck. They were followed by an E-2C Hawkeye radar surveillance aircraft.

With what looked like trouble in the offing, Captain McKenna also ordered the *Sides* to proceed at maximum speed to the area. Admiral Less directed the *Vincennes* to take tactical control of the *Sides* in addition to the *Montgomery*. The *Vincennes'* helicopter, Oceanlord 25, flew back near to the ship at high speed. When the *Vincennes* and the *Montgomery* sailed together into the vicinity of the Iranian boats, they saw that there were two groups of Boghammers. One group was about four miles away. The *Vincennes'* 25mm light automatic cannon kept them covered, although the boats were outside of the guns' range.

The two large 5-inch guns on the *Vincennes* were "centerlined," as opposed to tracking the boats, so that the big cruiser did not display an overtly threatening appearance. However, fire control targeting solutions were developed for the guns. Five of the six Iranian boats in the southernmost group headed away from the American ships, toward the entrance to the strait. The sixth drifted down the starboard side of the *Vincennes*. It carried on its bow what was described as a recoilless rifle (more likely a rocket launcher), which was not manned. The boat's crew appeared to be relaxed and slouching around. Most of the other group of Boghammers had retreated from international waters into nearby Iranian territorial waters, but several turned toward the *Vincennes* and the *Montgomery*.

The U.S. ships were still heading toward the Iranian craft, and, at 9:37 A.M., the *Vincennes* crossed into the Iranian declared war zone. The Boghammers had been swirling around in the haze about three or four nautical miles away. The small craft were difficult to track with sensors, but at least two appeared to turn, increase speed, and head toward the *Vincennes*. The commanding officer of the *Montgomery* saw the boats head toward the *Vincennes* at what he estimated to be a speed of 20–30 knots. Lookouts on the *Vincennes* reported that Boghammers were closing on the ship. Captain Rogers later said, "Just as I was about to clear the area, three of the northerly group reversed course and commenced closing *Vincennes* and *Montgomery* at approximately 17 knots."[7]

At 9:39 A.M., the *Vincennes* requested permission from McKenna and Admiral Less (whose instructions were being relayed through Captain Watkins) to open fire with its 5-inch guns. Admiral Less asked the *Vincennes* to verify that the boats were not leaving the area. The *Vincennes* answered that the boats were closing and increasing speed. At 9:41 A.M., came the approval: "Take Boghammer group with guns. I say again, take Boghammer group with guns."[8] A sonar man on watch heard what sounded like bullets ricocheting off the hull of the ship. Lookouts reported to the bridge that the Boghammers were firing at the *Vincennes*. Lookouts on the *Montgomery* reported small arms fire from the boats.

The two 5-inch guns on the *Vincennes* and the single 5-inch gun on the *Montgomery* opened up on the Iranian small boats. Captain Rogers said that the first round fired by the *Vincennes* exploded above a gunboat and destroyed it.[9] Guns firing, the U.S. warships continued forward toward the Iranian boats.

Some 50 miles away, on the Iranian mainland, Iran Air Flight 655 was sitting on the tarmac at Bandar Abbas airport. It had been scheduled to depart at 9:20 A.M. for a short hop across the Gulf to Dubai, but had been delayed. The plane was an Airbus, a jet with a 300-passenger capacity. During the stop in Bandar Abbas, the crew of 16 remained on board the jetliner. Two hundred and forty seven passengers walked across the field from the Bandar Abbas terminal to board the plane. Many were lugging cheap suitcases, which they anticipated filling up with purchases in Dubai. Some were shoppers, others small businessmen looking to stock up on inventory. Iranians often packed weekend flights from Iran to Dubai in order to buy low-priced electronic goods and jewelry—items often unavailable in wartime Iran. Other passengers were Iranian expatriates who lived in the UAE and were returning after going to Iran on business or to visit relatives.

The pilot, Captain Mohsen Rezaian, went through his preflight checklist before taking off. Captain Rezaian, 38 years old, had been trained by Boeing, and for a while had lived in the United States. He had married an Iran Air stewardess in a "modern," i.e. unarranged, marriage. The couple had three young daughters, one of whom had been born in Oklahoma. Because of the worsening conditions in Iran, Captain Rezaian had sent his family to live in West Germany.

Air Traffic Control (ATC) centers in Iran were notified through a "red alert" procedure when military activities posed a risk to civilian aircraft. When a "red alert" was in effect, the ATCs would not give clearance to civil aircraft to fly through the affected airspace. There was a shootout now taking place between the *Vincennes* and the Iranian gunboats, but Iranian authorities had issued no "red alert." It is unclear whether the small boats had not reported the surface action or if they had been unable to contact their command ashore. Iran Air Flight 655 was given take-off clearance by the Bandar Abbas tower, which radioed, "Have a nice flight."

At 9:47 A.M., having been delayed 20 minutes due to an immigration problem involving a passenger, Iran Air Flight 655 took off from runway 21 and began climbing straight ahead en route to Dubai. Almost immediately thereafter, the AN/SPY-IA AEGIS radar system on the *Vincennes* picked up a contact, which had taken off from the combined military and civilian airfield at Bandar Abbas, some 47 miles away from the ship. The unusually long-range radar detection of the low altitude contact was due to the favorable atmospheric conditions present at the time.

When the air contact first appeared, based on the fact that the take-off coincided with the surface action, the *Vincennes* Tactical Information Coordinator, Petty Officer John Leach, called out "Possible Padre" (Iranian F-4 Phantom fighter) over the anti-air warfare communications net. However, using an identification friend-or-foe (IFF) interrogator, the *Vincennes* picked up the contact "squawking" a Mode III IFF signal of the type assigned to civilian traffic. As the contact flew past the Iranian coastline and over the Gulf, the *Vincennes* assigned it Track Number (TN) 4474 and reported it to other ships over the Navy data link. USS *Sides* also picked up the contact squawking the civilian Mode III IFF signal.

The identification supervisor (IDS) on the *Vincennes*, Petty Officer Richard Anderson interrogated the incoming contact with a UPX-29 IFF system, which was separate from the ship's Aegis system. Using his remote control indicator (RCI), Anderson had initially picked up the Mode III response, a normal civil aircraft transponder code. However, Anderson "hit" the contact again, and this time he picked up a military

Mode II-1100 code from the same line of bearing (direction relative to the ship). The only radar contact on that bearing was TN 4474. Anderson then consulted a list of IFF codes kept at his console, ones that had been picked up from aircraft by the *Vincennes* or other U.S. warships. He saw that an Iranian F-14 fighter flying out of Bandar Abbas had used Mode II-1100 about two weeks before.

Anderson got on the *Vincennes* internal communications net and warned "all stations" that TN 4474 was squawking a Mode II IFF signal and "breaks as an F-14."[10] Anderson also called out loud, off the net, to the ship's Tactical Action Officer (TAO) to make sure he heard the report. Anderson told the Tactical Information Coordinator (TIC), Petty Officer John Leach: "I have a Mode II, 1100 on that track which also correlates to an F-14." Leach called out the identification "Astro" (Iranian F-14), based on Anderson's IFF response and on what he thought was a similar identification that had been called out by the ship's intelligence section. Anderson thought he heard the intelligence section say, "That track is possibly an F-14." The "intelligence section" was the ship's Signals Exploitation Space (SSES), which was physically separated from the CIC. It collected and evaluated signals intelligence on a real-time basis. The Petty Officer who supervised the SSES later denied making any such call. However, several CIC crewmen were under the impression that the F-14 identification had come from that source.

The USS *Sides* had assigned track number TN 4131 to the approaching contact that had taken off from Bandar Abbas. The *Sides* had assigned its track number slightly after the *Vincennes* had assigned TN 4474 to the same contact. The *Sides* did not correlate the two tracks and reported TN 4131 over the net. The more sophisticated *Vincennes* system did correlate the two track numbers, recognized that they were duplicates and, as first to correlate, dropped its own track number in favor of TN 4131. On the *Vincennes*, the contact now showed up as TN 4131. At his console on the *Vincennes*, Petty Officer Anderson consulted a commercial air schedule, provided via the Fleet Intel Center, to see if TN 4131 corresponded to any scheduled civilian flight out of Bandar Abbas. Because Iran Air was running 27 minutes late, the contact didn't seem to correspond to any of the scheduled flights on the list.

On board the *Sides*, Commander Carlson was standing between his Tactical Action Officer and his Weapons Control Officer. He asked about the contact, "Do we have it?" "Yes, Sir, we've got skin, it's a good contact," was the reply. (That is, the *Sides*' search radar signal was being reflected back by the metal "skin" of the air contact.) Commander Carlson observed that the contact was at around 3,000 feet in altitude, running 350 knots. He asked his ESM (electronic support measures) talker if the contact was putting out any electronic (radar) emissions. "No, sir, she's cold nose. Nothin' on her," was the reply.[11] (That is, the nose-mounted radar on the aircraft was not sending out a signal.)

The *Vincennes* was also keeping a close eye on another air contact. This one was an Iranian P-3 Orion maritime surveillance aircraft flying some 64 miles to the west of the ship. The *Vincennes* Military Air Distress (MAD) operator challenged the P-3 on the MAD frequency (243 Mhz), requesting that the Iranian "Papa Three" state its intentions and that it keep clear of the U.S. warship. The Iranian P-3 responded to the U.S. challenge stating, "Our intention is search mission . . . we keep clear of your unit." The *Vincennes* told the P-3 to stay 50 miles away from it.

Lieutenant Clay Zocher, the *Vincennes*' ship anti-air warfare coordinator, ordered the radio operators to challenge TN 4131 over the Military Air Distress (MAD) and International Air Distress (IAD) frequencies. At 9:49 A.M., the *Vincennes* issued its first warning to the contact over the MAD frequency, using the call sign "unidentified Iranian aircraft." The *Vincennes* gave the course, speed and altitude of the aircraft and requested that it state its intention. As a civilian aircraft, Iran Air 655 did not carry a radio capable of being tuned to the 243 Mhz MAD frequency, and the *Vincennes* received no reply.

The *Vincennes*' International Air Distress (IAD) operator next challenged the aircraft over the IAD frequency (121.5 Mhz). Using the call sign "unidentified aircraft," the operator gave the speed and course of the contact, and warned that if it maintained its current course it would be steering into danger. The *Vincennes*' operator requested the contact to immediately change to a different course. The Airbus had two VHF radios aboard; both were capable of picking up the 121.5 MHz IAD frequency. In September 1986, Iran Air had issued a notice to flight crews operating in the Gulf area, requiring them to monitor frequency 121.5 at all times. Iran Air 655 had been in contact with the Bandar Abbas tower and Tehran ATC over one of its two VHF radios on other channels, but there was no response to the *Vincennes* challenge on IAD.

It was now 9:50 A.M. The *Vincennes* was still hotly engaged in the ongoing surface action against the Iranian speedboats. Iran Air 655 was some 34 miles away from the cruiser, climbing to 6,000 feet and still heading directly toward it. The identification supervisor on the *Vincennes* had seen both Mode III (Civilian) and Mode II (Military) IFF "squawks" from TN 4131. Multiple personnel in the CIC, including the officer standing behind Rogers, Lieutenant William Montfort, also heard an IFF Mode II, or F-14, call over the internal communication net. However, the Aegis system was recording no Mode II military signal, only a Mode III civilian signal. Although a long distance away, the Iranian P-3 aircraft now turned inbound toward the *Vincennes*. It was around this time that the *Vincennes'* forward 5-inch gun mount went out of action, its bore fouled with a round stuck in it. The cruiser still had one big gun that was functioning. Captain Rogers anxiously ordered the Tactical Action Officer, Lieutenant Commander Vic Guillory, to "Bring that aft gun to bear now!"[12]

Sitting next to Captain Rogers in the *Vincennes* CIC, Lieutenant Commander Scott Lustig was acting in the dual roles of *Vincennes* anti-air warfare officer and force anti-air warfare. That is, he was coordinating the air defense of the other U.S. ships in the area, as well as being responsible for the air defense of his own ship. He was also communicating information on the surface action to the JTFME. Lieutenant Commander Lustig reported to the JTFME flagship that the *Vincennes* had an inbound F-14 that was ignoring radioed challenges. The *Vincennes* Own Ship Display Assistant (OSDA) had tagged TN 4131 as an F-14 on the AEGIS large-screen display, a 42-inch-square screen.

The display did not show the altitude of the "F-14," but it did show that it was headed directly toward the *Vincennes*. The *Vincennes'* MAD frequency radio operator issued another challenge and another request for a course change to "Iranian aircraft" over the MAD frequency that Iran Air 655 could not receive. Iran Air 655 was now some 28 miles from the *Vincennes*. Lieutenant Commander Lustig, believing that TN 4131 was an Iranian F-14, indicated his intention to engage it at a 20-nautical-mile range unless it turned away. Lustig asked Admiral Less over the radio for his concurrence. Admiral Less agreed, but ordered the *Vincennes* to warn the aircraft again before firing. Lieutenant Zocher ordered the radio operators to issue continuous challenges to TN 4131 until the *Vincennes* engaged it.

On the USS *Sides*, Captain Carlson was thunderstruck when he heard *Vincennes* announce its intention to shoot down the contact at 20 miles. He said to the people around him, "Why, what the hell is he doing?" Carlson had accepted the F-14 identification of the contact, but saw it now climbing past 7,000 feet and did not consider it a threat. In his mind, he said, "Maybe I'm not looking at this right. You know, he's got this Aegis cruiser. He's got an intelligence team aboard. He must know something I don't know."[13]

At this time, the *Vincennes*' Tactical Action Officer, Lieutenant Commander Vic Guillory, was sharply maneuvering the ship, using 30 degrees rudder, in order to bring the functioning aft 5-inch gun to bear on the Iranian small boats. Although it slowed from 30 knots to around 17 knots to turn, the ship heeled way over as it did so. In the CIC, the high speed maneuvering caused books, publications, and loose equipment to fall from desks and consoles as the crew dealt simultaneously with the Iranian small boats and the incoming air contact. The large screen displays in the darkened CIC flickered as the gun fired. Around this time, the *Vincennes* crossed into Iranian territorial waters in the vicinity of Hengam Island. The *Vincennes* issued additional warnings on the Military Air Distress and the International Air Distress frequencies.

The Iranian airliner was climbing through 7,000 feet altitude and squawking the Mode III commercial signal. USS *Sides* had the commercial signal and was reading the correct altitude. Two operators on the *Sides* evaluated TN 4131 track as a commercial "Haj," or pilgrimage flight. Standing behind Rogers was Lieutenant William Montfort, the Combat Information Officer. Montfort observed TN 4131 slowly climbing between 8,000–9,000 feet inside the commercial air corridor and said, "Possible COMAIR" (i.e. commercial flight) to Rogers and Lustig. Captain Rogers acknowledged the statement by raising his hand.

The other U.S. Navy warship engaged in the surface action against the Iranian small boats, USS *Elmer Montgomery*, wasn't able to pick up the approaching unidentified air contact on its own radar. USS *Sides* did have radar contact. Although the contact was crossing with respect to the *Sides*, Commander Carlson ordered a missile fire control radar to illuminate the aircraft. Iranian fighters were equipped with radar warning receivers which could detect a fire control radar locking on and alert the pilot. A radar lock-on would usually be expected to precipitate some sort of response, often an abrupt course or altitude change. Civilian aircraft did not carry radar-warning receivers and hence would be unaware of a radar lock-on. The *Sides* locked its fire control radar on TN 4131. There was no reaction from the aircraft.

The *Vincennes* continued to challenge the incoming track. Another warning was read out to "Iranian aircraft, fighter" on the Military Air Distress frequency that Flight 655 could not receive. The *Vincennes* anti-air warfare coordinator, Lieutenant Zocher, requested and received permission to illuminate TN 4131 with a fire control radar as it approached a range of 20 miles. The International Air Distress (IAD) operator issued yet another warning to "unidentified aircraft" on the IAD frequency that Flight 655 could receive, but which it was apparently not monitoring. Yet another MAD frequency warning was read out to "Iranian F-14."

It was 9:53 A.M. The Iran Air Flight 655 was climbing through 10,500 feet to 11,230 feet altitude and was 16 nautical miles away from the *Vincennes*. It was still heading toward the ship. The Aegis cruiser could pick up no radar signal from the contact on its SLQ-32 electronic support measures (ESM) system. A radar signal put out by the aircraft could have been correlated to signals in the ESM system's library and would have pointed to the aircraft's identity.

The Airbus carried a weather/navigation radar whose signals the SLQ-32 could pick up and identify. However, the aircraft was flying "cold nose," with no signal from its forward mounted radar. Apparently the flight crew had seen no need to turn it on, given the favorable weather conditions prevailing for the short hop across the Gulf. Accordingly, neither the *Vincennes*, the *Montgomery*, nor the *Sides* had been able to detect any electronic emissions from TN 4131. Rogers asked the operators again to verify that there were no electronic emissions from the contact. "Negative, negative, Captain. We've got nothing!" was the reply.[14] The IAD operator on the *Vincennes* was preparing to give another warning when the *Sides* issued a challenge to TN 4131 on the IAD frequency, addressed to "unidentified aircraft" and requesting a course change.

In the USS *Sides* CIC, there was growing excitement and shouting about "Comair" from two enlisted console operators, who thought the aircraft was a twice-a-week commercial "haj" flight. The CIC officer walked over and told them to "shut up." The *Sides*' CO, Commander Carlson, was not aware of the ruckus the two CIC crewmen were kicking up about "Comair." He thought that TN 4131 was an F-14 fighter, but not a threat. When he had verbally evaluated it as a "non-threat" to his ship, Carlton's TAO had given him a quizzical look. Carlson had explained his reasoning: The contact's course would not take it on a "closest point of approach" (CPA) to the *Sides* which would make it a danger; it was identified as an F-14 air-to-air fighter which lacked anti-surface warfare capability; it lacked any radar emissions which correlated with a military aircraft; and its relatively high altitude did not fit with the flight profile of a ship attack. "He's climbing. He's slow. I don't see any radar emissions. He's in the middle of a commercial envelope, and there is no precedent for any kind of attack by an F-14 against surface ships. So, non-threat," reckoned Commander Carlson.[15]

The *Vincennes* MAD operator issued another warning on the military frequency. Turning from the surface battle to the air contact, Captain Rogers asked, "What is 4474 doing?" Flight 655 was still climbing, which is exactly what the Aegis system showed. Up until 9:52 A.M., the altitude information on the contact being passed to Captain Rogers had been accurate. Now, according to later recollections, ominous reports of descending altitude were beginning to come over the internal net as the contact continued to head directly toward the *Vincennes*. Petty Officer Leach, the TIC, was interjecting reports on the ship's command communication circuit every time he had the opportunity to do so. As he later put it, "taking every open shot" so as to make sure they were staying informed, "[not] getting too sidetracked by the surface engagement where they were forgetting about the guy coming in." As the contact continued to close, he was reported to have been yelling out loud.[16]

Commander Lustig, who was running the air engagement, subject to Captain Rogers ultimate control, passed the reports of descending altitude and increasing speed to Captain Rogers without correlating the track on his Large Scale Display "picture" to a small digital (numerical) display in front of him, which showed Flight 655 climbing. Lustig also passed on, as a fact, a report that the incoming aircraft had veered from its flight path into an "attack profile." In contrast to what was being reported to Captain Rogers, the Airbus was still climbing past 12,000 feet.

At 9:54 A.M., the blue-and-white-colored jetliner was 12 nautical miles from the *Vincennes*, flying a mile off the centerline of a 10-mile wide commercial air corridor called "Amber 59." The *Vincennes* Missile System Supervisor (MSS) asked for and received confirmation from Lieutenant Zocher on the "take" order for the incoming aircraft. Commander Lustig hit the assign Standard missile button, which sent the order to the Missile System Supervisor, who then hit the firing authorize button. With the air contact now at a 10 nautical mile range, the system took over, initialized the missiles, and fired. A Standard anti-aircraft missile streaked into the sky, followed shortly by a second one. At that moment, Bandar Abbas took a position call from Flight 655, told it to contact Tehran Control, and to "have a nice flight." The Airbus replied, "Thank you, good day."

With both missiles in the air and heading to their target, the MAD operator issued a final challenge to "Iranian aircraft," requesting an immediate change in course. It was still possible to destroy the missiles in flight if the target responded. It did not. Some twenty seconds after launch, the first anti-aircraft missile exploded close below the airliner, between the wing and the tail. The second missile rapidly followed. Shrapnel sprayed an engine and the aft fuselage. The exploding missile warheads blew off the left wing and the tail.

The Commanding Officer of the USS *Montgomery* was on the bridge of his ship. He saw the flash of impact, and then saw the Airbus descending toward the sea in a rapid, flat spin with one wing and the tail missing. The jet crew and many of the passengers would have been still belted into their seats as the missiles exploded near the airliner. However, airlines in the Middle East were notorious for their poor seat-belt discipline. There were probably a fair number of passengers who had unbuckled immediately after takeoff. A few may have been killed or injured as shrapnel sprayed the aft fuselage. The unbelted passengers were probably sucked out of the now tailless aircraft through the open aft fuselage.

For the majority, the world must have tilted downward with a sickening lurch and whirled around and around as the stricken jet started to break up and spin toward the Gulf, some 12,000 feet below. It took little more than a horror-filled minute before the Airbus impacted the surface of the water, about six and a half miles east of Hengham Island. The airliner hit with tremendous velocity, killing everyone onboard. Aboard the USS *Sides*, Combat Information Center personnel shouted, "He shot down COMAIR!"[17]

The USS *Sides* itself came close to shooting down another Iranian aircraft. This one had departed Bandar Abbas at 9:56 A.M., flying the same course as the plane just shot down by the *Vincennes*. The USS *Sides* reported its missile fire control radar was locked on the approaching target and she intended to shoot it down.[18] However, based on the contact's slow speed and constant climb, the JTFME flag plot on board the USS *Coronado* in Bahrain evaluated the aircraft as either a P-3 or a commercial airliner. Captain Watkins told the *Sides* to hold its "weapons tight." Eventually, the contact turned away to the northwest. It was later identified as an Iranian military C-130 transport flying to Lavan Island.

The battle against the gunboats was winding down. Only two could still be seen on the *Vincennes* radar; the rest had either been sunk or had withdrawn out of range. At 10:03 A.M., the cruiser's still-functioning aft gun ceased firing. The ship had fired a total of 72 5-inch rounds at the Iranian boats. The *Montgomery* continued to fire for a while longer. A few minutes later it reported a "confirmed kill" on one of the small boats. At 10:19 A.M., the *Vincennes* reported to the JTFME that it had shot down an Iranian F-14 fighter. A minute later, two more inbound air contacts were picked up at a range of 43 nautical miles. These were Iranian F-4 fighters that, at first, flew toward the *Vincennes*. They tried to lock their nose-mounted fire control radars on the U.S. warship. The *Vincennes* used its electronic warfare system to jam their radars and broke several Iranian attempts to lock on the ship. The *Vincennes* had been withdrawing slightly to the south, and, at 10:32 A.M., it exited the Iranian-declared war zone.

Iranian search and rescue units were starting to arrive in the vicinity, but they didn't have the crash location of the fallen Airbus. Numerous small Iranian boats and tugs joined in the search effort over the next several hours. Sometime during this period, the *Vincennes* picked up Iranian radio calls over bridge-to-bridge VHF, accusing the U.S. of shooting down a passenger aircraft and threatening that "we are ready to answer for your actions."[19]

Admiral Less had received a report that an Iranian airliner was overdue at Dubai, and the awful truth was starting to dawn. As Captain Rogers would recount in his book, "Over the next hour and a half reports of a continuing search for an overdue civilian carrier continued to filter in. We had launched two missiles, and there was an aircraft missing. It was painful but not difficult for me to put the facts together."[20] Around mid-afternoon, Captain Rogers drafted a message to Admiral Less recapping the events of the day. It closed with the statement, "I and I alone am fully responsible for the actions of the *Vincennes*."[21]

In Dubai, dozens of distraught and sometimes frantic relatives and friends of those onboard the flight gathered at the airport clamoring for information. Iran Air officials laboriously compiled a handwritten passenger manifesto and passed out copies. Only when they saw the names on the list did the people anxiously waiting in Dubai know at last the fate of their loved ones. The blows fell with an enormous weight on some. Eleven members of one family were lost, ten of another. A young Indian doctor living in Iran lost six relatives. A Gulf Air employee in Dubai lost four brothers.[22] The Pakistani naval attaché, his wife and two daughters, had also been on board.

Abdul Amam Hassanpoor, an Iranian Coast Guard officer in Bandar Abbas, set out with several colleagues in a small boat to recover bodies at the crash site. He found some split open and others torn apart, either by the missile blast or crash impact. Unable to pull the bodies aboard, the crew tied a dozen together with rope and towed them to a large Navy recovery vessel. Pictures of the grotesque scene, with the gaggle of mostly naked bodies floating behind the boat went around the world. "For three days, I was sick, believe," said Hassanpoor. "It was a horrible picture. The men and women, they are no neck, no head. What can I say?"[23]

The mostly intact forward fuselage of the Airbus sank rapidly but probably retained some buoyancy. It appears to have drifted away from the original crash site. The Iranians searched only that location and never could find it. The fuselage held the bodies of the majority of the passengers and the flight data recorders. What the searchers did find were the severed wing and tail sections and some smaller debris. It is likely that most of the bodies recovered were those of unbelted passengers who had been pulled out of the plane as it descended. Their loose Middle Eastern clothing was probably stripped away by the rushing airstream as they fell from altitude, which was why many of the bodies were found floating nude.

The U.S. public got its first official word on the tragic event from the Chairman of the Joint Chiefs of Staff, Admiral William Crowe. He held a hastily convened press conference on the afternoon of July 3. Admiral Crowe expressed the U.S. government's deep regret over the incident and then gave a rundown on the sequence of events. He stated that the airliner was four to five miles outside of its prescribed air corridor, that it was traveling at high speed, that it had been sent numerous warnings, and that it had been descending in altitude. Admiral Crowe stated that, based on the information the local commanders had available, they had sufficient reasons to believe their units were in jeopardy and that they had fired in self defense. Asked if this was an accident waiting to happen, Admiral Crowe replied, "If a country is going to wage combat operations in a certain area and then send a commercial airliner into the area during that, of course it's an accident waiting to happen."[24]

Based on the information available to them at the time, the American people overwhelmingly concluded that the *Vincennes* was justified in shooting down the Iranian airliner. Seventy-one percent of those surveyed in a Washington Post-ABC News Poll thought that the captain of the *Vincennes* was justified in taking the action he did, while 23 percent did not. Seventy-four percent of those surveyed thought Iran was more to blame for the incident than the U.S., while 14 percent thought the U.S. was more to blame. The incident triggered a "rally around the boys in the Gulf" reaction, with a two-thirds majority approving of the way President Reagan was "handling the situation involving the U.S. Navy in the Persian Gulf."[25]

As it turned out, most of the major elements in the account given by Admiral Crowe were wrong. However, public reaction was strongly influenced by the initial version of events, which dominated the news in the critical first days after the action. The delayed release of the facts, a kind of trickle-down truth, helped attenuate the shock. Another factor present in the initial U.S. public reaction was the reduced level of sympathy toward the victims, which was an unfortunate by-product of the strong and continued animosity held by most of the U.S. public toward Iran. This hostility apparently created a psychological distance from the victims which insulated many Americans from the raw impact of the human tragedy caused by the shoot-down. A British newspaper reporter gave a Greek-American doorman in New York the news that 290 civilians had been killed when a U.S. warship had shot down an airliner. Dismayed, the doorman replied, "That's terrible. Where were they from?" Iran, came the reply. "Oh, well it's not so bad," said the doorman.[26] In fact, most Americans did feel badly over the loss of life, but it cannot be denied that their response was tempered by the fact that it had been an Iranian plane that had been shot down.

Administration strategy for handling the tragedy was to apologize for what happened, calling it unavoidable under the circumstances, but to continue on with business as usual. Congressional reaction varied, with many members calling on the administration to "review" its overall policy in the Gulf. However, public and bi-partisan Congressional support for that policy had steadily been growing, a trend that was not reversed by the Iran Air tragedy. Accordingly, there was little incentive for the administration to rethink its policy, much less abandon it.

In an effort to maximize the world's exposure to the tragedy and to further embarrass the U.S., Iran swiftly granted visas to journalists requesting permission to travel to the country. In Bandar Abbas, the recovered bodies of victims were displayed in a refrigerated produce warehouse being used as a makeshift morgue. Those previously identified lay in wooden coffins. Those still awaiting identification were in plastic body bags, which were opened for viewing by reporters and for filming by TV cameras.

The Bandar Abbas airport manager, who lost some members of his own family on the Airbus, bitterly told reporters, "When you see those dead bodies, you will see the human rights that Reagan insists on."[27] Some of the recovered bodies were dismembered, and grisly body parts were also displayed. Others seemed almost lifelike. One coffin held a three-year old girl wearing a green dress and white pinafore. Two bright gold bangles were on her arm, and her feet were still in white socks and tiny black shoes. Her equally small brother lay next to her. One young mother lay clutching her baby, forever frozen in a last embrace. "We found them together, so they must stay together," said an Iranian official.[28]

Nobody knew what Iran's reaction to the tragedy would be, but many braced for a possible rampage of terrorist revenge attacks. In a message broadcast over Tehran radio, Ayatollah Hussein Ali Montazeri, Khomeini's designated successor, took a hard line position in favor of violent retaliation. He urged Khomeini to order "revolutionary forces and resistance cells inside and outside the country to target America's material, political, economic and military interests."[29] Iranian president Ali Khameini wrote to heads of state that Iran had the "right to avenge the blood" of the victims of the attack, and was quoted as calling President Reagan and his administration "criminals and murderers."[30]

The more moderate or pragmatic approach was, as usual, advocated by Parliament Speaker Rafsanjani. The latter had been working to reduce Iran's isolation by improving its relations with other countries, and was generally seen as trying to steer it toward an end to the war with Iraq. The U.S. shoot-down of Iran Air 655 might have been a serious setback to Rafsanjani's efforts, strengthening the hand of the more radical factions in the internal tug of war over the direction of Iranian policy. Though in truth, Iran's maneuvering room was limited.

Conventional military attacks on U.S. forces had virtually no prospect of success. Terrorist strikes would inevitably bring heavy U.S. retaliation, adding to the woes of a nation suffering from increasing economic distress and one grown weary of a war in which the tide was turning against them. There was no explosion of popular demand for revenge. Most Iranians appeared to have been more shocked and bewildered than angry. "The people are hurt, but they're not hysterical," said a Western businessman living in Iran.[31]

Ayatollah Khomeini finally made clear the direction of Iran's response in a radio broadcast in which he responded to Montazeri's call for violent action by advising the latter to go along with Rafsanjani's more moderate position.

President Reagan had expressed his "deep regret" over the loss of life in a five-paragraph note delivered to the Swiss Embassy in Tehran on the day of the tragedy. On July 11, President Reagan announced that the U.S. would pay compensation to the families of the 290 people killed on Iran Air flight 655. In the words of a White House spokesman, the president was "personally saddened at the tragic death of the innocent" and had decided to offer compensation in keeping with "the humanitarian traditions of our nation."[32] The administration said that the payments would be made directly to the individuals and not to the government of Iran. The payments were described as "ex gratia"—purely a gesture by the offering country and implying no admission of guilt. As to assigning blame for the tragedy, that would depend a great deal on the outcome of a massive investigation getting underway in Bahrain.

CHAPTER 20

"I DEEPLY REGRET THE OUTCOME, BUT NOT THE DECISION"

The formal investigation into the circumstances surrounding the downing of Iran Air Flight 655 by the *Vincennes* was headed by Rear Admiral William M. Fogarty, Central Command's Director of Policy and Plans. The investigation team poured through the extensive data generated by the Aegis system, and took voluminous testimony. Under the circumstances, there was a great deal of pressure to soon come up with some answers about what had happened. An Investigation Report, commonly known as the "Fogarty Report," was handed to General Crist on July 28, 1988. It ran some 1,000 pages long with supporting documents, including 300 exhibits and appendices. A declassified version, only a small fraction of the full report, was released to the public in August.

The Fogarty Report noted that "time compression played a significant role in the incident," with Captain Rogers having only three minutes and forty seconds from the time he first became aware of the incoming aircraft until he made his decision to engage it.[1] Further, since he was in the middle of the surface battle against the Iranian small boats and devoting his attention to that action, Captain Rogers had very little time to personally verify the information being provided to him by his CIC team.

Among the factors which influenced Captain Rogers' decision, the Fogarty Report listed the fact that the aircraft had taken off from a joint military and civilian airfield; that the track was heading directly toward the *Vincennes*; that the aircraft was off the center line of the commercial air corridor, as opposed to other civilian aircraft previously observed by the *Vincennes*; that the reported altitude of the aircraft was below that previously observed for civilian aircraft; that the aircraft appeared to veer toward the USS *Montgomery*; that the track was reported increasing in speed and decreasing in altitude as it closed on the *Vincennes*; that the ESM system had not picked up a radar signature from the aircraft (i.e. it had neither a civilian nor a military radar signal), and Iranian F-14 fighters had been previously reported flying with their radars off; that the aircraft did not respond to verbal warnings on the military and civilian air distress frequencies; that the aircraft was reported "squawking" an IFF mode associated with Iranian military aircraft; that it appeared to be maneuvering into attack position; and that the *Vincennes* had been warned about increased hostile activity over the July 4th weekend.

In a statement to the investigators Captain Rogers had said, "I deeply regret the outcome, but not the decision."[2]

A startling finding of the Fogarty report was that two of the factors leading to the shoot-down, and two critical ones at that—the aircraft's reported military IFF signal and reported descending altitude—were directly contradicted by the Aegis system data. The recorded data showed that the aircraft never squawked anything but the civilian Mode III IFF signal, and never did anything but climb continuously from the time it took off until the time it was shot down. In trying to reconcile the discrepancies between what members of the *Vincennes* CIC team thought they saw and what the data actually showed, the Fogarty Report identified a likely technical explanation for the IFF error. In what was its most striking finding, the report pointed to "combat stress" as the culprit in the misreading of the airliner's flight profile. The report concluded that, "stress, task fixation, and unconscious distortion of data may have played a major role in the incident."[3]

In an endorsement of the Fogarty Report, JCS Chairman Admiral Crowe noted, "By far, the most puzzling mistake to me was the ultimate misreading of altitude."[4] Admiral Fogarty later testified before Congress, "I was unable to reconcile the fact that the tapes from the *Vincennes* showed a continuous ascent in altitude whereas at the final last seconds there was a call of decreasing."[5] Unable to resolve the clear discrepancies between the retrieved Aegis data and the CIC crew perceptions, the investigators had turned to possible psychological factors and brought in USN Medical Corps personnel who studied combat stress. Their conclusion was that the "TIC appeared to have distorted the data flow in an unconscious attempt to make available evidence fit a preconceived scenario ('scenario fulfillment')."[6]

An endorsement by Central Command's General Crist noted that a report by two Navy medical personnel contained the most reasonable explanation for the altitude misread. General Crist wrote that the medical report indicated that the altitude mistake "was induced by a combination of physiological fatigue, combat operations, stress and tensions which can adversely affect performance and mission execution."[7] Quoting the medical report, Crist wrote, "Since the TIC has no doubt that the aircraft is an Iranian F-14, heading toward the ship, and is not acknowledging repeated warnings, the mind may reject incongruent data and facilitate misperception which promote internal consistency."[8]

With the *Vincennes* in action against the Iranian gunboats and its forward 5-inch gun jammed, the ship had put its rudder over 30 degrees at speed, causing it to heel over as it swung into high-speed turns in order to bring its functioning aft 5-inch gun to bear on the Iranian craft. The CIC crew had been tossed about with unsecured manuals and equipment falling around them. In that atmosphere, with the pounding of the 5-inch gun, the threats posed by the gunboats and the incoming aircraft, there was certainly stress on a crew experiencing combat for the first time. Crews on Aegis ships did train constantly with tapes, which ran the system through numerous simulated battle situations. Still, as one Pentagon officer noted, "The excitement factor is missing in such drills, because regardless of the realism of the simulation it is just that, a simulation of the real thing."[9]

Captain Rogers said that the Aegis data recorded operators pushing buttons four to six times a second during moments of peak intensity.[10] Looking to stress as the source of the disparities between recollections and actual data, Congress heard testimony from a distinguished panel of behavioral scientists. They testified on the effect that expectations can have on sustaining a hypothesis, i.e. that people will often persist in seeing what they expect to see or what they are told they will see, rather than what is actually there. Questions were raised about the need for training on the operation of a complicated system in a stressful environment. It was charged that the Navy had not adequately supported research on decision-making under stress.

Duly chastised, the Navy went on to pour millions of dollars into a major research initiative called Tactical Decision Making Under Stress (TADMUS), in an effort to avoid future *Vincennes*-like incidents. The *Vincennes'* Aegis system itself came in for a great deal of criticism, with the shoot-down being held up as a stunning illustration of the limits of technology and the Navy's misplaced reliance on it. Critics argued that the sophistication of modem weapons had outstripped the capacity of operators to manage them. In fact, as it turned out, alleged flaws in the Aegis system had virtually nothing to do with the shoot-down of the Iran Air jet.

Some critics faulted the Aegis system because the radar return "blips" on the Aegis display were digitally processed and of a uniform size as opposed to the varying size of blips shown on analog displays. These critics seemed to think that, if the *Vincennes* had been able to see raw, unprocessed radar returns, it might have been able to distinguish the large aircraft from a smaller fighter. The problem with that theory is that while the size of an aircraft is a factor in its radar return, the radar cross sections of aircraft vary greatly with their shape and other characteristics. Broad, flat metallic planes are good radar reflectors. For instance, the large antenna in the nose of the F-14 fighter reflects back a large radar signature. The size of the "blip" was simply not a reliable indication of the type of aircraft being tracked.

A Navy expert on the Aegis system testified in Congress that, "There is no radar system right now which can positively identify the size of a radar contact."[11] The Fogarty report concluded, "The Aegis Combat System's performance was excellent—it functioned as designed. Had the CO [commanding officer] USS *Vincennes* used the information generated by his C&D [Command and Decision] system as the sole source of his tactical information, the CO might not have engaged TN 4131."[12]

One of the single most critical inputs into the information stream being evaluated by the *Vincennes* CIC staff was the identification of the incoming air contact as an Iranian F-14 fighter. That identification was planted early in the minds of the CIC crewmen, and went on to take firm root.

Two crewmen particularly affected were the Tactical Information Coordinator (TIC), Petty Officer Leach, and the Force Anti-Air Warfare Coordinator (FAAWC), Lieutenant Commander Lustig. The misidentification of the Airbus as an F-14 fighter originated in a response received by the *Vincennes* UPX-29 IFF (identification, friend or foe) system, not a part of Aegis, when it was used to interrogate the air contact. The identification supervisor (IDS), Petty Officer Anderson, had received two different replies: one a civilian Mode III, the other a Mode II associated with military aircraft. (An Iranian F-14 fighter had squawked that very code some two weeks previously.) In fact, Iran Air Flight 655 had squawked only the civilian Mode III from the time it took off until the time it was shot down. The *Vincennes*'s Aegis system never recorded anything but the civilian Mode III IFF signal.

The most likely explanation for the existence of the two different signals picked up by the IFF system was that, in addition to the Mode III it picked up from the jetliner, it also reportedly picked up a military Mode II signal from an Iranian military aircraft, probably a C-130 transport, preparing to take off from Bandar Abbas. The C-130 later took off squawking Mode II, right around the time the *Vincennes*' missiles were exploding near Flight 655. This was, in fact, the C-130 that had almost been shot down in turn by the USS *Sides*. An aircraft on the runway at Bandar Abbas would have been on the same line of bearing (direction relative to the ship) as Iran Air Flight 655, so the remote control indicator (RCI) had aligned the IFF interrogator in the right direction to pick it up.

Further, since the UPX-29 system was a manual system, it did not correlate automatically with the air contact displayed on the *Vincennes* radar screens. The range gate, i.e. the range from within which it would pick up signals, had to be set by the system operator. In this case, the operator (Anderson) had left his range gate covering Bandar Abbas for some 90 seconds, during which time Flight 655, the only radar contact he could see on that bearing, flew toward the *Vincennes*. The range gate determined the size of the "interrogation box" or "window" seen by the system. Here, that box covered both Iran Air 655 and the aircraft on the ground at Bandar Abbas. That coverage could have led to the operator miscorrelating the signal from the aircraft on the ground, which could not be seen by the Aegis radar, with Iran Air Flight 655, the only radar contact on that bearing.

The atmospheric phenomena known as "ducting" was present that day and also contributed to the miscorrelation, since the IFF signal and response traveled much further than expected. Normal atmospheric propagation of the IFF signals would have limited the distance they traveled, cutting off the signal from Bandar Abbas. If the range gate had been continuously reset so that it shrank along with the decreasing range of the incoming airliner, it would have cut off any signal from Bandar Abbas.

An organizational change may also have played a part in the events of July 3, 1988. In anticipation of the *Vincennes* assuming a Gulf role as force anti-air warfare coordinator, and because of the inexperience of the ship's own anti-air warfare officer, Captain Rogers had restructured the *Vincennes* battle organization. The "Golf Whisky," or GW position, was the force anti-air warfare commander. That is, it was responsible for organizing and executing the air defense of a given force of ships. On July 3, those ships were the USS *Sides* and USS *Montgomery*. Lieutenant Commander Scott Lustig, who Rogers considered his best anti-air warfare officer, had served in the "GW" slot. As such, he sat at a console to Captain Rogers' left and in front of his own Large Screen Display. Rogers had assigned Lustig the primary responsibility for the *Vincennes* own air defense, as well as force air defense. The *Vincennes* anti-air warfare coordinator, the inexperienced Lieutenant Clay Zocher, normally would have held that responsibility; instead he functioned essentially as a console operator.

Lt. Commander Lustig was also tasked with handling communications with the JTFME command, relaying both the surface and air tactical picture from the *Vincennes* and the air picture as to the *Sides* and *Montgomery*. On July 3, Lieutenant Commander Lustig was so engrossed in communicating with the JTFME that he had to have been distracted from giving his full attention to the ship's air defense. Since the primary responsibility for that role had been lifted from Zocher, essentially nobody was able to provide an independent check and assessment of the misinformation on the incoming contact which was being put out with increasing urgency by the IDS and TIC (Petty Officers Leach and Anderson). The Fogarty Report concluded that Lustig had "lost his ability to independently assess the actual profile and ID of TN 4131."[13]

It also appears that the TIC Petty Officer perceived Lieutenant Zocher as distracted by his attempts to illuminate the contact with the fire control radar. Accordingly, he felt the need to take up the slack and was much more assertive in warning about the incoming contact, which he saw as descending toward the ship.

It was widely reported that Lieutenant Zocher had difficulty in illuminating the inbound contact. Zocher was relatively inexperienced on the AAWC console. He had only begun sitting at it a month previously when Commander Lustig had been shifted off of it. However, his problem with illuminating the contact may have had more to do with the fact that an enlisted man, not the officer sitting at the AAWC console, had previously performed the action. The procedure had been changed only a few days earlier to require an officer to take the action, since illuminating a contact with fire control radar was considered an escalatory step under the Rules of Engagement. Thus, Zocher had virtually no experience with that particular console operation.

The Fogarty Report had described the *Vincennes* crew as being "in the highest state of training and readiness."[14] However, a 30-minute videotape of the ship in action during the July 3 shoot-down of the Airbus led some to conclude otherwise. Shot by a Navy camcorder team, the tape showed the ship's 5-inch gun firing at the Iranian speedboats and the Standard anti-aircraft missiles being launched at the Airbus. What generated strong negative reactions from several serving and retired naval officers was the tape of the bridge crew in action. The darkened Combat Information Center below decks was the electronic nerve center of the ship and Captain Rogers' location. It should not be confused with the bridge, where ships' captains used to station themselves prior to the advent of advanced electronic systems.

The videotape clearly showed that most of the bridge crew were not wearing protective gear such as helmets and anti-flash garb. "Can you imagine, one hit would have scorched them all," declared a retired Admiral. "This tape should be shown at every damage control and surface warfare school as an example of what can not be allowed to happen!" was the emphatic reaction of another officer.[15]

Aside from being unprotected, few crewmen were in the same uniform. Some were wearing tee shirts. A retired Admiral described the variously attired crew as having the appearance of a "come-as-you-are party."[16] The bridge also seemed excessively noisy. Officers appeared to be wandering around, and watertight doors were constantly being opened and closed. One retired Admiral observed, "If you can't manage the flow of information, you cannot control the ship. With the commanding officer running things down in the Combat Information Center, things should have been very quiet on the bridge. Instead, the bridge crew looked like it was conducting an independent war. They simply weren't trained for combat and drilled in the basic skills for fighting the ship."[17]

The Fogarty board considered recommending action against officers as high as Rear Admiral Anthony A. Less, Commander of the JTFME. Admiral Less had given Rogers permission to fire, but had left the actual decision up to him. In the end, no such recommendations were made. The report absolved Captain Rogers from any direct blame since he relied on others to furnish him with the critical information that led to his decision to fire on the contact. While attributing serious mistakes to "human error" brought on by the stress and confusion of battle, the report did not recommend action against any of those who made those errors. Some observers thought the decision made it clear that the military would seek to punish those who failed to act in the face of a perceived threat while giving the nod to those who did act. The obvious example was the recommendation to court-martial several of the *Stark* officers after the Iraqi attack.

The decision not to recommend action against the *Vincennes* officers is at least arguable. The decision to decorate some of the officers, however, reflected extremely poor judgment. Mark L. Collier, pilot of the *Vincennes'* "Oceanlord 25" helicopter, was awarded the Air Medal for saving his crew and aircraft by executing evasive maneuvering when Iranian fire passed within 100 yards of the helicopter. Leaving aside the question of whether Lieutenant Collier was "evading" what were only warning shots, he had apparently violated his orders by approaching much closer to the Iranians than authorized. This action is likely what precipitated the Iranian shots and initiated the chain of events that ultimately led to the tragic shoot-down. The helicopter was there to use its radar to establish a picture on the small boat activity, which would be passed to nearby ships though the data link. It certainly did not need to approach as close as it did to accomplish its mission. Under the circumstances, the award of a medal seems inappropriate, to say the least.

Lt. Commander Lustig, to whom General Crist wished to issue a non-punitive letter of reprimand, was awarded the Navy Commendation Medal for "heroic achievement" for his ability to quickly and precisely complete the missile firing procedure.

While not mentioned in the Fogarty Report, there was another, often overlooked, factor that contributed to the shoot-down of Iran Air 655: the policy decision made by the Reagan administration to expand the U.S. mission in the Gulf. Following Operation Praying Mantis, U.S. forces had begun providing "distress assistance" to third party shipping under certain circumstances. The events of July 3, 1988 had their origin in concerns over potential attacks by Iranian gunboats against just such shipping. USS *Montgomery* was watching the situation and the *Vincennes'* helicopter had been dispatched to the vicinity to provide a data link picture on the Iranian small boat activity.

No re-flagged tankers were in the area at the time, only third party shipping. It seems unlikely that the series of events that culminated in the shoot-down of Flight 655 would even have begun if the U.S. forces had retained only their original narrow mission.

While there is no doubt that a highly unusual conjunction of circumstances had resulted in the *Vincennes* shooting down Iran Air Flight 655, the situation in the Gulf was absolutely fraught with potential for similar disasters. Prior to the Airbus tragedy, one senior U.S. officer had said, "Our biggest fear is being sucker-punched like the *Stark*." In some ways, such as more effective damage control equipment and more rigorous training for Gulf service, the *Stark* attack had had a positive effect. However, there was a real downside. The prospect of taking serious damage and suffering dozens of killed, as had the *Stark*, haunted U.S. commanders in the Gulf.

Associated Press correspondent Richard Pyle worked out of the Gulf throughout the Earnest Will operation, and had the opportunity to go onboard numerous U.S. warships. He found a common pattern among their commanding officers. Virtually every one told him the same thing: *his* ship was not going to be caught in a surprise attack like the *Stark*. The problem was that the short flight time of anti-ship missiles meant that critical decisions had to be made in split seconds. The net result was that U.S. ships were sometimes on a hair-trigger alert. They were also routinely sailing under busy commercial air corridors. It was a dangerous combination. Speaking about the downing of the Iranian airliner, a UAE air controller said, "This was an accident waiting to happen."[18]

There had already been some near misses. On June 8, 1988, a British Airways Boeing 747, which had left London, was on its final approach to Dubai. Some 40 miles out from Dubai, the aircraft was also heading toward the USS *Halyburton*. The U.S. warship warned the civilian aircraft to change course by immediately veering out of its flight path. The Dubai air traffic controller told the pilot to ignore the warning and land normally. The pilot refused to turn. Had he done so, the airliner would have flown into the path of a second passenger jet taking off from nearby Sharjah International Airport. The result might have been a mid-air collision. The Dubai ATC then sharply warned the *Halyburton* that it was endangering the lives of civilian air travelers.[19]

The Fogarty Report faulted the Iranians for allowing the airliner "to fly a relatively low altitude air route in close proximity to hostilities that had been ongoing for several hours."[20] This conclusion requires an elastic definition of hostilities, one that seems to stretch far enough to cover the nonviolent harassment of a neutral ship earlier in the morning. The first action that could more legitimately be characterized as "hostile" occurred at approximately 9:15 A.M.. when shots were fired at or near the *Vincennes'* helicopter. There was then a near half-hour pause before the surface engagement began. The small boats commenced their high-speed run toward the *Vincennes* at approximately 9:42 A.M., followed shortly thereafter by exchanges of fire. These were the real "hostilities." The Airbus took off five minutes after they had commenced.

It is not clear if the small boats were in radio communication with their headquarters or if they had time, in the midst of their high-speed maneuvering while engaging the U.S. ships, to call in that an action had commenced. Any such call would then have to have been relayed to the Bandar Abbas civilian ATC. Given the short lead-time and potential difficulties, it is not at all surprising that a warning was not sent or received in time to hold the flight.

Given the heavy air traffic in the Gulf, along with the incidents that had occurred between U.S. warships and civilian airliners, the question was raised about why the JTFME had not taken more positive steps to de-conflict commercial air traffic, other than issuing the post-*Stark* attack Notice to Airmen (NOTAM). In a statement that does not appear to have drawn any published reaction, the Fogarty Report mentioned, "The first time the CJTFME promulgated commercial airline flight information to ships in the Persian Gulf Area was on 28 June 1988."[21] Thus, in a hair-trigger operation being partly conducted under extremely busy commercial air corridors, the JTFME had gone almost a year before it had gotten around to putting out the airline schedules.

Left to their own devices, U.S. ships in the Gulf had cumulatively built up their own unofficial information sheets, with scheduled flight times and IFF "breaks." Copies of the "gouge" were hand-carried between ships. One ship's CO said that the unofficial information "saved our cookies many times." One reason the JTFME finally issued an official guide was because of the pressure for one from below. Still, the sheer volume of air traffic in the Gulf, running as it did to some 900–1,000 flights per week, made it difficult to keep track of airline schedules. The track density often exceeded the capability of most ships' systems to process and display information in a timely manner. This was a particular concern in the narrow Strait of Hormuz where the time available to identify and react to a contact was minimal.

U.S. warships' lack of ability to reliably communicate with aircraft and air traffic control facilities was recognized as a serious shortfall. The International Civil Aviation Organization report on the shoot-down of Flight 655 noted, "There was no coordination between United States warships and the civil ATS units responsible for the provision of air traffic services within the various flight information regions in the Gulf area."[22] The Joint Task Force Middle East now sought to establish communications links with Air Traffic Control Centers in the region. The idea was that when the VHF communications with an aircraft were unsuccessful, the ships would be able to contact the ATCs to obtain their assistance in identifying and dealing with it.

Each U.S. ship would now be required to identify a member of each of its Combat Information Center watch teams as cognizant with civil aviation. This member of the watch team, known as the Civilian Air Identification Supervisor, had to be well versed on scheduled flights in the area, airways, and commercial air communication. He would have access to civilian ATC's via VHF radio.

The effectiveness of at least one of the measures, which had been implemented after the shoot-down, was quickly illustrated. In late August 1988, the guided-missile frigate USS *Vandegrift* was sailing off of Dubai when it picked up a radar contact at 4,000 feet, descending and heading toward the ship. The contact was squawking a civilian IFF code, but not responding to radio calls. As the aircraft closed on the ship, deck officers with binoculars could see that the plane was painted in a military camouflage pattern. "We couldn't make out who it was," said Commander Eric Utegaard, the captain of the *Vandegrift* recalled. "I just picked up the phone to Dubai [air traffic control] tower. They said it was a UAE C-130 [military transport plane]."

The post-*Vincennes* shoot-down remedial actions, particularly those relating to communications with air traffic control centers, show what should have been done all along. Too bad the *Vincennes* hadn't been able to just "pick up the phone" and call an air traffic control center. The JTFME's lapses were indeed among the many factors in the tragedy, ones on which the investigators trod very lightly.

In fairness, if U.S. forces focused on the prevention of another *Stark*-type attack, while paying inadequate attention to the possibility of a civil aircraft disaster, there seems even less excuse for some other parties, who had to be aware of the same near misses. For example, the air traffic control centers which might have done a better job monitoring the civilian distress frequency (and relaying warship calls to airliners), to say nothing of Iran Air's crews, who apparently made a point of pride out of not doing so. Captain Massoud Razeui, an Iran Air pilot who had often flown the downed Airbus, said that he normally ignored identification calls from American warships.[23]

Houssein Pirouzi, the manager of the Bandar Abbas civil airport, said, "The Americans have no right to be in the Gulf challenging our legitimate right to fly our air routes. Why should we reply to them?"[24] An Iranian flight attendant, who had flown on flight 655 a few weeks before the shoot-down, recalled, "The captain was joking with the crew. The Americans came on the radio four times warning us to keep away from the route. We were laughing about it; we thought it was funny."[25]

The Convention on International Civil Aviation (to which Iran was a party) provided that commercial aircraft "shall continuously guard the VHF emergency frequency 121.5 MHz in areas or over routes where the possibility of interception of aircraft or other hazardous situations exist and a requirement has been established by the appropriate authority." In this case, the U.S. NOTAM warning of September 1987 had established the requirement. The Airbus crew may have been communicating with Bandar Abbas at the time one of the IAD warnings was issued by the *Vincennes*, but not when the other three were issued. Either they weren't monitoring the IAD frequency or did not realize it was their flight that was being challenged. It would appear that the former is more likely.

In addition to its passengers and crew, the tragedy of flight 655 may have also engulfed more innocent lives. On December 21, 1988, a bomb concealed in an unaccompanied bag on board Pan Am Flight 103, a Boeing 747 flying from London to New York, exploded at 31,000 feet over Locherbie, Scotland. Airliner debris and bodies rained down on the village. All 259 people on board the jetliner and 11 more on the ground were killed. The fate that befell these victims was every bit as horrendous as that which befell those on Iran Air Flight 655. U.S. and U.K. investigators concluded that Libyan-supported terrorists had planted the bomb. Much later, a special tribunal agreed to by Libya would convict one of these men. At the time, there was suspicion that Iran had extracted vengeance for the Airbus shoot-down by the *Vincennes*.

There were reports from seemingly credible sources that Ayatollah Khomeini had ordered the bombing of the American jet in retaliation for the shoot-down of the Iranian airbus. The different conclusion reached by the U.S. and U.K. authorities, notwithstanding, the suspicion lingers that the bombing of Pan Am Flight 103 was indeed an Iranian-inspired act of eye-for-an-eye revenge for the *Vincennes* shoot-down of Iran Air Flight 655. It is possible that another such act even extended into the United States.

The first generation of Japanese minivans imported into the U.S. were derived from light delivery vehicles, which had no need for passenger access between the front seats and the rear. Accordingly, they mounted their engines and transmissions between and behind the front seats. This is a fact of automotive trivia, but one that may have saved the life of Captain Rogers' wife, Sharon, when a bomb blew up her Toyota van in March 1989.

Sharon Rogers was stopped at a San Diego intersection when an explosion rocked her vehicle, slamming her forward. The initial blast was followed by another a few seconds later as the gas tank went up. Sharon Rogers managed to free herself from her seatbelt and escape the burning van. The blast had resulted from the detonation of a large pipe bomb placed under the vehicle and behind the front seat. Fortunately, the bulk of the transmission had apparently shielded Mrs. Rogers from the worst of the blast. The vehicle became engulfed in flames and was a total loss.

Given the circumstances, authorities naturally suspected that the bombing was an act of terrorist retribution for the downing of Iran Air Flight 655 by USS *Vincennes* under the command of Captain Rogers. The FBI and Naval Investigative Service (NIS) undertook a thorough investigation. It was reported that Sharon Rogers had received a threatening call in July 1988 from someone she thought might have been Middle Eastern, who asked, "Are you the wife of the murderer?" Frightened, she had hung up. It was also reported that Rogers and his family had received at least two telephone death threats from callers who said they were acting in response to the jetliner's destruction.[26]

The case took a bizarre twist later that year when an Eastern Airlines pilot, who apparently had a personal grudge against Captain Rogers, claimed that the bombing might have resulted from an affair between Captain Rogers and a Maryland woman. The pilot's wife was now estranged and had named Rogers and the other woman as potential witnesses in her divorce proceedings. The pilot made the highly improbable claim to FBI investigators that the bombing may have been an attempt by Rogers or the other woman to kill Sharon Rogers. The

FBI did administer a lie detector test to Captain Rogers, asking if he had ever considered killing his wife. The agency ultimately closed the investigation without being able to reach any conclusions as to who had bombed the van.[27]

The fallout from the *Vincennes* incident eventually settled, with most seeming to accept the explanation that combat stress had induced the "scenario fulfillment" syndrome among some of the CIC crewmen. Captain Rogers never bought it. In November 1988, back in San Diego, he had said that the doctors who cited combat stress as a principal factor in the mistakes never interviewed the *Vincennes* crewmen. Rogers said that a second psychiatric team later examined the crew and said that stress was not a factor.[28] However, it would take some time before a seemingly viable alternative explanation was to fully surface. Some alternative explanations for other aspects of what actually happened on July 3, 1988 would also surface in time.

CHAPTER 21

SEA OF LIES?

Over the years, the *Vincennes'* shoot-down of Iran Air flight 655 has generated a multitude of newspaper and magazine articles, a book by Captain Rogers, several television news and investigation programs, and further Congressional hearings. Shrill accusations have been made and a supertanker load of ink has been spilled. The *Vincennes* incident bids fair to become the military equivalent of those great civilian controversies such as the Kennedy assassination, which feature a steady flow of new "revelations," new theories, and seemingly endless re-revised revisionism.

When the shoot-down occurred, it naturally spawned numerous stories dealing with the causes of the tragedy, many by instant experts. These tended to initially focus on the apparent failures of the high-tech Aegis system. With the publication of the Fogarty Report, attention swung toward the performance of individuals under stress and the adequacy of the man/machine interface under stressful conditions. In 1989, the commanding officer of USS *Sides*, Commander David R. Carlson, emerged as the leading critic of, and in fact, virtually the only active-service Navy public critic of the actions of Captain Rogers. Commander Carlson's comments appeared as a letter in the September 1989 issue of the *Proceedings* of the U.S. Naval Institute. Commander Carlson wrote:

> Having watched the performance of the *Vincennes* for a month before the incident, my impression was clearly that an atmosphere of restraint was not her long suit. Her actions appeared to be consistently aggressive, and had become a topic of wardroom conversation. "Who's driving the problem in *Vincennes*?" was a

question asked on numerous occasions prior to 3 July. "Robo Cruiser" was the un-amusing nickname that someone jokingly came up with for her, and it stuck.[1]

Commander Carlson said that he held the "minority view," that the *Vincennes* helicopter drew fire because it was a nuisance to the Iranian small boats, and that the *Vincennes* had seen an opportunity for action and pressed the Commander Middle East Force for permission to open fire on them. When Commander Carlson heard that permission granted, he had turned to his number two officer and given two thumbs down. He has been doing so ever since.

In 1992, *Newsweek* magazine published an explosive cover story in its July 13 issue entitled "Sea of Lies," charging that, "The Pentagon's official investigation into the incident, the Fogarty Report, is a pastiche of omissions, half-truths and outright deceptions. It was a cover-up approved at the top by Admiral William Crowe, then Chairman of the Joint Chiefs of Staff."[2]

The ABC News show, *Nightline*, echoed these charges in a show broadcast on July 1, 1992. A key element of these stories was a strained and ultimately unconvincing effort to link the *Vincennes* shoot-down to a "secret war" being fought in the Gulf by U.S. forces. The stories' sensational accusations were notably short on verifiable sources. Nevertheless, they did raise important questions in several areas and brought to light some aspects of the tragedy that had not really come to the public's previous attention. The stories sparked a hearing before the House Armed Services Committee, which further developed the publicly available account of the events that took place on July 3, 1988.

As far as the so-called "secret war" was concerned, the *Newsweek* story charged that, in addition to the *Iran Ajr*, a second Iranian minelayer, the *Rakish*, had also been seized by U.S. forces. It was also charged that radio messages from a fake tanker, the *Stoval*, had been used to lure out the Iranian gunboats on the morning of July 3, 1988, and that former JTFME commander Admiral Dennis Brooks had sent a 200-page report on "extra-legal" operations in the Gulf to Navy Secretary Lawrence Garrett.

Newsweek was forced to retract the second minelayer story when it turned out that the *Rakish* was the pre-revolutionary name of the *Iran Ajr*. In fact, the word "Rakish" was still painted across the *Iran Ajr's* stern at the time of its capture, which may have led to the confusion of the story's authors. A radio call from a ship identifying itself as the Liberian tanker *Stoval* was mentioned in the classified version of the Fogarty Report. There was no *Stoval* in the Liberian registry. However, the Iranian gunboats were already out in the Strait at the time that a radio call from the "*Stoval*" was logged, so they had not been lured out by it. The most likely explanation is that another merchant ship or tanker used the name in an effort to hide its identity; a practice sometimes resorted to in the Gulf. There is no evidence that the U.S. ever used such a decoy scheme.

In his 1992 House testimony, Admiral Crowe pointed out that the U.S. wanted to keep the Iranian boats in port, not lure them out. He witheringly noted: "In any event, I don't understand what purpose a fictitious ship would have served. The Iranians hear the transmission, come out and find no ship. What do they do then? Perhaps for lack of anything else to do, they would attack an American warship and fall right into our trap? Not likely. I find the whole scenario silly."[3]

The practice of using two patrol boats to simulate the radar signature of a larger ship was mentioned in a June 21, 1988 oral history interview with Lieutenant Jonathan G. Rourke, the Operations Officer at the time for the Special Warfare Task Unit in the Gulf. At one point, Lieutenant Roarke was asked about trying to make two patrol boats look like a merchant ship. Lieutenant Roarke said that the practice was known as "deceptive gliding" and was intended to draw a response from the Iranians, such as radio transmissions, which "intel types" could make something of. Asked if the practice was meant to provoke an attack, Roarke replied: "No, it's not meant to provoke attack. Maybe in the back of all sailors' minds . . . they would like for that to happen . . . but that's not the intent of it by any stretch of the imagination. They're just out there to do deceptive gliding, to get intel and information and see what they can do."[4]

Perhaps some of the boat crews thought the purpose of the tactic was to draw out the Iranians, and these crewmen had passed the idea on to visitors. Obviously, the operational commanders weren't trying to lure out the Iranians and, in fact, that scenario never seems to have occurred.

Admiral Crowe also testified that Admiral Brooks told him that he had sent a letter, not a report, to the Secretary of the Navy and that it was a private matter between the two parties. Admiral Crowe said he talked to Secretary Garrett, who described the letter as a communication from a disgruntled officer. Admiral Crowe had considered Admiral Brooks' performance as the JTFME commander unsatisfactory. Brooks had finally requested relief from his assignment and had been replaced by Admiral Less. The resignation was a face-saving gesture for his removal.

Newsweek charged that the Pentagon had concealed the fact that the *Vincennes* had been in Iranian territorial waters at the time of the shoot-down, "in clear violation of international law." ABC accused "the entire executive branch of government, from the President on down" of being involved in a cover-up concerning the location of the ship.[5] Similar accusations were leveled at the Navy, the Pentagon, and the State Department. It was also claimed that the *Vincennes*' helicopter was in Iranian waters when the gunboats fired the shots near it, and that the *Vincennes* had been in Iranian waters when it opened fire on those boats. It was pointed out that, in his 1988 testimony before Congress, Admiral Fogarty had presented radar screen pictures from the *Vincennes*, which did not show Iran's small Hengham Island. It was charged that this island had been deliberately deleted from the pictures in order to disguise the fact that the *Vincennes* was in Iran's territorial waters. Captain Rogers had repeatedly denied being in Iranian waters.

In fact, the *Vincennes* had crossed into Iran's territorial waters (twelve-mile limit) during the surface action and was approximately nine and a half miles from Hengham Island when it shot down Iran Air Flight 655. That information was contained in the classified version of the Fogarty Report delivered to Congress, but not in the publicly released portion. The question of the *Vincennes*' location had not been raised at the various news conferences held by defense officials and the information had not been volunteered. Full data on the *Vincennes* location had been made available to the International Civil Aviation Organization (ICAO), which incorporated it in their report issued to the public in March 1989. The location of the ship in Iranian waters is accurately shown on a chart in that report.

In his 1992 congressional testimony, a by-then retired Admiral Crowe gave two reasons why the *Vincennes*' location was redacted from the publicly released report. First, it would have disclosed the fact that the U.S. rules of engagement allowed warships to enter territorial waters under certain circumstances. Second, it could only have exacerbated an already highly inflamed situation to reveal that a warship located in Iran's own waters had shot down Flight 655.[6]

These concerns were well taken, particularly the second one. The main problem with the charges over the *Vincennes'* location is that it is hard to see how its crossing into Iran's waters made any real difference in the tragedy. If the ship had been in the airliner's flight path, but two and one-half miles further off Hengham Island, the circumstances that led to the shoot-down would have essentially been the same. As Admiral Crowe put it in his testimony: "So what has become a central point in the so-called cover-up didn't seem terribly important at the time, or throughout the past four years, to either the verdict or Congress. The reason is simple—it was never viewed as a significant issue." The ICAO report had not thought it important enough to mention this aspect of the shoot-down.[7]

Captain Rogers had apparently been operating under a misconception as to his location, based on his view of the Aegis large screen display (LSD) in the CIC. The LSD was not a navigational display and did not show nearby landmasses based on radar returns. Rather, the system had land data programmed into it to give some sense of location relative to the air and sea contacts which it was accurately depicting, based on their actual radar returns. Hengham Island was simply not in the Aegis database, which lacked the memory capacity to hold that much detailed navigational information. Hence, Rogers was convinced that he had not entered Iranian waters some minutes into the surface battle.[8]

As to the location of the *Vincennes'* helicopter, no evidence was presented to support the claim that it was in Iranian waters. The Fogarty Report and a study by the Naval War College stated otherwise. The charge was simply not proven. The *Vincennes'* helicopter did approach closer to the Iranian boats than it was permitted under its rules of engagement. Those orders specified that helicopters stay at least four miles away from Iranian craft. This was for the helicopters' own protection, particularly against hand-held anti-aircraft missiles such as SAM-7's or Stingers. In a sworn statement to the Fogarty Investigation, the pilot, Lieutenant Mark Collier, conceded that he had been one to two miles closer to the boats than allowed by his ROE's.[9] This unusually close approach likely prompted the burst of Iranian fire, whether directed at the U.S. helicopter or fired as a "keep away" warning.

It was also claimed that the *Vincennes* had entered Iranian waters before commencing fire on the Iranian gunboats. However, a sworn statement by the *Vincennes* navigator indicates that mounts 51 and 52 "lit-off," i.e. started firing prior to entering those waters.[10] The charge that the *Vincennes* violated international law when it entered Iranian waters is not so easily resolved. In defense against that claim, it was said that the *Vincennes* had been exercising its right of self-defense under Article 51 of the United Nations charter, which allowed a warship to enter sovereign territory in the course of defending itself. The larger question raised by this issue is: just who was the real aggressor and who was really defending themselves on the morning of July 3, 1988?

The "Sea of Lies" story described Captain Rogers as overeager and longing to see action. It said that, according to several high-ranking officers, Rogers was widely regarded as "trigger happy." Commander Carlson's "Robo Cruiser" theme was picked up and amplified. In fact, the actions of the *Vincennes* prior to the small boat engagement do look like a ship trying hard to get into some action. Three times that morning the *Vincennes* had gone to general quarters and steamed at high speed toward Iranian small boats. The first occasion was at 6:33 A.M. when the *Vincennes* had raced at speeds up to 32 knots to support the USS *Montgomery*, which had reported groups of small boats near its position. Again, at 8:18 A.M., the *Vincennes* had headed toward the swarming Iranian boats at high speed, before reportedly being ordered back by the Commander, Joint Task Force Middle East. Finally, when shots were fired near its helicopter, the *Vincennes* surged at full power not just up to the *Montgomery* but on into the vicinity of the Iranian boats.

No one has ever given a good reason for the *Vincennes* to go charging at full speed for at least some 20 minutes up to the Iranian small boats that had fired near its helicopter. In his book, Captain Rogers only relates that he turned north to close on the helicopter. The Fogarty Report doesn't give any rationale either, only noting rather blandly that the *Vincennes* proceeded to the vicinity of the boats. This key question was probably slighted for a very good reason: there wasn't any good reason for the *Vincennes* to run up to the Iranian boats, unless it was looking for the chance to get into a fight. Lieutenant Colonel David Evans, USMC (Ret.), military correspondent for the *Chicago Tribune*, asked Captain Rogers about it in a 1993 telephone interview. Captain Rogers replied, "I wanted to get him [my helicopter] back under my air defense umbrella. That's why I was heading north."[11]

This is a weak rationale. The helicopter faced no air threat whatsoever. Thus, it had no need to be under the *Vincennes'* air defense umbrella, which, as Colonel Evans pointed out, it was already under anyway since it was within range of the *Vincennes* anti-aircraft missiles. The helicopter had nothing to fear from the Iranian boats since it rapidly flew away from them, and from the relatively short range of their light automatic weapons. The helicopter withdrew at twice the speed the boats could manage, not that they tried to follow it anyway.

A better way to handle such incidents had been demonstrated in late December 1987, when an unarmed SH-60 helicopter based on USS *Elrod* had shots fired in its vicinity when it ventured near Iranian small boats attacking a merchant vessel. The helicopter didn't stick around to determine if it was being fired on directly or if it had only received a warning. It flew back to the *Elrod* a few miles away. The Captain of the *Elrod* apparently felt no need to go charging up to the Iranian boats at full speed and nothing came of the incident.[12] Rogers would later write that his closure on *Montgomery* "was anything but a desire to place his ship in harm's way."[13] The Commanding Officer of another U.S. warship in the Gulf at the time felt otherwise: "I think that's EXACTLY why he hauled ass and departed station without ASUWC [anti-surface warfare commander] authority."

If there weren't any good reasons to race up to the gunboats, there were good reasons not to. Earlier in the day on July 3, 1988, USS *Montgomery* had found itself alone in the vicinity of numerous Iranian small boats. Captain Rogers quoted a report to him that the *Montgomery* had "its nose in a beehive." By charging into a position close to the boats that had fired near its helicopter, the *Vincennes* was now putting its own nose in a beehive. Why it would choose to do so is not at all obvious. The *Vincennes* was unarmored. Light automatic weapons fire could punch right through its thin skin. Captain Rogers later wrote that the shoulder-launched rocket propelled grenades fired from Iranian boats "could severely damage the superstructure and certainly kill or injure crew members."[14]

While Captain Rogers gave that observation as a reason for his concern over a possible "swarm" attack by numerous small boats, others might see it as a good reason not to put one's "nose in a beehive" in the first place. Captain Rogers said he felt strongly about his crew and that, "I knew every man personally and was proud to be their skipper."[15] Yet it would be some of these men, members of "Team 49," who stood to be left dead or maimed if a gunboat attack got through his defenses and hit the ship. One might think that concerns over the crew would dictate that such risks only be taken when unavoidable.

Aside from the risks to the ship and its crew, putting the *Vincennes* into action against small gunboats raised the question of the appropriate tactical employment of an Aegis air defense cruiser. In 1988 Senate hearings, Senator John McCain had asked Admiral Fogarty, "Admiral, should a ship that expensive be committed in that scenario from your subjective viewpoint?"[16] It was a good question.

Critics had charged that introducing a ship into the Gulf with ultra sophisticated air defense electronics systems, but which was vulnerable to the less sophisticated weapons used by the Iranians in their ship attacks, was a serious mistake. The notion drew a variety of metaphors for inappropriate use from opponents. One critic compared the deployment of the *Vincennes* to the Gulf with taking a Porsche to the bazaar.[17] Putting the *Vincennes* in there, said military analyst Edward Luttwak, "is like chasing flies with a big hammer."[18] One senior Admiral had asked, "Why would you want to put a diamond in a pigsty?"[19]

What was an open ocean, saturation-attack, air defense cruiser like the *Vincennes* doing in the narrow confines of the Gulf? It was certainly there to provide anti-aircraft defense against the Silkworm. As has been recounted, the reason put forward when the ship was deployed was the construction of the underground Silkworm launch site at Khusestak. Supposedly, the lack of the advance warning otherwise provided by visible pre-launch activity at open sites put a premium on the short-notice defensive ability of U.S. ships to shoot down the missiles. Hence, the need to deploy a cruiser equipped with the Navy's premier air defense system, the Aegis.

However, when looked at closely, this rationale doesn't really hold up. The Silkworm launching sites were regularly "imaged" by reconnaissance aircraft and satellites. On occasion, U.S. P-3 Orion maritime patrol aircraft or ship-based helicopters might have a view of some of the sites using binoculars. Still, in the end, the launch sites were simply not being kept under real-time visual surveillance. In any case, most of the fixed concrete launch pads along the Strait had rear tunnels leading to the launcher, which concealed visual observation of pre-launch activity. Earnest Will convoys were usually timed to pass through the Strait at night, further limiting visual observation. The only pre-launch indications that could reliably be counted on were the electronic signals being given out by targeting radars locking on ships. The fact that a launch site was buried made no difference in these electronic signals.

The Khuestak site was not even expected to be operational until late summer or early fall, yet the *Vincennes* had been suddenly yanked out of a fleet exercise during the course of its normal training cycle, two months early. It was sped on a 32-day 13,000-mile dash from San Diego to the Gulf with a planned arrival date at the Strait of Hormuz of not later than May 18, 1988. The *Vincennes* even claimed a trans-Pacific speed record for the run. As Captain Rogers would write:

> The navy is pretty deliberate in maintaining operational schedules such as the thirty-day stand-down period before deployment. That time may be reduced but it is rarely cut out completely. To yank a ship out of her work-up cycle before deployment is almost unheard of. Deployments were accelerated during Desert Shield/Desert Storm, but no deployment before or since then has been as rapid as that of the *Vincennes* on that April night in 1988.[20]

As to why the *Vincennes* had been so hurriedly dispatched, Captain Rogers noted: "The complete rationale was not made available to me until well after our departure. However, it was obvious that a decision such as this was serious and decided at the highest levels of government."[21]

Indeed, what could have caused such high level concern? On the afternoon of April 18, 1988, during Operation Praying Mantis, the Iranians had crossed the dreaded "Silkworm threshold" and actually fired the missiles at U.S. ships and Mobile Sea Bases. Less than 48 hours later, on April 20, 1988, the *Vincennes* was ordered to the Gulf with extraordinary haste. Faced now with the real possibility of more Silkworm attacks, the U.S. Navy was bolstering its anti-missile capabilities on an emergency basis. That is why the *Vincennes* was in the Gulf. If the Khuestak bunker had been the real concern, an Aegis cruiser would not have been needed in the Gulf for at least another two months. Clearly, the construction of the bunker was being used as a cover story for the real reason the *Vincennes* had been rushed to the Gulf.

During the September 1988 Senate hearings, Rear Admiral Robert T. Kelly, Vice Director for Operations, Joint Staff, followed up an answer given by Admiral Fogarty to Senator John Glenn's question about the appropriate deployment of an Aegis cruiser. Admiral Kelly said, "I would just like to add, sir, that the reason the *Vincennes* was sent over there resulted from the engagement that occurred on the 18th of April."[22] The significance of that one remark was completely lost in the voluminous testimony generated at the various hearings on every aspect of the tragedy. Addressing the use of an Aegis cruiser in the Gulf, Joint Chiefs Chairman Admiral Crowe wrote in August 1988 that the Silkworm was an "awesome weapon" and that: "The most capable platform in the U.S. inventory for handling this threat is the Aegis cruiser. It makes the greatest sense to me to utilize the best available platform against the greatest threat."[23] Left unsaid was that the U.S. forces had already been forced to confront that threat once and wanted all the help they could get if they had to do so again. Admiral Crowe may have been sensitive on this point because apparently he was the one who had decided to dispatch an Aegis cruiser to the Gulf, possibly on the recommendation of General Crist.

The Rules of Engagement (ROE) under which the *Vincennes* operated when it steamed up to the Iranian gunboats on July 3 were not spelled out in the Fogarty Report. However, it is obvious that U.S. ships were allowed, if not required, to act in self-defense when "hostile intent" was shown. What constituted "hostile intent" was also not spelled out. A report to Congress in June 1987 by then Secretary of Defense Caspar Weinberger on security arrangements in the Gulf gave a definition that was likely close to or on the mark:

> Hostile intent: The threat of imminent use of force against friendly forces, for instance, any aircraft or surface ship that maneuvers into a position where it could fire a missile, drop a bomb, or use gunfire on a ship is demonstrating evidence of hostile intent. Also, a radar lock-on to a ship from any weapons system fire control radar that can guide missiles or gunfire is demonstrating hostile intent. This includes lock-on by land-based missile systems that use radar.[24]

When the *Vincennes* opened fire, at least two of the Iranian small boats were closing on the U.S. warship. It certainly appeared that the boats were maneuvering into a position where they could use gunfire against the Aegis cruiser. Captain Kearny, commanding officer of the USS *Montgomery*, testified that two of the Boghammers "headed right at *Vincennes*" at "20–30 knots." Thus, the decision to open fire on the closing boats seems to have been a prudent defensive measure in accordance with the ROE. It also makes the Iranians look like the aggressors. However, in assessing the actions of the various parties, it only seems fair to allow the Iranians to operate under the same ROEs as the Americans. In that light, the question then becomes, who showed "hostile intent" first? The two big warships with a combined displacement of some 15,000 tons, carrying over 600 men, armed with heavy, long-range 5-inch guns, and which came charging out of the haze toward the Iranian craft at 30 knots, or the two small boats with a combined displacement of maybe 12 tons, carrying 10 or 12 men, and armed only with light weapons, which pulled out of a larger group of boats and turned toward the big ships, which, incidentally, were still making their own high speed runs toward them?

While it is true that the *Vincennes* did not open fire until after two of the Iranian boats commenced high-speed runs toward it, it appears that Captain Rogers may have been trying to get permission to open fire even before the two evidenced hostile intent by turning and heading toward him. Captain Rogers had requested authority from the JTFME at 9:39 A.M., claiming that the gunboats were closing on the U.S. ships. Permission to fire was granted at 9:41 A.M. The *Vincennes* opened fire at 9:43 A.M. The exact time the Iranian boats turned toward the *Vincennes* was not in the publicly released version of the Fogarty Report. However, in his 1992 Congressional testimony, Admiral Crowe stated: "We actually know that they turned around toward *Vincennes* at time 09:42," several minutes after the *Vincennes* had first requested permission to open fire.[25]

The simple fact that Captain Rogers had gotten on the radio and asked for permission to open fire belies the notion that the *Vincennes* was under immediate threat. If two boats were making a high-speed run at his ship, Captain Rogers had ample authority under the Rules of Engagement to defend his ship and open fire without getting permission, in what Commander Carlson described as "a time consuming request that was passed through two levels of the chain of command and required the answering of several questions."[26]

The JTFME staff did not normally oversee tactical actions and did not interfere with decisions being made on the spot. Rogers simply had no need to ask for permission to fire in self-defense. It looks suspiciously like he was trying to cover himself by getting authority to open fire in a situation where, had he done so on his own, he would have been hard pressed to justify his actions. One critic has suggested that Captain

Rogers may have been trying to take advantage of the fact that Admiral Less' flag plot did not have a tactical data link picture of the actual situation in the Strait. In fact, the command ship had a "JOTS" terminal, which copied the data link with a lag of a few seconds. This near real-time picture would have been adequate to monitor the unfolding situation. However, on July 3 it was not working properly. It is unclear if Captain Rogers was even aware of the problem, and it is highly speculative that he sought to take deliberate advantage of it. Nevertheless, the Commander of the JTFME and the Commodore of DESRON 25 had to rely on Rogers' description of the circumstances he faced, though these did not really justify opening fire when he sought permission to do so.

The Commander of the JTFME had requested that the *Vincennes* verify that the small boats were not leaving the area. The *Vincennes* reported that the boats were approaching the two U.S. ships. The *Vincennes* made this claim and secured permission to fire before the 9:42 time given by Admiral Crowe as the point at which the boats turned and headed toward the *Vincennes* and *Montgomery*.

It is worth noting that the Navy has yet to release the geographic track files, which would allow the movements of the *Vincennes*, *Montgomery*, and the Iranian boats to be traced with complete accuracy.

After firing on the two Iranian boats which had headed toward them and forcing them to break off their runs, it would seem the U.S. ships could have broken off the engagement and safely withdrawn from the vicinity. One of the USS *Sides*' officers had muttered, "Why doesn't he just push his rudder over and get his ass out of there?"[27] Instead, the *Vincennes* gives every appearance of having chased retreating Iranian boats into Iranian waters at 30 knots, even though it had to swing violently back and forth to bring its functioning aft five-inch gun to bear. If the *Vincennes* had broken off the engagement, it could have sailed away smoothly with the aft gun providing good defensive coverage in case it was needed.

Why was Captain Rogers apparently so anxious to get into a surface engagement against the Iranians? His actions have been variously attributed to a desire to test himself; to get his "combat action" ticket punched to aid his promotion prospects; to the fact that he was a true warrior; or because he was basically a loose cannon. In fairness, it might be added that the opportunity to exercise professional skills in command of a "supership" in action would be a lifetime opportunity for a career naval officer. The sources of individual motivation can be quite obscure. In the end, discourses of this sort can only remain speculative.

However, there is little doubt about Rogers' aggressiveness. Rogers had written numerous messages to the JTFME Commander, Admiral Less, urging him to use the *Vincennes* aggressively. One of these said that the ship should "go into harm's way for which she was intended."[28] One individual described Rogers as a "real gentleman, but as aggressive as a bulldog." An officer who was acquainted with Rogers prior to the Airbus shoot-down was of the opinion that Rogers was desperate to make Admiral and was so determined to make his reputation at any price that, "If anyone was going to screw anything up, he was." Another officer who conducted war games with him recalled, "He always shot first and asked questions later."

Yet another officer who came in contact with Captain Rogers while enrolled in the Commanders' Tactical Training Course at Tactical Training Group, Pacific wrote, "Captain Rogers was a difficult student. He wasn't interested in the expertise of the instructors and had the disconcerting habit of violating the Rules of Engagement in the war games. I was horrified, but not surprised, to learn *Vincennes* had mistakenly shot down an airliner."[29] That Captain Rogers was willing to violate the ROE during simulations, where one might expect more discretion, suggests not the smooth actions of a make-no-waves organizational climber but rather those of a genuinely aggressive, rough-side-out fighter. One who was, in fact, too aggressive for the political environment of the Gulf.

Commodore McKenna's immediate predecessor as DESRON commander in the Gulf, Commodore Donald Dyer, had warned the commanding officers of U.S. warships not to come into the Gulf like a gunfighter walking through the doors of a western saloon. Unfortunately, that was probably an apt characterization of the attitude manifested by the *Vincennes* under Captain Rogers. When the *Vincennes* arrived in the Gulf, the "Golf Whisky," or anti-air warfare coordinator, was USS *Wainwright*, under Captain James Chandler.

The *Vincennes* announced that it was now the "Golf Whisky." Tussles broke out between the two ships over the AAWC (anti-air warfare coordinator) role. The CO of another U.S. warship in the Gulf recalled, "We saw *Vincennes* capture track reporting for air contacts and, on several occasions, try to wrest control of the air picture from *Wainwright*. This was a frequent occurrence at the enlisted track management level. We also observed *Vincennes* getting kicked off the AAWC net by CJTFME because of her constant interference with *Wainwright* trying to coordinate the picture as AAWC." Captain Chandler had contacted the JTFME, which told Rogers that *Wainwright* would retain the "GW" role through its scheduled departure in about a week. Of Captain Rogers, Captain Chandler observed in a conversation with several officers that, "Before it's over, this guy is going to cause trouble."

An operations officer on Commodore McKenna's CDS-25 staff later claimed that he had had an extremely difficult time controlling the *Vincennes*' movements. The ship didn't follow standard operating procedure while assigned to them. It frequently departed its assigned area without permission, was not responsive to radio call-ups, provided little feedback, and basically ignored CDS-25, causing McKenna great frustration.

This behavior probably contributed to what some came to perceive as the "Aegis arrogance" displayed by the *Vincennes*. There was more involved. Aegis ships were the most technologically advanced ships in the Navy, well ahead of anything else deployed to the Gulf. They were populated by an elite crew—as perceived by outsiders and the crews themselves. An Aegis assignment was considered a fast track for promotion. Naturally, there was some professional jealousy involved. One observer described the reaction of other crews to an Aegis cruiser in terms of average high school students enviously watching the star quarterback walking down the hall with the prom queen on his arm.

Captain Rogers had demonstrated a proclivity toward aggressive behavior on the *Vincennes*' very first patrol in the Gulf. At around 9:15 A.M. on June 2, the patrolling *Vincennes* was on the scene when the *Alborz*, one of Iran's two remaining operational *Saam*-class frigates, stopped a large bulk carrier, the *Vevey*, in Omani waters. The *Vincennes* had sounded general quarters, radioed Admiral Less, and described what was happening. No distress call from the ship had been received and the *Vincennes* was directed to remain within visual range and to continue reporting. Captain Rogers later said, "Sensitive ground was being broken."[30]

What he meant by that ground is not clear. The year before, the commander of the Iranian Navy had claimed that 1,200 ships had been boarded by the end of April (1987) and 30 cargoes seized. While the claims were exaggerated, there had been hundreds of boardings, with several cargoes and at least one ship itself seized.[31] The *Alborz* put a boarding party on the *Vevey*. Shortly thereafter, the cargo ship, with some boarders still on it, and the Iranian frigate got underway, apparently heading to Bandar Abbas. The Iranian frigate positioned itself between the *Vincennes* and the merchant ship. A *Vincennes* helicopter observed the scene.

The USS *Sides*, commanded by Captain Robert Hattan, was transiting the Gulf to rendezvous with an inbound merchant vessel and observed the *Vincennes* positioned close to the *Alborz*. Captain Hattan was in the process of turning over his command to Commander Carlson, who was also on board. The Iranian stop and search operation was considered legitimate by the U.S., though taking a ship into port to inspect its cargo was unusual. At the direction of the JTFME, the *Vincennes* took tactical control of the transiting *Sides*. Captain Hattan recalled, "Rogers wanted me to fall astern of the Iranian frigate by about 1,500 yards. I came up on the radio circuit and protested the order from the *Vincennes*. I felt that falling in behind the Iranian [warship] would inflame the situation."[32]

Commander Carlson described the *Vincennes* as "all over" the Iranian ship. There were now two U.S. warships near the *Alborz*. Two other U.S. ships were leaving the Gulf. A U.S. P-3 Orion reconnaissance aircraft was scheduled to fly over the area. "The Iranians' captain would be seeing all sorts of inbound ships on his radar scope and he was all alone," observed Commander Carlson.[33] One of the U.S. ships passing in the vicinity was the cruiser USS *Wainwright*, under Captain Chandler. It's tour over; *Wainwright* was on its way out of the Gulf. On the command frequency, Captain Chandler could hear the discussion going on between the *Vincennes* and the JTFME. With the situation looking serious, Admiral Less called *Wainwright* and told Captain Chandler to cover the *Vincennes* by targeting the Iranian frigate for a Harpoon anti-ship missile launch. USS *Wainwright* could see both ships clearly on its radar screens. It developed a targeting solution on the *Alborz* for its Harpoons.

Near noon, a white-colored chartered "Huey" helicopter carrying an NBC News crew made a pass over the bow of the *Alborz* and drew two long warning bursts of machine-gun fire from the increasingly nervous Iranians. The *Vincennes* observed several guns on the frigate tracking the helicopter. The aft gun mount on the *Alborz* was tracking the U.S. ship. The *Vincennes* got on bridge-to-bridge radio and warned the frigate to retrain its guns away from him, which it did. "Hattan was very concerned that Rogers was going to spook the Iranian skipper into doing something stupid. He wanted out and recommended de-escalation in no uncertain terms," said Carlson.[34]

Captain Hattan was not the only one. After listening in to the radio transmissions between the *Vincennes* and the *Alborz*, Captain Chandler called Admiral Less and told him that he thought what was going on was outside the scope of the U.S. rules of engagement. Admiral Less called about a minute later and detached the *Sides* from the *Vincennes'* control and ordered the *Vincennes* to back off and simply observe the Iranian activity. The *Vincennes* paced the *Alborz* and the *Vevey*, following them across the Iranian declared war zone at 12:40 P.M. This action may have violated the U.S. Rules of Engagement, which reportedly forbade crossing into the exclusion zone, except if hostile forces presented an imminent threat. The *Alborz* and *Vevey* then entered Iranian territorial waters. The *Vincennes* finally departed around 3:30 P.M. The *Vevey* and its cargo, which turned out to be bathroom tile, were released the next day.

The overall picture that emerges does not cast Captain Rogers' actions in a flattering light. Here was a ship that had been rushed to the Gulf on an emergency basis following the Silkworm attacks on U.S. forces during Operation Praying Mantis. Since the Iranians had now demonstrated their willingness to fire the missiles at U.S. forces, it made sense to dispatch a highly capable air defense ship to the Gulf as a shield against future attacks. As an Aegis cruiser, the *Vincennes* carried highly complex and sophisticated electronics for its air defense system, one designed to deal with open ocean saturation air and missile attacks. It offered superior anti-air warfare and air picture management capabilities, which were drawn on its "Golf Whisky" or force anti-air coordinator role. As has been mentioned numerous times, the Gulf at this time was an extremely delicate political environment. Indeed, the demonstrated willingness of the Iranians to risk U.S. retaliation by crossing the "Silkworm Threshold" had ratcheted the situation upward in its potential for a violent explosion.

To say the least, these considerations should have led the commanding officer of the *Vincennes* to act with caution in the case of potential action against Iranian small boats. While the *Vincennes* shared its vulnerability to light weapons fire with other U.S. warships, it was not the kind of general-purpose frigate or destroyer used for convoy escorts. In its assigned role as anti-air warfare coordinator, one would normally have expected it to hang back and provide an air defense umbrella to other ships, not expose its complex systems to damage in the forefront of a surface action. And what was this high-tech air defense cruiser actually doing in the Gulf? Under Captain Rogers, it appears to have been charging around looking for every opportunity to precipitate some kind of surface action against the Iranians.

On July 3, it had twice gone rushing up toward Iranian gunboats on its own initiative before being yanked back. On the third try, the *Vincennes* made it and finally got to fire its guns in anger. Of course, no one, including Captain Rogers, would have logically expected his actions to lead to the tragedy of Iran Air Flight 655—though even a small-scale action with Iranian gunboats was fraught with the potential for escalation and was considered no small matter by U.S. authorities.

Admiral Less had awakened Joint Chiefs Chairman Admiral Crowe at 3:18 A.M. in Washington with a call to let him know that the *Vincennes* had gotten into a shootout with the Iranian boats.[35] An action with some Iranian small boats under murky circumstances might not have, of itself, stirred up a strong Iranian reaction. Not that Captain Rogers deserves any points for judgment on that score since his general approach appears to have been indiscriminate. The near incident with the *Alborz* on June 2 involved one of the only two remaining effective major Iranian naval units. Any shooting incident involving that ship would certainly have risked serious consequences. All this was, of course, taking place right in the middle of the "Silkworm envelope," the one within which the *Vincennes* was supposed to provide protection to other ships in case things got out of hand as they had on April 18.

When an Aegis cruiser had been dispatched to the Gulf, the JTFME thought it was getting a handy fire extinguisher. Instead, in the *Vincennes*, it got something closer to a fire starter; one whose high friction contacts with the Iranians were striking sparks which threatened to ignite the dry tinder so abundant in the region. Captain Rogers obviously holds a different view. When the *Vincennes* returned to San Diego, he told reporters that he did not mean to diminish the magnitude of the tragedy, but characterized the surface battle as a textbook example of a naval engagement. "We had a lot go right. Everyone is focusing on what went wrong," he said.[36]

Apparently sensitive to the charges of over-aggressiveness, Captain Rogers has taken some pains to downplay that aspect of his behavior. In his book account, after the *Vincennes* helicopter is fired on, he states, "The klaxon sounded general quarters again and we turned north."[37]

Note the passive voice. It is almost as if, as Captain of the *Vincennes*, he had not been the one who had ordered general quarters sounded and sent the ship surging north. In his book, Rogers says that a group of seven boats, identified as those from which the shots had been fired near his helicopter, "had by now closed within four miles of the *Vincennes* and the *Montgomery*."[38]

No, the *Vincennes* and the *Montgomery* had closed within four miles of those boats. In his interview for the July 1, 1992, *Nightline* show, Captain Rogers said, "We asked permission to fire a warning shot."[39] There is no evidence that the *Vincennes* sought permission to or tried to fire a warning shot. Upon the *Vincennes'* return to San Diego in October, Rogers claimed that his first shot was a direct hit, bursting right over an Iranian boat and killing the occupants. Also, in his book, Captain Rogers gives the date of the *Alborz* incident as June 14, whereas it actually occurred on June 2, the date of his first patrol in the Gulf. It is possible this change was an effort to avoid giving the impression that he was excessively aggressive from the very beginning of his stay in the Gulf. Captain Rogers' chief service critic, Commander David Carlson, noted, "If the story is told as it actually happened, then Rogers comes across as a loose cannon on his first patrol. A junior four-striper [Hattan] had to set him straight and calm things down."[40]

With regard to the small boats, Captain Rogers had testified, " Just as I was about to clear the area, three of the northerly group reversed course and commenced closing *Vincennes* and *Montgomery* at approximately 17 knots."[41]

The investigators apparently accepted this version, with the Fogarty Report stating that Captain Rogers "was initially prepared to disengage from the small boats when they appeared to present no further threat to his units," and that he only changed his mind when they began to close on him.[42] These statements make it sound like Rogers only reluctantly decided to engage when directly threatened. However, they beg the obvious question: Why charge up to the boats in the first place and then, allegedly, be prepared to turn away since they presented no threat? They most assuredly presented no threat before the *Vincennes* raced over ten miles to their vicinity. In partial response to the allegations that Captain Rogers was the aggressor, a now-retired Admiral Crowe claimed in his 1992 Congressional testimony that Rogers had acted with considerable restraint:

He didn't go after every Boghammer. As a matter of fact, when the helicopter was shot at—and this sort of surprised me—when the helicopter was linking back the radar picture to the ship, they were able to identify a specific group of boats that had shot at the helicopter and the Aegis was able to pretty well keep track of those boats through the entire transit, despite all the other activity going on and so forth. They ultimately engaged the boats that they had identified as having shot at the helicopter after some other events happened as well.[43]

In fact, the engagement against the small boats was justified only on the grounds that they were demonstrating hostile intent toward the U.S. ships by heading in their direction. Whether those boats had previously fired near the helicopter, or had not, had no bearing at all on a decision to engage them in self-defense. During his 1992 Senate appearance, Admiral Crowe responded to a question about Captain Rogers being known as "sort of a feisty, trigger-happy kind of guy" by referring to the much lamented triumph of the administrator over the warrior in today's military culture. In part, Admiral Crowe replied:

In fact, since I've been a senior officer in the Navy, one of the things that has been the bane of my existence is I am constantly told that we are producing managers and administrators instead of warriors, and then when we see a warrior come up on the scene, we're told that we should produce a manager and administrator and not a warrior. Some of our commanding officers are aggressive and some are not. Some are cautious and some are not.[44]

It need only be added that some commanding officers' actions in the Gulf were informed by at least some sense of their mission in the context of overall U.S. policy objectives. One officer's actions were not. Whatever the motivation, getting into a surface action against the Iranians appeared to be at the top of Captain Rogers' agenda. That purpose was in direct conflict with the nature of his ship and its assigned role in the Gulf. It was in direct conflict with the interests of his crew, who stood to take unnecessary loss. It was in direct conflict with the interest of his commander, Admiral Less, whose JTFME operations in the Gulf sought to keep a lid on Iranian actions, not provoke them. Finally, it was in direct conflict with the U.S. foreign policy goal in the Gulf of reassuring the Gulf States but not getting into a major confrontation with Iran. A professional naval officer—the highest-ranking officer commanding a warship in the Gulf, no less—owes more to his service and his country than to indulge his appetite for action in a delicate political environment in contradiction to any sense of his mission.

In his endorsement on the Fogarty Report, Joint Chiefs Chairman Crowe noted that Iran must share responsibility for the tragedy, and "Given the fact that the surface engagement was initiated by the Iranians, I believe that the actions of Iran were the proximate cause of this accident and would argue that Iran must bear the principal responsibility for the tragedy."[45]

Admiral Crowe may have gone too far in putting principal responsibility on the party that initiated the surface action. After all, it was a highly improbable, if not bizarre, chain of circumstances that led to the accidental shoot-down of the airliner. Some of the many links in that chain were forged by chance, others by choice. The decision to initiate the surface action was one of the latter, and the party who made it does indeed carry a heavy share of the responsibility for the tragedy. However, it is difficult not to see that party as Captain Will Rogers III of the USS *Vincennes*.

Aside from the surface action, the "Sea of Lies" story raised new claims about the air engagement. *Newsweek* stated that there had been enough time—barely—to call in Navy F-14 fighters to identify the air contact prior to the *Vincennes* shooting it down, but that, even though the F-14 pilots were "itching" to close on it, the carrier air group commander held them off in order to allow Captain Rogers to "fight his own battle."[46]

The U.S. F-14's arrived at a rendezvous area outside the Gulf, known as station Alpha, some 58 miles southeast of the *Vincennes*' location. The commander of the carrier air group ordered the aircraft to remain at station Alpha and to go no further north because, as one of the F-14 pilots later paraphrased him, "There are a lot of people in there and we don't know exactly what's going on."[47]

In 1992 Congressional testimony, Admiral Crowe cited the views of an Aegis expert who said that, with the F-14's some 58 miles away and orbiting at 390 knots, "To close and identify the Airbus in five minutes would have been virtually impossible, even if the communication and de-confliction problems could have been resolved."[48] The key here was really the de-confliction problem. With the *Vincennes* about to fire its anti-aircraft missiles, there was simply too much risk of a friendly fire "blue-on-blue" engagement if the F-14's had been vectored into the vicinity of the action. It also appears to be highly questionable whether they could have gotten there in sufficient time to positively identify the airliner and warn off the *Vincennes*.

Another aspect of the situation ignored by critics is that of the operational command of the F-14s. They were under the operational control of the carrier battle group, not the *Vincennes*. The Navy fighters were on the other side of the "seam" between the JTFME and the carrier battle group. The *Vincennes* had no authority over them. Captain Rogers could not simply have called them directly and told them to "Come in here and defend me." He would have had to have gone to the battle group and gotten it to hand off control of the jets.

Questions were also raised, both at the time of the shoot-down and later, about whether an F-14 fighter even presented enough of a threat to the *Vincennes* to justify the latter shooting down a contact it had identified as one. Captain Rogers stated in his book that, "We were also told, 'The F-14 deployment represents an increased threat to allied forces."[49] Captain Rogers did not identify the source of this warning. The Fogarty Report noted that the *Vincennes* had been advised that F-14's had been deployed to Bandar Abbas and that the deployment represented an increased threat to allied *aircraft* [emphasis added] in the Strait, southern Gulf, and Gulf of Oman.[50]

A seemingly incoming F-14 did present two potential threats to the *Vincennes*. One was through a suicide attack, with the aircraft diving into the ship. Admiral Crowe testified that the U.S. "had been receiving reports for over a year that Iran was considering kamikaze-style attacks on our ships and actually configuring aircraft for the mission."[51] The Revolutionary Guard Corps had acquired Swiss Pilatus PC-7 light training aircraft and were reported to have trained in suicide attacks using them.

However, a little cool reflection, something for which there was simply no time in the *Vincennes* CIC during the July 3 action, might have led to the conclusion that an F-14 was not a likely vehicle for a suicide attack. Iran only possessed a few operational F-14's, and these were being called upon to defend against increasingly wide-ranging Iraqi air attacks. Clearly, that was why they had been deployed south to Bandar

Abbas in the first place. The F-14 was the most advanced and complicated aircraft in Iran's inventory. As such, Iran's most competent and
experienced regular air force pilots would have flown it. It is quite likely that these pilots had belonged to the pre-revolutionary air force and
had received their training on the aircraft under the Shah. All in all,
these well-educated and technically skilled pilots would seem to have
been poor candidates for suicide attacks. Likewise, as one of Iran's few
remaining sophisticated air defense aircraft, an F-14 would have been
an unlikely vehicle for such an attack. Less than a year earlier, an
Iranian F-14 pilot had told a reporter, "We have two missions: to kill
Iraqis and to save our planes."[52]

The F-14 also presented a potential threat as a platform for air-to-
surface weapons. The F-14 was originally designed as a pure air-to-air
fighter/interceptor. Its air-to-air missiles presented little or no threat to
ships, leaving only its short-range (several thousand yards, at most) 20-
mm Vulcan cannon for use against the *Vincennes*. Critics were quick to
note the weak threat presented by an air-to-air fighter. "An F-14 nine
miles away at 9,000 feet just isn't a threat to a big ship," said a veteran
U.S. aviator.[53] However, there had been intelligence reports that Iran
had been reconfiguring its F-14's to add an anti-surface capability
through the use of "Maverick" TV-guided missiles and large "Eagle"
unguided rockets. Admiral Fogarty testified that Rogers had been
advised that F-14's represented an air-to-surface threat, not only with
iron bombs but also from missiles which could have a stand-off release
range of 12 to 13 miles. It might also be recalled that, at one point during Operation Praying Mantis, U.S. Navy F-14's had been ordered to
attack Iranian Boghammers with their 20mm cannon.

The USS *Sides*' evaluation of the air contact thought to be an F-14
as a "non-threat" was widely mentioned by critics. Less noted was that
the contact was evaluated as a non-threat to the *Sides*, then located
some eighteen nautical miles to the northeast of the *Vincennes*. In addition to the supposed lack of F-14 anti-surface capability, that evaluation
was also based on the fact that the contact was not heading toward the
Sides, but toward the *Vincennes*. The *Sides* also correctly saw the contact climbing; the *Vincennes* reportedly thought it was descending. In
the end, it is hard to see how Captain Rogers and his CIC crew could
view an F-14 closing toward them in the middle of a surface action
against Iranian gunboats as anything but a threat. One can't help but
think that the real problem for many of the critics who claimed that an

F-14 was not a threat was that the contact had turned out to be a civilian airliner and not an F-14 at all. If the *Vincennes* had actually shot down an F-14, one doubts that many of these critics would have been heard from.

Many felt that a critical factor in the decision to shoot down the air contact was the perception that it was descending toward the *Vincennes*. Perhaps the most highly publicized conclusion of the Fogarty Report was that combat stress had induced the *Vincennes* crewmen to see something they might have expected to see but which had not, in fact, occurred. Few would argue that the ability of individuals to process information is degraded by stress. A Navy officer who served with Riverine forces in Vietnam said that, "Stress can override your faculties. You see what you want to see and hear what you want to hear."[54] Thus, the *Vincennes* CIC crewmen, who were convinced that they were about to be attacked by an Iranian F-14 fighter heading directly toward them during a surface battle, also testified they saw the aircraft descending toward them even though it did not. This is the "scenario fulfillment" theory espoused by the Fogarty Report. However, there is an alternative explanation, one that has been gaining increasing ground in the years since the incident.

On the morning it shot down Flight 655, the *Vincennes* had been linked into a Naval Tactical Data Systems (NTDS) Link 11 net in the Southern Gulf. The net allowed participating units (including U.S. and allied ships and aircraft) to exchange data in real time via high frequency radio. Contacts were assigned four-digit track numbers from a block of numbers specific to the ship or aircraft reporting the contact.

In the Aegis system, a console operator can obtain information on the contact's speed, range, altitude, etc. by "hooking" it with a track ball designation and button push (i.e. pointing and clicking) or punching in the track number on a key pad. This information is continuously updated by the unit reporting on the contact and appears as strings of numbers on the operator's small character readout screen (CRO), not on the larger radar screen displays at the console or on the four Aegis large-scale displays.

The *Vincennes* and *Sides* had both detected the unidentified contact taking off from Bandar Abbas. The *Vincennes* assigned the contact Track Number (TN) 4474. The *Sides* had picked up the same aircraft approximately one minute later and assigned it TN 4131. A link controller system manages the data link. The system automatically correlated TN 4131 and TN 4474 as the same contact. The *Vincennes* was "first to correlate" the two numbers as the same contact, so, under its protocols, the *Vincennes'* system adopted TN 4131 as the common track number and dropped TN 4474. Captain Rogers would not have been aware of the automatic correlation.

Meanwhile, over 100 nautical miles away in the Gulf of Oman/ North Arabian Sea, a Navy A-6E Intruder attack aircraft had been picked up on the radar of the destroyer USS *Spruance*, also sailing in that area. The A-6E had been launched by the aircraft carrier USS *Forrestal* to fly a surface combat air patrol (SUCAP) mission. When the *Spruance* picked up the A-6E, in a highly unlikely coincidence, it had assigned the contact Track Number (TN) 4474, the same number first assigned to its unidentified air contact in the Strait of Hormuz by the *Vincennes*. Ships operating together under common command are not assigned the same block of numbers from which to draw track numbers. However, *Spruance* was operating under the command of the carrier battle group, which belonged to the Seventh Fleet, while the *Vincennes* fell under the operational command of the Joint Task Force Middle East (JTFME). Each command had separate "taskers" assigning track number blocks. Unfortunately, at the Strait of Hormuz, ships from the separate commands could share a common data link, and as occurred here, common or overlapping blocks of track numbers. This is obviously a formula for trouble.

The U.S. warships operating in the Strait, i.e., the *Vincennes* and *Sides* (*Montgomery* was not link capable), shared a data link among themselves but were too far away to net into the link being shared by the ships in the Gulf of Oman/North Arabian Sea.

The Royal Navy Type-42 destroyer HMS *Manchester* was in the Gulf of Oman link and thus carried the A-6E under TN 4474, as reported by *Spruance*. At the time of the *Vincennes* air engagement, HMS *Manchester* was heading into the Strait and entered into the data link being shared by the *Vincennes*. When it did so, HMS *Manchester* carried TN 4474 with it back into that link. Only this TN 4474 was the designation for the A-6E Intruder, an aircraft said to have been accelerating and descending in altitude, not climbing like Iran Air Flight 655.

When the unidentified, but assumed hostile, air contact inbound to the *Vincennes* was 20 nautical miles away from the ship, unaware that the original TN 4474 designation had automatically been dropped in favor of TN 4131, Captain Rogers had asked, "What is 4474 doing?"

The Aegis system data link later confirmed that a Force Console operator (FC-1) had hooked TN 4474 for five seconds. The only information the system held on TN 4474 was for the A-6E in the Gulf of Oman, being relayed through HMS *Manchester*. The system data on Iran Flight 655 was under TN 4131. Investigators later determined that this data accurately showed that aircraft climbing. However, if an operator or operators had looked at data shown for TN 4474 on their CRO's, they might have seen numbers showing an aircraft descending and accelerating. In fact, this is exactly what the TIC, the IDS, and several other CIC crewmen recollected seeing, but which the retrieved Aegis data did not show for TN 4131.

The information reviewed by the Fogarty investigators essentially fell into two classes. The "hard" data recorded by the Aegis system and the recollections of the *Vincennes* CIC crewmen, based on interviews. The Fogarty team was never able to reconcile the two. Unable to resolve the discrepancy, the Fogarty investigators had turned to psychologists and gotten the explanation: "scenario fulfillment." Under great stress, the CIC crewmen had somehow seen what they expected to see. The possibility has since been raised that they were correctly reading information on the wrong track number: TN 4474.

As has been noted, Captain Rogers never did buy off on the Fogarty conclusion. In 1992, Air Force Captain Kristen Ann Dotterway completed her Master's Thesis at the Naval Postgraduate School in Monterey, California. The thesis, which in part relied on Captain Rogers' cooperation, took a different approach than the Fogarty Investigation. Captain Dotterway did a systematic analysis of the *Vincennes* data. The "system" data and the "recollected" data were gathered in the form of a database, which was then plotted out in various forms.

In examining the results, Captain Dotterway was able to point to an apparent pattern in the relationship between the system and the recollected data. What the CIC crewmen recalled and what the system data showed on the altitude and speed of the unidentified contact closing on the ship were actually quite consistent up until 9:52 A.M. After that point, the recollections and the system data diverged. The system showed the contact continuing to climb, the crewmen recollected it descending.[55]

What had happened at 9:52 A.M.? At that time, or slightly before, HMS *Manchester* had entered the *Vincennes* data link, bringing with it

TN 4474. An operator on the FC-1 console had "hooked" TN 4474. Captain Rogers had asked, "What is 4474 doing?" Two explanations have been put forth to account for the divergence between system data and CIC crew recollections.

The Fogarty Report suggests that some *Vincennes* CIC crewmen looked at their digital displays, which showed TN 4131 climbing, but under the stress of combat action, and convinced they were about to be attacked by an F -14 fighter, saw the altitude of the contact decreasing as it closed on the ship. The other explanation, put forth by Captain Rogers, and tested but not refuted in Captain Dotterway's thesis, holds that the CIC crew were reading the wrong track number: TN 4474, an aircraft that actually was decreasing in altitude.

The Chief of Naval Operations, Admiral Carlyle H. Trost, had directed that a medical team composed of psychiatrists and psychologists from the Portsmouth Naval Hospital go to the *Vincennes* and spend up to 30 days evaluating the crew for post-traumatic stress. Commander John Matecvun headed the three-man team. The team quickly determined that the crew was psychologically prepared for operations in a hostile environment and made no recommendations for changes in crew or procedures. The team left after three days. The team's evaluation of the crew did not necessarily bear on the Fogarty conclusion, since "scenario fulfillment" might only show up under the specific circumstances that induced it, and not be reflected in the crew's later psychological condition. However, what was of interest with regard to the Fogarty conclusion was the team's response to a question posed by Captain Rogers, about "how five people at five separate consoles could see something that hard data did not support?"

The response noted in part: "That five or more combatants, some with prior combat experience, most with extensive equipment experience, all viewing separate displays for cognitively significant periods of time would have the same perceptual distortion or misinterpretation of data is highly implausible."[56]

At first, it does appears that the more probable explanation for the discrepancy between the system data on TN 4131 and what CIC crewmen recollected seeing was that the data-link system had ended up playing a kind of electronic shell game with track numbers. The resulting confusion then figured prominently among the factors contributing to the tragedy. However, it is simply impossible for any track number mix-up to have led to a misreading of altitude.

The track number theory requires that, when the Force Console operator (FC-l) brought up TN 4474, other CIC console operators, guided by Captain Rogers question, "What is TN 4474 doing?" also looked at that track number on their displays and accurately saw it descending. Implicit in the theory is that TN 4474 was displayed on the other consoles. In fact, it was not. When the FC-1 hooked TN 4474, he brought it up on his display only. It did not come up on any of the other operator displays. Here, at least, there is hard data. All console actions on the *Vincennes* were recorded moment by moment. What the operators had on their displays, what contacts they took under close control, and what buttons they punched were all recorded on tape. TN 4474 never appeared on any other consoles. Those operators were not confused at all. They were always focused on the right track: TN 4131.

The FC-1 (and FC-2) were enlisted men whose positions would have supported force commanders, had they been embarked on *Vincennes*. None were present on July 3. Accordingly, the operators had no assigned tasks and were simply sitting and watching as events unfolded. They did not participate at all in the CIC actions that day. When Rogers asked about TN 4474, the FC-1 checked to see what the Captain was asking about and "hooked" TN 4474. He was the only person in the CIC who had it on his display, and he held it for five seconds. The FC-1 looked at it and saw it was way to the south. It was obviously not the right contact, so he dropped it.

The team reviewing the Aegis data during the investigation did not ignore the existence of the two TN 4474's. They informed Admiral Fogarty. They looked at what the contact was doing, and they looked at which tracks the console operators were looking at, and for how long. Their conclusion was that the existence of the second TN 4474 had had absolutely no effect on the outcome of the events that day. Another group, which in light of the *Vincennes* tragedy, looked at possible changes for the Navy to make, determined that there was no need to change its procedure for correlating duplicate track numbers.

The duplicate track number issue had, in fact, come up during the formal hearings held during the Fogarty investigation. These were primarily directed at Captain Rogers and Commander Lustig. The attorney representing Captain Rogers clearly saw exculpatory potential for his client in a data link problem caused by duplicate track numbers. He seized on it in the hearings and, in the words of one observer, "wouldn't let go." Captain Rogers went on to make a rather glancing reference to the dual track numbers in his book. In the years since, the theory has been picking up steam.

One can certainly see why. It was, after all, an amazing coincidence that the same track number briefly assigned to the Airbus by the *Vincennes* reappeared for another aircraft in the North Arabian Sea. The fact that this duplicate track number was then carried into the Gulf data link during the course of the *Vincennes* engagement seems to promise a highly intriguing line of inquiry. However, when pursued a short distance, it runs smack into a brick wall. Captain Dotterway's thesis work did show an apparent change in the recollected flight profile of the contact at around 9:52 A.M. However, it cannot be overstressed that the "data" being plotted was only after-the-fact recollections.

Fogarty investigators had done a plot of their own. Using a large sheet of wall-mounted white paper, they had plotted out the testimony given under oath by the men in the *Vincennes* CIC. A look at plotted testimony yielded what one investigator thought was the most telling bit of information they found: the plotted points were all over the sheet of paper. They showed no consistency, except in one area—the altitude of the contact at intercept. Here, the testimony of several of the men was consistent . . . and wrong.

The whole discussion about the CIC crewmen seeing the contact descending is off base. There is, in fact, no real evidence that more than one person in the *Vincennes* CIC saw, thought, or called out that the contact was descending. The limited information released in the public version of the Fogarty report, as well as misunderstandings and logical leaps, have fused into a kind of quasi-mythical account of what happened in the *Vincennes* CIC, one that has dominated discussion over the years. It will be necessary to peel off several layers of that account to get a closer look at *Vincennes'* realities.

CHAPTER 22

"GIVE ME THE KEY. GIVE ME THE KEY."

After testifying at the formal hearings being held by the Fogarty Commission in Bahrain, several of the *Vincennes*'s Combat Information Center (CIC) petty officers went upstairs to where investigation team members were reviewing the data generated by the Aegis system. The crewmen sat down with the investigators and went over the recordings made in the CIC. One of the young petty officers had testified under oath earlier that morning that he had seen the incoming air contact descend toward the *Vincennes*. After reviewing the data and listening to the audiotapes, he was stunned. "That's my voice," he said, "I was reading it [the correct altitude] from close control, so that's what I saw. But three hours ago, I testified to something completely different. He turned with a look of absolute horror on his face and said, "Did I cause this to happen?"

What that petty officer had encountered, and he was probably the first to do so, was the discrepancy between the recorded Aegis data and some of the CIC crew's recollections on the behavior of the incoming air contact. That discrepancy would go on to bedevil the investigators, with the Fogarty report ultimately resolving it by resorting to the "scenario fulfillment" theory. As previously described, that theory maintained that combat stress had induced some of the *Vincennes*' CIC crewmen to see a climbing aircraft as descending toward them—thus, fulfilling the scenario they thought they were experiencing: an attack on their ship by an Iranian F-14 fighter.

The duplicate track number theory, discussed in the last chapter, attempts to substitute a data link technical glitch for the unnerving prospect of CIC crewmen seeing "up" as "down" under stress.

However, the track number theory fails for a number of reasons. There is, however, another form of "scenario fulfillment," one different from that suggested by the Fogarty Report. One that seems to be a more plausible explanation for the difference between the recollections of multiple crewmen and the recorded data.

Both Captain Rogers and Commander Lustig testified that they heard calls of descending altitude toward the end of the engagement. These calls appear to have come from only one individual, the Tactical Information Coordinator (TIC). However, several other crewmen later testified that they, too, had seen the contact descending in those last minutes. The TIC petty officer may have been suffering from scenario fulfillment, as suggested by the Fogarty Report. There certainly are other possibilities, however.

For example, in an anxious state, he may have been confusing decreasing range with decreasing altitude. Alternatively, Rogers and Lustig themselves may have confused accurate range calls with altitude. Rogers' perceptions may have owed more to what he was hearing from Lustig than to anything he was hearing directly. Alternatively, the TIC may not have been reading the small alphanumerical CRO display showing altitude at all. Rather, looking at the contact coming in on his large circular radar display, and again, in an anxious state, he may have thought the aircraft was coming down as well as in. Are these possibilities any less likely than the TIC looking directly at ascending numbers on his CRO and seeing them as descending? What seems to lend a good deal of weight to the Fogarty Report's scenario fulfillment theory were the recollections by other CIC crewmen that they, too, saw the contact descending.

As to those recollections, all external voice channels on the *Vincennes* were recorded. Higher authority imposed this requirement in order to capture any International Air Distress (IAD) or Military Air Distress (MAD) warnings issued by the ship. Internal channels were not recorded. Because of the numerous external nets in use (IAD, MAD, force AAW, ASUW [anti-surface warfare]), the *Vincennes'* standard voice recording system did not have the capacity to allot a channel to the MAD frequency. As an expedient, a large "boom box" type cassette tape recorder was used to record MAD transmissions. It was secured by adhesive tape to the console of the Air Radar Controller (ARC), the operator for the SPS-49 radar. The boom box had a voice-activated microphone.

Because of the high ambient noise level generated in the *Vincennes* CIC during the July 3 engagement, the boom box recorded continuously. Neither the system recordings on the external nets nor the cassette tape recording of what was, in effect, an open air mike on the boom box, picked up anyone calling out that the air contact was descending toward the ship.

Calls made by the TIC were over the internal net and were also perhaps shouted out loud enough to be heard by some. The internal net was not recorded, and the boom box did not catch any such calls made out loud. It is possible they were masked by other sounds, although the calls of decreasing range can be heard. Still, while it is questionable, it is at least possible that the TIC did make these calls, thinking that the contact was descending. The same cannot be said for the other crewmen's recollections.

The Fogarty investigators carefully walked the CIC console operators through the computer printouts of data generated by the Aegis system side-by-side with the voice recordings made on four external nets and by the boom box. Where the retrieved Aegis system data showed that the air contact was at 9,000 feet, the voices on the time-tagged audio recordings said that it was at 9,000 feet. The voice tapes were never at a variance with the Aegis system data. Every single recorded voice report was consistent with the system data. It is, of course, possible that inconsistent calls by some of these men were made over the unrecorded internal nets such as those made by the TIC. However, those calls would not only have been inconsistent with the system data, but inconsistent with what some of the same console operators were saying over the external nets.

Where did the recollections of decreasing altitude on the part of the CIC crewmen come from? It is a standard procedure during practice anti-aircraft engagements against drone targets to record altitude, range, and bearing when an anti-aircraft missile intercepts the target. Investigators going onboard the *Vincennes* discovered that a senior chief in the CIC had written in grease pencil on the large display screen of his PPI console located next to the ship's AAWC position, the following notation:

7800'
Mode II, 1100

The airliner had actually been at 13,500 feet when it was hit. The audiotape recorded by the boom box during the engagement carries the sound of voices in the CIC getting louder as the air contact closed on the *Vincennes*. When the anti-aircraft missiles leave the launch rails, there is total silence until about the time the Aegis system would have given a "kill" alert. Then, there are sounds of relief, which last for a few seconds before the normal buzz of activity resumes. The system data showed that the senior chief had "hooked" TN 4131 at this time, at which point the fatally damaged Airbus was plunging to the surface.

The extremely tense atmosphere in the CIC can probably explain the 7,800-foot altitude written on his display, as the crew appeared to have almost frozen in anticipation of the aircraft's being intercepted by the two missiles. The silence on the tape probably reflects a kind of collective holding of breath and suspension of activity as the missiles streak toward what is perceived as an incoming threat. Intercept is followed by a short period of relief, a kind of collective exhalation of breath. It was shortly after this point that the chief hooked TN 4131. The recorded Aegis data indicated that he picked up an altitude of around 6,500 feet for the contact as it plunged toward the surface of the Gulf. Where he got the 7,800 feet recorded on his display is unclear. Possibly he heard someone call out that altitude just prior to hooking the contact himself. In any case, he wrote down 7,800 feet in extremely large letters on the screen.

On the afternoon of July 3, after it was realized that the *Vincennes* had shot down a civilian airliner and not a F-14 fighter, the CIC officers and enlisted men were told to go and write down their own versions of what they had seen happen. The officers went to their cabins. The CIC petty officers shared their berthing spaces with other crewmen, so they were sent back to the *Vincennes* CIC to write up their accounts.

It seems quite possible that, shortly after the engagement and/or when they returned to the CIC in the afternoon to write up their accounts, the CIC petty officers saw the 7,800' altitude notation written on the senior chief's display. It is also possible that one of the men pointed it out to the others. Upon seeing the numbers, the men may well have formed the impression that the aircraft was at that altitude when it was hit by the *Vincennes*' missiles. If this seems a bit too speculative, consider: numerous CIC crewmen later testified under oath that the aircraft was at exactly 7,800 feet when it was intercepted. The recollections of four of these men were noted in the publicly released Fogarty Report. Several others, who were not mentioned in the report, had also testified that the contact was at exactly 7,800 feet. It was not possible for all of these men to have gotten that altitude from their own displays when normal activity resumed in the CIC shortly after intercept. The consoles on the *Vincennes*, which was a "Baseline I" Aegis cruiser, were time-synched in two groups. Half on one "pulse" of updated information, half on another. Thus, the 7,800 feet altitude could only have been seen on one-half of the consoles. The other half would have been updated on a different cycle and would have displayed a significantly different altitude for the plunging airliner. It was impossible for all the CIC crewmen who testified it was at 7,800 feet to have seen that height on their displays.

The senior chief's notation may have carried considerable weight among the CIC crew since they considered him highly experienced and reliable. These men later testified that they had seen the aircraft at higher altitudes. They recalled warnings being given when it was at 10,000 feet and 11,000 feet. They remembered it being at 13,000 feet. When they saw the senior chief's notation of 7,800 feet, their minds may well have anchored to that number. Certainly it showed up in their later testimony. The 49 ADT recalled that at 10 nautical miles out, the contact was at 7,800 feet. "That," he said, "I haven't been able to get out of my mind."

The men were aware that, earlier in the engagement, the contact had been at significantly greater altitudes. The 7,800-foot number, coming as it did from an individual they considered a highly reliable source, might have driven them toward the logical conclusion that the aircraft had been descending when hit. That altitude may also have been a subject of discussion among the men. It might have been along the lines of: "You can see why we had to shoot it down. It was descending toward us." The TIC may have strongly maintained that he saw the contact descending. If he did, his representations might also have influenced the men.

There is one other opinion on this. One of the Fogarty investigators, a father, thought that some of the crewmen testifying to having seen the contact descending reminded him of obviously guilty children nevertheless steadfastly maintaining their innocence. It was his opinion, and his alone, that the men had been strongly influenced during their meeting in the CIC. The scenario here would have run along the lines of: "You see those numbers? 7,800 feet and Mode II. We saw a fighter coming down at us. That's our story, and we're all gonna stick to it!"

During the hearings, the CIC petty officers had testified under oath that they had seen the contact descending toward them. Admiral Fogarty sat through all of the testimony. He was personally convinced that these men were telling the truth. Given that assumption, the only way for the report writers to square those recollections with the Aegis data was to suggest that the crewmen had suffered an inversion of reality under stress and had seen a climbing contact descending. The CIC crewmen may very well have believed that they were accurately recalling what they saw, but the evidence suggests that they were wrong. Not just wrong about the altitude of the contact, as we know for certain, but wrong about what they had actually seen during the engagement.

As one of the investigation team members put it, "I personally do not believe that they saw the contact descending when they decided to fire. They knew how to read those consoles. It was only after the fact, when they tried to put the picture together. The senior chief was considered an extremely reliable person. When they started to put the pieces together, they saw the altitude written by the senior enlisted guy and it sort of became part of their memory."

The psychiatrist called in by the Fogarty team had said, to paraphrase him, that "scenario fulfillment" affects your memory (emphasis added) more than your actions. Actions are your reactions to the events of the moment. Scenario fulfillment means putting the pieces back together in a way so as to reconcile what you did. This then was probably the real "scenario fulfillment." Not CIC crewmen looking at their displays under stress and seeing "down" for "up." This is what another member of the investigation team later described as "pure fiction." But instead, distorted after-the-fact recollections had been influenced by the senior chief's 7,800 foot altitude notation and by the need to justify their actions which had resulted in a terrible tragedy. With the possible exception of the TIC, those men had not seen the aircraft descending during the engagement. What they did, with real conviction, was later remember it descending toward them.

Stress then, did not cause *Vincennes*' CIC crewmen to believe that the aircraft was descending toward them. Yet, it was shot down. It was shot down because it had been identified as an Iranian F-14 fighter which was approaching weapons release point, the critical range at which it could launch air-to-ground weapons, notably the Maverick TV-guided missiles it may have been modified to carry. Even at its true altitude, the aircraft was well within the Maverick's launch envelope, which extended up to 25,000 feet.

Captain Rogers' decision to shoot down the plane was based on the information that was available to him. Preoccupied with the surface battle, he had very little time to personally verify that information. As Admiral Crowe put it, "That these officers relied on information from their combat team is not only reasonable, but is an absolute necessity in a pressure-packed environment."[1]

The information Captain Rogers relied on was derived from raw data which had been received and processed in the Combat Information Center. It is here, in the *Vincennes'* CIC, that there were failures in the handling and processing of that data which ultimately had a significant impact on the outcome of events. Indeed, it seems possible that, if the CIC crew had handled the same information differently, it might well have yielded a decision not to engage.

Much has been made over the effect of stress on the *Vincennes'* crew. Such stress has often been pointed to as a causative factor in the decision to shoot down the air contact, particularly in connection with the widely reported perception that the aircraft was descending toward the ship. As has been discussed, with one possible exception, it does not appear that the crewmen perceived the aircraft descending during the engagement. Nevertheless, stress certainly did affect the performance of the *Vincennes'* CIC crew.

Indeed, among at least some of the CIC crew, it seems to have produced a state of high anxiety and a near chaotic communications net. The open mike boom box recorded an increasingly noisy CIC as the action came to a climax. According to one source who listened to the tape, "You could hear the fear in their voices." Against their standing orders, theoretically a court-martial offense, some crewmen abandoned the communication nets they were supposed to be on and went to the command net instead. The TIC broke in with excited reports on the incoming contact. At one point, he was virtually shouting out warnings over the net. A former Aegis cruiser commander said, "A CIC should be like a surgical ward. Activity should be measured, precise, and professional." That was hardly the case aboard *Vincennes*.

The *Vincennes* was not the only ship to have faced a stressful situation in the Gulf. When the *Samuel Roberts* hit the Iranian mine on April 14, listeners on the radio net were amazed at the calm way the ship reported the mine strike. The *Roberts* had almost been blown in half, had suffered personnel casualties, and was experiencing severe flooding, fires, and smoke. In that condition, and still in the middle of a minefield, the ship continued to matter-of-factly report its situation. The crew fought exactly as trained to save the ship. During Operation Praying Mantis, Surface Action Group "C" had faced an inbound Harpoon anti-ship missile fired by the Iranian missile boat *Joshan*. There was an audiotape here, too. This one was recorded on the bridge of the USS *Simpson*. The voices of Captain McTigue (*Simpson*) and Commander Chandler (*Wainwright*) stayed even in tone throughout the engagement. Both commanding officers thought that their CIC crews had performed superbly—calmly and professionally going about their tasks.

In the northern Gulf, USS *Gary* had faced an incoming Silkworm missile on April 18. During the engagement, *Gary* had to worry about running into nearby shoal water while moving at high speed between the missile and the Mobile Sea Bases it was protecting. It also had to be very careful not to hit either of the sea bases with its 76mm gun when it began firing at the missile. Lieutenant Tom Wetherall, who had been on the ship's bridge that day, later recalled:

> Remembering what the bridge of GARY was like during the attack is the proudest moment in my memory of my Navy career. Eighteen men on the bridge, all in complete battle dress with flak jackets, flash hoods, flash gloves and helmets, all completely quiet, all doing their jobs and silently shitting bricks. GARY had trained right and these men did exactly what they were trained to do. When compared to the video shot on the bridge of VINCENNES several months later, with their bridge wing doors open, no battle dress and everyone whooping and hollering as they fired their missiles, it just reminded me how really good GARY was.[2]

By way of comparison to the situations those other ships found themselves in, the *Vincennes* and the *Montgomery* were chasing and firing on small boats in a surface action. The Iranian speedboats appear to have been too far away at this point to hit the U.S. ships with their light weapons, although it was certainly possible that they might turn and desperately try to close the range. The *Vincennes* was heeling as it turned from side to side in order to bring its aft 5-inch gun to bear, and loose items in the CIC slid about. The large screen displays flickered when the gun fired. Then, an unidentified air contact, initially identified as an Iranian fighter, flew directly toward the ship.

For all the talk about busy Gulf skies, at the time, the *Vincennes* actually faced an extremely simple air picture. Other than the inbound contact and a distant Iranian P-3 patrol aircraft, the air radar screens were empty. There were no other contacts to sort through, identify or de-conflict. Describing Aegis anti-air engagement simulations, an Aegis expert said, "When you've watched one of these things work. . . . I've seen them when they're surrounded on all sides. Everything in the world coming at them. A calm CIC cannot be overwhelmed by 20 things coming at them." Chasing the Iranian boats, the *Vincennes* CIC crew had one thing coming at them.

This was, no doubt, a stressful situation. It is not easy to quantify such stress. However, in general, it is difficult to judge that the *Vincennes* experienced any greater stress than the other ships mentioned. Yet that stress seems to have had a highly disproportionate effect on the functioning of the *Vincennes* CIC crew. The question is: why?

Men who successfully deal with combat situations are obviously aware, at one level, of the danger they face. To function efficiently in a life-threatening environment, they must hold their fears in check, "silently shitting bricks," and perform their assigned tasks. The traditional tools used by the military to try to ensure successful performance under stress are training and discipline. The actions of the *Vincennes* bridge crew during the engagement may indicate the level of discipline on the ship.

A Navy camera crew recorded those actions. That video shows a noisy bridge with watertight doors frequently being opened and closed as men come and go. The video also shows the bridge crew, variously, and in some cases improperly, attired, looking like what one retired Admiral described as a "come-as-you-are party." Navy Captain Keith F. Amacker had been the Executive Officer on the USS *Sides* under Commander David Carlson. Based on the video, Captain Amacker later described the *Vincennes* bridge crew as "a group of sailors at general quarters . . . lounging around and acting like giddy football fans."[3]

There was no videotape of the *Vincennes* CIC crew in action. However, the boom box audiotape did record a high level of noise, with fear manifesting itself in several voices. While not conclusive, the bridge video may well indicate an overall level of ship's discipline that fell short of the mark. Captain Rogers appears to have been about as popular with the crews that served under him as he was unpopular with his fellow commanding officers, who tended to resent his elbows-out style.

One officer who served under Rogers remarked that he was the best-liked commanding officer he'd ever had. Being well liked is not necessarily inimical to good discipline. Still, after reading Captain Rogers' book, Captain Amacker judged, "One gets the picture of a command where success is based on how much the crew loves the captain. The 'hug 'em and love 'em' style of leadership espoused by Captain Rogers accepts whatever level of performance the crew is willing to serve up, in order to have good morale. Mediocrity is the normal result."[4]

As to training, a U.S. Army officer with extensive helicopter combat experience remarked, "If you do very demanding, very realistic training, when you get into a real situation, no switch comes on making you say, 'Whoa! This is for real!' Instead, what you do is react exactly the way you were trained. There is no time to shop and think." That sounds like a pretty good description of what happened on the *Roberts*, the *Simpson*, the *Wainwright*, and the *Gary*—But not on the *Vincennes*, where the mental "switch" apparently did come on among one or more crewmen.

In fact, there appear to have been serious training shortcomings on the *Vincennes*. These were, in part, reflected in the setup of the ship's CIC organization. That setup was, in turn, a major factor in the crew's inability to properly deal with the situation they faced on July 3, 1988. As has been mentioned, under the "GW" organization, Commander Lustig had been made the force anti-air warfare coordinator (AAWC) while, at the same time, retaining his responsibility as ship anti-air warfare coordinator. He had previously been assigned the own-ship AAWC position. Rogers' predecessor in command of *Vincennes*, Captain George N. Gee, had assigned separate officers to the force AAWC and own-ship AAWC positions.

In Captain Gee's CIC organization, the force AAWC officer's function was limited to coordinating the air defense of a given force of ships. Perhaps it is an indication of the relative importance with which Captain Gee viewed the tasks that the officer he assigned to that position was not as senior as Commander Lustig, who held the own ship AAWC slot. The force AAWC officer was under the supervision of an officer senior to Commander Lustig.

Captain Rogers had implemented the *Vincennes* "GW" organization during the ship's transit from San Diego to Subic Bay, slightly more than two months before the shoot-down. A member of the Fogarty team later described the move as "a big mistake." Captain Rogers had actually moved both the surface warfare and the own-ship AAWC responsibilities onto the shoulders of the individuals sitting to his immediate left and right. Instead of letting "surface run surface," from the middle of the consoles to his left rear, Rogers had shifted the function to his Tactical Action Officer (TAO), Vic Guillory, who sat to his right before the large screen displays. Instead of letting "air run air," from the center console in "air alley," to his right rear, Rogers had combined that function with the force AAWC role and assigned it to Commander Lustig, who sat to his left.

Rogers said that he wanted his best "war fighters" sitting beside him. A member of the Fogarty team observed that, "Rogers is a control guy. He wanted the functions falling to hand, right and left, where he could reach out and grab them. . . . He wanted the key people where he could touch them." In so doing, Rogers relegated the individuals who sat at the console positions which normally had the surface warfare and own-ship AAWC responsibilities to the role of button pushers. Instead of, in part, overseeing the surface warfare function, the TAO now had the prime responsibility for it. However, the mechanical operations of the console still had to be performed. The operator at the TAO's direction now did these. When he had been own-ship AAWC, Commander Lustig had operated the AAWC console himself. Now, with his ship AAWC responsibility combined with the force AAWC role, he sat up front. Lieutenant Zocher now sat at the AAWC console, physically operating it at Lustig's direction. Zocher was completely outside of the decision loop.

As noted, Captain Rogers' predecessor in command of the *Vincennes* was Captain George N. Gee. The latter was well regarded and would go on to achieve flag rank. Captain Gee had worked up the *Vincennes* commissioning crew and was considered a good team builder. Unfortunately, in the four months or so prior to its Gulf deployment, the *Vincennes* crew would see a substantial turnover. Even worse, the cruiser was pulled out of its training cycle two months early and rushed to the Gulf because of the Iranian Silkworm attacks during Operation Praying Mantis. Thus, the ship Captain Rogers took to the Gulf had many new crewmen who had neither been able to work together nor complete a normal training cycle for Gulf duty.

Further exacerbating the situation, Captain Rogers himself had not been able to complete the Aegis training school. In fact, he was at the time, and for at least a dozen years thereafter, the only officer to have commanded an operationally deployed Aegis cruiser without having completed the school. Once again, he would have done so had the ship not been pulled out early. Captain Rogers' reorganization of the *Vincennes* CIC may have reflected the fact that he had not completed the Aegis training. One observer noted, "He was never told things were organized this way for a specific reason and that, if you don't do things this way, you can screw up."

Captain Rogers was hardly responsible for the decision to rush the *Vincennes* to the Gulf, thereby curtailing its training cycle and preventing him from completing the Aegis school. He had clearly been placed in an undesirable situation with regard to his own and his crew's training levels. His unfortunate reorganization of the CIC may have been, at least in part, a product of those circumstances. However, other actions taken by Rogers may have had further negative effects on his crew's proficiency.

In the Gulf, Rogers had concluded that his department heads—key officers Vic Guillory and Scott Lustig—had too much paperwork to do, so he had them quit standing routine watch in the CIC. Thus, these men were deprived of the experience of operating firsthand in the Gulf environment. The result was that, when the *Vincennes* got into battle, the two officers in the most critical decision-making positions under Rogers had the least real-world Gulf experience.

Prior to Rogers taking over the *Vincennes*, an officer who evaluated the crew's performance hit them up in several areas related to good teamwork. One of these was that the crewmen didn't identify themselves when communicating over the internal nets. The men didn't question what was being reported over the nets, nor did they ask for follow-up information. Unless crews practice this procedure all the time, they tend not to do it under stress. It can be a serious problem because voices and even the hearing of them change under stress. One observer said, "Parties who are like brothers may not recognize each other's voices."

Captain Gee, the ship's commanding officer at the time, was considered to be a good team builder, so the evaluation may have reflected problems generated by turnover in the ship's original crew. During his time in command prior to the July 3 action, including the admittedly truncated training cycle, Captain Rogers does not appear to have rectified the problem. That problem would manifest itself during the July 3 engagement, first in the critical initial misidentification of the air contact as an Iranian F-14 fighter.

The Identification Supervisor (IDS) may have picked up a military-associated Mode II, 1100 IFF response using the non-Aegis RCI. Intelligence said this was a hostile indicator. The IDS was the only individual in the CIC who could have seen that response. The IDS, without identifying himself, called over the internal radio net that the contact was an F-14, or that he had picked up a military Mode II, 1100 signal, or maybe both. Recollections were unclear as to which. Several CIC crewmen later testified that they had heard an F-14 or Mode 1100 call. The TIC re-interrogated the contact with the Aegis system and picked up only a civilian Mode III response.

It should again be pointed out that there is no hard data whatsoever backing up the receipt of even this single "momentary" Mode II signal. The IDS initially testified that he had seen the Mode II signal on the Aegis Command and Decision (C&D) system. That system was recorded, and the recorded data from that system held no such signal. The theory that the IDS picked up a Mode II signal from Bandar Abbas airfield is just that: a theory. The alternative would be that, without any IFF signal, he just called out that it was a fighter when he saw the contact taking off from a mixed-use civilian/military base and heading directly toward the U.S. ships which were engaging the Iranian boats. There were some recollections by other crewmen that they heard a Mode II call. It seems more likely that the IDS did, in fact, pick up a brief Mode II signal and called out an F-14 identification, possibly also calling out Mode II, 1100.

Whatever he called out over the net, the IDS did not identify himself by his name or position, i.e.: "Smith, IDS." Several crewmen later testified that they thought that the F-14 call had come from the Ship's Signals and Exploitation Space (SSES). The only crewman who knew that the source of the F-14 identification had been the IDS was the Tactical Information Coordinator (TIC). He had immediately re-interrogated the contact with the Aegis IFF and had gotten a civilian Mode III response. Nevertheless, he did not question the IDS' call. The TIC was being trained by the IDS, and he assumed the IDS had more information than he did.

The validity of the fighter call was greatly amplified in the minds of several CIC crewmen because they thought it came from the SSES. The failure of the IDS to properly identify himself facilitated that confusion. The SSES, filled with what an observer called "highly classified crypto/intel stuff," was in the business of monitoring radio communications.

The *Vincennes'* SSES had a Farsi speaker on board, so it could have identified a contact as an Iranian fighter by, say, intercepting a radio conversation between the pilot and a ground controller. The level of reliability that people attach to a piece of information is obviously dependent on its source. The SSES was considered to be a very authoritative source. According to a member of the Fogarty team, "When they thought the call came from SSES, they took it for gospel truth." Another said that they had "asked countless military who were in the Gulf at the time and they said if an ID call was received from SSES, they wouldn't question it. They would accept it without question."

An interesting point raised by one former CO who served in the Gulf is why wasn't the *Vincennes'* SSES monitoring the Air Traffic Control frequency? Those conversations were conducted in English. The SSES could possibly have picked up way point calls or other communications between the aircraft and the ATC's. Such information might have allowed the CIC to correlate the radar contact with the civilian flight. This particular CO had frequently heard Iran Air Flight 655. In his experience, it was not unusual for that flight to be 10 to 30 minutes off schedule.

The fact that the F-14 identification was accepted virtually without question early on was a critical element, if not the single most critical element, in the process leading to a decision to engage. CIC officers and crew may have had F-14's on the mind. On the afternoon of the previous day, July 2, two Iranian F-14's had approached the cruiser USS *Halsey*. The fighters had closed to within seven nautical miles of the ship before repeated radio warnings and the use of fire control radars to illuminate the jets persuaded them to turn away. The *Vincennes'* CIC crew were well aware of the incident. On a total of seven occasions within the previous three weeks, Iranian F-14's had been challenged by U.S. ships.

The call that the aircraft was an Iranian fighter was heard by Commander Lustig, who was acting in the dual roles of both force anti-air warfare officer (AAWC) and ship AAWC. As the force AAWC (the "GW" or "Gulf Whiskey"), Commander Lustig was responsible for coordinating and directing the air defense of the *Vincennes*, the *Montgomery*, and the *Sides*. That air defense coordination and direction should not have presented burdensome problems. The *Sides*, some 18 miles away, faced no potential threat until after the Airbus was shot down. The *Montgomery*, positioned near the *Vincennes*, faced a common threat in the single incoming air contact. Therefore, Commander Lustig did not have to concern himself with distinct air threats to the other ships.

He was, however, burdened with the duty of being the primary telephone talker for situation reports being made to JTFME. Thus, not only was Commander Lustig relaying the air picture to Admiral Less on his flagship anchored in Bahrain, he was also relaying the surface picture, i.e. information about the ongoing battle against the small boats. He had an earphone for net 15, the internal CIC command net in one ear. Instead of the earphone for internal net 12 in the other ear, as he would have had if he had only the ship AAWC responsibility at the AAWC console, he now had an earphone for the external Force net. That net went to the Commander, JTFME and to the other ships in the force, the *Sides* and the *Montgomery*. Commander Lustig was giving instructions to Lieutenant Zocher over net 15. Lieutenant Zocher, who now operated the AAWC console, was communicating with the other crewmen in "air alley" over net 12.

Commander Lustig appears to have "bought in" from the beginning on the misidentification of the air contact as an F-14. General Crist later noted, "He accepted without question the combined reports of the TIC and IDS as confirming an F-14." Commander Lustig later said that this judgment was based on the intelligence warnings, the deployment of F-14's to Bandar Abbas, the fact that the Mode II 1100 IFF signals had previously been squawked by Iranian F-14's, and because the Iranian P-3 was possibly targeting the U.S. ship.

The *Vincennes* "GW" organization had moved Commander Lustig to a position where his responsibility for communicating the air and surface picture to the JTFME had to seriously detract from his ability to concentrate on evaluating the potential threat presented by the incoming air contact. Things were happening fast and Commander Lustig does not appear to have taken a second look at the IFF identification of the contact.

If the *Vincennes* CIC organization had not been changed, Commander Lustig would have been sitting at the ship AAWC console back in "air alley." It is possible that, in his former position and undistracted by his "GW" duties, he might not have immediately bought off on the F -14 misidentification of the air contact. He might have looked at his CRO display and seen only the civilian Mode III IFF signal attributed to the contact. He might have gone back to the IDS to double check and elicited the crucial fact that he was the source of the original "F-14" call, not the SSES. Further, he might have learned from the IDS that the Mode II IFF signal had only been picked up momentarily, followed continuously by the civilian Mode III.

Instead, with the "F-14" 28 miles away, Commander Lustig requested approval from Admiral Less to shoot it down at a range of twenty miles if it continued inbound. Admiral Less approved, if the contact continued to ignore radioed warnings. Which it did, probably because the Iran Air flight crew were not monitoring the International Air Distress frequency, as they should have been. In light of all the attention paid the alleged calls later that the contact was descending toward the ship, it cannot be overemphasized that Commander Lustig had sought, and been granted, approval to shoot down the contact while it was clearly seen by all as climbing, not descending. No question of descending altitude affected Commander Lustig's decision or Admiral Less' approval. It was purely the identification as an F-14 fighter on an inbound flight path.

The contact, now labeled an F-14 on the large screen displays, continued inbound heedless of the various warnings the *Vincennes* was sending out. Commander Lustig was responsible for defending the *Vincennes* and the *Montgomery* from air attack. He wanted to meet that responsibility by shooting the plane down. Captain Rogers was more focused on the surface battle. His large screen display was set at only a 16 nautical mile range, whereas Commander Lustig had his set at 64 nautical miles to get the air picture. Captain Rogers could easily look over at Commander Lustig's screen. He later said that, although he was largely focused on his display, he did occasionally look over at Commander Lustig's.

Some ten years later, a now-retired Will Rogers visited the Aegis computer center in Dahlgren, Virginia. He ran through the recorded tapes of the action for the first time. At several points he said that the Iranian boats ought to be about this far away. When checked, they were. According to an individual who was present, "He still had the surface action burned into his brain." Captain Rogers appears to have harbored enough uncertainty about the identity of the air contact to override Commander Lustig and to deny him the authority to shoot at the 20-mile point approved by Admiral Less.

The incoming contact was within the bounds of the 20-mile wide "Amber 59" civilian air corridor, flying to the west of the centerline.

The aircraft's flight path within the air corridor did not keep it a constant distance from the centerline. Rather, it increasingly diverged from the centerline, taking it more toward the *Vincennes* and *Montgomery*. At 9:53 A.M., while approximately 18 miles from *Vincennes*, Flight 655 passed the "MOBET" navigational waypoint. The Iran Air jet called Bandar Abbas and reported position "MOBET." At that waypoint, civil aircraft routinely made a three-degree turn. Flight 655 made the turn.

Several crewmen in the *Vincennes* CIC noticed the small course change. They did not know about "MOBET," which did not appear in the air corridor displayed on the *Vincennes* radar screens, nor did they know about the usual three-degree turn there. The arrow-shaped "speed leader" on the radar display, the symbol for the contact whose "shaft" lengthened with its speed, now pointed directly at *Montgomery*. The small course change could be seen as a final fine adjustment by the "F-14" before making an attack run at the U.S. ships.

The CIC "air alley" petty officers had watched as the "F-14" ominously continued inbound undisturbed. Instead of the comforting and familiar presence of Commander Lustig at the AAWC console in "air alley," there sat the relatively inexperienced Lieutenant Zocher. Ordered by Commander Lustig to illuminate the contact with a fire control radar, Lieutenant Zocher was fumbling with the unfamiliar procedure. The two petty officers, the IDS and the TIC, were becoming increasingly apprehensive about the ship's ability to defend itself against what appeared to be an incoming air attack. The familiar figure of the experienced Commander Lustig, with whom they had trained and in whom they had a great deal of confidence, no longer sat near them at the AAWC console. His reassuring voice could no longer be heard on Net 12, the internal air net. What they could hear was Commander Lustig asking out loud for permission from Captain Rogers to shoot down the incoming "fighter."

Commander Lustig kept requesting, "Give me the key. Give me the key, skipper. Give me the key." Anxious to defend the ship, he was asking Captain Rogers to turn the firing inhibit key located next to the commanding officer's console. Turning the key would authorize the launch of the ship's anti-aircraft missiles. At the same time, the CIC crewmen could also hear Lieutenant Zocher, unable to illuminate the contact, being coached by the Missile Systems Supervisor (MSS) on how to perform the console operation. The men had to have become increasing worried, wondering for God's sake when are they going to shoot?

And can Zocher even do what he has to do when we do shoot? Captain Rogers appeared to be preoccupied with the surface battle and did not seem to be paying much attention to the air threat.

The contact was closing on the ship at a rate of five or six miles per minute. Still the ship would not act to defend itself. Captain Rogers kept holding off from firing, now trying to get more information on the aircraft's identity. At the same time, the ship's most experienced anti-air warfare officer could be heard repeatedly requesting, "Give me the key. Give me the key."

Before he even got the details on the engagement, the psychiatrist called in by the Fogarty team said that, when you have a group forced to deal with multiple events, often one person, and often a person who does not have authority over the group, will emerge to try to focus the group's attention and efforts. On the *Vincennes*, that person was the TIC petty officer. The effect was probably magnified by what the "air alley" petty officers perceived as a vacuum at their own ship AAWC position.

In this instance, human nature abhorred a vacuum at a position holding the responsibility for protecting the crewmen's lives in the face of what appeared to be an imminent threat. As the Fogarty Report described it, the "perception that there was a weak and inexperienced leader at the AAWC position led to the emergence of the TIC in a leadership role." The TIC "jumped net" to the command net (net 15). Without identifying himself, he broke into the net, in his words, "to make sure that they were staying informed and . . . not getting too sidetracked by the surface engagement where they were forgetting about the guy coming in." The TIC reported that the contact was increasing its speed, heading toward *Vincennes*. Possibly he reported it decreasing in altitude. The TIC began shouting out the alarming reports as the contact closed on the U.S. ships.

At this point, and probably well before, one of the experienced senior officers in the CIC should have exerted some authority and seen that proper communication procedures were being strictly followed. An observer who had been present during an Aegis training exercise held some years later recalled a CIC crew that was starting to lose it. The exercise involved the live firing of a missile by the mostly inexperienced crew, which included a young ensign fresh out of the Naval Academy among their number. As they approached the firing point, the CIC crew was "going wobbly" and ignoring standard procedures.

The Captain was on the bridge for the exercise, not in the CIC.

Suddenly, his deep bass voice came rumbling over the communications net. "OK people, let's settle down and do it the way we're trained to do it." The CIC quickly pulled itself together and went on to successfully conduct the firing exercise. On the *Vincennes*, nobody's voice came over the net to remind the CIC that they could do it right. Logically, this would have been Commander Lustig, if he had not been moved to his dual responsibility position and further burdened with the additional duty of being the telephone talker to the JTFME. Rogers himself was probably too preoccupied with his first concern, the surface engagement, to perform the task.

The alarming reports coming from the CIC were heard by Commander Lustig. He passed them on to Captain Rogers, telling him that the aircraft had veered from its flight path into an attack profile heading directly toward *Vincennes*. Commander Lustig did not personally verify the information. The CRO at his position showed that the contact was continuing to climb, as indeed, did the CRO at the TIC's position.

When asked about this contradictory data during the subsequent investigation, Commander Lustig defended his actions, stating that he "came to the realization that the data to me doesn't mean anything, because I reacted to people that I thought that . . . I knew that I had operated with that were reliable . . . and when they reported at short range they had a decreasing altitude, increasing speed, I had no reason to doubt them." As Commander Lustig put it, "I had to make a split-second recommendation to the commanding officer, and I did."[5]

It was now up to Captain Rogers. There is more than a little justification for seeing him as a loose cannon in precipitating the surface action now underway against the Iranian boats. It would be logical to assume that the same approach was carried over to his decision to shoot down the incoming air contact. However, that would not seem to have been the case. In contrast to his eagerness to get into the surface action, Captain Rogers appears to have only reluctantly fired on the air contact. An anti-air engagement was apparently not at all what he had in mind when he got into the shootout with the boats.

Rogers had overridden Commander Lustig's decision to shoot the contact at 20 miles. The "F-14" was now almost at the point where it could fire the air-to-surface missiles it might be carrying. In his endorsement to the Fogarty Report, General Crist noted: "In the final minute and forty seconds, the AAW tells his Captain, as a fact, that the aircraft has veered from the flight path into an attack profile and is rapidly descending towards USS *Vincennes*." Captain Rogers later testified that his confidence in Commander Lustig confirmed to him that the aircraft was, in fact, a threat.

Only seven minutes elapsed between the time the air contact was picked up and when the decision was made to fire the missiles. From the time Captain Rogers was personally made aware of the contact as a possible threat to when he made his decision, only three minutes and forty seconds elapsed. Preoccupied with the surface battle, Captain Rogers had very little time to personally verify the partially incorrect information being passed to him. He later testified that he had great faith in the "GW" organization he had set up in the *Vincennes* CIC.

In fact, he had unknowingly erected a fragile organizational structure, one whose ability to process data and provide accurate information to him essentially collapsed when subjected to a level of stress that other ships had been able to handle without difficulty. Contrary to the impression held by many, one of the real myths of the *Vincennes* is that the CIC crew had panicked. There had been fear, but more than anything else there had been confusion. And, more than anything else, that confusion had centered not on the final flight profile of the incoming contact, but on its identification as an F-14 fighter, and particularly on the source of that identification.

The information being passed to Rogers, with one exception, seemed to confirm that the contact was a threat to his ship. The only bit of negative feedback Rogers got was when Lieutenant Montfort had said, "Possible Commair." That one opinion was not enough to stem the swelling and urgent stream of contrary information that flowed over and around him. Under heavy pressure to act, Rogers seems to have stayed calm and tried to think things through. He was in the middle of a surface action. The air contact had taken off from a combined military/civilian airfield and had headed directly toward *Vincennes* and *Montgomery*.

An Iranian P-3 surveillance aircraft in the vicinity had turned inbound, possibly vectoring an air attack on the U.S. ships in support of the gunboats. There had been an identification of the aircraft as an F-14 fighter. Rogers zeroed in on the aircraft's radar signal, asking for electronic readouts in an attempt to positively identify the contact. There were none.

Under his Rules of Engagement, Captain Rogers' first responsibility was to protect his ship and his crew. Apparently, an enemy fighter was inbound and perhaps also descending toward *Vincennes* and *Montgomery*. He had waited until almost the last possible minute, looking for indications that the air contact was not a threat. He didn't get them. The fate of the *Stark*, which had failed to act in the face of a potential threat, had to weigh heavily on his mind. Captain Rogers reached up to the console over his head and "gave the key," authorizing the launch of his anti-aircraft missiles.

It was not a grand act of folly. Rather as one suspects of many, if not most, disasters, it was the cumulative result of numerous smaller errors, not all of which were committed on the *Vincennes*. To this day, the Iranian government maintains that the U.S. deliberately shot down the airliner.

CHAPTER 23

"THEY DON'T FIGHT LIKE IRANIANS ANYMORE"

Chief Warrant Officer Chris Dodd, an Army Task Force 118 helicopter pilot, was relaxing on the deck of the Mobile Sea Base Hercules. The base was hosting a "steel beach" picnic on the afternoon of July 12, 1988. The frigate USS *Nicholas* (FFG-47) was tied up alongside the Mobile Sea Base to take on water at the time. Seamen from the *Nicholas* joined the Marines, the special boat squadron sailors, the SEALs, and the Army aviation crews for a welcome break in routine. Many of the men were wearing comfortable garb of PT shorts, tee shirts, and sneakers.

The picnic was well underway when General Quarters sounded. The alarm was not followed by an announcement that this was a drill. It had also sounded during a scheduled picnic. Dodd figured this was for real and began to pull his flight gear on. The order now came for the OH-58D helicopters to be rolled out from their hangers. The *Nicholas* was going to battle stations with crewmen scrambling back aboard. The frigate did a quick disconnect from the Hercules.

Two Iranian speedboats had raced out of Farsi Island and attacked the 81,282-ton Panamanian-flag tanker *Universal Monarch*. The ship's captain radioed a distress call that had been picked up by U.S. forces. Rockets had hit the tanker in the engine room and its decks had been raked by heavy machine-gun fire. The ship had suffered some damage to its hull, and a fire had broken out in its engine room. Fortunately, there had been no casualties among its crew. The attack out of Farsi was unusual and may have been fueled by Iranian anger over the Airbus shoot-down nine days before. Under the U.S. "distress assistance" policy, the ship was eligible for help from U.S. forces.

Two AH-58D's on the Hercules were rolled out from their hangers and began running through their pre-flight equipment tests. Dodd's aircraft checked out, but the built-in test equipment on the other one showed a weapons system failure. Nevertheless, both aircraft launched, with Dodd flying trail. A TF-160 Blackhawk also took off from the Hercules. There was a detachment of two AH-58D's onboard the *Nicholas*. One of these also registered a systems failure when it ran through its pre-flight checks. That chopper aborted, but the other one launched from the frigate. The *Nicholas* itself got underway and headed out at flank speed.

It was near dusk as the U.S. helicopters approached the scene of the attack, about 20 miles west of Farsi. They were near the Iranian exclusion zone, which the pilots had superimposed on their navigation display by the expedient of plotting its waypoints and then connecting them. Dodd was ordered to verify the damage on the *Universal Monarch*. He made a pass alongside, at a distance of a few hundred yards, and could see smoke pouring out of holes that had been blasted in the ship's stern. Crewmen from the stricken ship were on deck waving at the U.S. helicopters. The *Nicholas* was closing and had picked up a flickering radar return from a contact that appeared to be departing the area. The Army helicopters were vectored to investigate and to visually identify the contact.

From his right seat position, Dodd was flying the second AH-58D in the lead formation. His copilot was Al Hosely. Having launched hurriedly, both men were still wearing their sneakers, not their regulation flight boots. The OH-58D from the *Nicholas* was to the rear with the Blackhawk. Dodd was straining to see the contact in the haze. The water was glassy smooth, and he was able to spot the wake left by a boat. Peering ahead into the dusk, he could see two small boats. He could also see a flashing light from one of the boats. Realizing what the light was, Dodd called out to his copilot, "I think those m---f---ers are shooting at us!"

Hosely was looking through his thermal sight. The heat signature from the hot outboard engines on the boats must have washed out the muzzle flashes. Hosely couldn't see them through the sight, so he answered, "No, they're not." Hosely lifted his head from the thermal sight display and looked out through the cockpit canopy. Both pilots saw the blinking light again. This time they were both sure that they were taking fire. The original idea had been simply to verify that these were the Iranian boats that had attacked the *Universal Monarch*, and to return with video footage of the craft. The helicopters had not planned to engage them, but the fact that the Iranians had taken them under fire had changed that.

The flight lead confirmed what his built-in test equipment had shown at takeoff: his weapons systems were down. He probably should not have been out there at all. However, with the prospect of action ahead, he had refused to take "no" as an answer from his system. Now, he had no choice.

He pulled out of the way as Dodd flew at a slow speed of thirty knots toward the Iranian gunboats. At an altitude of 50 feet and at a range of 1,000–1,5000 meters, Dodd could see that the two boats were zigzagging back and forth as they fired at the helicopters. The boats were Boston whaler-types mounting heavy machine guns. One of them also appeared to have a multiple rocket launcher on it. Probably this had been fired at the *Universal Monarch*. Dodd could also see the heavy machine gun bullets fired at them by the Iranian boats splashing in the water in front of his helicopter.

The AH-58D carried seven 2.75-inch rockets. Four of these had high explosive (HE) warheads, the other three carried flechette warheads. Al Hosely's heart was pounding. The adrenalin pumping through his system heightened his senses as he called out the range using measurements from his laser rangefinder. Dodd loosened off two HE rounds at the boats. The first went long, the second short. Having bracketed the boats, Dodd adjusted to get on target, and rapidly punched out the three flechette rockets and a single HE. The warheads on the flechette rockets contained dozens of nail-like lethal steel darts embedded in a matrix material binding them together.

When the warhead detonated downrange in the vicinity of the target, the explosion propelled the lethal darts out like a giant shotgun blast. The matrix material holding the darts together was pulverized into a fine reddish powder, which was also blown out by the blast. The powdered material created a "halo effect" or smoke ring in the air. If the helicopter maintained its firing position, the pilots could look through the smoke ring and see the area that had been impacted by the flechettes. Dodd could see the two Iranian boats, which were close together, right inside the smoke rings generated by his rocket warheads. His sixth rocket, the one with an HE warhead, landed between the two Iranian boats, which were then about fifty feet apart.

The *Nicholas* ordered the helicopters to cease fire and break off the action before Dodd could fire his last rocket. He looked to his right to clear for a turn away from the engagement area and saw the TF-160 Blackhawk only two rotor disc diameters away. The Blackhawk had been supposed to hang back with the AH-58D from the *Nicholas*. Instead it had closed up, even in the face of the Iranian fire. It felt really good to have the Blackhawk right there in case it was needed for a rescue pick-up. Dodd felt a surge of admiration for the TF-160 pilot. Hosely thought the engagement had gone exactly the same as their training scenarios prior to deployment. Dodd couldn't determine the effect of the rockets on the gunboats at the time.

Intelligence later indicated that the shower of deadly flechettes, ripping into the crews exposed on the open boats, had killed seven Iranians and wounded two others. One boat had been destroyed and the other disabled. The rocket barrage had only lasted a few seconds. The Iranians later mounted a search and rescue operation out of Farsi. The *Nicholas* spent the night circling and protecting the stricken tanker until it was taken under tow by a salvage tug the next day.

Obviously, the "Tanker War" was still going on. However, the crucial events in the Gulf region were taking place on land. For six years, the Iraqis had barely been hanging on against Iran. More recently, the Iraqis had been standing solidly on the defensive. The highly successful Iraqi attack on Al-Faw in April 1988 indicated that Saddam Hussein's army had finally been able to put together the elements of a formula for tactical offensive success against the Iranians. Wresting the initiative away from the Iranians, the Iraqis would attack four more times, pushing the Iranians out of occupied areas of Iraq and, at least on a temporary basis, carrying the ground war back into Iran again.

The Iraqi attacks were set-piece affairs, which had been carefully rehearsed using models and sometimes full-scale mock-ups of Iranian positions. They were preceded by a massive buildup of supplies to support the operations. The Iraqis also used a surprise or deception plan to mislead the Iranians as to the location of the coming offensive. At the point of attack, the Iraqis brought to bear a strong numerical superiority and an overwhelming material superiority, particularly in armor and aircraft, including helicopter gunships.

There was also a marked qualitative improvement in Iraqi forces through the use of elite Republican Guards units that had received extensive combined arms training. Finally, chemical weapons were used to cause casualties and sow confusion and panic among the Iranians. As an American military officer later described it, the results of the Iraqi effort were impressive:

> In the first battle, 17–18 April [1988], the Iraqis retook the Al-Faw peninsula. . . . The second battle saw Iran surrender land around the pressure point of Basra. The Iranians had seized this territory in 1987, after a desperate campaign that went on for over three weeks and cost them some 70,000 casualties. The Iraqis took it back in seven hours. . . . One month later, the Iraqis struck at Majinoon, the site of the Middle East's largest undeveloped oil fields. . . . Again the Iraqis retook it in a matter of hours. . . . The fourth battle occurred in the vicinity of Dehloran and effectively removed any remaining threat toward Baghdad. In the fifth and final battle, the Iraqis drove some 40 miles into Iran to Qasr-e Sherin/Kennanshah. Iraq's military commanders, apparently, were prepared to penetrate farther, but were recalled by the civilian leadership. . . .[1]

At Majnoon, an Iraqi soldier said, "We attacked for six, maybe eight hours. Then the Persians just got up and ran away." Another Iraqi soldier, nursing a wounded hand, said, "I am tired, but I am not so scared of the enemy as I was. They don't fight like Iranians anymore."[2]

The Iraqis may have gotten their act together for their offensives, but what was really critical to the outcome was the perilous state of Iranian forces by 1988. Iranian military morale had sagged badly under the exhausting burdens of a long war, massive casualties, and the widespread Iraqi use of chemical weapons. The Iranian Revolutionary Guards were particularly vulnerable to the chemical attacks because their beards made a tight fit of gas masks difficult. High summer temperatures made the wearing of masks and other protective clothing all but unbearable. Iraqi Foreign Minister Tariq Aziz shrugged off Western criticism of Iraq's gas warfare: "There were different views on the matter from different angles. You are living on a civilized continent. You are living on a peaceful continent."[3]

The sporadic and often token resistance put up by the Iranians before they abandoned their positions made it obvious that they had lost much of their will to fight at the time of the Iraqi offensives. Many were clearly disenchanted with the war and had been waiting to surrender at the first opportunity. The Iranians also abandoned large amounts of military equipment, much of it intact. The Iraqis gleefully displayed immense quantities of Israeli military equipment that had been supplied to Iran. The Iraqis' war booty also included nearly 17,000 Iranian caskets, which were finding fewer and fewer willing takers.

The Iranian revolution had unleashed the powerful forces of a resurgent Shiite faith, and at first there seemed to be no height to which the soaring aspirations of the revolutionaries could not carry them. Iran was being recast as an Islamic Republic. The Great Satan had been successfully defied. The foreign invader had been stopped and then thrown back in large measure by volunteers fired with the spirit of self-sacrifice. In time, however, the laws of political gravity gradually asserted themselves. Revolutionary fervor slowly sank under the grinding burden of eight years of war.

For some time, palpable war weariness had been spreading over Iran. The costly failure of the offensives launched at Basra with the expectation of a decisive victory was a turning point. "The psychology in Iran changed dramatically after Basra," said a U.S. intelligence analyst. "They were militarily bankrupt and demoralized."[4] Cracks began to appear in the religious foundation for the sacrifices demanded by the war. In October 1987, Grand Ayatollah Qami of Mashhad had declared that there was no truth in the promise that those who died in the war against Iraq would get to heaven.

The better off families, who could afford it, were sending their sons abroad before they reached the age of 16 in order to escape military service. Draft evaders and army deserters were turning up in increasing numbers in neighboring countries. Working class and peasant families were holding their sons back from martyrdom on the battlefield. The Iranians even tried to draw on expatriates of military age living in the UAE, resulting, in the words of the American consul in Dubai, in "a sudden noticeable increase in the applications of unaccompanied Iranian men who profess an urge to tour the States."

In late February 1988, Iraq had begun raining SCUD missiles on Tehran. The missiles were Soviet-made SCUD-B's modified by the Iraqis by trading off warhead size for fuel tankage to extend their range in order to reach the Iranian capital. Over the next seven weeks, some 140 missiles fell on the city. The missile attacks, which came without any warning, had a devastating psychological effect on Iran. Many stores and government offices closed. Schools closed. At least a quarter, and perhaps as many as a half, of the capital's population of 12 million fled. One Tehran resident said:

> It was the war of the cities more than anything else which broke the morale of the Iranian people. When the missiles were falling, everyone fled into the mountains outside the city. Tehran was like a ghost town. . . .The worst thing was that you had no idea of when a missile would land. You can't see or hear one coming. I was at home when one fell five hundred meters away from our house. The same evening we left we knew the war would have to end soon. We wanted it to end because the Iranian people had already lost enough.[5]

The Iranian upper and middle classes had never particularly cared for the clerical regime. However, the revolution had mined a rich vein of support among the rural peasantry and the urban poor. Now, even that was playing out.

Near the end of the war, a young soldier who went to Tehran following his obligatory military service experienced a great letdown. "In Tehran, it was wedding parties. Two of my friends had been martyred. And there, in the same alley with their funeral, was a wedding party. At the front, it was Islam and the war. Here in Tehran people were talking about fashions and music. On the Voice of America we could hear Iranian people asking for new records to be played. In Tehran, nobody cared about the war."[6]

A somewhat bitter American joke of the time asked, "How do you identify an Iranian moderate? Answer: He's the one who's run out of ammunition." By mid-1988, Iran was running out of ammunition, both the material kind and, more importantly, the moral kind. Iran could either accept the U N. cease-fire now or be pummeled by further Iraqi attacks and eventually be forced into a humiliating peace. The handwriting was on the wall, though it is doubtful that Ayatollah Khomeini, sitting isolated in his compound at Jamaran ("haven of snakes"), could read it.* Others, however, could see it clearly. On July 18, Parliament Speaker Rasfanjani and Khomeini's son Ahmad visited Khomeini in an effort to convince him to end the war. They argued that the continuation of the conflict seemed to threaten the Islamic revolution itself. It was on that basis that Khomeini finally abandoned his uncompromising position and approved an end to the war.

The shoot-down of Iran Air flight 655 had stirred a surprisingly mild Iranian reaction. True, there were denunciations and demonstrations, but a populace numbed by eight years of heavy wartime casualties seemed to have lost the capacity to generate massive outrage over the incident. Rafsanjani claimed that the shoot-down was not a mistake but "a warning rather than anything else."[7]

Rafsanjani probably did not believe the shoot-down had been deliberate, but, as a clever politician maneuvering Iran toward accepting a cease-fire, that interpretation lent weight to the argument that the U.S. and other Western powers were moving against Iran. The subsequent failure of the U.N. Security Council to condemn the U.S. action deflated Iranian expectations that there would be a wave of international outrage directed against the U.S., and brutally drove home the depth of its international isolation. Rafsanjani would claim that the downing of the passenger plane was a "turning point" in Iranian thinking because it showed that the U.S. was ready to commit "immense crimes" if Iran pursued the war.[8] Some had feared that the shoot-down of the Airbus would wreck the apparently fragile chance for peace in the region; however, the effect may have run in the opposite direction.

Iraq proclaimed a "great victory" in the war with Iran. After the announcement of the cease-fire agreement, jubilant Iraqis fired tens of thousands of rounds of ammunition into the sky over Baghdad in a wild celebration. Iraqis danced on the beds of pickup trucks and waved palm fronds from car windows. Some beat drums and sang, as others danced in the streets. Arab delegations began arriving in Baghdad to congratulate Saddam Hussein. Kuwait presented him with a miniature mosque cast in pure gold. The mood in Tehran was relieved but hardly joyful. On August 10, more than one million people marched in Tehran in support of Khomeini's acceptance of the cease-fire.

As for the "Tanker War," some 441 ships had been hit during the Iran-Iraq conflict. Several ships were hit five and six times. The unfortunate *Filikon L* was hit twice, once by Iran and once by Iraq. 239 of the ships hit (around 58 per cent) were tankers. 115 ships were sunk or written off in the total loss, constructive total loss, or compromised settlement categories by insurers.[9] Various estimates of losses put them at around $2.5 billion. Iraqi ship attacks were estimated to have cost 329 lives, Iran's 60.

On August 20, Iraq literally tested the waters of the Gulf by bringing in its first merchant ship in many months, the roll-on/roll-off transport *Khawla*. Iranian warships shadowed the ship, but they did not interfere with its transit.

The cease-fire declared on August 20 may have halted attacks on merchant ships and other hostilities in the Gulf, but as a U.S. Navy officer put it, "Mines don't know there's peace going on."[10] No new mines were being laid, but a "residual" threat remained, and sweeping operations against the moored mines continued.

However, the threat was shifting to floating mines that had broken loose from their moorings in the northern Gulf and were drifting south through the sea lanes. There were still mine incidents. The Liberian flag tanker *Pegasus I* struck a mine in December. In January 1989, a dhow from Bahrain hit a mine, killing its captain. In January 1991, on the eve of Desert Storm, the Cypriot-flag freighter *Demetra Beauty* struck what was probably an old Iranian mine in the Gulf of Oman.

The general level of attention paid to events in the Gulf by the American public had not been particularly high on a sustained basis, though it had spiked with incidents such as the *Stark* attack and the *Vincennes'* shoot-down of Flight 655. To a lesser extent, the *Bridgeton* mining, the capture of the *Iran Ajr*, Operation Nimble Archer, and Operation Praying Mantis got a reasonable amount of notice. With the cease-fire in effect, the Gulf seemed to completely vanish from public consciousness.

Some would always remember. Nancy Erwin lost her son Steven, a sonar technician on the *Stark*. In the year following, she always wore a pin with a gold star on a blue background. When asked about the pin, she would tell people that her son had been killed on the *Stark*. A blank stare was the reaction she frequently got. "I remember because my son was killed, but the country does not remember," she said.[11] On May 17, 1988, in Mayport, Florida, the USS *Antrim* had carried families and friends of the victims of the attack for a "service of remembrance." A wreath had been cast upon the sea, and family members at the fantail scattered flowers on the water. Two buglers sounded the mournful cry of "Taps." *Stark* crewman Tim Porter suffered flashbacks about the attack and feelings of guilt because he had survived but had been unable to save his best friend, Terry Weldon. Three years after the attack, Porter would hang himself in a Veterans' hospital. His family mourned him as the 38th victim of the *Stark* attack.

Some would remember for a while, too, in Iran. On April 19, 1989, a year after Operation Praying Mantis, six Iranian Navy ships sailed into the Gulf to the vicinity of the sunken *Sahand* and laid a wreath during a memorial service.

The Kuwaiti tankers began "de-flagging" in April 1989. The Kuwaitis allowed five of the ships to remain under the American flag, registered to the Glen Eagle Company. The 81,000-ton *Surf City* was one of those ships. Loaded with diesel and naphtha, the tanker blew up in February 1990 after having survived dozens of trips through the war-torn Gulf unscathed. Ironically, USS *Simpson*, with Jim McTigue in command, was back in the Gulf and actually sailing with the *Surf City* near the Strait. It was a beautiful, clear morning when a crewman reported to McTigue, "Captain, it just blew up!" "What did?" asked McTigue. "The *Surf City*," was the answer. McTigue went up to look and saw the whole tanker engulfed in a fireball. The explosion claimed several lives and rendered the ship a total loss.

With the end of the war, Saddam Hussein turned to unfinished business. The day after the cease-fire went into effect, the Iraqi air force began attacking Kurdish villages with bombs, rockets, and poison gas. An amazing string of helicopter crashes began claiming the lives of Iraqi generals whose popularity had been boosted by the war, giving them some potential to become rivals to Saddam. Cooperation with the U.S. ceased virtually overnight. Iraq erected a war memorial in Baghdad consisting of enormous swords crossed over a broad boulevard. The memorial was cast using metal from melted Iranian helmets and armor. The hands holding the swords were modeled using impressions from Saddam. Along a one-mile stretch of the Shatt al-Arab, Saddam erected 90 life-sized statues of Iraqi officers killed in the war. The outstretched arms of the statues pointed accusingly across the water toward Iran.

The war had ended with Iraq still maintaining its claim to the entire Shatt al-Arab waterway. In August 1990, facing the American-led coalition lined up against him following his invasion of Kuwait, and hoping to secure his Iranian flank, Saddam relinquished his claim, the nominal cause for the long war he had started.

END NOTES

INTRODUCTION
1. John Bullock and Harvey Morris, *The Gulf War: Its Origins, History and Consequences,* (London, England, 1989), 150.
2. Christopher Thomas, "Grief and pride haunt a cemetery for young soldiers from Gulf War," in *The Times (London)* (February 2, 1978), 7.

Chapter 1: THE STARK DISASTER
1. Grant Sharp, Rear Admiral, USN, *Formal Investigation Into the Circumstances Surrounding the Attack on the USS Stark (FFG 31) on 17 May 1987* (June 12, 1987), 12.
2. Ibid., 13.
3. John Fritz, "Stark's sailors will remember victims of ships' 'day from hell,'" in *Florida Times Union Online* (May 16, 1997) http://www.Jacksonville.com.
4. Ibid.
5. Ed Margnuson, "A Shouted Alarm, A Fiery Blast," in *Time* (June 1, 1987), 20.
6. William Lowther and James Mills, "The Deadly Mistake," in *MACLEANS* (June 1, 1987), 19.
7. Steve Crane, "Wounds heal for Stark sailor, but not the memory," in *The Washington Times* (July 10, 1987), A-1.
8. David Fairbank White, "How They Saved the Stark," in *Parade Magazine* (February 12, 1989), 6.
9. Fritz, "Stark's sailors will remember victims of ships' 'day from hell,'" Ibid.
10. Rear Admiral United States Navy (Retired) Harold Bernsen, telephone interview with author

11. Jeffrey L. Levinson and Randy L. Edwards, *Missile Inbound: The attack on the Stark in the Persian Gulf* (Annapolis, MD.,1997), 20.

12. White, "How They Saved the Stark," 4–6.

13. James Kitfield, "Firefighting: Have the Lessons of the Stark Been Learned?" in *Military Forum* (March 1988), 23.

14. "Scarred Stark Body Back Home," in Houston Chronicle News Service, *Houston Chronicle* (August 6, 1987), 4.

15. Levinson and Edwards, *Missile Inbound: The attack on the Stark in the Persian Gulf*, 36.

16. "Scarred Stark Body Back Home," 4.

17. Michael Dobbs, "Crews' Families Share Relief, Grief and Anger," in *The Washington Post* (May 20, 1987), A-23.

18. Richard R. Steward, "In grieving Florida port, reporters are viewed as outsiders," in *The Boston Globe* (May 21, 1987), Sect. 1–23.

19. Jennifer Holmes, "Intruding on Grief: does the public really have a need to know?" in *Fine Line: The Newsletter On Journalism Ethics* (September 1989), 2, 5.

20. Dobbs, "Crews' Families Share Relief, Grief and Anger," A-23.

21. Alfonso Navarez, "Jersey Family Grieves Loss of Happy-Go-Lucky Son," in *The New York Times* (May 20, 1987), A-13.

22. Dobbs, "Crews' Families Share Relief, Grief and Anger," A-23.

23. Patrick E. Tyler, "A Family's Last Reunion," in the *Washington Post* (May 21, 1987), A-62.

24. William Matthews, "A Year Hasn't Washed Away Loss of Stark Sailors," in *Navy Times* (May 30, 1988) 4.

25. David Hoffman, "President Gives Eulogy for 37 Killed in Attack on U.S. Ship; Men Hailed for "Extraordinary Act," in *The Washington Post* (May 23, 1987), A-6.

Chapter 2: TARGET: KUWAIT

1. Elaine Sciolino, "Iraq's Tanker War May Miss Mark," in *The New York Times* (January 20, 1985), D-5.

2. John Vincour, "Iran Said to Develop Reflector That Fools Exocets," in *The New York Times* (July 6, 1984), A-3.

3. Paul Lewis, "Iraqi Exocet Hit Tanker but Failed," in the *New York Times* (June 26, 1984), A-3.

4. John Kifner, "U.S. Move in the Gulf: More Firmly on Iraq's Side," in *The New York Times* (June 12, 1987), A-14.

5. Dilip Hiro, *The longest war: The Iran-Iraq Military Conflict* (New York, NY., 1991), 214.

6. Laurie Mylrole and Judith Miller, *Saddam Hussein and the Crisis in*

The Gulf (New York, NY, 1990),122.

7. John Kifner, "Fleet in the Gulf: Outcome of Furor Over Iran . . . or a Move to Draw U.S. Into War," in *The New York Times* (June 4, 1987), A-8.

8. "A Soviet Show of force to Iran," in *The Philadelphia Inquirer* (June 6, 1987), 8.

9. Bernard Gwertzman, "Offer By the U.S. to Guard Tankers In Gulf Reported," in the *New York Times* (May 17, 1984), A-1.

10. Drew Middleton, "Iran And The Strait: Threat Is Discounted," in *The New York Times* (March 3, 1984), A-3.

11. Stephen Engelberg, "Iran And Iraq Gor 'Doctored Data', U.S. Officials Say," in *The New York Times* (January 12, 1987), A-1.

12. James McCartney, "How the U.S. Stumbled Upon Kuwait," in the *Philadelphia Inquirer* (June 28, 1987), E-2.

13. Elaine Sciolino, "A Showdown in Gulf War?" in *The New York Times* (May 26, 1987), A-5.

14. McCartney, "How the U.S. Stumbled Upon Kuwait," E-2.

15. Department of State Message from U.S. Embassy in Kuwait to Secretary of State, "Subject: Chronology of Silkworm attacks on Kuwait in 1987, October 25, 1987."

16. McCartney, "How the U.S. Stumbled Upon Kuwait," E-2.

17. Statement by President Reagan, 19 May 1987 *State Department Current Documents, 1987, #262.*

Chapter 3: QUESTIONS ARE RAISED

1. Levinson and Edwards, *Missile Inbound: The attack on the Stark in the Persian Gulf*, 101.

2. Ibid, 92-93. See chapter five generally.

3. Ibid, 91. Citing Sharp Report transcript at page 407.

4. Tamar Jacoby with Eleanor Cliff and Robert B. Cullen, "A Questionable Policy," in *Newsweek* (June 1, 1987), 22.

5. Molly Moore, "Gulf Attack Stirs Doubt on Defensive Capability," in *The Washington Post* (May 25, 1987), A-16.

6. Mark Thompson, "Until May Attack, Some Ships in Gulf Had No Antimissile Michael Valhos, "The Stark Report," in *Proceedings: Naval Review Annual Issue* (1988), 67.

7. Gun, Sources Say," in *Philadelphia Inquirer* (July 12, 1987), A-4.

8. Commander Steven M. Lanoux, "Letter in Comment Discussion Section, *Proceedings* (December 1992), 19.

9. Levinson and Edwards, *Missile Inbound: The attack on the Stark in the Persian Gulf,* 8.

10. Gilbert Gaul and Dan Stets, "Navy Knew of Fire Hazards 4 Years Before Stark," in *Philadelphia Enquirer* (September 20, 1987), A-1.
11. Levinson and Edwards, *Missile Inbound: The attack on the Stark in the Persian Gulf*, 112.
12. Salvador Mafe Huertas, "In his own words..." in *Air Forces Monthly* (February 1991), 10–11.
13. George C. Wilson, "USS Stark Had Only Seconds to React," in the *Washington Post* (June 4, 1987), A-3.
14. Richard Mackenzie, "Technical error aboard jet blamed for attack on Stark," in *The Washington Times* (July 17, 1987), A-1–2.
15. Robert Fisk, "Flying the flag with discretion in Gulf minefield," in *The Times (London)* (June 22, 1987), 7C.
16. "Iran Claims Role in Stark Attack," in *The Washington Times* (June 5, 1987) A-8.
17. "The attack on USS Stark: Baghdad tries to shift the blame," *The Times (London)* (May 20, 1987), 7E.
18. Harry Anderson et al, "Simmering About the Saudis," in *Newsweek* (June 15, 1987), 33.
19. Molly Moore, "Two Officers on USS Start Are Allowed to Quit by Navy," in *The Washington Post* (July 28, 1987), A-1.
20. "Brindel: Engine test ban needed in Gulf," Houston Chronicle News Service, *Houston Chronicle* (July 29, 1987) 4.
21. James M. Dorsey, "3rd Stark officer disciplined, but allowed to stay in Navy," in *The Washington Times* (July 29, 1987), A-6.
22. Warren Strobel, "Experts see Stark as victim of policy," in the *Washington Times* (May 21, 1987) A-7.
23. Jacob Lamar et al, "Why Did This Happen," in *Time* (June 1, 1987), 19.
24. "Weinberger calls attack on frigate indiscriminate," Associated Press, *The Boston Globe* (May 21, 1987), 21.
25. Peter Ross Range et al, "The Tragic Cost of Commitment," in *U.S. News and World Report* (June 1, 1987), 17.
26. Ibid, 18.

Chapter 4: OPERATION EARNEST WILL
1. Caspar W. Weinberger, *Fighting For Peace, Seven Critical Years in the Pentagon* (New York, NY.,1990), 400.
2. Maxwell Orme Johnson, "Military Force in the Gulf War," in Christopher C. Joyner, ed., *The Persian Gulf, Lessons for Strategy Law and Diplomacy* (New York, NY, 1990), 32.
3. U.S. Congress, House. *National Security Policy Implications of United*

States Operations in the Persia Gulf Report of the Defense Policy Panel and the Investigations, Subcommittee on Armed Services, House of Representatives, One Hundredth Congress, First Session, July 1987.

4. George C. Wilson, "Tanker Escort Not a Big Risk, Crowe Asserts," in *The Washington Post* (June 6, 1987), A-1.

5. "IRAQ IS A KEY to the U.S. Persian Gulf Strategy, top officials believe," in the *Wall Street Journal Online–Washington Wire* (July 24, 1987), 1.

6. Richard Pyle, *Schwarzkopf in His Own Words, The Man, The Mission, The Triumph* (New York, NY., 1991), 50.

7. General George B. Crist, *End of Tour Report, 27 November 1985* (November 23, 1988), 1.

8. William J. Crowe, Jr. and David Chanoff, *The Line of Fire: From Washington to the Gulf; The Politics and Battles of the New Military* (New York, N., 1993), 108.

9. David B. Crist, *Operation Earnest Will: The United States in the Persian Gulf, 1986–1988* (Unpublished Thesis Florida State University, 1993), 62.

10. "Iran missiles in Gulf no surprise to U.S." in *Chicago Tribune* (June 16, 1987), Sect. 1, p. 2.

11. Molly Moore, "Navy Planes' Launch in Gulf Played Down, Link to Iranian Missile Activity Denied," in *The Washington Post* (July 7, 1987), A-12.

12. Richard Murphy, *International Shipping and the Iran-Iraq War,* United States Department of State, Current Policy No. 958, 2.

13. John Kifer, "U.S. Move in Gulf: More Firmly on Iraq's Side," *in The New York Times* (June 12, 1987), A-14.

14. Jonathan Broder, "Anxiety Follows U.S. into Gulf," in *Chicago Tribune* July 5, 1987), Sect. 1, p.3.

15. Ibid.

Chapter 5: AMBUSH

1. Patrick E. Tyler, "Reflagged Tankers Enter Persian Gulf," in *The Washington Post* (July 23, 1987), A-31.

2. Ibid.

3. James Dorsey, "Iranian Jets, Soviet Warship pass near convoy," in *The Washington Times* (July 24, 1987), A-1.

4. James Adams, with Marie Colvin and Amit Roy, "Running the Gauntlet," in the *Times (London)* (July 26, 1987), 25B.

5. Adams, Colvin and Roy, "Running the Gauntlet," 25.

6. James M. Dorsey, "Captain predicts Iran won't strike," in *The Washington Times* (July 22, 1987), A-1.

7. Adams, Colvin and Roy, "Running the Gauntlet," 25.

8. Dorsey, "Captain predicts Iran won't strike," A-1.

9. James M. Dorsey, "Gulf Convoy steams beyond missile threat," in *The Washington Times* (July 23, 1987), A-1.

10. Patrick E. Tyler, "U.S. Protected Kuwaiti Tankers Reach Halfway Point," in *The Washington Post* (July 24, 1987), A-16.

11. Ibid.

12. DOD, Media Pool Report from USS *Fox*.

13. "SS *Bridgeton*: The First Convoy," Interview with Captain Frank Seitz Jr., U.S. Merchant Marine in *Proceedings, Naval Review* (1988), 56.

14. Harry Anderson and Richard Sandza, et al, "A Sting in the Gulf," in *Newsweek* (August 3, 1987), 24.

15. Tim Ahern, "U.S. Officer radioed, 'We've been hit!'" in *Orlando Sentinel* (July 25, 1987), A-10.

16. "SS Bridgeton: The First Convoy," 56.

17. Patrick E. Tyler, "Reflagged Tanker Hits Gulf Mine," in *The Washington Post* (July 25, 1987), A-1.

18. "Sea Brotherhood: U.S. Ship Warns Soviet Vessel of Danger of Mines," in *Los Angeles Times* (July 25, 1987), A-10.

19. Tyler, "Reflagged Tanker Hits Gulf Mine," A-1.

20. White House Defends Escort," in *The San Diego Union* (July 25, 1987), 11.

21. Walter Isaacson, "Into Rough Water," in *Time* (August 10, 1987), 8.

22. Tyler, "Reflagged Tanker Hits Gulf Mine," A-1.

23. Robert Fisk, "Mined ship limps into Kuwait haven," in *The Times (London)* (July 25, 1987), 5.

24. Tyler, "Reflagged Tanker Hits Gulf Mine," A-1.

25. James O'Shea, "Navy didn't check for mines," in *Chicago Tribune* (July 27, 1987), Sect. 1-1.

26. Jacob V. Lamar, Jr., "Coping With the Unfathomable," in *Time* (August 10, 1987), 1.

27. Frederick Kempe, "Iran Exploits U.S. Reflagging in Gulf to Build Morale, Counter Iraqi Threat," in *The Wall Street Journal* (July 27, 1987), 16.

28. Robert Fisk, "US Navy's incompetence blown open by a single mine," in *The Times (London)* (July 27, 1987), 1C.

29. Shea, "Navy didn't check for mines," 1.

30. Patrick E. Tyler, "Mines Put Gulf Escort in Question," in *The Washington Post* (July 26, 1987) A-1.

31. *The Nunn Report*, Senate Armed Services Committee Report (June 29, 1987), 1474.

32. Isaacson, "Into Rough Water," 8.

33. John Moore, "Relearning a hard lesson of naval warfare," in *The Times* (London) (July 29, 1987), 12B.

34. "SS Bridgeton First Convoy," 52.

35. Weinberger, *Fighting for Peace*, 40.

36. "Reported Iranian Decision to Attack U.S. Targets," in Department of State Message from Secretary of State to Commander in Chief, U.S. Central Command (October 15, 1987).

37. Harold Bernsen, RADM, "Persian Gulf Update," in *Second Annual Naval Aviation Symposium* (May 6, 1988), 6.

38. O'Shea, "Navy didn't check for mines," Sect. 1-1.

39. "The USS Vincennes Public War, Secret War," *ABC News Nightline Transcript* (July 1, 1992), 6.

Chapter 6: RETHINKING

1. Lieutenant Jonathan G. Roarke, USN, *Transcript -Interview Conducted by Commander Charles Chadbourn and Doctor Michael Palmer, June 21, 1988*, Naval Historical Center, Washington, DC, 2.

2. Fay Willey, et al, "Oops We Forgot the Minesweepers," in *Newsweek* (August 10, 1987), 40.

3. James Hessman, "Mine Warfare: A Sweeping Assessment," in *Sea Power* (September 1987), 7.

4. Commander Bruce E. Dunscume, USN and Lt. Jimmie b. Ford, USN, *Transcript–Interviews* Conducted by Doctor Michael Palmer and Commander Charles Chadbourn, June 14, 1988, Naval Historical Center, Washington, DC, 39.

5. Hessman, "Mine Warfare: A Sweeping Assessment," 7.

6. Scott C. Truver, "Weapons that wait . . . and wait," in *Proceedings* (February 1988), 33.

7. Ibid., 32.

8. "U.S. helicopters secretly arrive in Persian Gulf," in the *Houston Chronicle* (August 17, 1987), 1.

9. James R. Giusti, "Sweeping the Gulf," in *Surface Warfare* (March-April 1988), 3.

10. Molly Moore, "Pentagon Concerned Gulf Operation is Open-Ended," in *The Washington Post* (August 23, 1987), A-14.

11. Harry Anderson, John Barry et al, "Settling In For a Long Stay," in *Newsweek* (September 28, 1987), 34.

Chapter 7: THE INVISIBLE HAND STRIKES AGAIN

1. Alan Cowell, "Iran Warns It Has Extended Maneuvers in Gulf," in *The*

New York Times (August 7, 1987), A-1.

2. Loren Jenkins, "Iran concluded Naval Exercises; Tehran Reports Antiship Missile Test, Practice Ramming by Boats," in *The Washington Post* (August 8, 1987), A-13.

3. Michael, Dyness, "Iran's Suicide Mentality Could Turn Rhetoric Into Bloodshed," in *The Times (London)* (August 7, 1987), 6C.

4. Ross Lauer, "Power Ken Politics," in *Macleans* (August 31, 1987), 15.

5. Molly Moore, "High Over Strait of Hormuz; It was The USS Stark Revisited," in *The Washington Post* (August 9, 1987), A-1.

6. Robert K. Wilcox, *Wings of Fury* (New York, NY, 1997), 201–202.

7. Lou Cannon and Molly Moore, "U.S. Officials won't Confirm Fighter Incident; 'We Don't Want to Escalate This Further'; One Aide Says," in the *Washington Post* (August 12, 1987), A-1.

8. Crist, *Operation Earnest Will: The United States in the Persian Gulf, 1986–1988*, 145.

9. Loren Jenkins, "Gulf Harbors Doubts About Naval Build-up, U.S. Presence Viewed as Raising Tensions," in *The Washington Post* (August 16, 1987), A-23.

10. Molly Moore and Don Oberdorfer, "Mine Field is Found in Shipping Channel," in –*The Washington Post* (July 29, 1987), A-1.

11. Loren Jenkins, "Explosions Rocks Saudi Plant on Persian Gulf, Ship Strikes Mine, Sinks Off Emirates," in *The Washington Post* (August 16, 1987), A-1.

12. David Wallen et al, "Minehunt," in *The Sunday Times* (August 16, 1987), SL-11.

13. "How the Gulf looked from the gondolas," in *The Economist* (June 13, 1987), 48.

14. Ibid.

15. "U.S. Cruiser Joins 6 Other Ships in Persian Gulf," in *Houston Chronicle* (June 2, 1987), Sect. 1-1.

16. Tom Morganthau et al, "In Deeper In The Gulf," in *Newsweek* (August 31, 1987), 16.

17. Edward Cody, "Europeans Send Mine Sweepers; French, British Ships to Patrol in Gulf Separately From U.S.," in *The Washington Post* (August 13, 1987), A-1.

18. Edward Cody, "Chain of Events In Persian Gulf Led Reluctant Allies to Join U.S.; Mine Blast, Politics of Western Europe Led to Forces Deployment," in *The Washington Post* (September 20, 1987), A-25.

19. Christopher Dickey, "The Method in Iran's Seeming Madness," in *Newsweek* (August 3, 1987), 26.

20. Edward Cody, "Iran Says It Mines The Gulf, Tehran Cites Need to

Guard Its Waters Denies Harm to Ships," in *The Washington Post* (August 21, 1987), A-1.
21. "Tankers leave Kuwait after convoy arrives," in the *Houston Chronicle* (August 23, 1987), 1.
22. John Kifner, "Iraqi Warplanes Resume Attacks on Iranian Shipping and Oilfields," in *The New York Times* (August 30, 1987), A-1.

Chapter 8: IN FLAGRANTE
1. Sam Seibert et al, "The 'Night Stalkers': Death in the Dark," in *Newsweek* (October 15, 1987), 26.
2. Melissa Healy, "Navy Ill-Equipped to Fight a Restricted War I Gulf," in *Los Angeles Times* (October 25, 1987), A-1.
3. This account generally draws on Dr. John W. Partin, "Special Operations Forces in Operation Earnest Will; Prime Chance I," U.S. Special Operations Command, History and Research Office, April 1998.
4. Partin, "Special Operations Forces in Operation Earnest Will; Prime Chance I," 52.
5. Ibid.,58.
6. Ibid.,60.
7. Ibid., 61.
8. Paul Frochlich, "In harm's way," in *All Hands* (March 1988), 4.
9. Partin, "Special Operations Forces in Operation Earnest Will; Prime Chance I," 62.
10. Russell Watson and John Barry, "A U.S. Ambush in the Gulf," in *Newsweek* (October 5, 1987), 24.

Chapter 9: FORT APACHE
1. Crist, *Operation Earnest Will: The United States in the Persian Gulf, 1986–1988*, 184.
2. Ibid., 205.
3. Patrick E. Tyler, "U.S. Rejects 'Floating Fortress' in Kuwaiti Waters," in *The Washington Post* (November 27, 1987), A-1.

Chapter 10: TURN AND ENGAGE
1. Peter I. Wikul, *Mobile Sea Base Hercules in the Northern Persian Gulf: Beirut Barracks II?* Marine Corps Command and Staff College, Student Paper, AY 1994-95, 22-23.
2. Partin, "Special Operations Forces in Operation Earnest Will; Prime Chance I," 68. Generally this chapter will draw on events recounted in this report.
3. Ibid.

4. Ibid., 69.
5. Ibid.
6. Ibid., 71.
7. Ibid., 72.
8. Ibid.
9. Crist, *Operation Earnest Will: The United States in the Persian Gulf, 1986 – 1988*, 192.
10. Partin, "Special Operations Forces in Operation Earnest Will; Prime Chance I," 73.
11. Roarke, *Transcript -Interview Conducted by Commander Charles Chadbourn and Doctor Michael Palmer, June 21, 1988*, 12–13.
12. John Walcott and Tim Carrington, "An Iranian Group Seizes U.S. Missiles From the Afghans," in *Wall Street Journal* (October 14, 1987), 5.
13. John H. Cushman, Jr., "U.S. Says Iranian Boats Hit in Gulf May Have Had American Missiles," in *The New York Times* (October 10, 1987), Sect., 1-1.
14. Molly Moore and David Ottaway, "Iran Said to Obtain U.S.-made Stingers: Afghan Rebels May Have Sold Missiles," in *The Washington Post* (October 10, 1987), A-1.

Chapter 11: NIMBLE ARCHER
1. Michael S. Serrill, "Silkworm Sting," in *Time* (October 26, 1987), 42.
2. Statement of Captain Hunt, paragraph 9, Exhibit 88, "Counter Memorial and Counter Claim submitted by the United States of America," June 23, 1997, *Supporting Documents, International Court of Justice Case Concerning Oil Platforms, Islamic Republic of Iran versus United States of America*.
3. Statement of Colin Eglington, paragraph 22, Exhibit 31, "Counter Memorial and Counter Claim submitted by the United States of America."
4. Kamran Khan, "Iranians Celebrate Missile Attack As Much-Needed 'Morale Booster,'" in *The Washington Post* (October 18, 1987), A-34.
5. David B. Ottaway and David Huffman, "Iranian Missile His U.S.-Flagged Ship at Kuwaiti Port; U.S. Condemns Attack; Reagan Advisers Confer," in *The Washington Post* (October 17, 1987), A-1.
6. "Gulf: Seriousness downplayed," in *The San Diego Union* (October 17, 1987), A-1.
7. John Walcott, "Abar and Israeli Officials Tell Shultz U.S. Should Stage Counterattack on Iran," in the *Wall Street Journal* (October 19, 1987), 23.
8. Michael S. Serrill, "Punch Counter Punch," in *Time* (November 2, 1987), 62.
9. May Lee, "Members Learn to Keep Naval Family Afloat When Sailors

Go to Sea," in *Los Angeles Times* (November 14, 1987), Sect. 1–28.

10. Partin, *Special Operations Forces in Operation Earnest Will, Prime Chance I*, 79.

11. Ibid., 80.

12. Geraldine Brooks and Tony Horowitz, "Vulnerable Dubai Applauds U.S. Action But Dreads Becoming Object of Iran's Ire," in the *Wall Street Journal* (October 22, 1987), 35.

13. Ibid.

14. Tom Masland, "Iran creates storm of rhetoric," in *The Chicago Tribune* (October 21, 1987), 1-5.

15. Lou Cannon and David B. Ottaway, "Officials Say Attack Shows U.S. Intends to Defend Interests," in the *Washington Post* (October 20, 1987), A-26.

16. John Kitner, "Missile Reportedly Fired by Iran Damages a Kuwaiti Tanker," in *The New York Times* (October 23, 1987), A-1.

17. Nabil Megalli, "Iran fight tests U.S. gunboat diplomacy," in the *Houston Chronicle* (October 25, 1987), Sect.1-30.

18. Crist, *Operation Earnest Will: The United States in the Persian Gulf, 1986-1988*, 78.

19. Commander Dennis R. Flynn, Interview conducted by Paul Stillwell, *Transcript–Oral History Collection* (January 25, 1988), Naval Historical Center, Washington D.C., 17.

20. Marie Colvin, "Egypt to help defend Kuwait," in the *Sunday Times* (October 25, 1987), 1.

Chapter 12: WE ARE THE BIG WINNERS IN THE GULF NOW

1. General George B. Crist, USMC, "Statement," U.S. Congress, House Committee on Appropriations, February 22, 1988.

2 .Crowe and Chanoff, *The Line of Fire: From Washington to the Gulf: The Politics and Battles of the New Military*, 188,189.

3. Youssef Ibrahim, "Raids Make Iran Import Refined Oil Products," in *The New York Times* (March 21, 1988), Sec. D-2.

4. Len Roberts, ed., *Lloyd's List International: After the Gulf War* (London, England, 1988, 32.

5. Captain Dallas Bethea, USN Retired, Author Interview.

6. Patrick E. Tyler, "U. S. Warning to Iraq to Control Planes or Risk Losing Them, in the *Washington Post* (February 23, 1988), A-17.

7. Ibid.

8. Ibid.

9. Rick Francona, *Ally to Adversary: An Eyewitness Account of Iraq's Fall from Grace* (Annapolis, MD, May 1999), 13.

10. Commander Earl W. Shaut, Interview conducted by Commander Charles Chadbourn, *Transcript–Oral History Collection* (June 16, 1988), Naval Historical Center, Washington D.C., 18.

11. "Iran says it fired on U.S. Helicopter Pentagon Casts Doubt on Claim," in *Boston Globe* (February 15, 1988), 4.

12. Lieutenant Scott Brinkman, USN, Interview conducted by Commander Charles Chadbourn, *Transcript* (June 17, 1988), Naval Historical Center, Washington, D.C., 10.

13. Commander Gary Stubblefield, Interview conducted by Commander Charles Chadbourn and Doctor Michael Palmer, *Transcript* (June 22, 1988), Naval Historical Center, Washington, D.C., 9.

14. Partin, *Special Operations Forces in Operation Earnest Will, Prime Chance I*, 102–103.

15. Group Interview, Troop B, 4th Squadron, 17th Cavalry, CW3 D.C. A. Carver, et al., conducted by Major Robert K. Wright Jr., *Transcript–Operations Desert Shield and Desert Story, DSIT AE 005*, February 13, 1991, 8.

16. Partin, *Special Operations Forces in Operation Earnest Will, Prime Chance I*, 99.

17. Gary Stubblefield and Hans Halberstadt, *Inside the U.S. Navy Seals* (Osceola, WI, 1995), 155.

18. Help in the Gulf, Help on the Hill," in *Newsweek* (February 29, 1988), 6.

Chapter 13: NO HIGHER HONOR

1. Richard Pyle, *DOD Media Pool Report filed from aboard USS O'Brien* (April 15, 1988).

2. Stewart Powell, *DOD Media Pool Report* (March 22, 1988).

3. Chuck Mussi, "To see the dawn," in *ALL HANDS* (August 1988), 4.

4. Lt. Kenneth A. Heine J.G., "This is No Drill," in *Surface Warfare* (July/August 1988), 3.

5. Mussi, "To see the dawn," 6.

6. Victoria Sharp, "Saving the Samuel B. Roberts, in *Fathom* (Fall 1988), 7.

7. George C. Wilson and Molly Moore, "Reagan Aides Weigh Response To Damaging of Ship in Gulf; Evidence Indicates Iran Placed Mines Found in Area," in *The Washington Post* (April 16, 1988), A-1.

8. Mussi, "To see the dawn," 8.

9. Ibid., 5, 6.

10. Ibid., 7.

11. "Iran Air Flight 655 Compensation," in *Hearings before the Defense Policy Panel of the Committee on Armed Services, House of Repre-*

sentatives (August 3 and 4, September 9, and October 6, 1988), 251.

12. Mussi, "To see the dawn," 7.

13. St. Steven Balisdell, J.G., "HSL-44 Detachment Five had a Blast in the Persian Gulf," in *Rotor Review* (August 1988), 55.

14. Mussi, "To see the dawn," 9.

15. Ibid., 10.

16. Heine, "This is No Drill," 4, 5.

17. Mussi, "To see the dawn," 10.

18. Heine, "This is No Drill," 5.

19. Brenda Mitchell, "Preparedness and Courage USS Samuel Roberts," in *On The Surface* (May 20, 1988), 4.

20. Heine, "This is No Drill," 5.

Chapter 14: A ONE-DAY WAR

1. Patrick E. Tyler, "Gulf Rules of Engagement a Dilemma for U.S.; American Ship Commanders Operate in Increasingly Dangerous War Zone," in *The Washington Post* (July 4, 1988), A-1.

2. USS Gary, Command History File, 1988.

3. Crist, *Operation Earnest Will: The United States in the Persian Gulf, 1986-1988*, 213.

4. "Operation Praying Mantis," in *Surface Warfare Magazine* November/December 1988), 16.

5. Captain J.B. Perkins, USN, "Operation Praying Mantis, The Surface View," in *Proceedings* (Naval Review Issue, 1989) 68.

6. Perkins, "Operation Praying Mantis, The Surface View," 69.

Chapter 15: "STOP YOUR ENGINES, I INTEND TO SINK YOU"

1. Patrick E. Tyler, "Iran Hits Back With Attack On Arab-Owned Oil Complex," in the *Washington Post* (April 19, 1988), A-1.

2. Mary Judice, "Local boat ducks rocket in gulf strike," in *The New Orleans Times Picayune* (April 19, 1988), Sect. 1-1.

3. Bill Coulter, "Texan on rig calls lack of injuries a miracle," in *Houston Chronicle* (April 19, 1988), Sect. 1-1.

4. Ibid.

5. Ibid.

6. Melinda Henneberger, "Oil rig damaged in Iranian attack had just become operational," in *The Dallas Morning News* (April 20, 1988), A-8.

7. Coulter, "Texan on rig calls lack of injuries a miracle," Sect. 1-1.

8. Sam Fletcher, "Rig hit by Iranians managed by Houston firm" in *The Houston Post* (April 19, 1988), B-1.

9. John H. Cushman, "President Gave Permission for Attack on Ships," in

The New York Times (April 22, 1988), A-8.
10. Peter Almond, "Iranian attack called bid for 'suicide'" in *The Washington Times* (April 20, 1988), A-5.

Chapter 16: "NONE OF THESE LADIES HAS A SCRATCH ON HER"
1. Richard Pyle, "Sometimes the Pool Works," in *Washington Journalism Review* (July/August 1988), 14.
2. "Operation Praying Mantis," in *Surface Warfare* (November/December 1988), 20.
3. Crowe, and Chanoff, *The Line of Fire: Form Washington to the Gulf; The Politics and Battles of the New Military*, 202.
4. Tim Carrington, "U.S. Navy Strikes Iranian Vessels, Oil Platforms in Persian Gulf," in *Wall Street Journal* (April 19, 1988), 12.
5. Patrick E. Tyler, "Iranian Setbacks, U.S. Naval Clash Cloud Future in Persian Gulf," in *The Washington Post* (April 20, 1988), A-22.
6. Islamic Republic News Agency, dispatch April 19, 1988.
7. Bob Levin and William Lowther, "Flare-up in the Gulf," in *MACLEANS* (May 2, 1988), 20.
8. Ibid.
9. Ibid.
10. John Cushman, Jr. "U.S. Weighs Expansion of Gulf Forces and Role, " in *The New York Times* (April 20, 1988) A-6.

Chapter 17: MULTIPLE SILKWORMS INBOUND THIS UNIT
1. Stubblefield and Haberstadt, *Inside the U.S. Navy Seals,* 165–166.
2. Ibid., 166
3. Ibid., 167.
4. Richard Pyle, *DOD Gulf Media Pool Report Number Thirteen, filed from USS Jack Williams.*
5. Ibid.
6. Ibid.
7. Molly Moore, "3 Iranian Mines Found, U.S. Ship Reports Silkworms Fired Monday," in *The Washington Post* (April 20, 1988), A-29.
8. Pyle, *DOD Gulf Media Pool Report Number Thirteen, filed from USS Jack Williams.*
9. Moore, "3 Iranian Mines Found, U.S. Ship Reports Silkworms Fired Monday," A-29.
10. Ibid.
11. Pyle, *DOD Gulf Media Pool Report Number Thirteen, filed from USS Jack Williams.*
12. Admiral H. Mustin, *Transcript Federal News Service News Conference*

(April 21, 1988), 12-1.

13. "Pentagon denial leaves questions on Iran missiles," in *The Baltimore Sun* (April 29, 1988).

14. Mustin, *Transcript Federal News Service News Conference,* 13-1.

15. "Silkworms reportedly fired at US ships," in *The Boston Globe* (April 28, 1988).

16. Brenda, Greeley, Jr., "U.S. Sinks Iranian Frigate in Persian Gulf Action," in *Aviation Week and Space Technology* (April 25, 1988), 20.

17. "No white flag hoisted/Iran is building new Silkworm missile site, U.S. commander says," in *Houston Chronicle* (June 2, 1988), Sect 1-18.

18. Joint Electronic Warfare Center, *Praying Mantis After Action Report* (July 1988).

19. Captain Dallas Bethea, USN Retired, Author Interview.

20. Peter Almond, "Iranian attack called bid for suicide," in *The Washington Times* (April 20, 1988), 5.

21. Ibid.

22. "Pentagon denial leaves questions on Iran missiles," in *The Baltimore Sun* (April 29, 1988).

23. Stubblefield and Haberstadt, *Inside the U.S. Navy Seals,* 168.

24. "Pentagon denial leaves questions on Iran missiles."

25. Pyle, *DOD Gulf Media Pool Report Number Thirteen, filed from USS Jack Williams.*

26. "Pentagon denial leaves questions on Iran missiles."

27. Tom Wetherall, Author Interview.

28. Pyle, "Sometimes the Pool Works," 16.

Chapter 18: POLICEMAN OF THE GULF?

1. Juan O. Tamayo, "Attack in the Persian Gulf/Iran shows signs of fatigue in 8th year of war," in *Houston Chronicle* (April 20, 1988), Sect. 1-12.

2. Admiral Anthony Less USN, Interview conducted by Doctor Mike Palmer and Commander Charles Chadbourne, *Transcript, Naval Historical Center* (June 17, 1988), 9.

3. Author interview with ship commanding officer.

4. Statement by Secretary of Defense Frank Carlucci on April 29, 1988, in *Department of State bulletin* (July 1988), 61.

5. Robert H. Hulman, USMC, Mark E. Wilson, USMC, and Donald E. Scott USMC, Interview Conducted by Commander Charles Chadbourn and Doctor Michael Palmer, June 22, 1988, Naval Historical Center, Washington D.C., Transcript, 7.

6. Stubblefield and Halberstadt, *Inside the US Navy Seals,* 164.

7. Molly Moore, "Iranian missile site will increase threat in Gulf," in

Houston Chronicle (July 1, 1988), Sect. 1-16.

8. "Iran Said to Fortify Key Strait," *The New York Times* (July 1, 1988), A-2.

Chapter 19: UNKNOWN ASSUMED HOSTILE

1. "Man loses 11 members of his family," in *Houston Chronicle* (July 4, 1988), Sect. 1-12.

2. Rogers, Rogers and Gregson, *Storm Center: The USS Vincennes and Iran Air Flight 655: A Personal Account of Tragedy and Terrorism*, 2.

3. Tom Burgess, "Vincennes' tragic day was promising at start," in *San Diego Union* (November 1, 1988) Sect. 1-16.

4. John Barry and Charles Roger, "Sea of Lies," in *Newsweek* (July 13, 1992), 29.

5. Ibid., 32.

6. Will Rogers III, Sharon Rogers, and Gene Gregson, *Storm Center: The USS Vincennes and Iran Air Flight 655: A Personal Account of Tragedy and Terorrism*, (Bethesda, MD, 1992), 1.

7. Ibid., 146.

8. Ibid., 9.

9. Burgess, "Vincennes' tragic day was promising at start," Sect. 1-16.

10. General George B. Crist USMC, "FIRST ENDORSEMENT on Read Admiral Fogarty's ltr. of 28 July 1988," (August 5, 1988), 4.

11. Lieutenant Colonel David Evans, Retired USMC, "Vincennes, A case study," in *Proceedings* (August 1993), 53.

12. Rogers, Rogers and Gregson, *Storm Center: The USS Vincennes and Iran Air Flight 655: A Personal Account of Tragedy and Terrorism*, 15.

13. Evans, "Vincennes, A case study," 49.

14. Ibid., 53.

15. Ibid.

16. Crist, "FIRST ENDORSEMENT on Rear Admiral Fogarty's ltr. of 28 July 1988," 3.

17. Evans, "Vincennes, A case study," 50.

18. Rogers, *Storm Center: The USS Vincennes and Iran Air Flight 655: A Personal Account of Tragedy and Terrorism*, 17.

19. Ibid., 19.

20. Ibid.

21. Ibid.

22. Bulloch and Morris, *The Gulf War: Its Origins, History and Consequences*, 245.

23. Edward Cody, "Strait's Waters Mix Tension, Grief, Naval Might," in *The Washington Post* (July 8, 1988), A-1.

24. "Statement by Joint Chiefs Chairman 'US Deeply Regrets This Incident … but Commanders On The Scene Believed Their Units Were In Jeopardy," in *The New York Times* (July 4, 1988), Sect. 1-4.
25. Lou Cannon, "Poll Finds Support For Ship's Action, U.S. Policy in Gulf," in *The Washington Post* (July 7, 1988), A-21.
26. "Iranians? Oh well, it's not so bad?" in *Sunday Times* (July 10, 1988), B-5.
27. Edward Cody, "Stacks of Bodies on Display," in *The Washington Post* (July 7, 1988), A-1.
28. Robert Fisk, "Appalling Silent Horror of an Iranian Cold Store," in *The Times (London)* (July 7, 1988), Sect. 1-10.
29. Edward Cody, "Reagan Apologizes to Iran for Downing of Jetliner; Tehran Official Cautions Against Hasty Revenge," in *The Washington Post* (July 6, 1988), A-1.
30. Yousef M. Ibrahim, "The Downing of Flight 655; As Iran Mourns, Khomeini Call for 'War' on U.S.," *New York Times* (July 5, 1988), A-9.
31. Geraldine Brooks, "Tehran Seeks Lever Against U.S. Policy, Not Revenge in Airliner Disaster's Wake," in *Wall Street Journal* (July 11, 1988), 15.
32. Steven U. Roberts, "U.S. Compensation Will Be Provided in Airbus Downing," in *The New York Times* (July 12, 1988) A-1.

Chapter 20: "I DEEPLY REGRET THE OUTCOME, BUT NOT THE DECISION"
1. Rear Admiral William Fogarty, *Formal Investigation into the Circumstances Surrounding the Downing of Iran Flight 655 on 3 July 1988* (Washington, DC, July 28, 1988), 151.
2. Rogers, Rogers and Gregson, *Storm Center: The USS Vincennes and Iran Air Flight 655: A Personal Account of Tragedy and Terrorism*, 144.
3. Fogarty, *Formal Investigation into the Circumstances Surrounding the Downing of Iran Flight 655 on 3 July 1988*, 45.
4. William J. Crowe, Jr., "Second Endorsement on Rear Admiral Fogarty ltr. of 28 July 1988," (August 18, 1988), 5.
5. "Investigation Into The Downing of An Iranian Airliner By The USS Vincennes," *Transcript U.S. Senate Committee on Armed Services* (September 8, 1988), 21.
6. Fogarty, *Formal Investigation into the Circumstances Surrounding the Downing of Iran Flight 655 on 3 July 1988*, 45.
7. Ibid., 3.
8. Crist, "FIRST ENDORSEMENT on Rear Admiral Fogarty's ltr. of 28 July 1988," 3.

9. Bernard E. Trainor, "Errors By A Tense U.S. Crew Led to Downing of Iran Air Jet," in *The New York Times* (August 3, 1988), A-1.

10. Rogers, Rogers and Gregson, *Storm Center: The USS Vincennes and Iran Air Flight 655: A Personal Account of Tragedy and Terrorism*, 6.

11. U.S. House of Representatives Committee on Armed Services, Defense Policy Panel, *Transcript of Testimony of Captain George N. Gee USN* (October 6, 1988), 181.

12. Fogarty, *Formal Investigation into the Circumstances Surrounding the Downing of Iran Flight 655 on 3 July 1988*, 43.

13. Ibid., 46.

14. Ibid., 18.

15. David Evans, "Videotape Tells a Tale of an Unready Vincennes Crew," in *Chicago Tribune* (December 2, 1988), Sect. 1-31.

16. Ibid.

17. Ibid.

18. Patrick E. Tyler, "Vincennes Cited in Earlier Incident; Gulf Air Controller Describes Threat of Airliner Collision," in *The Washington Post* (July 5, 1988), A-1.

19. Stephen Franklin, "Unfriendly Skies Loom over Gulf," in *Chicago Tribune* (July 10, 1988), Sect. 1-16.

20. Fogarty, *Formal Investigation into the Circumstances Surrounding the Downing of Iran Flight 655 on 3 July 1988*, 46.

21. Ibid., 17.

22. International Civil Aviation Organization, *Destruction of Iran Air Airbus A300 In the Vicinity of Qeshm Island, Islamic Republic of Iran on July 3, 1988* (November 1988), 24.

23. "2 mix ups preceded gulf air disaster," in *Chicago Tribune* (July 6, 1988), Sect. 1-8.

24. Robert Fisk, "Explosive mix of failures that send IR655 to disaster, The shooting down of the Iranian Airbus," in *The Times (London)* (July 8, 1988), 8.

25. Karen Young, "Sorrow Over Lost Friends," in *The Washington Post* (July 7, 1988), A-1.

26. "Van bombing probed as terrorism linked to Vincennes," in *Houston Chronicle* (March 12, 1989), A-3.

27. Author letter of inquiry and telephone discussion with San Diego FBI office.

28. Burgess, "Vincennes' tragic day was promising at start," 16.

Chapter 21: SEA OF LIES?

1. Commander David R. Carlson, "The Vincennes Incident," letter to

Proceedings (September 1989), 88.

2. John Barry and Charles Roger, "Sea of Lies," in *Newsweek* (July 13, 1992), 33.

3. U.S. Congress, House Committee on Armed Services, Investigations Subcommittee and The Defense Policy Panel, *Transcript – The July 3, 1988 Attack by the Vincennes on an Iranian Aircraft* (July 21, 1992), 15.

4. Lieutenant Jonathan G. Roarke USN, *Transcript - Interview with Commander Charles Chadbourn and Dr. Mike Palmer*, Naval Historical Center (Washington, DC, June 21, 1988), 17, 18.

5. "The USS Vincennes: Public War, Secret War," Transcript of *ABC News Nightline* (July 1, 1992) 3.

6. *Transcript–The July 3, 1988 Attack by the Vincennes on an Iranian Aircraft*, 10.

7. Ibid.

8. Richard J. Grunawalt, "USS Vincennes (CG49) and the Shoot-Down of Iranian Airbus Flt. 655," Memorandum for Dean, Center for Naval Warfare Studies, Naval War College (Newport, RI, September 18, 1992), 7.

9. Evans, "Vincennes, A case study," 51, 56.

10. Grunawalt, "USS Vincennes (CG49) and the Shoot-Down of Iranian Airbus Flt. 655," 8.

11. Evans, "Vincennes, A case study," 51.

12. "Iran Speedboats Fire Close to Copter of U.S. Gulf Force," in the *New York Times* (December 25, 1987), A-2.

13. Will Rogers, Letter to Author dated July 20, 2001, 2.

14. Rogers, Rogers and Gregson, *Storm Center: The USS Vincennes and Iran Air Flight 655: A Personal Account of Tragedy and Terrorism*, 10.

15. Ibid., 8.

16. "Investigation Into The Downing of An Iranian Airliner By The USS Vincennes," 32.

17. "Blunder in the Gulf," in *The Economist*" (July 9, 1988), 19.

18. Brian Duffy, Robert Kaylor and Peter Cary, "How Good is This Navy Anyway," in *U.S. News and World Report* (July 18, 1988), 18.

19. Crist, *Operation Earnest Will: The United States in The Persia Gulf, 1986–1988,* 233.

20. Rogers, Rogers and Gregson, *Storm Center: The USS* Vincennes *and Iran Air Flight 655: A Personal Account of Tragedy and Terrorism*, 73.

21. Ibid.

22. "Investigation Into the Downing of an Iranian Airliner by the USS Vincennes," 32.

23. Crowe, "Second Endorsement on Rear Admiral Fogarty ltr. of 28 July 1988," 8.

24. Secretary of Defense, *A Report to Congress on Security Arrangements in the Persian Gulf* (Washington, DC, June 15, 1987).

25. *Transcript–The July 3, 1988 Attack by the Vincennes on an Iranian Aircraft*, 18.

26. Carlson, "The Vincennes Incident," 92.

27. Barry and Roger, "Sea of Lies," 33.

28. Crist, *Operation Earnest Will: The United States in The Persia Gulf, 1986–1988*, 234.

29. Evans, "Vincennes: A case study," 55.

30. Rogers, Rogers and Gregson, *Storm Center: The USS* Vincennes *and Iran Air Flight 655: A Personal Account of Tragedy and Terrorism*, 88.

31. Martin S. Navias and E. R. Houton, *Tanker Wars: The Assault on Merchant Shipping During the Iran-Iraq Conflict, 1980–1988* (London, England, 1996), 160.

32. Evans, "Vincennes: A case study," 50.

33. Ibid.

34. Ibid.

35. Rogers, Rogers and Gregson, *Storm Center: The USS* Vincennes *and Iran Air Flight 655: A Personal Account of Tragedy and Terrorism*, 22.

36. Burgess, "Vincennes' tragic day was promising at start," 1.

37. Rogers, Rogers and Gregson, *Storm Center: The USS* Vincennes *and Iran Air Flight 655: A Personal Account of Tragedy and Terrorism*, 5.

38. Ibid., 9.

39. "The USS Vincennes: Public War, Secret War," 2.

40. Evans, "Vincennes: A case study," 50.

41. Rogers, Rogers and Gregson, *Storm Center: The USS* Vincennes *and Iran Air Flight 655: A Personal Account of Tragedy and Terrorism*, 146.

42. Fogarty, *Formal Investigation into the Circumstances Surrounding the Downing of Iran Flight 655 on 3 July 1988*, 26–27.

43. *Transcript–The July 3, 1988 Attack by the Vincennes on an Iranian Aircraft*, 17.

44. Ibid.

45. Crowe, "Second Endorsement on Rear Admiral Fogarty ltr. of 28 July 1988," 3.

46. Barry and Roger "Sea of Lies," 36.

47. Grunawalt, "USS Vincennes (CG49) and the Shoot-Down of Iranian Airbus Flt. 655," 11.

48. *Transcript–The July 3, 1988 Attack by the Vincennes on an Iranian Aircraft*, 13.

49. Rogers, Rogers and Gregson, *Storm Center: The USS* Vincennes *and Iran Air Flight 655: A Personal Account of Tragedy and Terrorism*, 12.

50. Fogarty, *Formal Investigation into the Circumstances Surrounding the Downing of Iran Flight 655 on 3 July 1988*, 11.

51. *Transcript–The July 3, 1988 Attack by the Vincennes on an Iranian Aircraft*, 14.

52. John Cushman, Jr. "In The Trenches in Iraq: Iran's Teen-Agers Dig In," in the *New York Times* (August 25, 1987), Sect. 1-1.

53. George C. Wilson, "Pilots Question Threat Posed by F-14; Warplane Designed to Attack Air Targets, Not Ships," in *The Washington Post* (July 6, 1988) A-1.

54. Trainor, "Errors By A Tense U.S. Crew Led to Downing of Iran Air Jet," A-1.

55. K.A. Dotterway, *Systemic Analysis of Complex Dynamic Systems: The Case of The USS Vincennes*, Unpublished Master's Thesis, Naval Postgraduate School (1992). See especially Sect. III, C, 4.

56. Rogers, Rogers and Gregson, *Storm Center: The USS* Vincennes *and Iran Air Flight 655: A Personal Account of Tragedy and Terrorism*, 161.

Chapter 22: "GIVE ME THE KEY, GIVE ME THE KEY"

1. Crowe, "Second Endorsement on Rear Admiral Fogarty ltr. of 28 July 1988," 6.

2. Tom Wetherall, Author Interview.

3. Captain Keith F. Amacher, USN, "Letter to Editor," in *Proceedings* (December 1989), 20.

4. Ibid.

5. Crowe, "Second Endorsement on Rear Admiral Fogarty ltr. of 28 July 1988," 3.

Chapter 23: THEY DON'T FIGHT LIKE IRANIANS ANYMORE"

1. Major John F. Antal, "The Iraqi Army Forged in the Gulf War," in *Military Review* (February 1991), 60.

2. Tony Horowitz, *Baghdad With a Map and Other Misadventures in Arabia* (New York, NY, January 1, 1992), 126.

3. Serge Schmemann, "Iraq Acknowledges Its Use of Gas But Says Iran Introduced It In War," in *The New York Times* (July 2, 1988), Sect. 1-3.

4. Bernard E. Trainor, "Basra Failure altered Iran's view on war, analysts say," in *Houston Chronicle* (July 19, 1988), Sect. 1-10.

5. Ian Brown, *Khomeini's Forgotten Sons*, (London, England, August 29, 1990), 36.

6. U.S. Naipaul, "After the Revolution," in the *New Yorker* (May 26, 1997), 50.

7. Edgar O'Ballance, *The Gulf War* (Washington, DC, 1988), 246.

8. Robert Pear, "Iran Action Linked to Anti-War Mood," in *The New York Times* (July 22, 1988), A-6.
9. Navias and Houton, *Tanker Ward: The Assault on Merchant Shipping During the Iran-Iraq Conflict, 1980–88,* 164.
10. "Drifting Mines Pose New Threat to Ships in the Persian Gulf," in *Journal of Commerce* (November 29, 1988), 1813.
11. William Matthews, "A Year Hasn't Washed Away Loss of Stark Sailors," in *Navy Times* (May 30, 1988), 4.

INDEX

ABC News, 91

Abu al-Bukush oil field, 211

Abu Musa Island, 66-67, 223-225, 227-230, 242, 253, 257, 295-296

"Aegis arrogance", 299, 342

Aegis radar system, 89, 296-297, 305-308, 315, 317-318, 329, 333, 336, 338, 344-345, 348, 351, 353, 355, 357, 359-361, 363, 365, 367-368, 372

Aerogulf, 226-227

Aerospatiale Company, 29

Afghanistan, 31

AIM-7 Sparrow air-to-air missile, 90

Air Medal, Collier, Lt. Mark, USMC, 322

Airborne Warning and Control aircraft (AWACS), 7-9, 16, 43-44, 51, 60, 68, 106, 129, 208, 228, 237, 280

aircraft, Iran:

C-130, 271-272, 276-277, 282-284, 310, 319

F-4 Phantom, 65-66, 89-90, 228, 236-237, 263, 276, 302

F-14 Tomcat, 296, 303, 305, 308, 310, 316-318, 351, 354, 357, 360, 362, 368- 369, 371-373, 375-376

P-3 Orion, 304-305, 365, 371, 376

SH-3, 119

aircraft, Iraq:

Mirage F-1, 8-10, 16, 41-44, 46-47, 49-52

Super Etandard fighter, 29, 51

TU-16 "Badger", 180

aircraft, Saudi Arabia:

F-15, 8

aircraft, United States:

A-6E Intruder, 208, 227-229, 243- 251, 253-256, 283, 300, 352-353

A-7E Corsair, 227, 246-247, 250- 251, 300

AH-1 Cobra helicopter, 114, 209, 256

AH-58 Warrior helicopter, 186

AH-58D Kiowa helicopter, 184-185, 380-382

AH-6 attack helicopter, 80-81, 103- 105, 107-108, 111-112, 132, 138- 142, 146, 149, 182, 184, 186

AH-64 Apache helicopter, 184

C-130, 278

C-141 Starlifter, 23

C-5A Galaxy, 79, 81, 84, 103

CH-46 helicopter, 113, 117, 146, 198, 205, 209, 213

E-2C Hawkeye, 89, 156, 209, 227-

228, 230, 243-247, 251, 254-255, 278, 300

E-3A "Sentry" Airborne Warning and Control aircraft (AWACS), 7, 60, 208

EA-6B Prowler, 87, 168, 208, 243-244, 269, 278

F-14 Tomcat, 89, 156, 208, 227-228, 243-244, 246, 253, 255, 271-272, 278, 300, 307, 349-350

F-4 Phantom, 246, 273

KA-6 tanker, 227

KC-10 tanker, 208-209, 227, 253

MH-6 observation helicopter, 80-81, 101, 103, 105, 107-111, 121, 132, 138-140, 142, 146, 149, 182, 184-186

MH-60, 219-221, 233, 257-258

Navy LAMPS, 182-183, 216, 218, 237

OH-58D helicopter, 184, 379

P-3C Orion, 58, 89, 106, 129, 336, 343

RH-53D minesweeping helicopter, 82

SH-2F LAMPS Mk I helicopter, 103, 138-139, 144, 209, 217, 231, 239, 241-242, 250, 272

SH-2J helicopter, 248

Navy SH-60 LAMPS III helicopter, 209, 217

SH-60B helicopter, 69, 128, 197, 211, 221, 335

UH-1 "Huey", 101, 213

UH-60 Blackhawk, 128, 132, 217-218, 241

UH-IN transports, 209

Al Ahmadi channel, port and terminal, 83, 96, 170

Al Rekkah, freighter, 64

Alborz, Iranian frigate, 342-346

Al-Faw peninsula, 5, 30, 32, 35, 151, 154, 172, 258, 264, 279-280, 283, 382-383

Algiers Accords of 1975, 1-2

Ali Khamenei, Iranian President, 88, 120-121, 153, 313

Ali Montazeri, Ayatollah Hussein, 313-314

Alvand, supertanker, 96

Amacker, Capt. Keith F., USN, 365-366

Amam Hassanpoor, Abdul, 311

American Red Cross, 22

Anderson, Cmdr. Samuel K., 288

Anderson, PO Richard, USN, 302-303, 318-320

Anita, 92, 94,

USS Antrim, (FFG-20), 49, 80, 103, 387

Arabian Sea, 58-59, 61, 84, 156, 163, 168, 175, 177, 300, 352, 356

Army Helicopter Improvement program, 185

Aspin, Les, 74

Atlantic Fleet, 53

Atlantic Fleet Mobile Training Team, 8

Atlantic Fleet Naval Special Warfare Task Unit, 127

Aviation Week, 277

Baghdad, Iraq, 31, 49, 60, 65, 181, 388

USS Bagley, (FF-1069), 217-219, 231-232, 237-239, 241

Bahrain, 7, 9, 16, 22-24, 54, 64, 68, 80-81, 96, 100, 114, 118, 122, 126, 130, 155, 168, 200, 209-210, 297-299, 309, 314, 357, 371

Bahrain Defense Forces Search and Rescue, 21

Ballad of the Jack Williams, 288

Bandar Abbas, 65, 89, 91, 106, 120, 168, 177, 206, 209, 228, 237, 242—243, 251, 254-257, 272,

291, 296-297, 301-304, 309, 311, 313, 319, 324, 326, 343, 349, 351, 371, 373
Bandar Abbas Naval Ammunition Depot, 61
Barbour, Lt. Carl S., USN, 14
Bareford, Mark, USN, 14
Basra, Iraq, 3, 5, 383-384
Bath Iron Works, 188, 201
Battle Group Foxtrot, 208
Bavle, Robert, 225
Beheresht, Firouz, 285
Beirut, Lebanon, 128-129
Belton, Betty, 23
Belton, Mack, 23
Berg, Lt. Cmdr. Paul D., 272
Bernsen, Rear Adm. Harold, 16, 24, 40-41, 68, 73, 91-92, 105-106, 108-109, 113, 126, 131, 135, 160, 175-177
Bethea, Capt. W. Dallas, 206-207, 261-263, 266-267, 273, 289
Bier, Cmdr. Gary, USN, 156-162
"Black Monday", 170
Blackburn, Gerry, 92
Blaisdell, Lt. Steven, 197
Bracca, CPO Douglas, USN, 166
Bridgeton, mining of, 63-65, 69-75, 78, 80-83, 86, 88, 92-93, 95-96, 98, 105, 124-125, 175
Brindel, Capt. Glen, 7-10, 13, 17, 20, 24; Adm. Sharp recommends dereliction of duty charges, 43; assessing blame, 46; blames equipment, 53; blames his subordinates, 43; brief of ROE, 43; command failure, 41; Moncrief's loyalty toward, 43; plan to court martial, 41; retires, 52; salvage tug to the rescue, 49; Sharp Report, 39-40
Brinkley, Maj. Clyde, USMC, 213
Bronze Star, Anderson, Cmdr. Samuel K., 288

Brooks, Adm. Dennis M., 85-86, 130-131, 156-157, 175-176, 177, 330-332
Brown and Root, 126-128
Brzezinski, Zbigniew, 72
Bubiyan Island, 30, 35, 172
Bucher, Capt. Lloyd, USN, 145
USS *Bunker Hill*, (CG-52), 168
Byrd, Senator Robert, 72

C-601 missile, 180
Caouette, Seaman Mark R., USN, 15
Carlson, Cmdr. David R., 303-308, 329-330, 334, 339, 343-344, 346, 365
Carlucci, Frank, 74, 228, 255-257, 286-293
Carter, President Jimmy, 72
Casey, William, 148
Central Intelligence Agency, 58-60, 90, 121, 134, 148
Chandler, Capt. James F., USN, 217-220, 230, 232-239, 341-342, 344, 364
USS *Chandler*, (DDG-996), 180-181
Chesapeake Shipping, Inc., 64
Chicago Tribune, 334
Clemenceau, French aircraft carrier, 93, 294
Clement, Lt. Cmdr. Robert, USN, 89-90
Clinefelter, S/CPO Gary, 24-25
Collier, Lt. Mark, USMC, 299, 322-333
"combat mindset", 45
Conklin, Lt. William A., USN, 15, 17-18
USS *Constellation*, (CV-64), 54, 61, 65, 89
Contingency Marine Air-Ground Task Force (MAGTF) 2-88, 212
Convention on International Civil Aviation, 326

USS *Conyngham,* (DDG-17), 21, 45
USS *Coontz,* (DDG-40), 8, 42, 45, 51
USS *Coronado,* (AGF-11), 207, 228, 269, 309
Covington, Cmdr. Craig, 211
Crescent Petroleum Company, 224, 226-227
Crist, Gen. George W., USMC, 57-59, 85, 103, 129, 175, 181, 213, 228, 277, 283, 295, 315, 317, 322, 371, 375
USS *Crommelin,* (FFG-37), 64-65, 69, 75, 87-88, 98
Crosby, CPO Earl, USN, 188-189
Crowe, Jr., Adm. William J., 130; Army helicopters on Navy ships, 103; attack on the USS *Gary,* 275-276, 287-288; *Bridgeton* attack, 71, 74, 76, 85, 87; Iran Air Disaster, 311-312, 316, 330-333, 338-340, 345-349, 363; *Iran Ajr,* 121-122; Mobile Sea Bases, 128, 131; Operation "Earnest Will", 56, 59; Operation "Nimble Archer", 155; Operation "Praying Mantis", 207, 255-256; relieves Adm. Brooks, 176-177
Cruz, EW2 Fernando, 191
Cyrano IV radar, 9, 46

Dahran, Saudi Arabia, 7, 146, 209, 274, 289
Dahulagiri, merchant ship, 298-299
David Taylor Model Basin, 202
De Zinnia, merchant ship, 95
DeAngelis, Robert, 23
Decca 68 search radar, 159
de-conflictation, 60, 179-181, 261, 273, 324, 349
Defense Intelligence Agency, 90, 148
Dejno, Mark, USN, 192
Demetra Beauty, freighter, 387

Dena, tanker, 178
Deramonde, Adm. Francois, 294
"Desert One", 101
Desert Storm, 387
Destroyer Squadron 9, 209
Destroyer Squadron 14, 64, 179
Destroyer Squadron 22, 241
Destroyer Squadron 25, 156, 298, 300, 340-342
Detachment 160 Aviation Group, 103
Diego Garcia, 84
Dodd, CPO Chris, USN, 379-382
Dotterway, Capt. Kristen Ann, USAF, 353-354, 356
Dubai, UAE, 31, 51, 74, 96, 201, 206, 297, 301-302, 310-311, 323, 325
Dyer, Capt. Donald, USN, 241-244, 255, 262, 272, 276, 288-289, 341

"Eager Glacier" program, 58, 134
USS *Elmer Montgomery,* (FF-1082), 296-301, 306-307, 309-310, 316, 320, 322, 334-335, 338, 340, 346, 352, 364, 370-373, 376-377
USS *Elrod,* (FFG-55), 335
embassy hostage crisis, 8
Emergency Escape Breathing Devices (EEB), 15, 21-22
Engler, Lt. Cmdr. Jim, USN, 227-230, 253-255
USS *Enterprise,* (CVN-55), 208-210, 227-229, 242, 244-246, 252, 271, 294-295
Erwin, Steve and Nancy, 24, 387
Etnyre, Cmdr. Terrance T., 211
Evancoe, Cmdr. Paul, USN, 77-79, 114-118, 127-128, 133, 135, 137-138, 142, 145-146
Evans, Lt. Col. David, USMC, 334
"exclusion zone", Iranian declared, 8, 50-51, 380

Exocet missile, 7, 9-13, 15-18, 21, 27-29, 34, 37, 41-42, 44, 46-48, 51, 53, 79

Explosive Ordnance Disposal (EOD), 21, 83, 113, 116, 122, 163-165, 167-168, 172, 205, 215

Failaka Island, 35, 172

Falklands War, 17, 48, 248

Farchain, Lt. Comdr. Mohammad, IR, 119-120

Farsi Island, 66, 68-69, 72-73, 75, 83, 112, 127, 130, 134, 136-137, 145, 147, 154-155, 178, 182, 184, 261-263, 270, 273-274, 379, 380, 382

Federal Bureau of Investigation, 327-328

Fereidoon oil field, 144-145

Ferran, Bill "Bear", USN, 89-90

Fifth Fleet, 100

Filikon L, tanker, 27, 386

"Filipino Monkey", 96-100

Firehammer, Lt. Robert, USN, 189

Fitzwater, Marvin, 62, 71, 90, 153

Flannigan, Dick, USN, 127

USS *Flatley*, (FFG-21), 112

flechette round, 117

Fogarty, Rear Adm. William M., 315-316, 332, 336-337, 350, 354-356, 362

Fogarty Commission, 357, 359, 370, 374

"Fogarty Report", 315-316, 318, 320-324, 329-334, 338-339, 346, 348-349, 351, 353-355, 357-358, 360-361, 366-367, 374

Ford, Kevin, USN, 195

USS *Forrestal*, (CV-59), 300, 352

Fortuneship L, tanker, 178

Forward Looking Infra-Red (FLIR) viewing device, 80, 101, 104, 107, 109, 111, 121, 132, 138-140, 142, 185-186, 244, 248-250, 253

Foster, Ernestine, 23

Foster, Vernon, USN, 23

USS *Fox*, (CG-33), 64-68, 70, 84

Fridley, Dick, USN, 202

Frost, George, USN, 200-201

Fujairah, UAE, 91-92, 95

Furuno surface radar, 132-133, 182

Gable, Timothy, USN, 15-16, 21

Gajan, Lt. Cmdr. Ray, USN, 9, 12, 17, 20, 39, 41, 43, 53

Garrett, Lawrence, 330-331

USS *Gary*, (FFG 51), 206-208, 261-270, 273-274, 277, 279-282, 289, 364, 366

Gas Al Minagish, tanker, 64

Gas King, tanker, 88, 96

Gas Kuwait, tanker, 189

Gas Prince, tanker, 64-65, 70, 75, 87

Gas Queen, tanker, 189

Gee, Capt. George N., USN, 366-368

Ghorbanifar, Manucher, 33

Glen Eagle Company, 388

Glenn, Senator John, 337

Goldwater-Nichols Defense Reorganization, 85

Grabowsky, Capt. Ted, 265

Grand Ayatollah Qami, 384

Great Britain, 93-94

Grenada, invasion of, 64

USS *Guadalcanal*, (LPH-7), 84, 98, 112-113, 117, 163, 168

Guillory, Lt. Cmdr. Vic, USN, 305-306, 367-368

Gulf of Kuwait, 92

Gulf of Oman, 58, 65, 88, 91, 93-94, 125, 154-155, 177, 218, 242, 349, 352-353

Gulf War, 289

USS *Halsey*, (DDG-97), 370

USS *Halyburton*, (FFG-40), 323

Hanks, Rear Adm. Robert, USN, 73
Hanson, Lt. (jg) William A., USN, 13
Harirud, tug, 123
Harpoon anti-ship missile, 17, 208, 232, 233, 235-236, 238-240, 243, 245-249, 253-254, 276-277, 280, 282-284, 286, 343, 364
Harris, Brent, USN, 161
Hartmann, Dr. Gregory K., 83
Hashemi Rafsanjani, Ali-Akbar, 30, 52, 62, 67, 75, 95-96, 121, 258-259, 313- 314, 385-386
Hastings, Capt. Thomas, USMC, 214
Hattan, Capt. Robert, 343-346
Havglimt, tanker, 206-207
USS *Hawes,* (FFG-53), 98, 122-123
Hawk anti-aircraft missile, 52, 129, 171-172, 254
Hays, Adm. Ronald J., 85
Hellifre laser-guided antitank missile, 185
Hengam Island, 306, 309, 332-333
Herat, Afghanistan, 148
Hill, Capt. Kenneth, USMC, 257
USS *Hoel*, (DDG-13), 156-159, 161-162, 168
Hoffman, Fred S., 169
Holloway, Stan, 77
Horriyat, tug, 119
Hosely, Al, 380, 381-382
House Armed Services Committee, 330
Huff, Lt. Roger, USMC, 299
Hunt, John, 152-153
Hunter, tug, 89, 96, 200
Hussein, Saddam, 1-3, 5, 29, 36, 50, 54, 178, 258, 382, 388

Ibn Rashid, Kuwaiti freighter, 54
International Air Distress, 304, 306-307, 358, 372
International Civil Aviation Organization, 325, 332

Iran Air Flight 655, (shoot down of), 297, 301-305, 307-310, 313-315, 319, 323, 325-327, 329, 332, 345, 351-353, 370, 372-373, 386-387
Iran air tragedy, 313, 315-318, 322, 326-327, 332
Iran Ajr, attack on, 106-107, 109-124, 126, 130, 146, 175, 186, 205, 240, 292, 330, 387
Iran Bayan, tanker, 177, 280
Iran: admits planting mines, 95; attacking tankers, 7, 27-29; attacks Kuwait, 29; crossed "Silkworm threshold", 259, 274-275; "exclusion zone" Iranian declared, 8, 50-51, 380; fires Silkworm into Kuwait, 35; increase exports of oil, 178; *Iran Ajr* response, 123, 313; Kharg Island oil terminal, 27; minelaying, 69, 71, 90, 95, 121, 190-194, 197, 205-206, 292-293; mines the *Bridgeton*, 69-72; navy frigates, 27; not looking for a confrontation, 67; oil exports, 7; oil production, 27; on defensive in gulf, 292; pressure on Kuwait, 35; revolution, 32; small boats, 68; supplies food for Mobile Support Base, 134; threats against shipping, 32; "Twin Pillars" policy, 31; warns it would use mines, 74
Iran-Contra scandal, 32-34, 36, 52
Iranian Islamic revolution, 30
Iranian National Shipping Lines, 106
Iranian Revolutionary Guard Corps (IRGC), 2, 27-28, 87-88, 94, 127, 137-138, 148, 151, 153, 155, 206, 210, 223, 225-227, 230, 240, 243, 257, 282, 293, 296, 298, 349, 382-383
Iranian Supreme Defense Council, 95

Iran-Iraq war, 1, 7, 27, 29, 31, 39, 56, 61

Iraq, 7, 27-28, 30, 32, 39-41, 51-52, 57, 73, 96, 179, 261

Islamic Republic, 33

Islamic Republic News Agency, 257

Italy, 94

Ivan Koroteyev, Soviet freighter, 31

USS *Iwo Jima*, (LHD-7), 84

USS *Jack Williams*, (FFG 24), 241-243, 248-251, 255, 257, 269-273, 275-279, 284, 288

Jackson, Bob, 225-226

Jane's Fighting Ships, 73

USS *Jarrett*, (FFG-33), 88, 98, 103, 106-113, 118, 120

USS *John A. Moore*, (FFG-19), 177, 186

USS *John Hancock*, (DD 981), 298

John Hopkins University, 202

USS *John Young*, (DD-973), 156, 161-162

Joint Chiefs of Staff, 53, 60, 86-87, 103, 121-122, 128, 148, 155, 176-177, 184, 207, 228, 275, 287, 330

Joint Task Force Middle East (JTFME), 85-86, 130, 156, 165, 175-177, 181, 190, 205-207, 228, 230, 232, 236-237, 243, 255, 262-263, 268-269, 281, 283, 292, 299, 305, 309-310, 320-321, 324-325, 330, 332, 334, 339-343, 345, 347, 349, 352, 371, 375

Jokar, tanker, 242

Jolly Rubino, container ship, 94

Jones, Lt. Dave, USN, 165

USS *Joseph Strauss*, (DDG 16), 63, 241, 243-244, 246, 248-249, 253, 269-273, 278-279, 284, 288

Joshan, Iranian patrol boat, 231-240, 246, 283, 285, 364

USS *Kansas City*, (AOR-3), 157

Karama Maersk, tanker, 296

Karen Island, 131, 273

Katrina Maersk, supertanker, 242

Kelly, Rear Adm. Robert, 337

Kelso II, Adm. Frank B., 53

Kennedy, Senator Ted, 55

Kharg Island, 27, 172, 231

Khark 4, tanker, 178

Khawla, transport, 387

Khayyam, tug, 119

Khomeini, Ayatollah Ruollah, 1-4, 153, 313-314, 326, 385

Khor Fakkan, UAE, 65, 91-92, 95, 209

Khorassani, Rajaie, 72

USS *Kidd*, (DDG-993), 64-65, 70, 73, 75-76, 87-88, 112, 122-123, 155-156, 161- 162, 168, 179

King Fahd, 154

Kiser, PO Steve and Barbara, 24

Kissinger, Henry, 31

Kosnick, Lt. Mark, USN, 209-210

Kouroosh, Iranian warship, (ex-USS *Kidd*) 156

Kuwait, 1, 29, 31, 59, 84, 88, 96, 126, 169-170; Iran attacks ships carrying oil, 7; Iran fires Silkworms at, 35; now an Iranian target, 171; played Soviet Union against the U.S., 56; re-flagging ships, 31, 34-36, 39, 54-59, 61-65, 68, 71, 73, 86-87, 103, 125, 151, 154, 171, 175, 177, 180, 189, 322, 388; Silkworm missile attack, 154; supports Iraq, 30

Kuwaiti Oil Tanker Company, 30, 64, 126, 200

USS *La Salle*, (AGF-3), 9, 16, 21, 51, 73, 81, 103, 105-107, 109, 112-113, 116, 118-120, 177, 268

Langston, Cmdr. Bud, USN, 243-
    246, 248, 251-253
Larak Island, 241, 253
Larak, Iranian ship, 256, 258
Larguier, Capt. "Izzy", USN, 156,
    159-160, 162
Lavan Island, 120
Leach, PO John, USN, 302-303, 308,
    318
USS *Leftwhich*, (DD-984), 156, 160-
    162
Leslie, Capt. Stephen, 257
Less, Rear Adm. Anthony, 175, 177,
    190, 193-194, 197, 203, 205,
    207, 209, 228, 236-237, 243-244,
    255, 273, 292, 294, 300-301,
    305, 310, 321, 332,
340-345, 347, 371-372
Lewis, Howard, USN, 116
Liquid Petroleum Gas (LPG) tankers,
    28, 59, 88
Llewellyn, Lt. David, USN, 199
"locking-on", 11-12, 41, 46, 66
London *Daily Times*, 73, 149
USS *Long Beach*, (CGN-9), 86, 156-
    157
Lustig, Lt. Cmdr. Scott, USN, 305-
    306, 308, 318, 320, 322, 355,
    358, 366-368, 370-373, 375-376
Luttwak, Edward, 336
USS *Lynde McCormick*, (DDG-8),
    209, 211-213, 216
Lyons, Adm. James A., 85

M-08 type mine, 91-92
Mahone, Gary, USN, 16, 21
Manama, Bahrain, 8, 39
HMS *Manchester*, 352-353
Mann, Cmdr. Edward, USN, 241
Marine Expeditionary Unit, Special
    Operations Capable, 77
Marine Special Operations Task Unit,
    78

Marine Squadron HML/A-167, 209
Marshal Chuykow, Soviet tanker, 35
Massey, Dwayne, USN, 22
Matecvun, Cmdr. John, 354
Mathews, Maj. Tom, USA, 80
Mathis, Captain William, USN, 65,
    67-68, 70
Matthews, Lt. Cmdr. Timothy, USN,
    197
Maverick TV-guided missile, 350
Mayport Naval Station, 22-24, 64
McCain, Senator John, 336
McFarland, Robert C., 33, 148
McKenna, Capt. Richard, USN, 298-
    301, 341-342
McLeod, William, USN, 15, 21
McTigue, Capt. James, USN, 182-
    183, 217-218, 233-235, 237-239,
    364, 388
USS *Merrill*, (DD-976), 209-216
Middle East Force, 9, 16, 19, 40-41,
    46, 58-60, 68, 73, 85, 91, 105,
    108, 112-114, 125-126, 135, 145,
    147, 160, 175-177, 181
Middle Shoals Buoy, action at, 138-
    139, 144-145, 147, 150, 176, 184
Mighty Servant II, heavy lift ship,
    201
Military Air Distress, 304, 306-307,
    358
Military Air Distress Frequency, 9-
    11, 16
Mina Al Ahmadi, port of, 30, 35, 59,
    65, 127, 151
mine countermeasures, 81-85, 92-95,
    99, 125
mine warfare, 82, 125, 190-194,
    197, 205, 292, 387
Mine Warfare School, 78
minefields, 292-293
minesweeping boats, 78, 82
Mir Hussein Moussavi, Iranian Prime
    Minister, 54, 72, 86

"Mirage Alley", 8
USS *Missouri*, (BB-63), 64, 86, 168
MK-68 Fire Control System, 157
MK-92 Fire Control System, 11
Mobile Sea Base, 126-127, 129-130, 133, 184-185, 208, 261, 264, 267-270, 277, 279-280, 287, 293, 337, 364; Hercules "Fort Apache", 127-135, 137-138, 142-147, 150, 178, 182, 186, 262-263, 268, 281, 288-289, 294, 379-380; Wimbrown VII, 127, 130-131, 176, 186, 217, 265, 273, 281, 287, 294
MODE II IFF Signal (Military), 303, 305, 318-319, 359, 369, 371-372
MODE III IFF Signal (Civilian), 302, 305-306, 316, 318-319, 369, 371-372
Moncrief, Lt. Basil, USN, 8-12, 17, 39-41, 43, 48, 52
Montfort, Lt. William, USN, 305-306, 376
Moore, John, 73
Moorer, Rear Adm. Thomas H., 53
Morandi, PO William, 15, 21
Mubarak oil field, 223-225, 227, 242-243, 284-285, 291
Mubarak, President, 173
Murphy, Daniel I., USN, 179
Murphy, Cmdr. Richard W., USN, 62, 71, 73
Mustin, Adm. Henry, 276

Namdoon, Nizar, 51
National Military Command Center, 268
National Security Agency, 90
National Security Council, 34-35, 61
Naval Forces Central Command, 85
Naval Institute Proceedings, 329
Naval Investigative Service, 327
naval special warfare boats, 79-80

Naval Special Warfare Group 1, 265
Naval Special Warfare Group 2, 77
Naval Special Warfare Task Unit, 217
Naval War College, 333
Navy Commendation Medal; Berg, Lt. Cmdr. Paul D., 273; Lustig, Lt. Cmdr. Scott, USN, 322
Navy Special Boat Units, 126, 134
Navy Squadron HM-14, 84
Needler, Lt. Cmdr. Mark, USN, 246-250
Newsweek, 81, 330, 332, 348
USS *Nicholas*, (FFG-47), 379-380, 382
Nicholson, Dan, USN, 198
Nightline, 330, 346
North Atlantic Treaty Organization, 82
Nortz, Lt. Cmdr. Joe, USN, 227
Nutwell, Capt. Robert M., USN, 211

Oakley, Robert, 35
USS *O'Brien*, (DD 975), 241, 249, 270-272, 282
Ocean City, tanker, 88, 96
Office of Naval Intelligence, 87
O'Keefe, Michael, USN, 14
Oman, 58, 89, 123
Operation "Earnest Will", 58-59, 62-64, 91, 95, 102, 123, 131, 151, 180, 187, 189, 208, 258, 292, 323, 336
Operation "Martyrdom", 87-88, 92
Operation "Nimble Archer", 155, 210, 219, 226, 279, 285, 387
Operation "Praying Mantis", 207, 209, 218, 241, 257, 259, 275, 277, 282-283, 286-287, 289, 291, 293-295, 322, 337, 344, 350, 364, 367, 387
Operation "Prime Chance II", 185
Operation "Prime Chance", 103

Organization of the Islamic
    Conference, 34-35
Oxygen Breathing Apparatus (OBA),
    19, 49, 66, 203

Pacific Command, 59, 85
Pacific Fleet, 53
Pacific Fleet SEAL Commandos, 241
Pan Am Flight 103, 326-327
Papadakis, Lt. Bob, USN, 243-246
Patrol Boat, Iran, (Boghammer), 140-
    143, 147, 150, 228-229, 231,
    242, 253, 300-301, 338, 347, 350
Patrol Boat, United States:
Mark III, 78, 122, 133, 137, 142;
Seafox, 103, 130, 138-139, 143;
Zodiac, 111, 121-122
Pegasus I, tanker, 387
Pentagon cover up, 259
People's Republic of China, 34
Perez, Alex, USN, 191
Perkins, Capt. James B., 209-213,
    215-216
Perot, Ross, 128
Perry, Chaplain Bill, 22
Persian Gulf, 1, 7, 27, 54, 59, 71-72,
    88, 93, 312, 324
Phalanx Close In Weapon System
    (CIWS), 11, 42, 45, 48, 53, 58,
    157-158, 265, 267
Phoenix air-to-air missile, 52
Pirouzi, Houssein, 326
Ponturier, Lt. Augustine, USN, 269-
    270
Porter, Timothy, USN, 15, 21, 387
Powell, Colin, 154
USS *Pueblo,* (AGER-2), 145
Pyle, Richard, 323

"Q" Route, 292-293
Qatar, 106, 123, 189
Qeshem Island, 271, 278, 295
Quainton, Anthony, 71

Queshem Island, 273, 278

Rakesh oil platform, 207, 216
Rakish, Iranian minelayer, 330
Rakow, Col. William M., USMC,
    212
USS *Raleigh*, (LPD-1), 78-80, 145-
    146
USS *Ranger*, (CV-61), 154, 156, 168
Rashadat oil platform, 155-156, 160,
    170-171, 221
Razeui, Massoud, 326
Reagan, President Ronald, and his
    administration, 24-25, 32-33, 36,
    53-55, 71, 84, 88, 90, 92-94, 96,
    113, 126, 148, 154, 170,
    203,205, 228, 275, 286, 293,
    312-314, 322
USS *Reasoner*, (FF 1063), 242, 259
Red Crescent Society, 146
Red Sea, 59
"Reef Point", 58, 89
USS *Reeves*, (CG-24), 84, 112
re-flagged Kuwaiti ships, 31, 34-36,
    39, 54-65, 68, 71, 73, 86-87, 103,
    125, 151, 154, 171, 175, 177,
    180, 189, 322, 388
Rehwald, Lt. (jg) Steve, 268
USS *Rentz*, (FFG-46), 168
USS *Reuben James*, (FFG-57), 180,
    218
Rezaian, Mohsen, 301-302
Richards, Cmdr. Tom, USN, 217,
    287
Rinn, Cmdr. Paul X., 187-203
Riydah, Saudi Arabia, 60
Roark, Lt. Jonathan USN, 142-146
Rockeye, cluster bomb, 253-254
Rogers, Capt. Will III, 298-301, 305-
    308, 310, 317, 328-329, 337,
    348, 353; aggressiveness, 341-359;
    bridge discipline, 366; control guy,
    367-368; crew stress issues, 367-

368; formal investigation, 315-317, 320-321, 327, 332-333, 354-355, 358, 373; his defense, 335-336, 339-340; loose cannon, 375-376; placing blame, 346; responsibility to protect ship and crew, 377; "Sea of Lies", 334, 352, 354-355; shootout with Iranian gunboats, 372, 374-376; shoots down Iran Air, 363, 373

Rogers, Rear Adm. David N., 49

Rostam oilfield, 155, 159, 163, 284, 292

Rourke, Lt. Jonathan G., 331

Rules of Engagement, 40-41, 43, 53, 89, 108, 188, 210, 245, 299, 321, 338-339, 341, 344, 377

Rush, Lt. Cmdr. Richard, USN, 232-234

Ryals, Earl and Susan, 23

SA-7 Strella anti-aircraft missile, 152, 172, 245, 253, 258

Sabalan, Iranian frigate, 206-208, 218, 236, 241-242, 244, 253-256, 275, 282-283, 286, 291

Sahand, Iranian frigate, 206, 245-246, 248-252, 254, 275, 282-285, 288, 291, 388

SAM-7 missile, 333

Samples, G/M Mark, 20

USS *Samuel Gompers*, (AD-37), 217-218

USS *Samuel Roberts*, (FFG-58), 187-189, 197, 200, 203, 209, 211, 217-218, 256, 363, 366; strikes a mine, 190-199, 201-203, 205

USS San Jose, (AFS-7), 189, 197, 200

Sandle, Kim, USN, 191, 196

Sarghoda, tanker, 297

Sasser, Senator James, 54

Sasson oil platform, 207, 210-211, 216-217, 219-220

Saudi Arabia, 7-8, 27, 29, 31, 52, 75, 84, 106, 126, 154, 171

Scan Bay, barge rig, 225, 227

"scenario fulfillment", 316, 328, 357-358, 362

Schork, Cmdr. John, USN, 247-249, 251-252

Schultz, George, 33-34, 154

SCUD missile, 258, 384

Sea Island terminal, attack on, 170-173, 293

Sea Isle City, tanker, attack on, 88, 96, 151-154, 279

Sea Killer anti-ship missile, 242, 251, 276, 282-283

"Sea of Lies", 334, 348, 352-357

Sea of Oman, 87

SEABAT team, 106-107, 109-110, 130-133, 138-139, 146, 148, 182-183, 211, 256-257

"Seafox," naval special warfare boats, 79

Seakiller missile, 27

Seely, Bernard, USN, 12-13

Seitz, Frank C., 64, 69-70, 74

Selah Oil Field, 242-243, 270, 279, 288

Senate Armed Services Committee, 56, 73

Senate Foreign Relations Committee, 55

Seventh Fleet, 85, 352

Shah Alum Shoals, 205, 292

Shah of Iran, 8, 34, 156

Sharp Report, 39-40, 43, 45, 48

Sharp, Rear Admiral Grant, 39, 43

Shatt al-Arab waterway, 1-2, 151, 258, 279, 388

HMS *Sheffield*, 16, 48

show-the-flag, 60

Shuaiba oil loading terminal, 151, 170

USS *Sides*, (FFG 14), 297-298, 300,

302-307, 309-310, 319-320, 329, 340, 343-334, 350-351, 365, 370-371

"Silkworm Envelope", 58, 67, 158, 242, 271, 273, 345

Silkworm missiles, attacks and issues, 34-35, 54, 56, 61-62, 65-68, 73, 87-89, 151-152, 154-155, 157-158, 170, 172, 177, 180-181, 255, 264-266, 269-271, 274-277, 279-282, 284, 286-289, 293, 295, 336-338, 344, 364, 367

Silkworm threshold, 259, 285-286, 337, 344

USS *Simpson*, (FFG-56), 182-183, 211, 217-221, 231-235, 237-239, 241, 273, 364, 366, 388

Sirri Island and oil platform, 96, 180, 207, 216, 218-219, 221, 230-232, 239

Sitra Bay, Bahrain, 21

Skipper bomb, 249-250, 284

SLQ-32 ECM system, 46-47

SM-1 missile, 237-238

SM-2ER missile, 237

Smith, Cmdr. Steve, 180-181

Soviet Navy, 82-83

Soviet Union, 31

Special Boat Unit 20, 77, 85, 114, 127, 134, 137, 142

special warfare task unit, 184, 331

USS *Spruance*, (DD-963), 352

SQQ-14 sonar, 84

Standard missile, 233-234, 308-309, 321

USS *Standley*, (CG-32), 112, 165, 168

USS *Stark*, (FFG-31), 37, 39, 175, 178, 196, 199, 203, 322-325, 377, 387; administration blames Iran, 53; assessing blame, 41-47, 49, 52, 54-55; attack on, 8-21, 27, 46, 52; attack took heavy tool of America's prestige, 48; bodies returned home, 23; Congress wakes up, 55; damage control, 14-21; decision not to prosecute officers, 53; de-confliction procedures, 60; demonstrated the hazards of inaction, 53; draws U.S. deeper into Gulf, 54; failure to sound General Quarters, 42; frigate design a mistake, 45; inside the Exclusion Zone, 51; Iraqi pilot did not hear warnings, 50; lack of "combat mindset", 45; "low end" ship, 48; not giving an aggressive impression, 42-43; Oliver Hazard Perry-class frigate, 47-48; one-fifth of crew dead, 17; Persian Gulf, 7-8; Reagan's eulogy, 24; resentment against the media, 22-23; retaliation for Iran-Contra, 52; Sharp Report, 40; towed by USS *Conyngham*, 21

stinger anti-aircraft missile, 17, 129, 143, 147-150, 158, 185, 265-266, 268-269, 294, 333

Stoval, tanker, 331

Strait of Hormuz, 28, 32, 34, 36, 54, 60-61, 65, 67, 84, 87-89, 91, 97, 99, 103, 125, 154-155, 157, 163, 168, 206-209, 227-228, 241-242, 248, 262, 264, 269-270, 273, 282,285, 291, 293, 295, 297, 324, 337, 352

Striker, tug, 89

Stubblefield, Cmdr. Gary, USN, 265-266, 273, 287, 294

Styx anti-ship missile, 34,

Sungari, Liberian tanker, 154

Super Rapid Bloom Off Board Chaff launcher (SRBOC), 10, 12, 42, 47

Surf City, tanker, 388

surface action group, 231-232, 233, 237

Surface Action Group "Alfa", 156, 159-160, 163, 168
Surface Action Group "Bravo", 207, 209-211, 216
Surface Action Group "Charlie", 207, 210, 216-217, 230, 237, 283, 364
Surface Action Group "Delta", 207-208, 241-244, 246, 248, 255-257, 262, 269-271, 276-277, 282-284, 289
surface combat air patrol (SUCAP), 208-209, 242, 244, 246, 255, 269, 285, 300, 352
Swiss Embassy, 314

Tactical Air Defense Alerting Radars, 293
Tactical Decision Making Under Stress (TADMUS), 317
"tanker war", 1, 7, 27-28, 32, 44, 57, 382, 386
Target Number 4131, 303-307, 318, 320, 351-355, 360
Target Number 4474, 303, 308, 351-355
Tariq Aziz, Iranian Deputy Foreign Minister, 49, 383
Task Force 118, 184-186, 266, 379-380, 382
Task Force 160, 101-103, 105-106, 109, 112, 115-117, 122, 125, 127, 131-132, 134, 137, 139, 143, 146, 148-150, 182-183, 185-186, 211, 217, 220, 231, 241, 256
Tehran, Iraq, 2, 31, 33, 35, 56, 75, 88, 95, 155, 285, 309, 313-314, 385
Texaco Caribbean, tanker, 91-92, 95
USS *Thatch*, (FFG-43), 138, 145-146, 156, 160, 163, 165, 167-168
Thatcher, Prime Minister Margaret, 93-94

Tilley, Mike, USN, 193, 201
Toricelli, Congressman Robert, 54
TOW II wire-guided anti-tank missile, 52, 130, 215
USS *Trenton*, (LPD-14), 197, 205, 209, 211-212, 256
Trost, Adm. Carlyle H., USN, 354
"Twin Pillars" policy, 31

Umm Al Maradex, Kuwaiti tanker, 151
United Arab Emirates, 60, 65, 91, 92, 95, 97, 161, 181, 206, 209, 211, 223- 225, 227-228, 230, 243, 248, 251, 270, 291, 297, 301
United States Government; declares neutrality in Iran-Iraq war, 61; goal to prevent Iran victory, 33; Gulf commitment a shambles, 275; Gulf situation needs a reappraisal, 86; Iranian hostages, 32-33; no retaliation for Sea Island attack, 171; not at war, but short of war, 44; pattern of a cover-up, 284, 332; position in the Gulf, 55; possibility of traffic shutdown in the Gulf, 36; pressure after Silkworm attack, 154; reaction to attack on Rushadat oil platform, 169; retaliation an appropriate response, 286; "secret war", 330; strategy for handling Iran Air tragedy, 312; "Twin Pillars" policy, 31; verge of unprecedented commitment, 27
United States Air Force, 7
United States Army: 82nd Airborne Division, 101, 293; 160th Special Operations Aviation Regiment, 80-81, 101
United States Army Special Forces, 81

United States Central Command (CENTCOM), 57-58, 86, 128, 181, 205, 269, 271, 277, 315, 317

U.S. Naval Institute *Proceedings*, 44, 46

United States Navy, lack of minesweepers, 73-75

U.S. Navy Sea, Air and Land Forces (SEAL), 78, 84-85, 112-116, 119, 134, 137, 144, 148, 156, 163, 165-168, 207, 210, 217, 219-220, 265

United Nations, 334

United Nations General Assembly, 120

United Nations Security Council, 31, 386

Universal Monarch, tanker, 379-381

Utegaard, Cmdr. Eric, USN, 325

USS *Valley Forge*, (CV-45), 88-89

Valliere, Lt. (jg) Michael, USN, 201

Van Hook, Lt. Gordan, USN, 199-200, 202

USS *Vandegrift*, (FFG-48), 325

Vevey, tanker, 342, 344

Ville d'Avers, French cargo ship, 93

USS *Vincennes*, (CG 49), 298-299, 343-344, 346, 349, 376; "Aegis arrogance", 299; arrives in the Gulf, 296; bridge discipline, 365; cover-up, 330, 332; crew stress issues, 318, 322, 328, 351, 357, 362-363, 365-366, 374; crossed into Iranian zone, 300-301, 306; en route to Bahrain, 297; fire guns in anger, 345; "Fogarty Report", 315-316, 318, 320-324, 329-334, 338-339, 346, 348-349, 351, 353-355, 357-358, 360-361, 366-367, 374; formal investigation, 315, 319-322, 324-330, 333, 335-337, 339-341, 348, 350-352, 356-357, 359-362, 365, 368, 370, 372-373, 375-377; in Iran waters, 332-334; intent to shoot down Iran Air, 305, 307-308; no actions against officers, 322; ordered to Gulf in haste, 337; Pan Am Flight 103 revenge, 327; psychological factors, 328, 351, 357, 362-363, 365, 374; scenario "scenario fulfillment", 328, 357-358, 362; "Sea of Lies", 352-357; "secret war", 330; sharp maneuvering, 306; shootout with Iranian gunboats, 301-302, 304-305, 310, 317, 334; shoots down Iran Air, 1, 309-312, 319, 323, 326, 329-330, 387; sticking nose in the wrong place, 299-300; tactical control of the area, 300; tracking Iranian P-3 Orion, 304-305; tracks Iran Air flight, 302-303, 305, 307; unable to detect electronic emissions from Iran Air, 307-308

Vlahos, Dr. Michael, 44

Vogel, Lt. Richard, 69

Voice of America, 385

"vulture tugs", 20

USS *Waddell*, (DDG-24), 16, 20-22, 45

USS *Wainwright*, (CG-28), 197, 200, 210, 217-220, 230-239, 256-257, 276, 283, 341-343, 364, 366

Walleye II guided glide bomb, 250, 284

"war-at-sea" strike group, 255

War Powers Act, 90, 123, 275

Warner, Senator John W., 82

Washington Post, 74

Washington Post / ABC poll, 170

Waters, Vice Adm. Robert L., USN, 82

Weaver, Wayne R., USN, 15

Webb, Navy Secretary James H., 23, 128

Webb, Lt. Cmdr. Paul, USN, 227

Weicker, Senator Lowell, 154

Weinberger, Caspar, 34, 37, 54-56, 74, 122, 128, 154, 162, 338

Welch, Larry, USN, 192

Weldon, Terry, 387

Wetherall, Lt. Tom, USN, 364

Wheeler, PO James, USN, 14

USS *Whidbey Island*, (LSD-41) 99

Wikul, Pete, USN, 114, 137

Willey, Maj. Barry, USA, 271

Willi Tide, supply vessel, 224-225

USS *William H. Standly*, (CG-32), 156

Yonkers, Captain David, USN, 63, 65-67, 70, 76, 123, 179

York Marine, tanker, 223-225, 291

Younis Khalis Islamic Party, 149

Zakhem, Ambassador Sam H., 16, 24, 123

Zeller, Rear Adm. Raymond G., 208, 210, 252, 295

Ziegler, Capt. Conway, USN, 105, 108

Zocher, Lt. Clay, USN, 304-305, 307-308, 320-321, 367, 371, 373-374